Kanji for Beginners Vol. 2
Learning Japanese Made Simple

Learn how to read, write and speak
Japanese with JLPT N4 Level Kanji

A Workbook for Self-Study

Dan Akiyama

JAPANESE FOR BEGINNERS | SYSTEMATIC LEARNING APPROACH

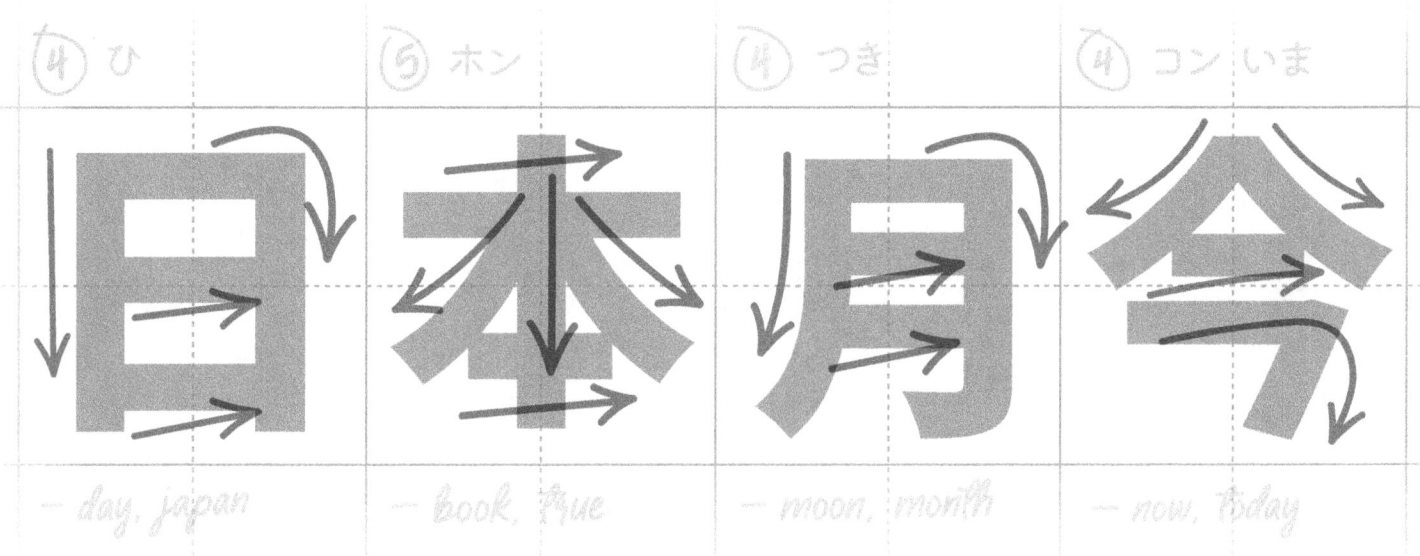

KANJI

FOR BEGINNERS
VOLUME 2

JLPT N4 KANJI

ひらがな
カタカナ
漢字

Detailed Study Sheets for 145 new Kanji!
Hundreds of Useful Terms and Vocabulary
Writing Instruction with Stroke Order Diagrams
Extra Tools to aid your Japanese Kanji Study

JAPANESE MADE SIMPLE®

BEGINNER'S GUIDES + INTEGRATED WORKBOOKS

///////////////////////

DAN AKIYAMA

Learning Japanese Made Simple
Kanji for Beginners Vol. 2 *(JLPT N4 Level)*

A Workbook for Self-Study
by Dan Akiyama

ISBN: Print 978-1-7393210-0-0 (Paperback)
First Edition

**Copyright © 2022 by Dan Akiyama.
All Rights Reserved.**

No part of the content within this publication may be reproduced, duplicated, stored in a retrieval system, or transmitted in any form or by any means, electronic, mechanical, photocopying, recording, scanning, or otherwise, except as provided by United States of America copyright law and fair use, without the prior written permission of the Publisher and author. You are not permitted to amend, distribute, sell, use, paraphrase, or quote any part of this publication without the author and Publisher's consent.

Limit of Liability/Disclaimer of Warranty:
The author and Publisher make no representations or warranties with respect to the accuracy or completeness of the contents of this work and expressly disclaim all warranties, including, without limitation, warranties of fitness for a particular purpose. No warranty may be created or extended by sales or promotional materials.

The advice and strategies contained herein may not be suitable for every situation. This work is published and sold with the understanding that the Publisher is not engaged in rendering medical, legal, or other professional advice or services. If professional assistance is required, the services of a competent professional should be sought. Neither the Publisher nor the author shall be liable for any damages arising from the information contained within this publication.

The fact that an individual, organization, or website is referred to in this work as either a citation and/or potential source of further information does not mean that the author or Publisher endorses the information from the individual, organization, or website that may provide, or recommendations that they/it may make.

Furthermore, readers should be aware that any websites listed in this work may have changed or disappeared between when this publication was written and when it is read.

Contents

1 Introduction — 007
- About this Book — 008
- Learning Japanese — 009
- Stroke Order Notes — 010
- Radicals & Components — 012
- Identifying Kanji — 014
- About Study Pages — 016

2 The N4 Kanji — 018
- Kanji Study Begins — 024
- Final Study Page — 168

3 Extra Study Tools — 169
- Writing Templates — 170
- Kanji Study Templates — 180
- Mini Flashcard Deck — 189

Note of Thanks! — 225

//////////////////////////////////// **PART 1**

Introduction

Welcome to the second volume of my *Kanji for Beginners* workbooks, part of the *Japanese Made Simple* series. It's aimed at those who have already completed my N5 level workbook, but it suitable for anybody that has memorized the kana scripts and begun studying kanji. It is designed to help you learn how to read, write, and pronounce 145 more Japanese kanji - those typically needed for the second *Japanese Language Proficiency Test*, the **JLPT N4**.

Those who are just beginning their Japanese language journey should start with an earlier volume in the series, where you will find introductions to different scripts, information about the way the language works, and some of the basics of Japanese grammar.

This book will focus on individual N4 kanji characters - the more demanding grammatical requirements of JLPT N4 will have to be covered separately. By the end of this workbook, you will have learned how to read, write and pronounce 145 new kanji, including lots of useful N4-level vocabulary assisting those preparing to take the N4 exam, and helping everybody else take their Japanese to the next level!

About this Book

Writing and spaced repetition remain one of the most effective tools for memorization, so this workbook provides space to practice your penmanship. This technique helps to build muscle memory and help make information stick.

Manual handwriting is a low priority when you learn about other foreign languages, such as French or Spanish, and it's a skill we use less and less frequently in our everyday lives. It plays a different role when studying Japanese - carefully follow the correct stroke order and practice often, pronouncing readings and vocabulary out loud. Developing neat written Japanese is an essential skill that you will begin to achieve quite naturally as part of this process - a little bonus, for your hard work and determination!

Writing in this Book

This workbook is for writing in, and while the paper is relatively good quality, you should try to avoid using any markers or pens with especially wet ink that is prone to bleeding. The pages are better suited to ballpoint pens, pencils, or even gel-based stationery, which should not transfer to the pages beneath.

Test your writing tools in the spaces below, checking how they affect the following pages:

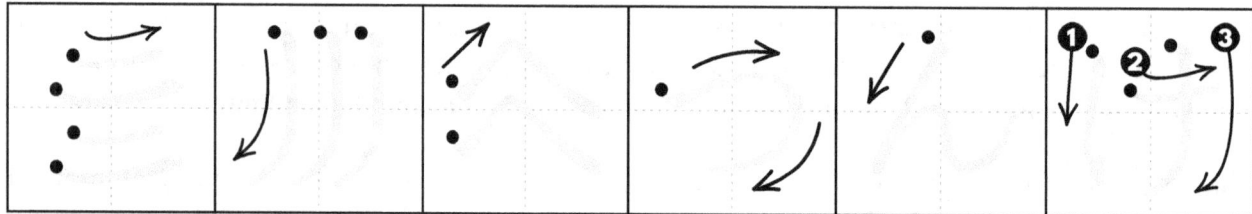

It may eventually be worth investing in a high-quality notebook for more advanced studies with traditional brush-style pens. Until then, my companion study books or regular paper should be fine. Brush pens require specialist paper but make writing more natural-looking.

The book is divided into sections to help structure your learning effectively:

Part 1

This chapter contains an overview of this book and some reference information for those studying kanji. You should already understand how the Japanese language is structured, the difference between each script, and, generally, how texts are written. Earlier books in the series cover these topics in more detail.

Part 2

After a brief look at the kanji characters covered in this book, the work begins. Learn about new kanji characters with 145 dedicated study pages, taking in stroke order, readings, vocabulary words, and more.

Part 3

The final section of the book features additional study tools, including a small section of extra blank writing grids. A separate notepad is always recommended for practicing your Japanese writing, but these sheets may be handy for repeating characters that you found particularly tricky. My companion writing pads are ideal for this, and they work well with flashcards to check whether you remember stroke orders or just for writing out essential vocabulary.

I have also included a template for studying other unfamiliar kanji that you encounter, with a similar layout to the N4 kanji study pages. Space is provided to record important kanji information, and these can be used at all stages of your study.

Finally, a section of double-sided pages that are designed to become *flashcards* - intended to be cut out and turned into a deck of helpful memory prompts. Feel free to make copies if you prefer not to remove pages. They might not be as large or durable as cards, but they are still handy and save any further cost.

Stroke Order

All learners should try to make time for kanji writing practice in their study schedules. Stroke order plays a crucial role in forming accurate and legible characters, just as it did with kana. That said, memorizing the stroke order for so many kanji, especially as you progress to the most complex characters with *upwards of 20+ strokes,* can become very time-consuming.

Most online resources and Japanese character dictionaries will often show you the stroke order and may include animations. When that information is not available, some generalized rules can be applied to almost every kanji, saving considerable time and effort. As with all aspects of Japanese, there are exceptions to the rules, so they may not always work perfectly. They should, however, cover more than nine out of ten kanji:

Work from top to bottom, and from left to right.

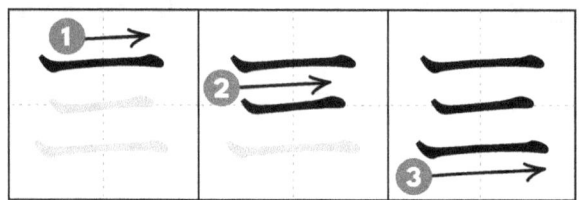 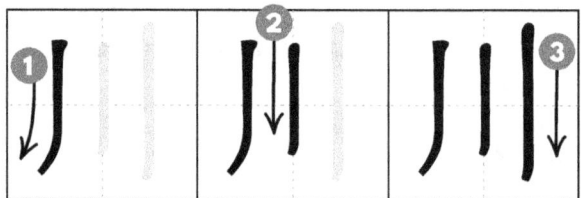

Horizontal lines first, then vertical.

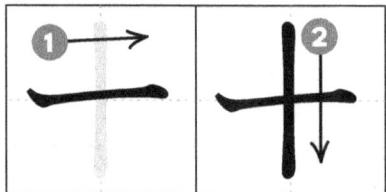 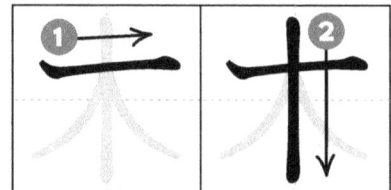

Vertical lines in the center, before strokes on the left and right.

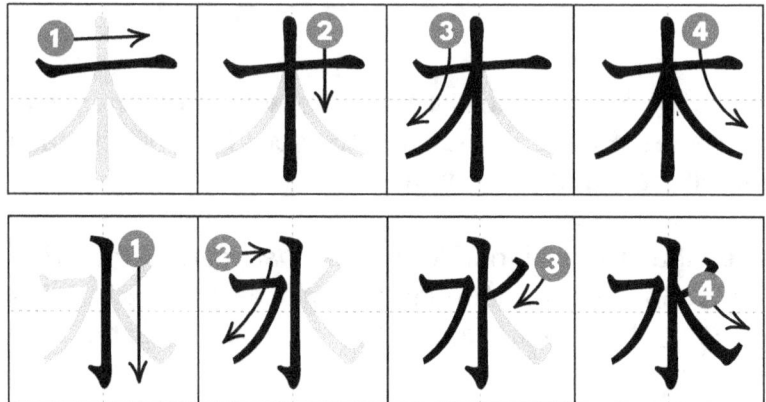

Boxes are three strokes, not four.

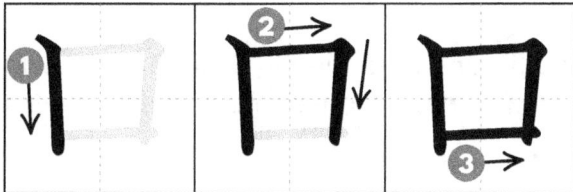

Outsides then inside (Boxes), before closing - but not C-shapes.

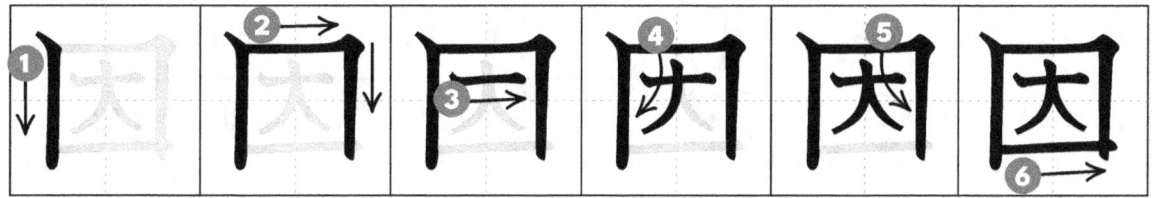

Lines overlapping lots of others come last (or later).

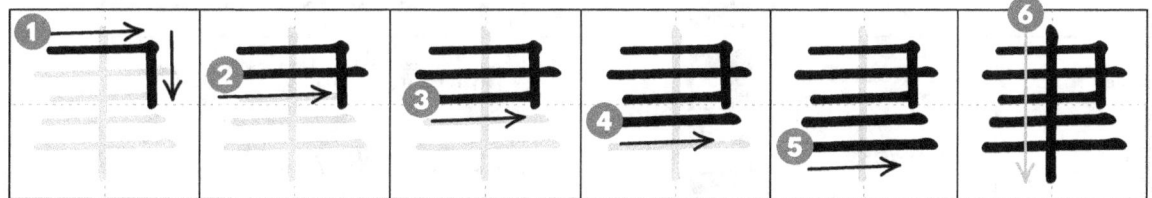

X-shapes, right > left diagonal lines before left > right (from top to bottom)

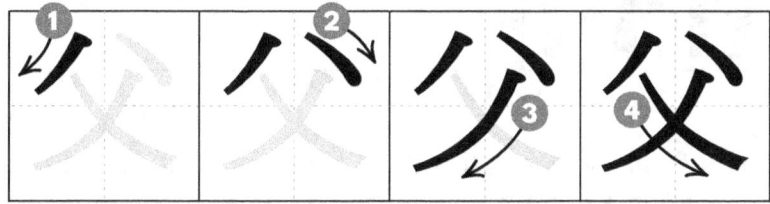

Dots/dashes on top of sections/kanji first, others at end.

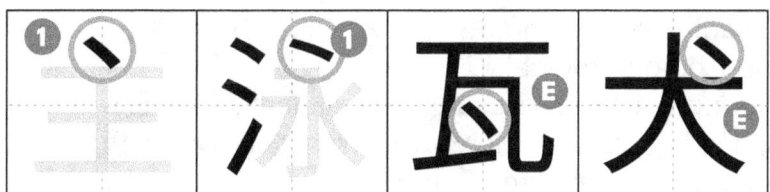

Underlining parts very last.

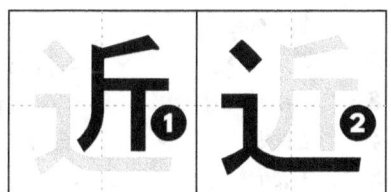

The same rules apply to even the most complex-looking kanji. Approach characters that appear to have multiple kanji using the steps above, component-by-component. Begin with the radical or kanji located in the upper-left corner or left side, and work towards the lower right corner. Muscle memory can soon take over with practice, and kanji stroke order will become an easier aspect of studying kanji.

Radical Placement

To find kanji in Japanese character dictionaries, you first need to identify which of its parts is the primary radical *(Bushu)*. Unless the kanji is made from a single shape *(therefore, it's also the radical)*, it will be in one of seven positions:

#	Name	Placement	Position	Examples
1	**Hen** 偏	Left side		言 (言) in 記, 扌(手) in 指
2	**Tsukuri** 旁	Right side		刂(刀) in 利, 力 in 助, 欠 in 歌
3	**Kanmuri** 冠	Upper		艹 (艸) in 花, 雨 in 雪, 穴 in 空
4	**Ashi** 脚	Lower		心 in 恋, 灬(火) in 点, 儿 in 免
5	**Tare** 垂	Northwest		厂 in 原, 尸 in 局, 广 in 店
6	**Nyō** 繞	Southwest		辶(辵) in 近, 走 in 起, 廴 in 建
7	**Kamae** 構	Enclosures (Various)		門 in 開, 囗 in 国, 勹 in 包

Most kanji contain multiple components from the KangXi radical list, making it difficult to determine where characters might be listed in a dictionary. The **twelve steps**, summarized below, will usually lead you to the correct part:

1	Whole	- Is the whole kanji a radical in and of itself ? (文, 長, & 黍)
2	Single	- There may only be one radical (丿 in 乃)
3	Enclosure	- A shape covering 2-4 sides is usually the radical (匚 in 医)
4	Left	- On left side, nothing above, below, or intersecting (木 in 板)
5	Right	- As above, but on the right side (彡 in 形)
6	Top	- Is there a clear upper radical? (大 in 奈)
7	Bottom	- Top may have 2+ but possibly one at bottom (刀 in 劈)
8	Top Left	- If not obvious from steps 1-7, check the top-left (土 in 報)
9	Top Right	- Still not sure, check the upper-right for a radical (口 in 呉)
10	Lower Right	- If still no radical, check lower-right (口 in 君)
11	Lower Left	- Lower-left (虫 in 虱). Also when all corners are radicals.
12	Inside	- Last step, sometimes obvious at start (大 in 夾, or 女 in 嬲)

Common Components & Variants

These lists contain frequently used *KangXi radicals* and components. Some radicals change shape and appearance when they occupy different positions in a kanji to fit into that space. These alternate versions are called *variants* and they can sometimes look very different from their original shapes *(shown alongside)*.

Radical nicknames can vary from one list to another - remember that the names are simply tools to assist in memorization and are not necessarily meanings. *Variants share the same nickname as the regular versions of characters but could be renamed:*

Radical	Strokes	Position	Meaning/Name
亠	2		lid, top
亻 (人)	2		person
人 (人)	2		person
儿	2		legs
冖	2		cover, crown
刂 (刀)	2		knife, sword
厂	2		cliff
口 (口)	3		mouth
囗	3		border
土 (土)	3		earth
女 (女)	3		woman
子 (子)	3		child, son
兦 (小)	3		small
丷 (小)	3		small
宀	3		roof, house
广	3		slanting roof
彳	3		step, street
艹 (艸)	3		grass
辶 (辵)	3		road, walk
阝 (邑)	3		village, country
阝 (阜)	3		hill, mound
忄 (心)	3		heart, mind
扌 (手)	3		hand
氵 (水)	3		water
犭 (犬)	3		beast
攵 (攴)	4		activity, hit
日 (日)	4		sun, day, time

Radical	Strokes	Position	Meaning/Name
月 (肉)	4		meat, flesh
朩 (木)	4		tree, wood
火 (火)	4		fire
灬 (火)	4		fire (boil)
王 (玉)	4		jewel, jade
礻 (示)	4		altar, festival
疒	5		sickness
目 (目)	5		eye
禾	5		grain
穴 (穴)	5		hole, cave
衤 (衣)	5		clothing
竹 (竹)	6		bamboo
米 (米)	6		rice
糹 (糸)	6		thread
虫 (虫)	6		worm, insect
行	6		to go
言 (言)	7		words, say
貝 (貝)	7		shell, property
走 (走)	7		to run
足 (足)	7		foot, leg
車 (車)	7		vehicle, wheel
金 (金)	8		metal, gold
門	8		gate, door
雨 (雨)	8		rain
頁	9		head, page
魚 (魚)	11		fish

Identifying Kanji

Learners of all levels will need to check the meaning of unfamiliar kanji sooner or later. No matter how advanced your studies, the way to lookup kanji remains the same.

The best method will depend on which medium you are using for study, but the most straightforward solution will usually be to search online. If you are using a computer, smartphone, or similar device, the process is simple. Many online kanji dictionaries such as **[jisho.org]** make it easy to find meanings and pronunciations, and you can simply *copy + paste* a kanji in the search bar to get started.

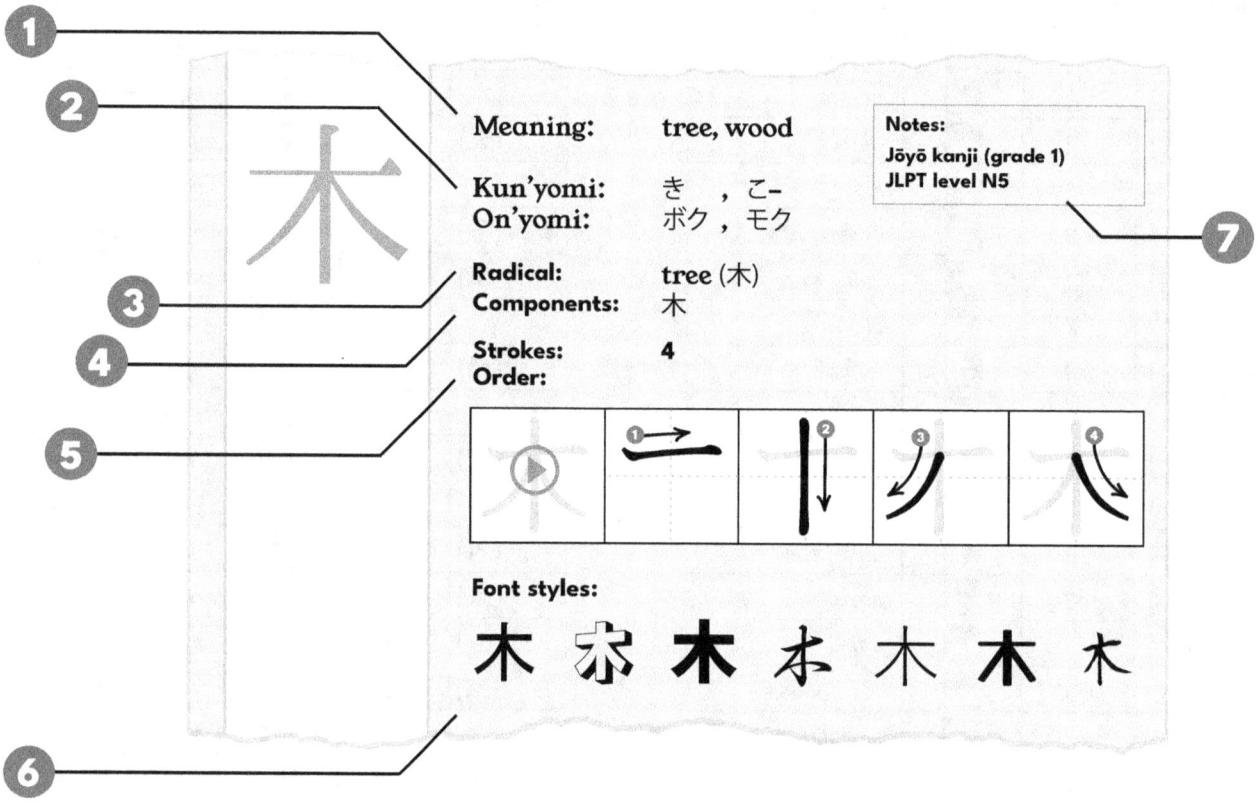

Above: the basic information typically found in online dictionaries (also see table, right)

Irrespective of the chosen method, you are usually provided with similar information upon finding the desired kanji. Some dictionaries show a bare minimum of information, while others can offer a lot more. It varies from one publication to the next, so you should consult reviews from other learners if you are unsure about the suitability of a particular dictionary for your level of knowledge. Those with extra information about using a kanji, with some example sentences or lists of compound words made with that character, are useful but contain fewer unique entries.

1	Meaning	There are many, but this will be the most common.
2	Readings	Most have multiple pronunciations, with 2 types: (a) Kun'yomi, the 'Japanese pronunciation' (b) On'yomi, so-called 'Chinese pronunciation'
3	Main Radical	The component used to index kanji in dictionaries.
4	Components	Like letters, used to make words (kanji), they are the basic building blocks of all kanji, called bushu.
5	Strokes/Order	The number of lines and the order they are written.
6	Font Styles *(sometimes)*	Variety of fonts displayed, often with a mix of both handwritten and modern, digital styles
7	Other data *(sometimes)*	Additional attributes that beginners may find useful, such as specific dictionary indices, etc.

Above: key for illustration of typical dictionary entries (see left page).

Suppose you need to look up a printed or handwritten kanji: in that case, those websites allow you to also browse and filter kanji by the components that you do recognize - even a single radical. It takes practice, especially when you are unsure which shapes are radicals, but these systems are generally intuitive, so they are worth trying next.

Another potential solution is to try software that can identify kanji written into them. You can either use a touch screen and your finger or draw the kanji with your computer mouse more crudely, and potential matches filter into view. Once again, *[jisho.org]* has this alternative function for times when you cannot *copy + paste* a character into a search engine.

Lastly, a traditional Japanese character dictionary will always be a sound investment. The most popular publications classify kanji by their primary radical, usually those in the *KangXi* list of radicals. Some may organize entries by the number of pen strokes it takes to write them. At the same time, some may use modified or alternative lists of radicals to index kanji, while others group kanji by the positions in which you find primary radicals.

Dictionaries aimed at learners with advanced kanji knowledge have longevity but can be challenging to use at earlier stages. Those aimed at beginners are easier to use but need replacing over time.

Learning the Kanji

The following section of the workbook contains study pages dedicated to the N4 kanji. An example of their layout and important features can be found below:

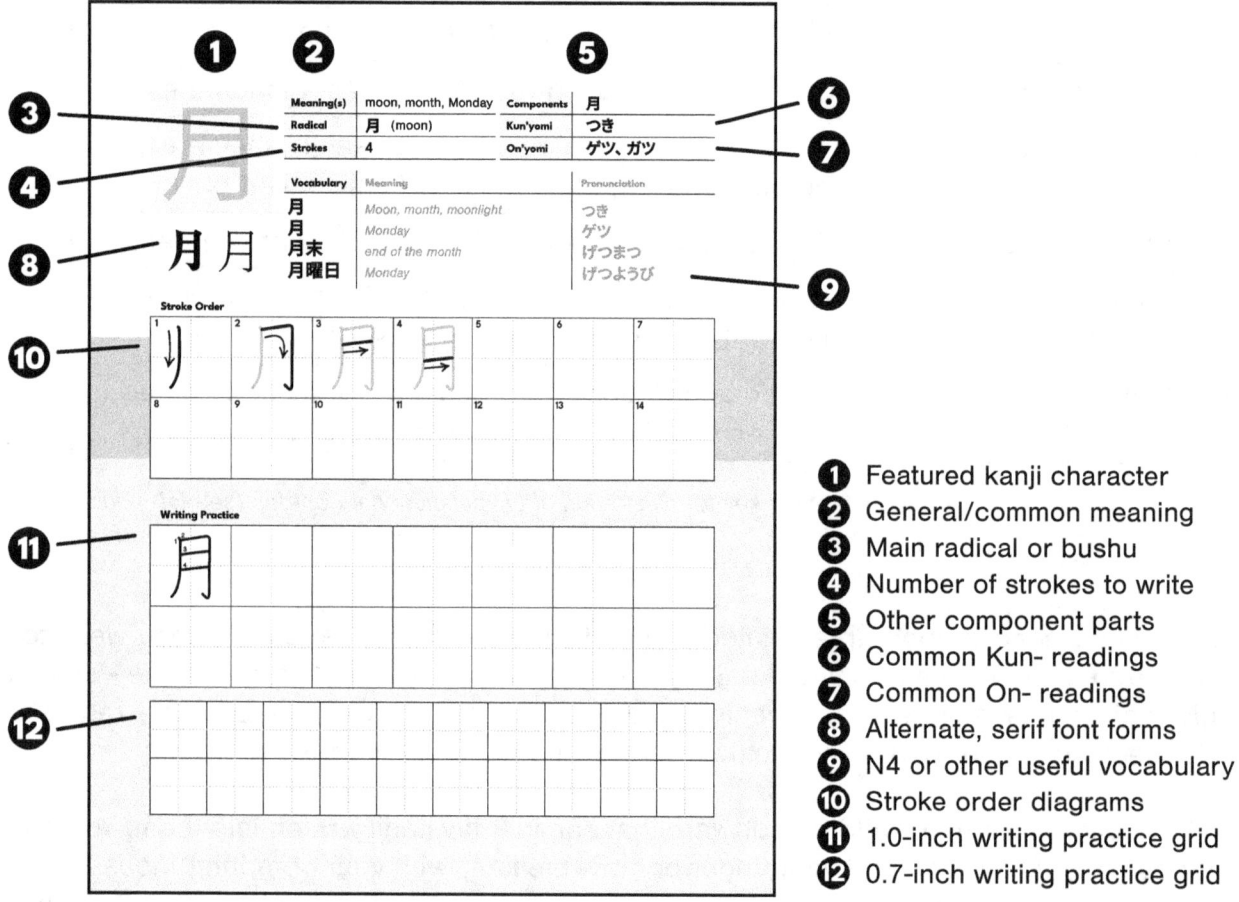

① Featured kanji character
② General/common meaning
③ Main radical or bushu
④ Number of strokes to write
⑤ Other component parts
⑥ Common Kun- readings
⑦ Common On- readings
⑧ Alternate, serif font forms
⑨ N4 or other useful vocabulary
⑩ Stroke order diagrams
⑪ 1.0-inch writing practice grid
⑫ 0.7-inch writing practice grid

Approaching each new kanji, practice pronunciation of the readings and look at the type of vocabulary it represents. As your studies advance, you will find you can often associate that new kanji with those you are about to learn. The repeating shapes and patterns will become more apparent over time - building kanji knowledge takes time - there are simply more things to remember for each one.

One study tactic that I find works well is re-writing or transferring the details for each kanji to a separate, blank study book. I created the Kanji Study Companion for this purpose, and have included some templates at the end of the book that you can copy for your own - but virtually any sort of notebook will work - structured, organized studies are more effective!

PART 2

The N4-Level Kanji

The next section contains detailed study pages for the following 145 Japanese kanji:

N4 Kanji	Basic Meaning	Radical
同	same, agree, equal	口
事	matter, thing, fact, business	亅
自	oneself	自
発	departure, discharge, start from	癶
者	someone, person	老 (耂)
地	ground, earth	土
業	vocation, arts, performance	木
方	direction, person, alternative	方
場	location, place	土
員	employee, member, number	口
開	open, unfold, unseal	門
力	power, strength, strong, strain	力
問	question, ask, problem	口
代	substitute, change, convert	人 (亻)
明	bright, light	日
動	move, motion, change	力
京	capital	亠
通	traffic, avenue, commute	辵 (辶, 辶, 辶)
理	logic, reason, justice, truth	玉 (王)
体	body, substance, object, reality	人 (亻)
田	rice field, rice paddy	田
主	lord, chief, master, main thing	丶
題	topic, subject	頁
意	idea, mind, heart, taste, thought	心 (忄, 㣺)

N4 Kanji	Basic Meaning	Radical
不	negative, non-, bad	一
作	make, prepare, build	人 (亻)
用	utilize, business, service, use, employ	用 (甩)
度	degrees, occurrence, time, counter for occurrences	广
強	strong	弓
公	public, prince, official, governmental	八
持	hold, have	手 (扌龵)
野	plains, field, rustic, civilian life	里
以	by means of, because, in view of, compared with	人 (亻)
思	think	心 (忄, 㣺)
家	house, home, family, professional, expert	宀
世	generation, world, public	one 一
正	correct, justice, righteous	止
院	institution, temple, mansion, school	(阝 left) 阜 (阝)
心	heart, mind, spirit	心 (忄, 㣺)
界	world, boundary	田
教	teach, faith, doctrine	攴 (攵)
文	sentence, literature, style, art	文
元	beginning, origin	儿
重	heavy, important, esteem, respect	里
近	near, early, akin, tantamount	辵 (辶, 辶, 辶)
考	consider, think over	老 (耂)
画	brush-stroke, picture	田
海	sea, ocean	水 (氵, 氺)
売	sell	士
知	know, wisdom	矢
集	gather, meet	隹
別	separate, branch off, diverge	刀 (刂)

N4 Kanji	Basic Meaning	Radical
物	thing, object, matter	牛(牜)
使	use, order, messenger, ambassador	人(亻)
品	goods, refinement, dignity, article	口
計	plot, plan, scheme, measure	言(訁)
死	death, die	歹(歺)
特	special	牛(牜)
私	private, I, me	禾
始	commence, begin	女
朝	morning	月
運	carry, luck, fate	辵(辶, 辶, 辶)
終	end, finish	糸(糹)
台	pedestal, a stand, counter for machines and vehicles	口
広	wide, broad, spacious	广
住	dwell, reside, live, inhabit	人(亻)
無	nothingness, none, ain't, nothing, nil, not	火(灬)
真	true, reality, Buddhist sect	目
有	possess, have, exist, happen	月
町	town, village, street	田
料	fee, materials	斗
工	craft, construction	工
建	build	廴
急	hurry, emergency, sudden, steep	心(忄, 㣺)
止	stop, halt	止
送	escort, send	辵(辶, 辶, 辶)
切	cut, cutoff, be sharp	刀(刂)
転	turn around, change	車
研	polish, study of, sharpen	石
究	research, study	穴

N4 Kanji	Basic Meaning	Radical
楽	music, comfort, ease	木
起	wake up, get up; rouse	走(走)
着	arrive, wear, counter for suits of clothing	目
病	ill, sick	疒
質	substance, quality, matter, temperament	貝
待	wait, depend on	彳
試	test, try, attempt, experiment	言(訁)
族	tribe, family	方
銀	silver	金(釒)
早	early, fast	日
映	reflect, reflection, projection	日
親	relative, familiarity	見
験	verification, effect, testing	馬
英	England, English, hero, outstanding	艸(艹)
医	doctor, medicine	匚
仕	attend, doing, official, serve	人(亻)
去	gone, past, quit, leave, elapse, eliminate	厶
味	flavor, taste	口
写	copy, describe	冖
字	character, letter, word	子
答	solution, answer	竹(⺮)
夜	night, evening	夕
音	sound, noise	音
注	pour, irrigate, shed (tears), flow into, concentrate on	水(氵,氺)
帰	homecoming, arrive at, lead to, result in	巾
歌	song, sing	欠
悪	bad, evil, wrong	心(忄,㣺)
図	map, drawing, plan, extraordinary	囗

N4 Kanji	Basic Meaning	Radical
室	room, apartment, chamber, greenhouse, cellar	宀
歩	walk, counter for steps	止
風	wind, air, style, manner	風
紙	paper	糸(糹)
黒	black	黒
春	spring	日
赤	red	赤
青	blue	青(靑)
館	building, mansion, large building, palace	食(飠)
屋	roof, house, shop, dealer, seller	尸
色	color	色
走	run	走(赱)
秋	autumn, fall	禾
夏	summer	夂
習	learn	羽
洋	ocean, sea, foreign, Western style	水(氵, 氺)
旅	trip, travel	方
服	clothing, admit, obey	月
夕	evening	夕
借	borrow, rent	人(亻)
曜	weekday	日
肉	meat	肉(月)
貸	lend	貝
堂	public chamber, hall	土
鳥	bird, chicken	鳥
飯	meal, rice	食(飠)
勉	exertion, endeavor, effort	力
冬	winter	冫

N4 Kanji	Basic Meaning	Radical
昼	daytime, noon	日
茶	tea	艸(艹)
弟	younger brother	弓
牛	cow	牛(牜)
兄	elder brother	儿
犬	dog	犬(犭)
妹	younger sister	女
姉	elder sister	女
漢	China	水(氵, 氺)

Meaning(s)	same, agree, equal	Components	一 冂 口
Radical	口 (mouth, opening)	Kun'yomi	おな.じ
Strokes	6	On'yomi	ドウ

Vocabulary	Meaning	Pronunciation
同じ	same, identical, equal, uniform	おなじ
同	the same, the said, likewise	ドウ
合同	combination, union, incorporation	ゴウドウ
同じく	in the same way, like, likewise	おなじく

Stroke Order

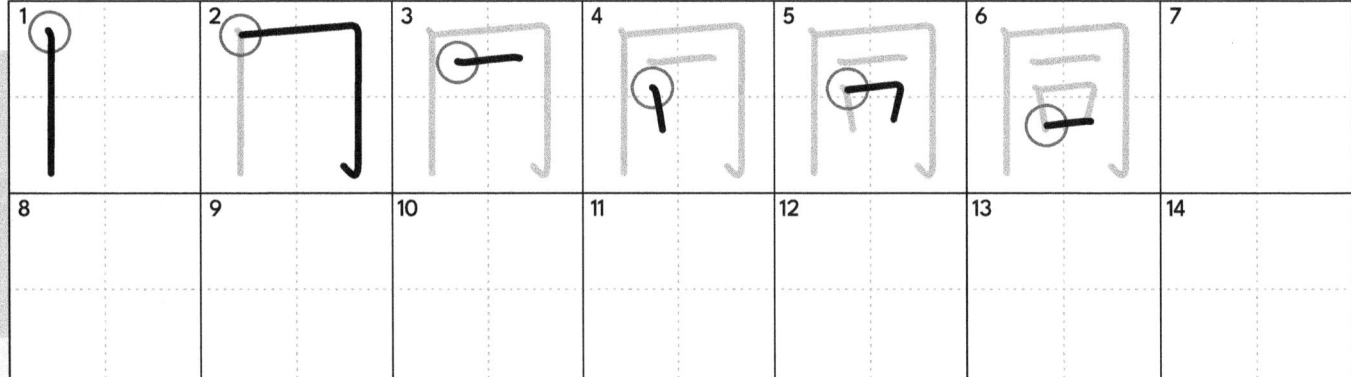

Writing Practice

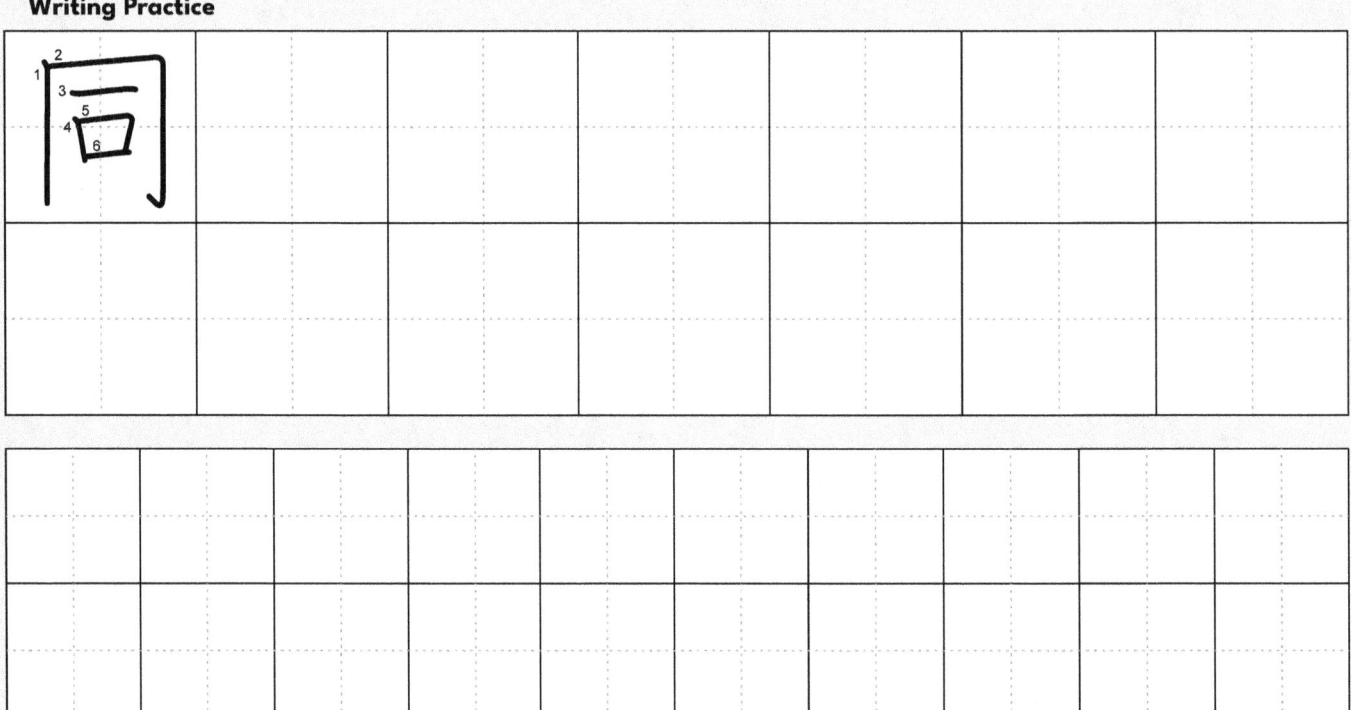

Meaning(s)	matter, thing, fact	Components	一 亅 口 ヨ
Radical	亅 (hook)	Kun'yomi	こと、つか.う、つか.える
Strokes	8	On'yomi	ジ、ズ

Vocabulary	Meaning	Pronunciation
事	thing, matter, incident, occurrence,	こと
神事	Shinto ritual	しんじ
有事	emergency	ユウジ
事業	project, enterprise, business	ジギョウ

Stroke Order

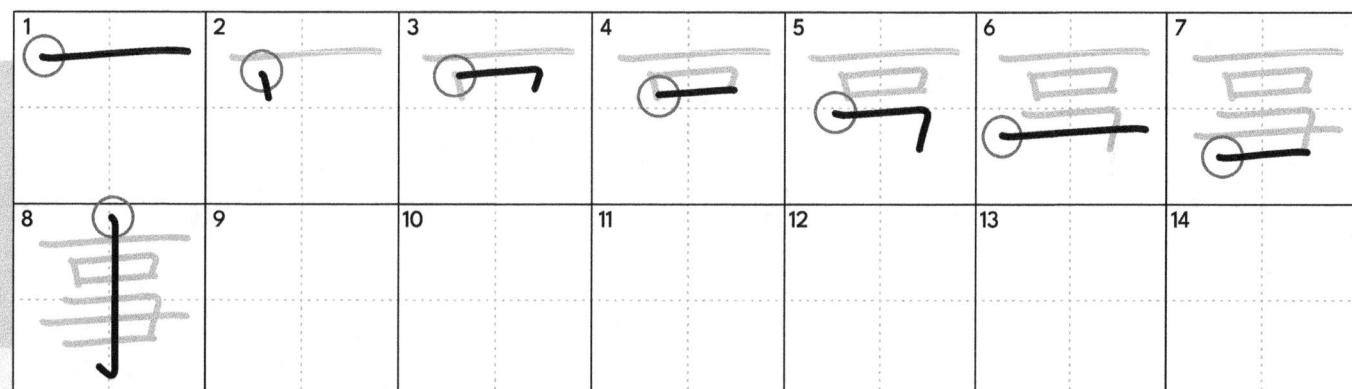

Writing Practice

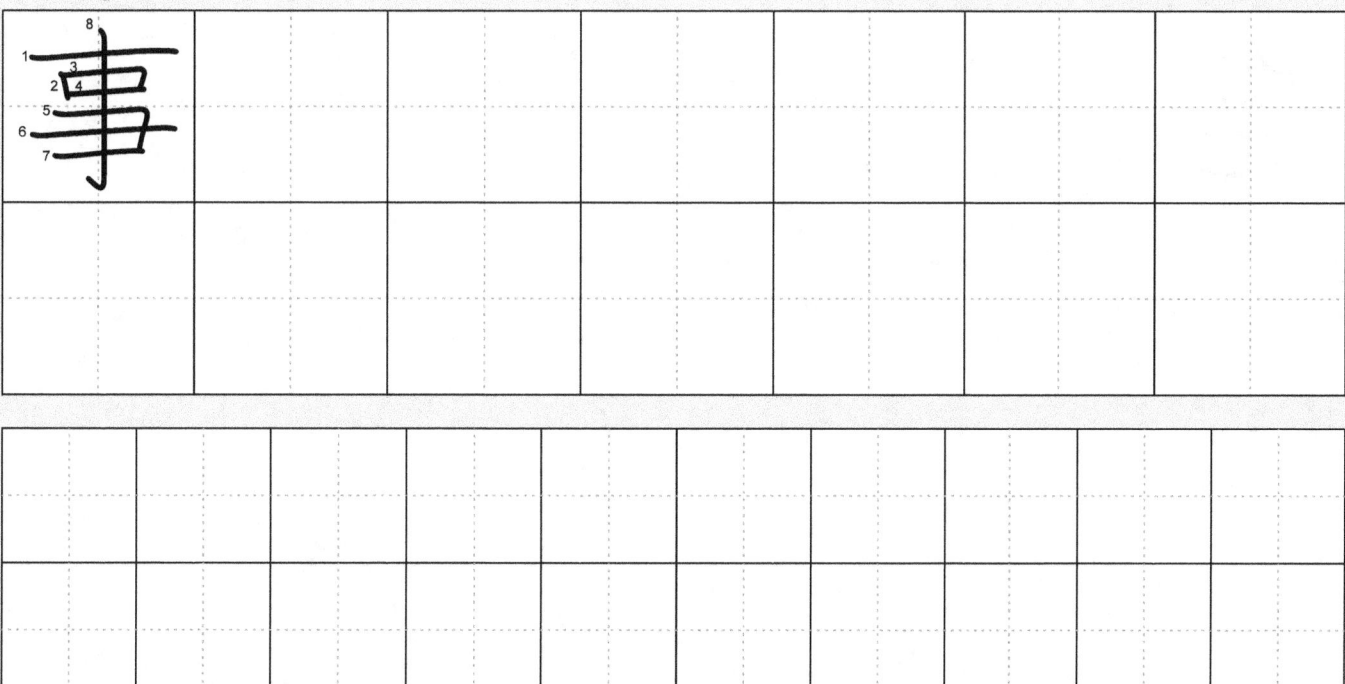

Meaning(s)	oneself	Components	目 自
Radical	自 (self)	Kun'yomi	みずか.ら、おの.ずから
Strokes	6	On'yomi	ジ、シ

Vocabulary	Meaning	Pronunciation
自然	nature, natural, spontaneous, automatic	シゼン
出自	origin, birthplace, descent	シュツジ
自ら	for oneself, personally, in person	みずから
自ずから	naturally, in due course, by itself	おのずから

Stroke Order

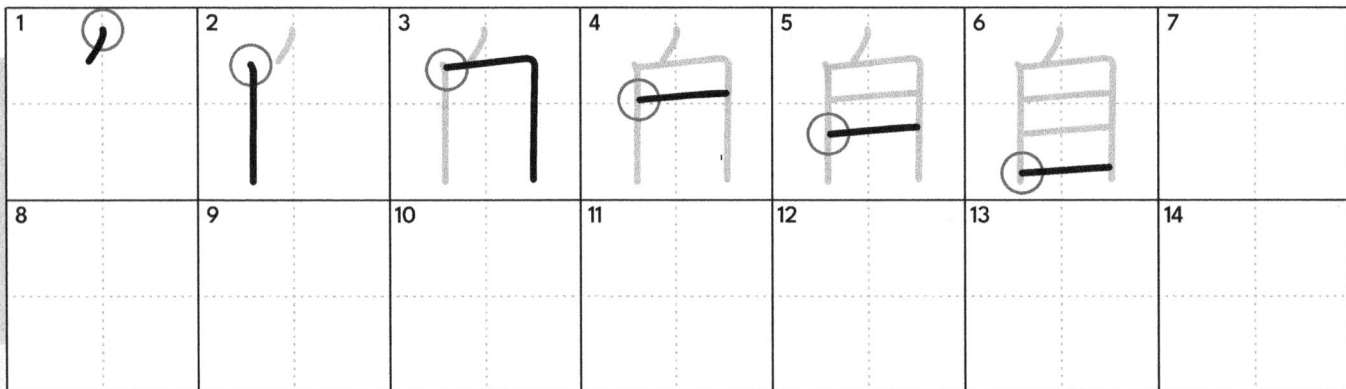

Writing Practice

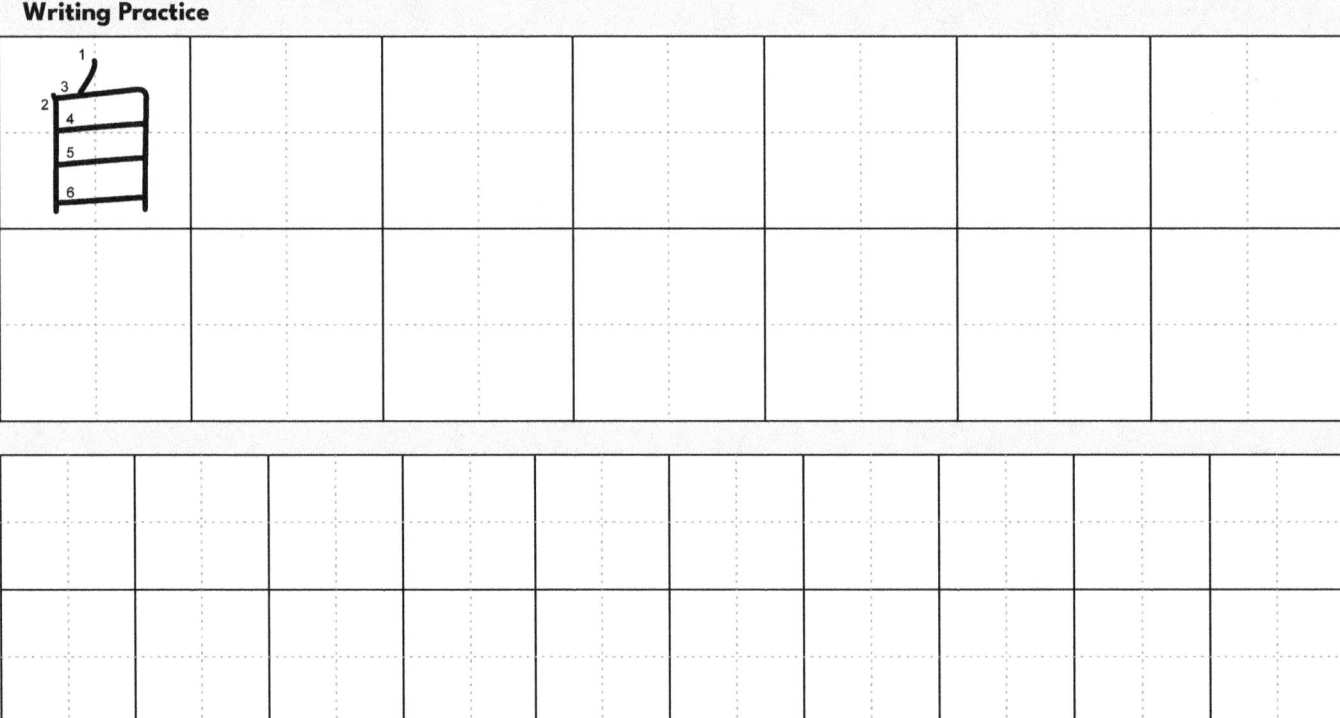

Meaning(s)	departure, discharge	Components	二 ル 癶
Radical	癶 (footsteps)	Kun'yomi	た.つ、あば.く、おこ.る
Strokes	9	On'yomi	ハツ、ホツ

Vocabulary	Meaning	Pronunciation
発	departure, departing from ..., leaving at ...	ハツ
発熱	generation of heat, (attack of) fever	ハツネツ
偶発	sudden outbreak, accidental	グウハツ
暴く	to disclose, to divulge, to expose	あばく

Stroke Order

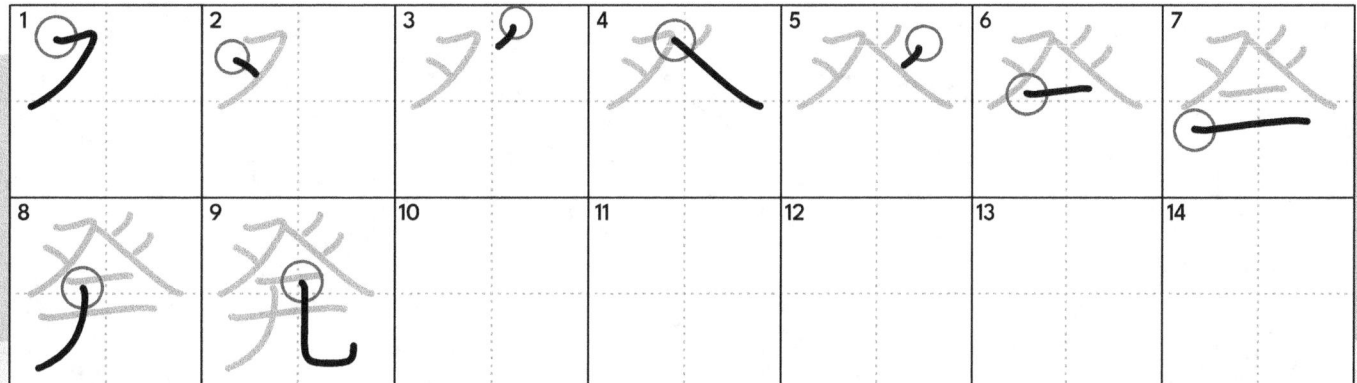

Writing Practice

Meaning(s)	someone, person	Components	老 日
Radical	老 (耂) (old)	Kun'yomi	もの
Strokes	8	On'yomi	シャ

Vocabulary	Meaning	Pronunciation
者	person	もの
芸者	geisha, professional female entertainer	ゲイシャ
者ども	you, people	ものども
若い者	young person, young people, youth	わかいもの

Stroke Order

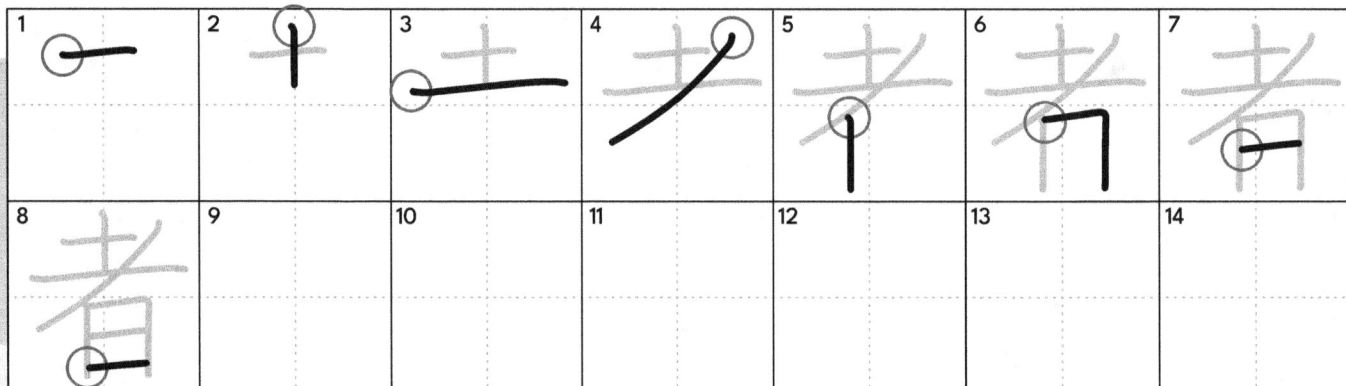

Writing Practice

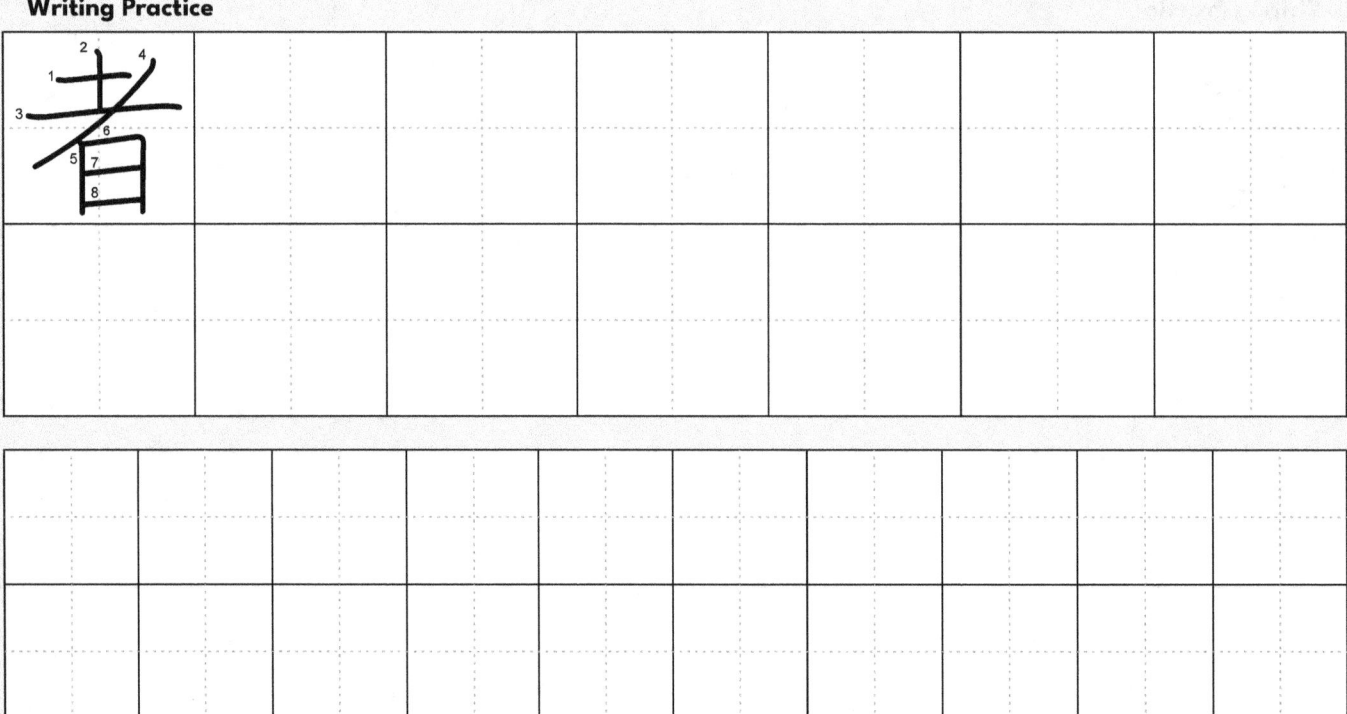

Meaning(s)	ground, earth	Components	土 也
Radical	土 (earth)	Kun'yomi	
Strokes	6	On'yomi	チ、ジ

Vocabulary	Meaning	Pronunciation
地	earth, ground, land, soil, place, territory	チ
地位	(social) position, status, standing	チイ
地	ground, land, earth, soil, the local area	ジ
下地	groundwork, foundation, aptitude	シタジ

Stroke Order

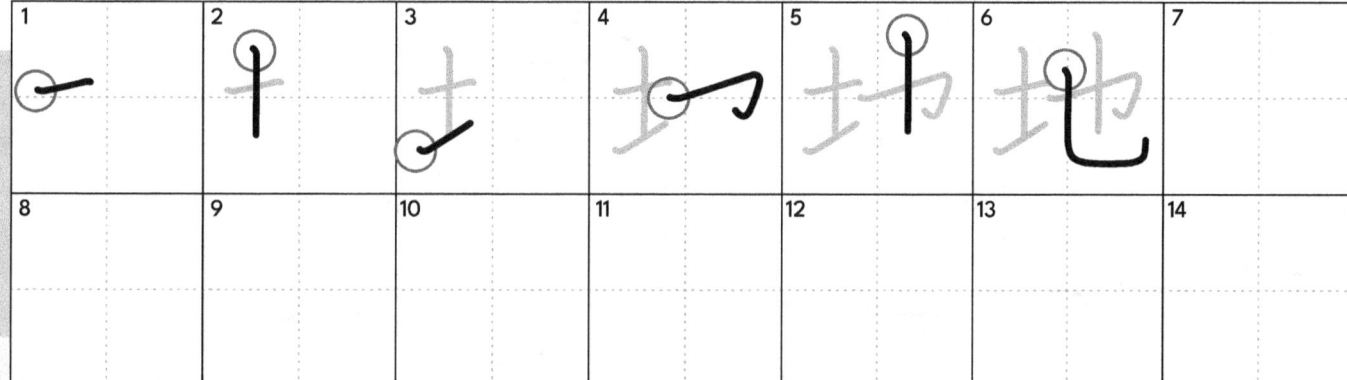

Writing Practice

Meaning(s)	business, performance	Components	一丨丼木王羊丵
Radical	木 (tree)	Kun'yomi	わざ
Strokes	13	On'yomi	ギョウ、ゴウ

Vocabulary	Meaning	Pronunciation
業	work, business, company, agency	ギョウ
業	deed, act, work, performance	わざ
業界	business world, (the) industry	ギョウカイ
業因	karma	ゴウ

Stroke Order

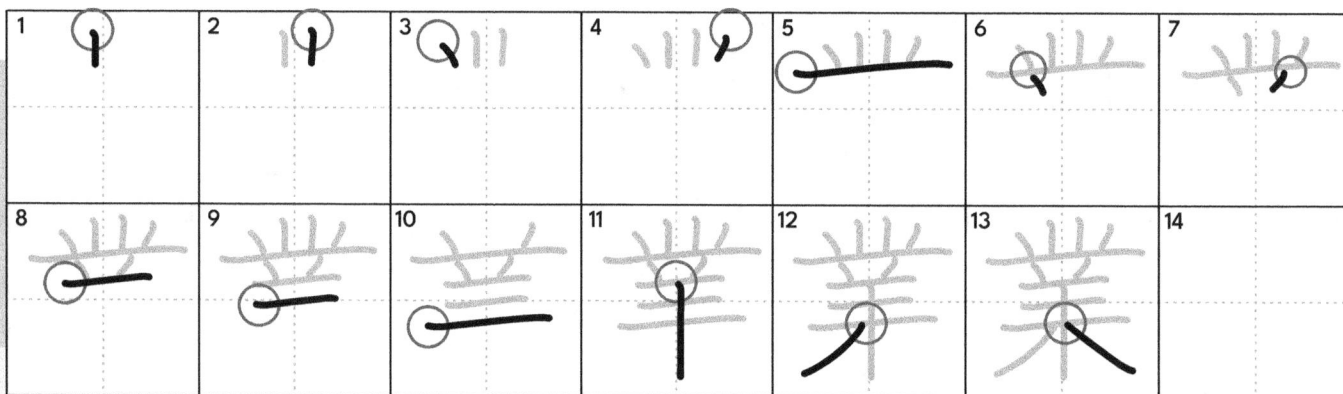

Writing Practice

方

Meaning(s)	direction, person, alternative	Components	方
Radical	方 (square)	Kun'yomi	かた、-かた、-がた
Strokes	4	On'yomi	ホウ

Vocabulary	Meaning	Pronunciation
方	direction, way, side, area (direction)	ホウ
途方	way, destination, reason	トホウ
方々	people, (all) persons, everyone	かたがた
親方	master, boss, chief, foreman, supervisor	おやかた

Stroke Order

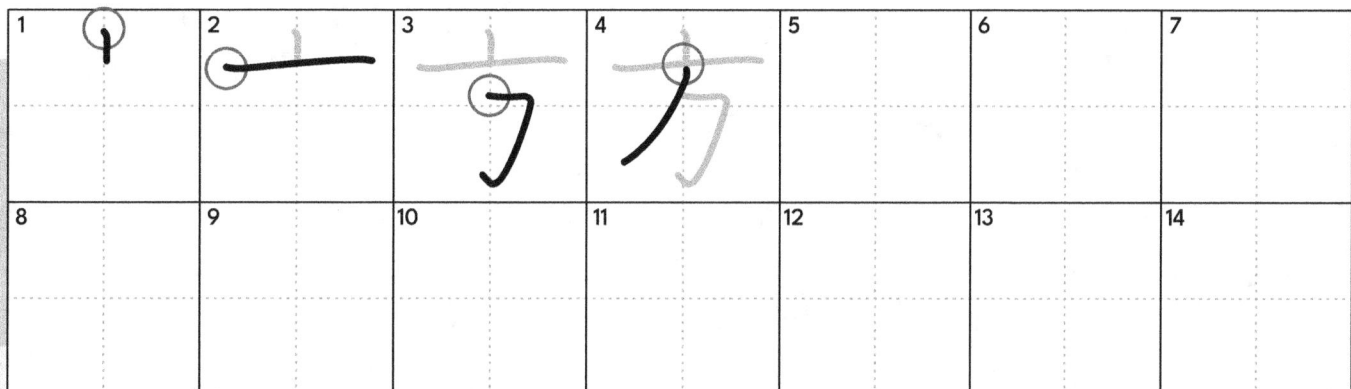

Writing Practice

Meaning(s)	location, place	Components	一 土 日 勿
Radical	土 (earth)	Kun'yomi	ば
Strokes	12	On'yomi	ジョウ、チョウ

Vocabulary	Meaning	Pronunciation
場	place, spot, space, field, discipline, sphere	ば
場	place, spot, grounds, arena, stadium	ジョウ
場合	case, situation	ばあい
場外	outside the hall (or stadium, market, etc.)	ジョウガイ

Stroke Order

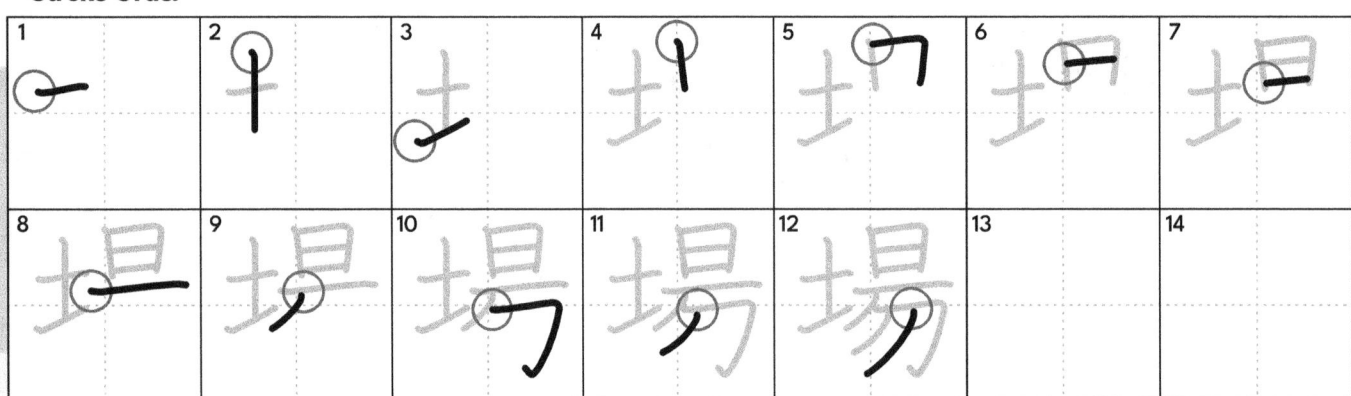

Writing Practice

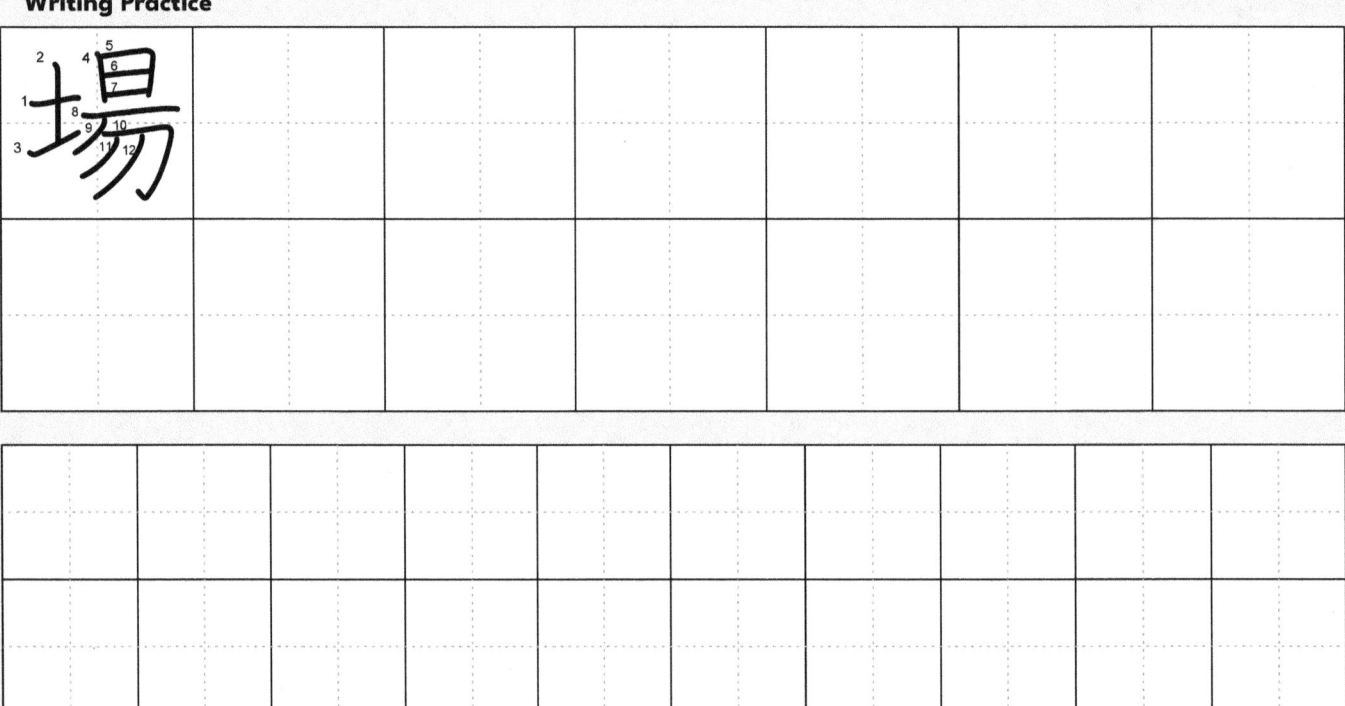

Meaning(s)	employee, member	Components	八口目貝
Radical	口 (mouth)	Kun'yomi	
Strokes	10	On'yomi	イン

Vocabulary	Meaning	Pronunciation
員	member	イン
員数	(total) number (of people or things)	インズウ
随員	member of an entourage, attendant	ズイイン
執行委員	executive committee	シッコウイイン

Stroke Order

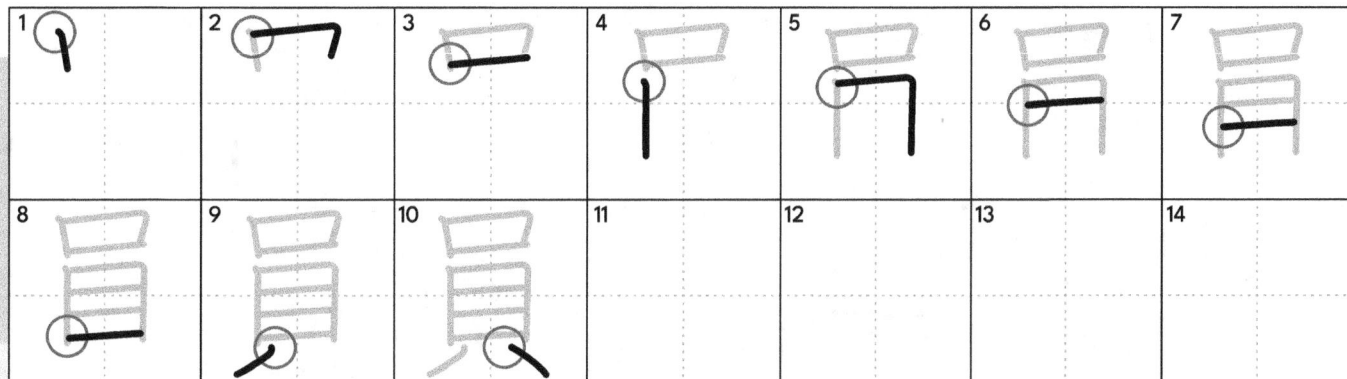

Writing Practice

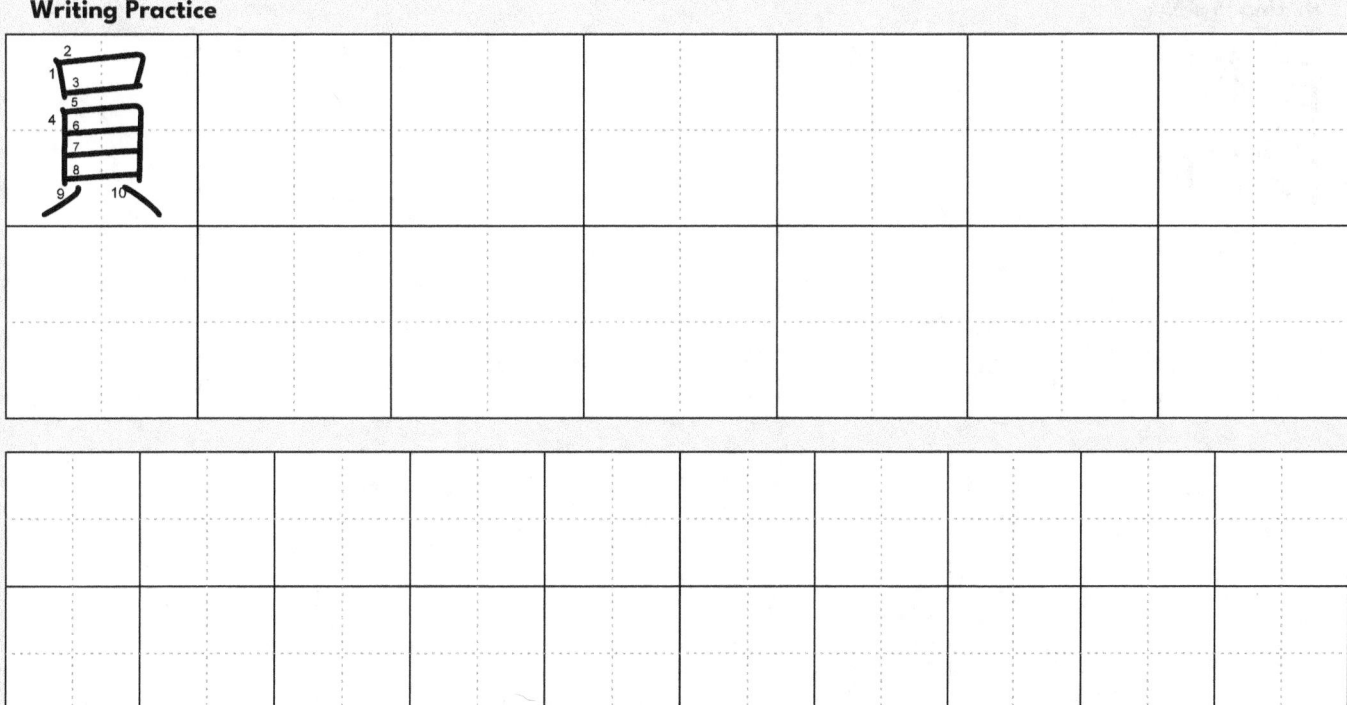

Meaning(s)	open, unfold, unseal	Components	一ノ二廾門
Radical	門 (gate)	Kun'yomi	ひら(く)、あ(ける)
Strokes	12	On'yomi	カイ

Vocabulary	Meaning	Pronunciation
開く	to open, to undo, to unseal, to unpack	ひらく
開花	flowering, blooming, blossoming	カイカ
開ける	to open out (of a view, scenery, etc.)	ひらける
ひらける	to open (a door, etc.), to unwrap	あける

Stroke Order

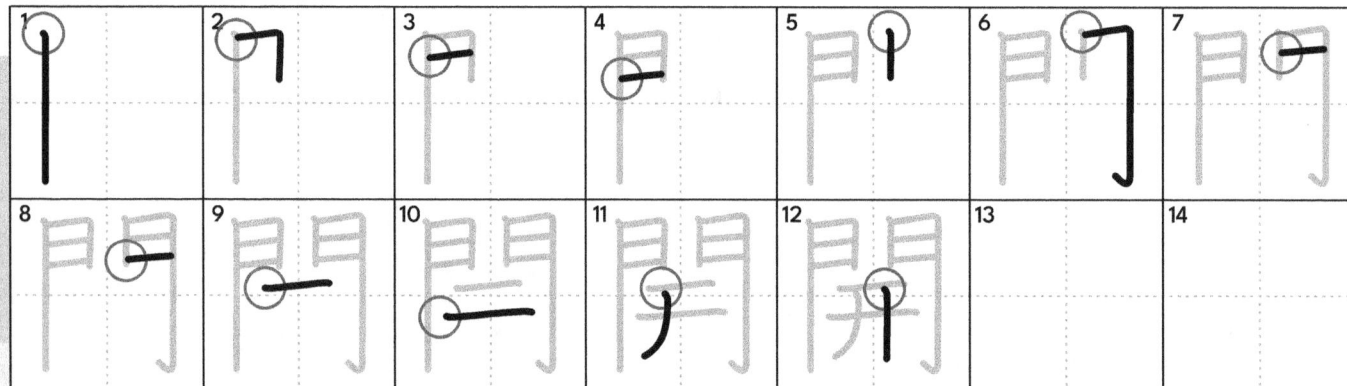

Writing Practice

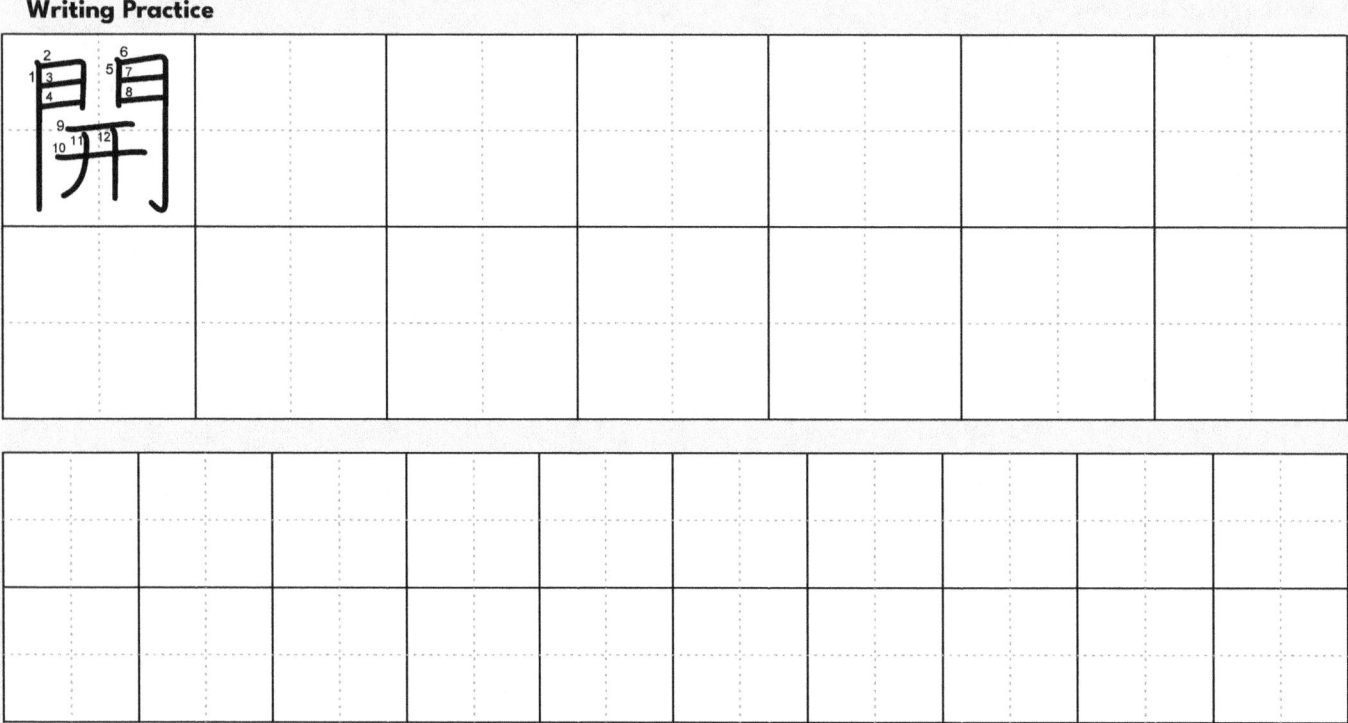

Meaning(s)	power, strength, strong	Components	力
Radical	力 (power, force)	Kun'yomi	ちから
Strokes	2	On'yomi	リョク、リキ

Vocabulary	Meaning	Pronunciation
力	force, strength, might, energy, capability	ちから
力	strength, power, proficiency, ability	リョク
力強い	powerful, strong, forceful, encouraging	ちからづよい
力学	mechanics, dynamics	リキガク

Stroke Order

Writing Practice

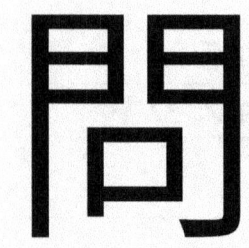

Meaning(s)	question, ask, problem	Components	口 門
Radical	口 (mouth)	Kun'yomi	と(う)
Strokes	11	On'yomi	モン

Vocabulary	Meaning		Pronunciation
問	counter for questions		モン
問う	to ask, to inquire, to accuse of		とう
更問	follow-up question		さらとい
設問	posing a question		セツモン

Stroke Order

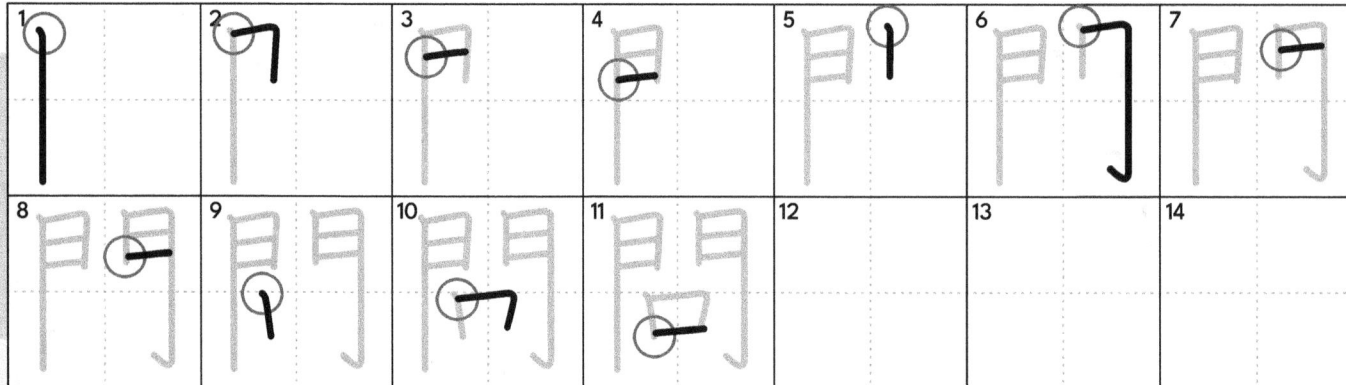

Writing Practice

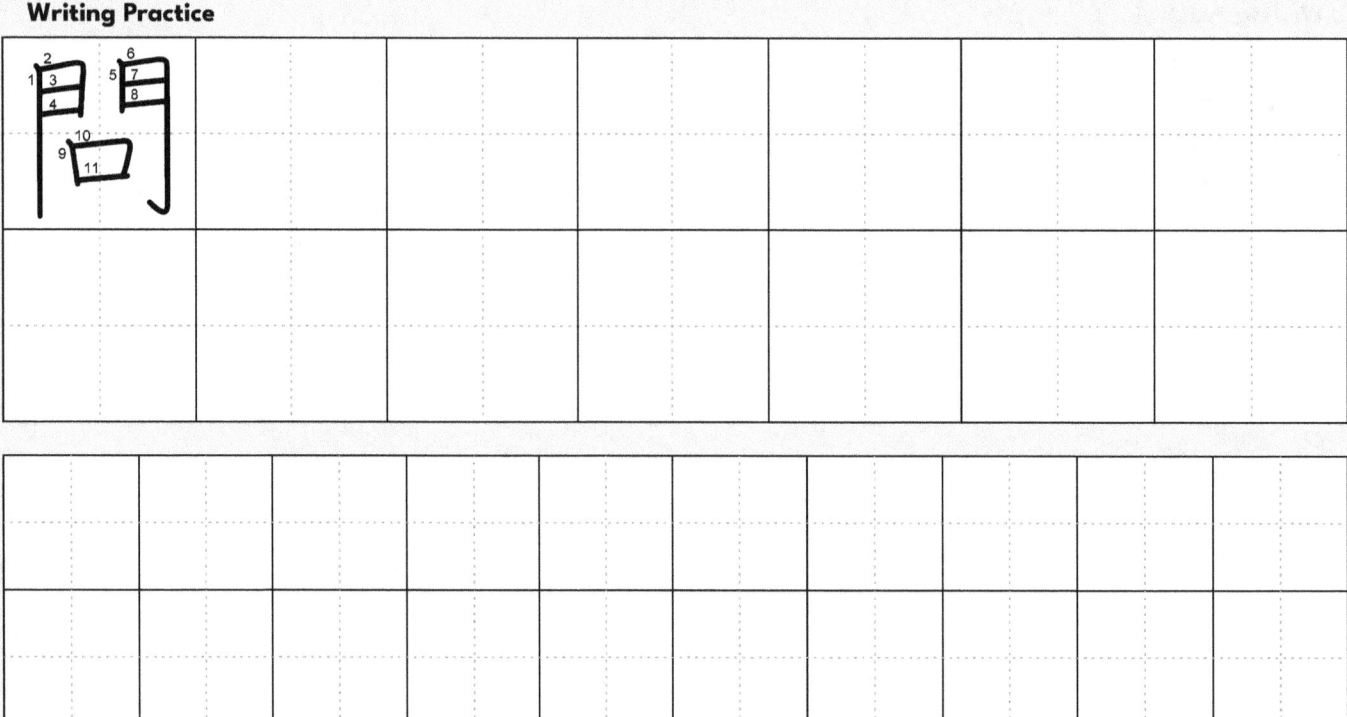

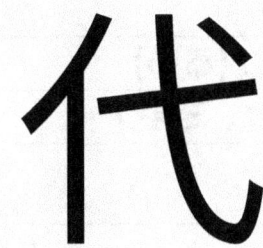

Meaning(s)	substitute, change	Components	化 弋
Radical	人 (亻) (human)	Kun'yomi	か(わり)
Strokes	5	On'yomi	ダイ

Vocabulary	Meaning	Pronunciation
代	charge, cost, price, generation, age	ダイ
代わり	substitute, replacement, proxy	かわり
大時代	old-fashioned, antiquated	オオジダイ
希代	uncommon, rare, extraordinary	キタイ

Stroke Order

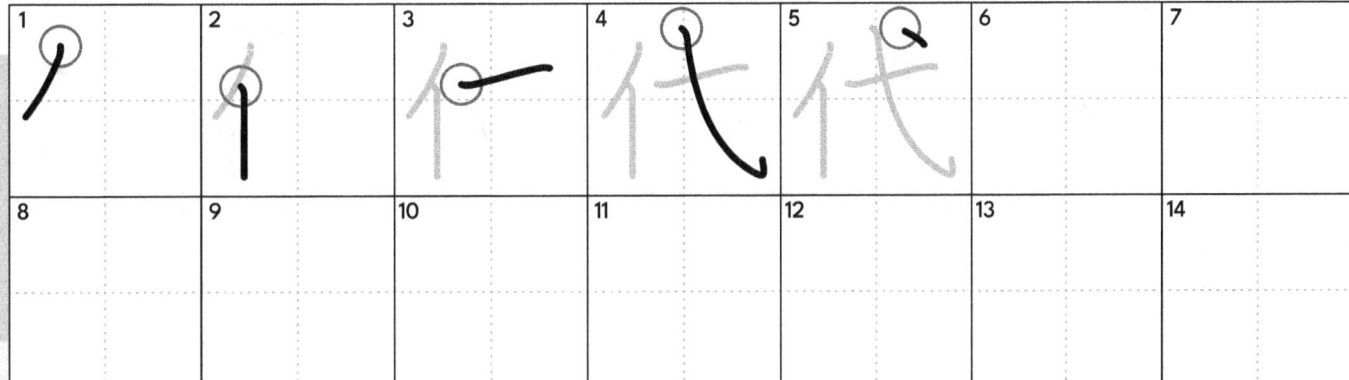

Writing Practice

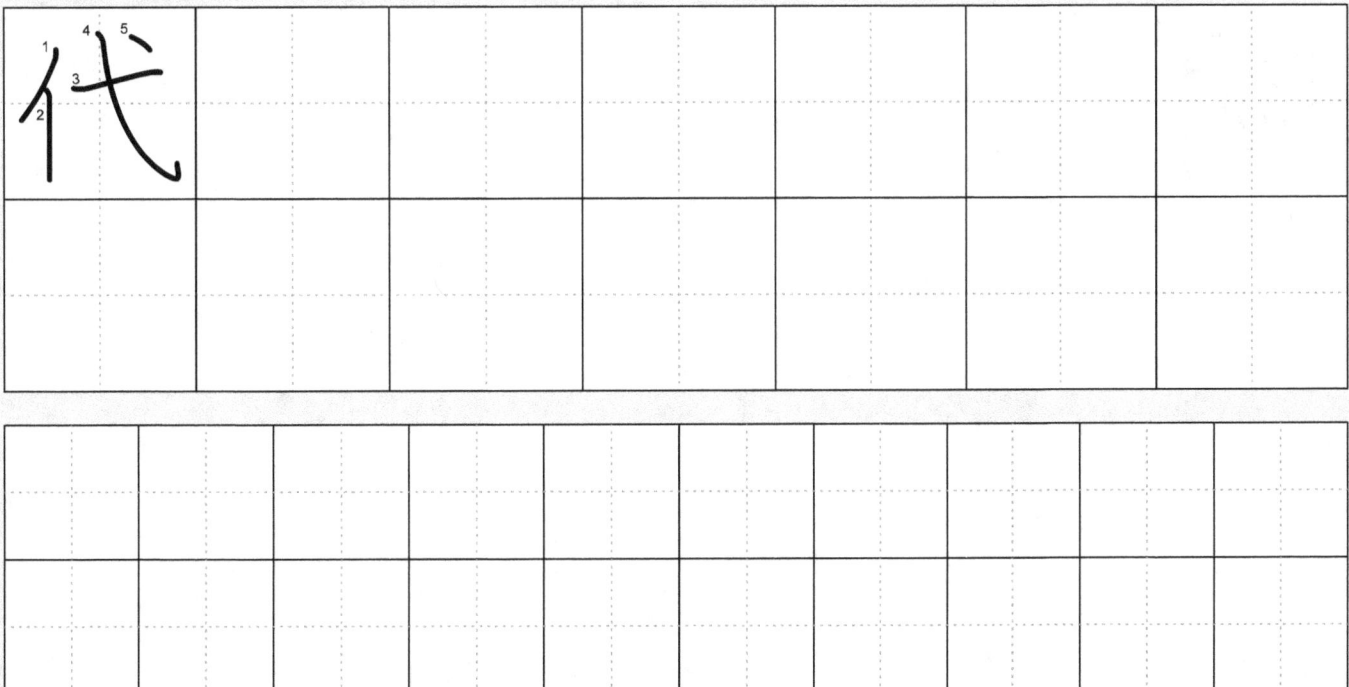

Meaning(s)	bright, light	**Components**	日 月
Radical	日 (sun, day)	**Kun'yomi**	あか(るい)
Strokes	8	**On'yomi**	メイ、ミョウ

Vocabulary	Meaning	Pronunciation
明かり	light, illumination, glow, gleam	あかり
明るい	light, well-lit, well-lighted, bright (of a colour)	あかるい
明	brightness, discernment, insight	メイ
光明	bright light, hope, bright future	コウミョウ

Stroke Order

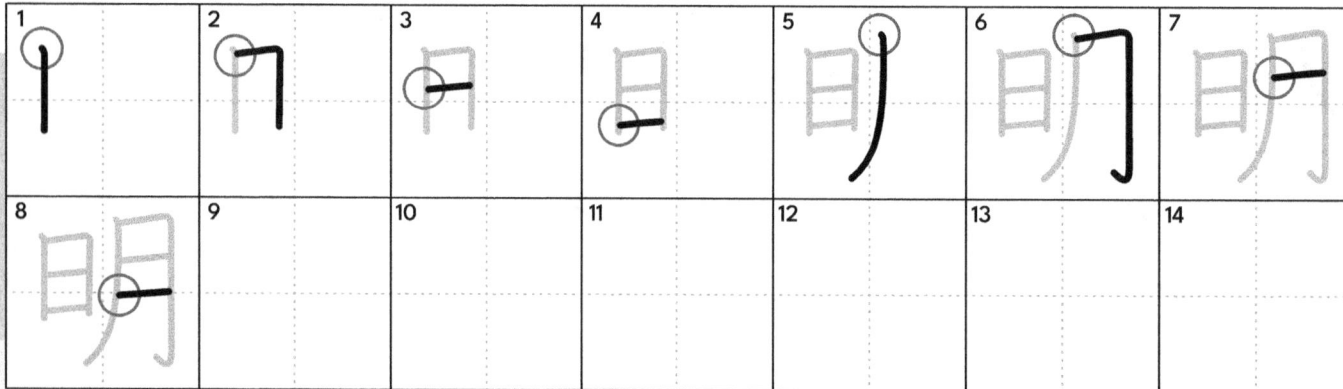

Writing Practice

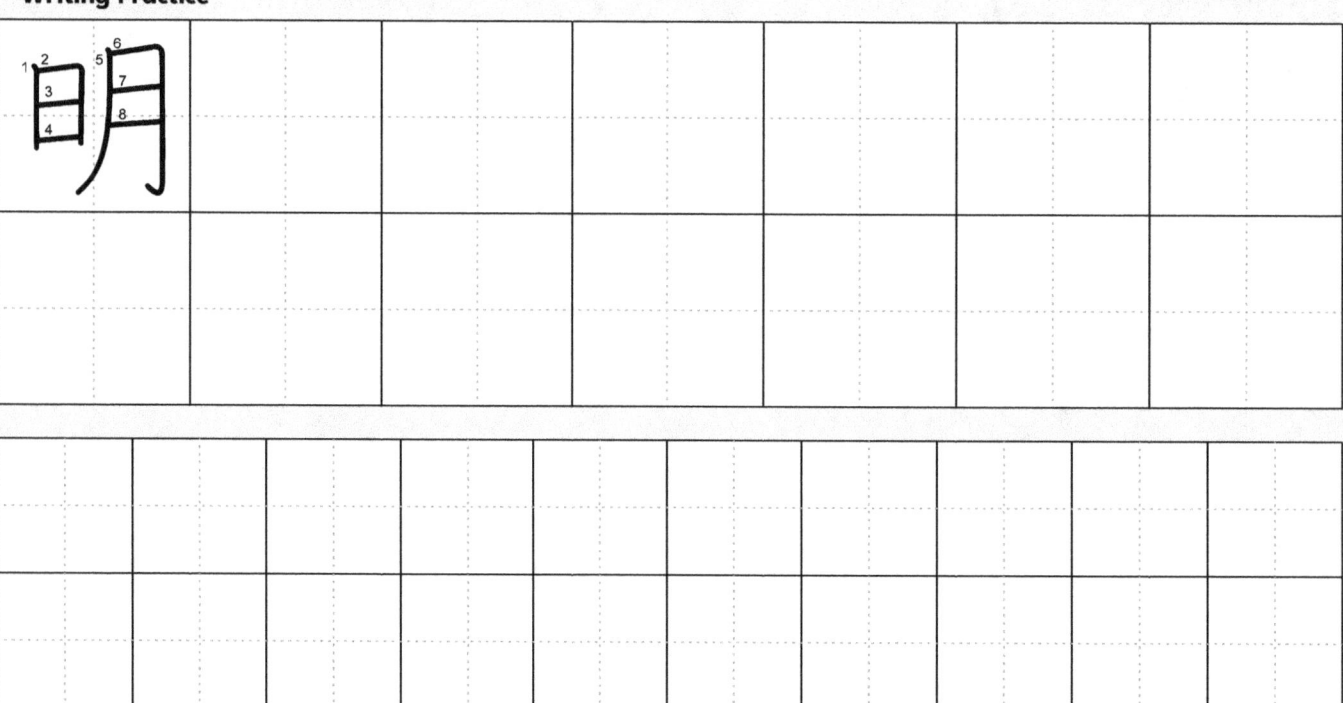

Meaning(s)	move, motion, change	Components	一 丨 ノ カ 日 里
Radical	力 (power)	Kun'yomi	うご.く、うご.かす
Strokes	11	On'yomi	ドウ

Vocabulary	Meaning		Pronunciation
動く	to move, to stir, to shift, to shake		うごく
動かす	to move, to shift, to stir, to budge		うごかす
動	motion		ドウ
異動	(personnel) change, transfer		イドウ

Stroke Order

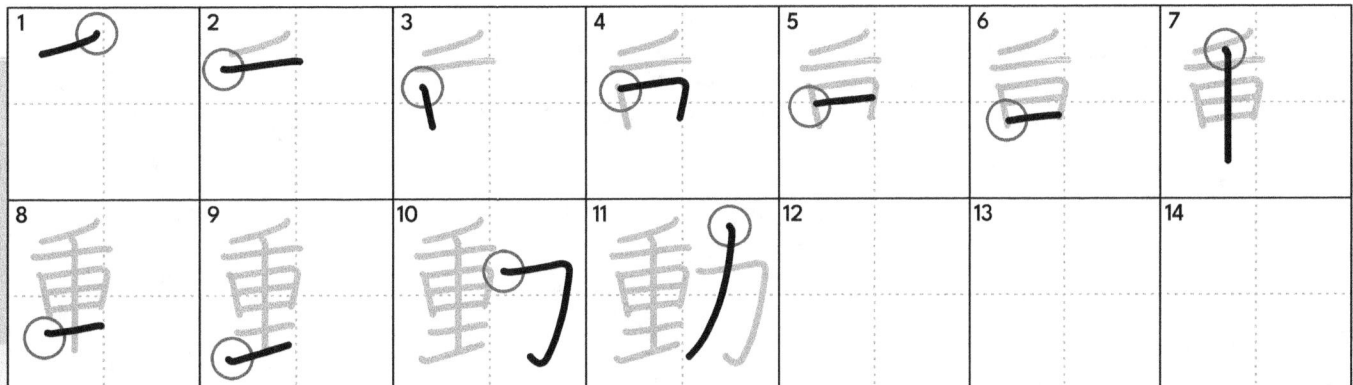

Writing Practice

Meaning(s)	capital	Components	亠 口 小
Radical	亠 (lid)	Kun'yomi	みやこ
Strokes	8	On'yomi	キョウ、ケイ、キン

Vocabulary	Meaning	Pronunciation
都	capital (esp. Kyoto, Japan's former capital)	みやこ
京	imperial capital (esp. Kyoto)	キョウ
京都	Kyoto (city, prefecture)	キョウト
英京	British capital, London	エイキョウ

Stroke Order

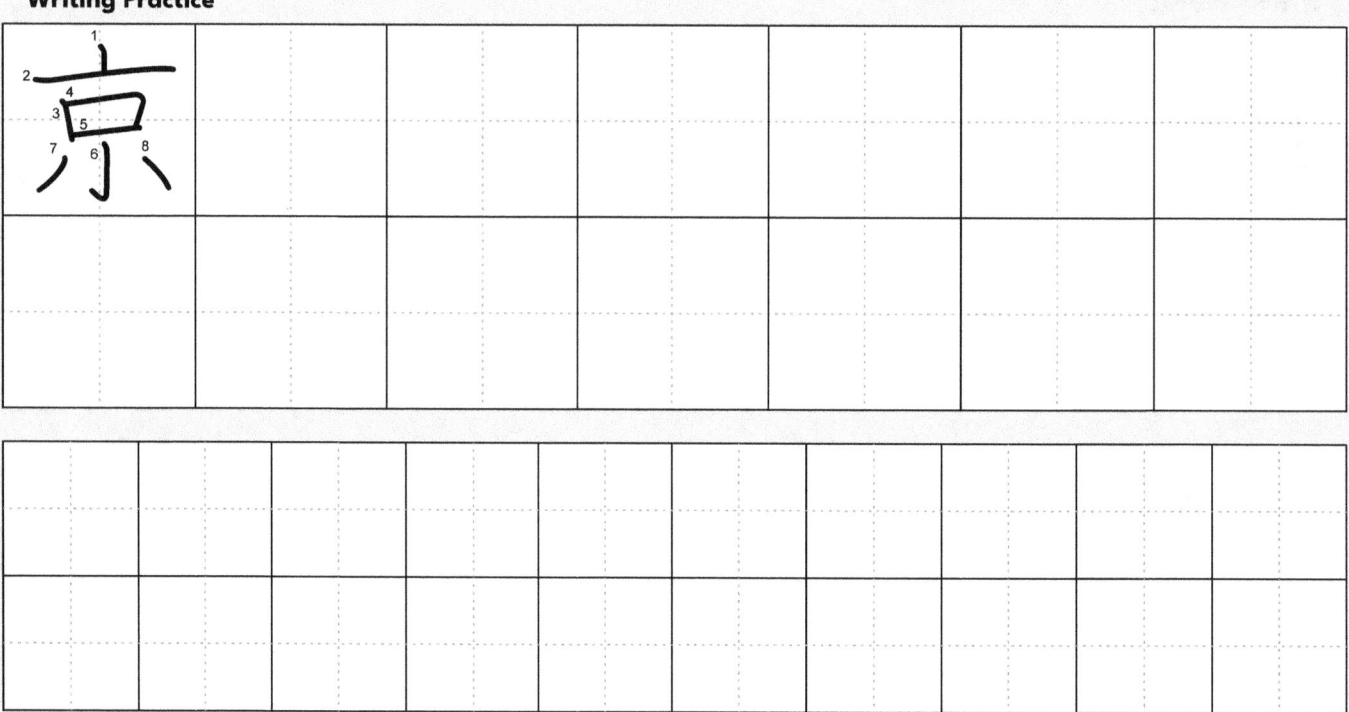

Writing Practice

Meaning(s)	traffic, commute, ave.	Components	マ 込 用
Radical	辵 (辶, 辶) (walk)	Kun'yomi	とお(る)、かよ(う)
Strokes	10	On'yomi	ツウ

Vocabulary	Meaning	Pronunciation
通る	to go by, to go past, to go along	とおる
通り	avenue, street, way, road	とおり
通	authority, expert, connoisseur	ツウ
通う	to go back and forth between	かよう

Stroke Order

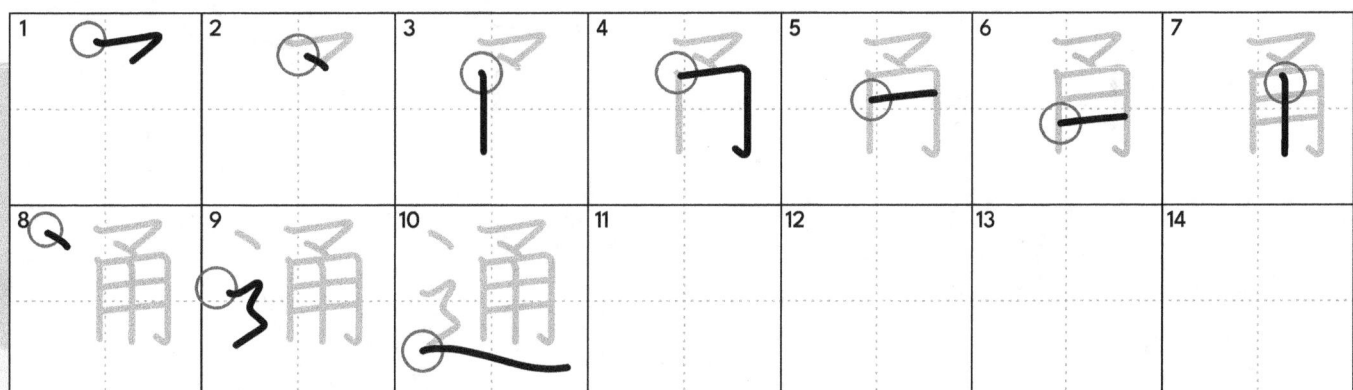

Writing Practice

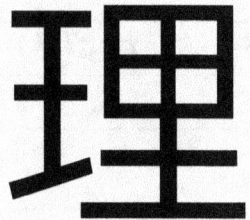

Meaning(s)	arrangement, reason	Components	王 里
Radical	玉 (王) (jade (king))	Kun'yomi	ことわり
Strokes	11	On'yomi	リ

Vocabulary	Meaning	Pronunciation
理	reason, logic, sense	ことわり
理	reason, principle, logic, general principle	リ
理科	science (inc. mathematics, medicine, etc.)	リカ
経理	accounting, administration (of money)	ケイリ

Stroke Order

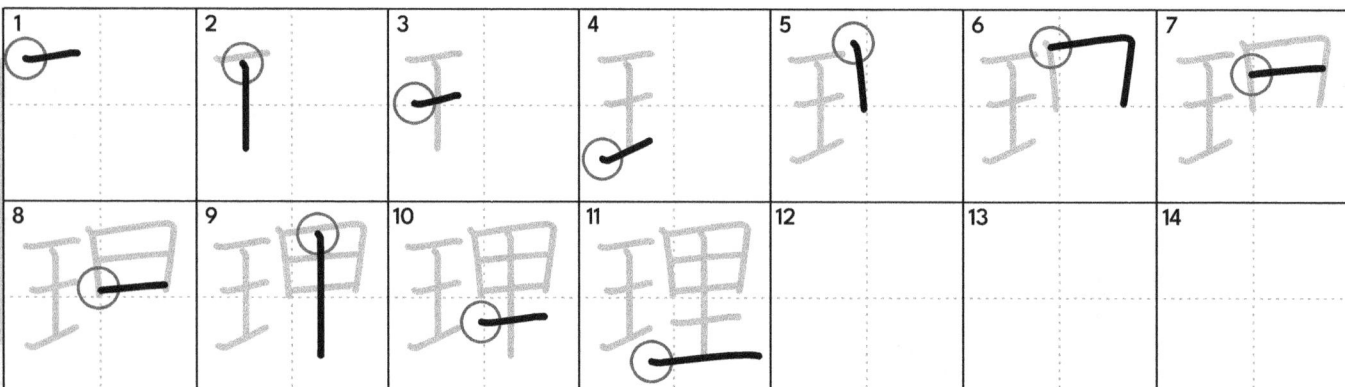

Writing Practice

Meaning(s)	body, substance	**Components**	一 化 木
Radical	人 (亻) (human)	**Kun'yomi**	からだ
Strokes	7	**On'yomi**	タイ

Vocabulary	Meaning	Pronunciation
体	body, torso, trunk, build, physique	からだ
体	body, physique, posture, shape, form	タイ
体育	physical education, PE, gym (class)	タイイク
風体	appearance, look, dress	フウテイ

Stroke Order

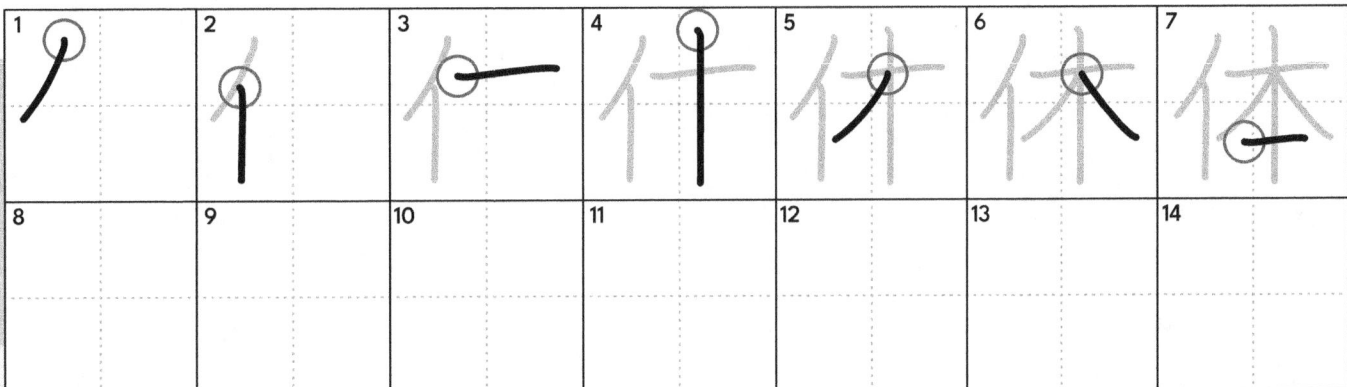

Writing Practice

Meaning(s)	rice field, rice paddy	Components	田
Radical	田 (field)	Kun'yomi	た
Strokes	5	On'yomi	デン

Vocabulary	Meaning	Pronunciation
田	rice field	た
田畑	fields (of rice and other crops)	タハタ
田園	the country, countryside	デンエン
田植え	rice planting	たうえ

Stroke Order

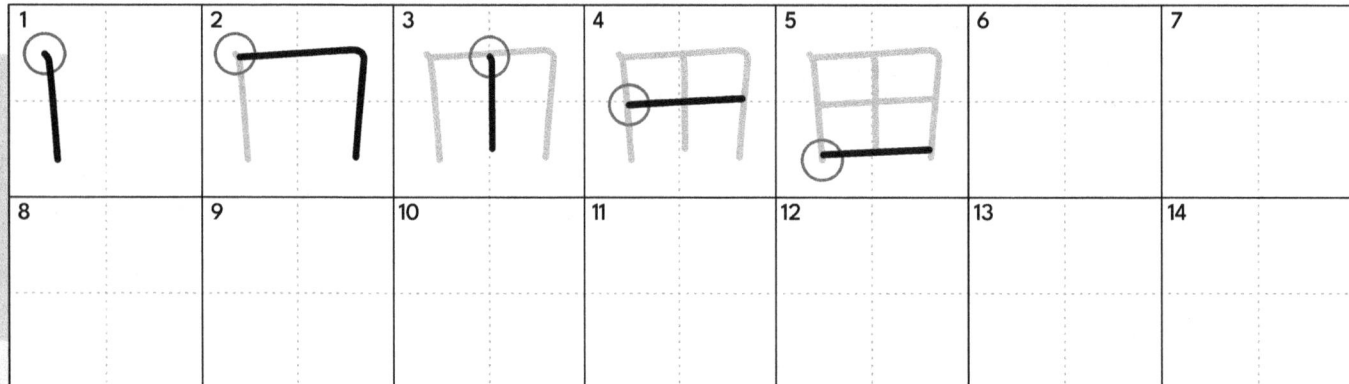

Writing Practice

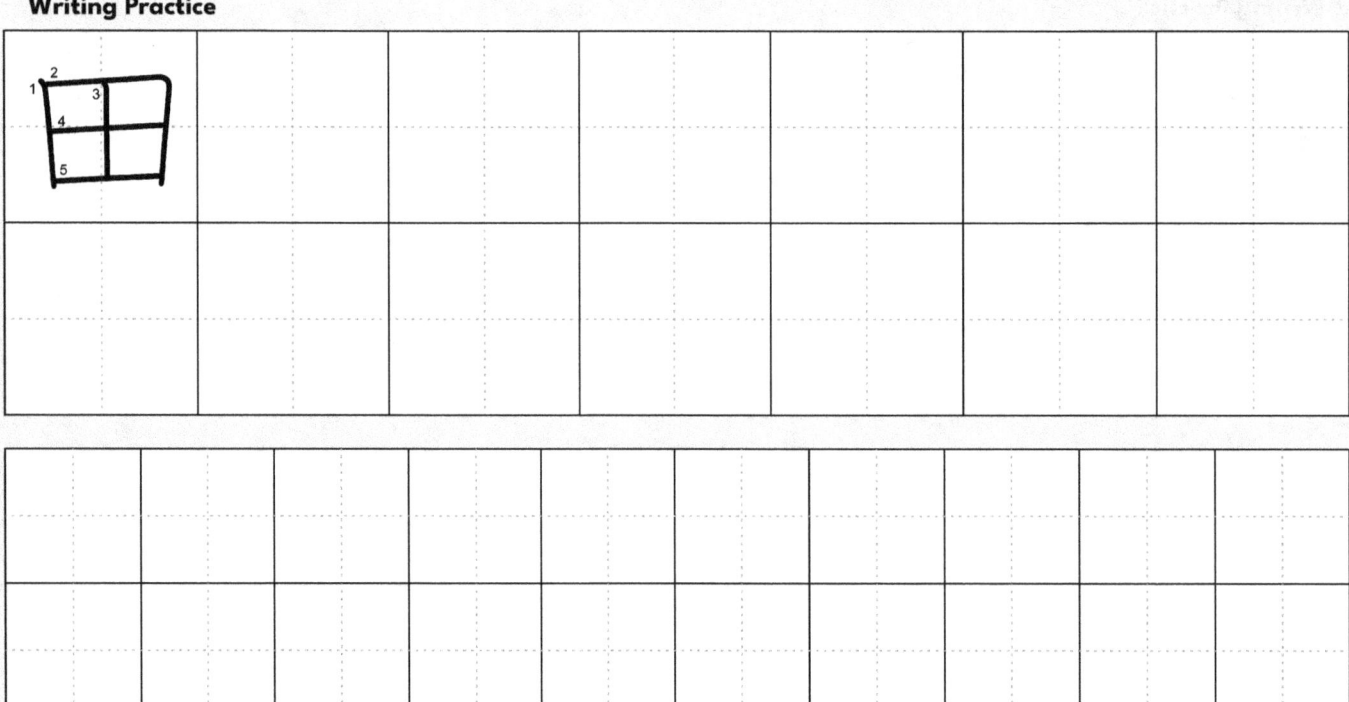

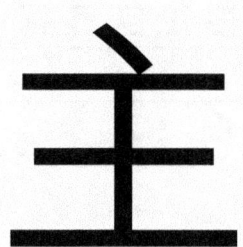

Meaning(s)	lord, chief, master	Components	一ノ干乞
Radical	丶 (dot)	Kun'yomi	ぬし、おも
Strokes	5	On'yomi	シュ

Vocabulary	Meaning	Pronunciation
主	head (of a household, etc.), leader, master	ぬし
主	chief, main, principal, important	おも
主	(one's) master, the main thing, majority	シュ
主に	mainly, primarily	おもに

Stroke Order

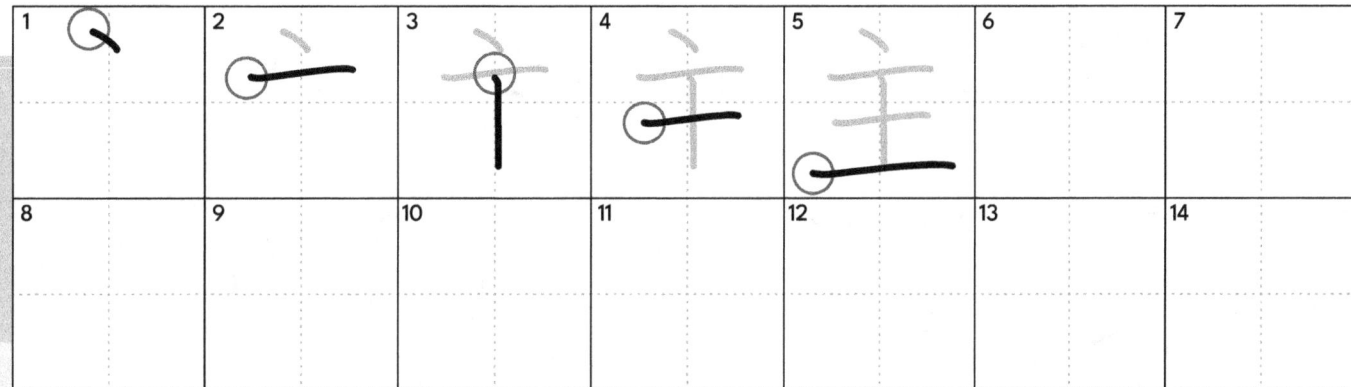

Writing Practice

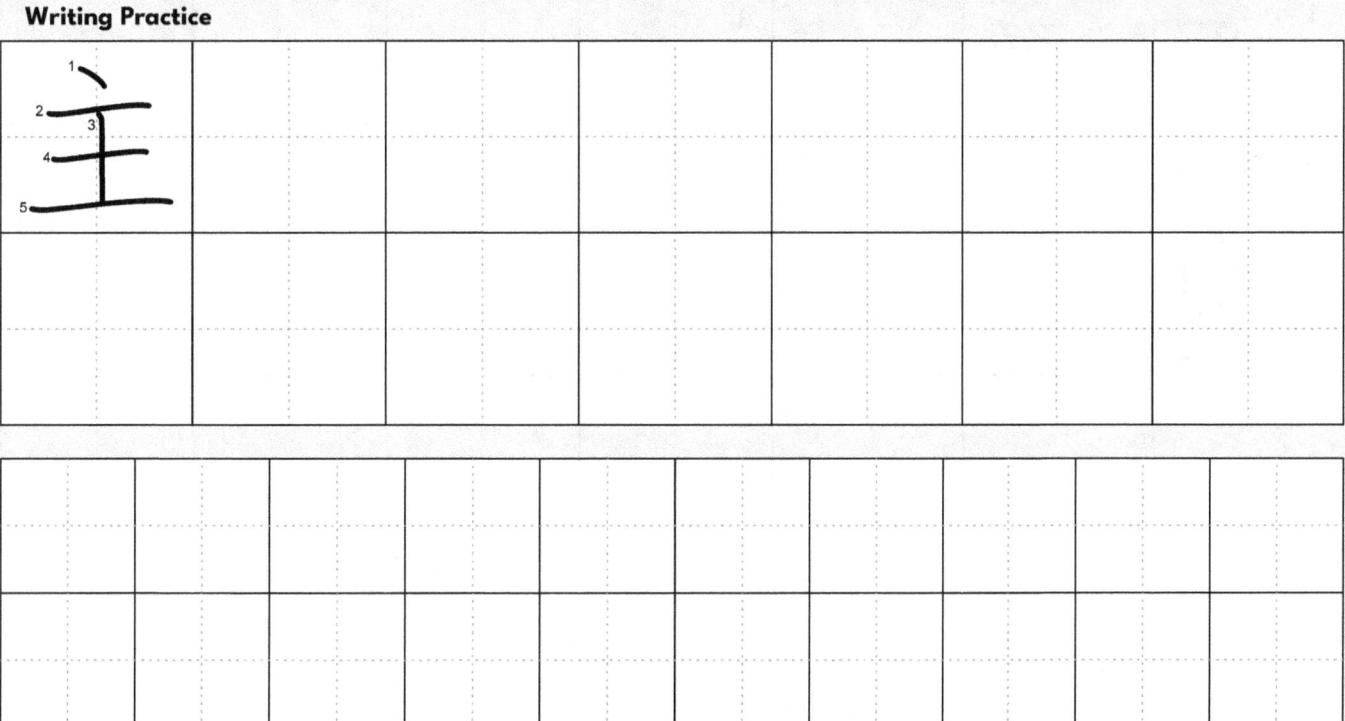

Meaning(s)	topic, subject		Components	八 日 疋 目 貝 頁
Radical	頁 (leaf)		Kun'yomi	
Strokes	18		On'yomi	ダイ

Vocabulary	Meaning	Pronunciation
題	title, subject, theme, topic	ダイ
題材	subject, theme	ダイザイ
表題	title, index, heading, headline, caption	ヒョウダイ
命題	proposition, thesis, notion, theory	メイダイ

Stroke Order

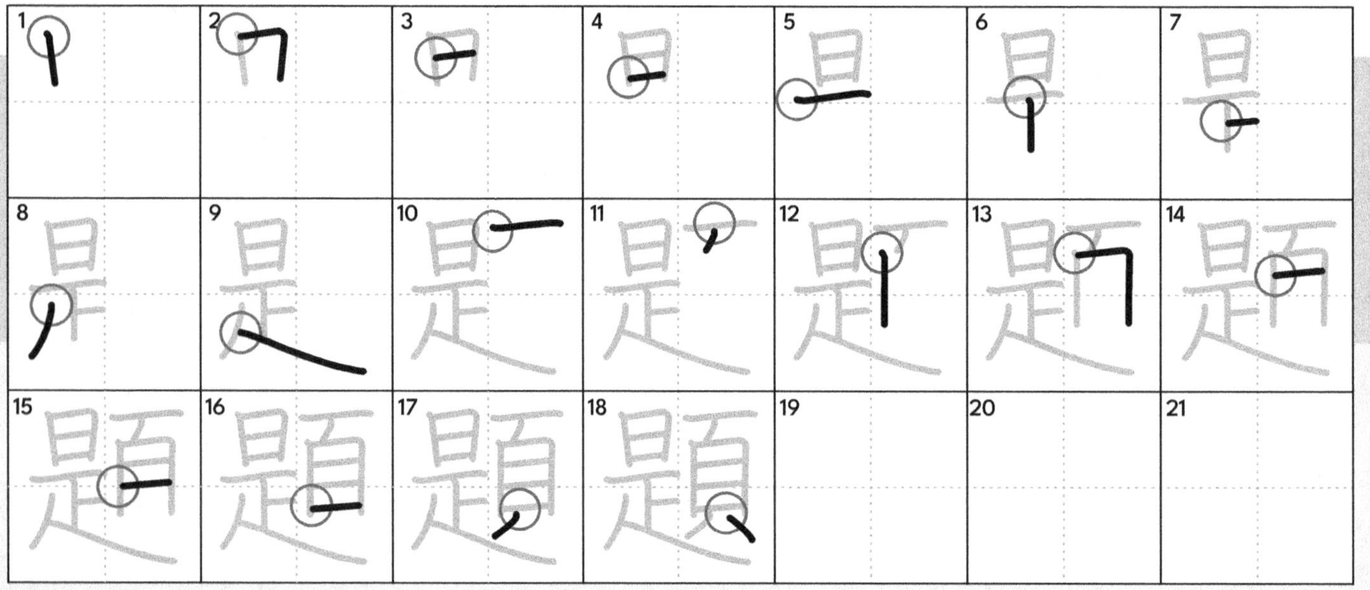

Writing Practice

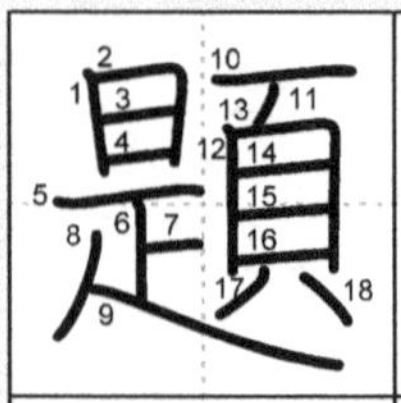

Meaning(s)	idea, mind, heart	Components	心日立音
Radical	心 (忄, 㣺) (heart)	Kun'yomi	
Strokes	13	On'yomi	イ

Vocabulary	Meaning		Pronunciation
意	feelings, thoughts, meaning		イ
意外	unexpected, surprising		イガイ
賛意	approval, assent		サンイ
総意	consensus, collective will		ソウイ

Stroke Order

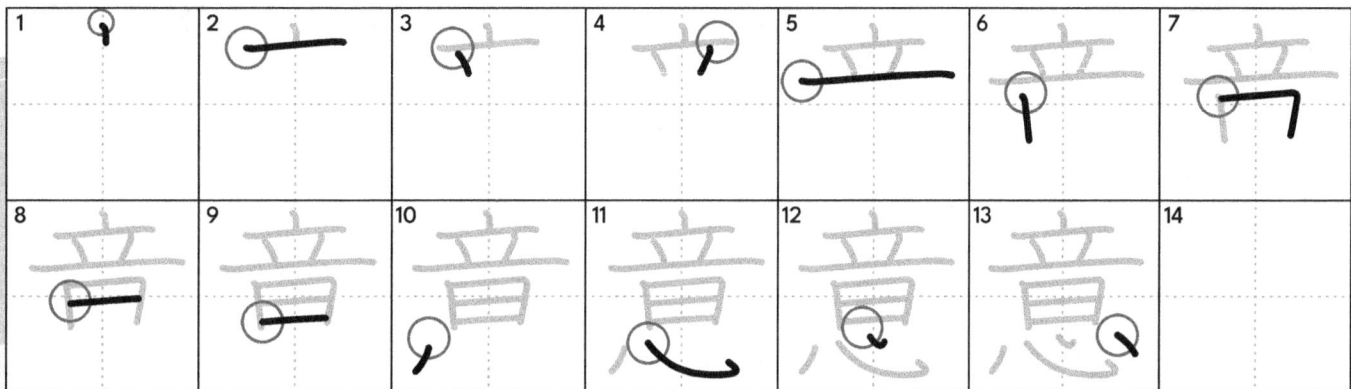

Writing Practice

Meaning(s)	negative, non-, bad		Components	一 丨 丶 ノ
Radical	一 (one)		Kun'yomi	
Strokes	4		On'yomi	フ、ブ

Vocabulary	Meaning	Pronunciation
不	un-, non-, negative prefix	フ
不安	anxiety, uneasiness, worry	フアン
意味不	of uncertain meaning, ambiguous	イミフ
不気味	weird, ominous, eerie, uncanny	ブキミ

Stroke Order

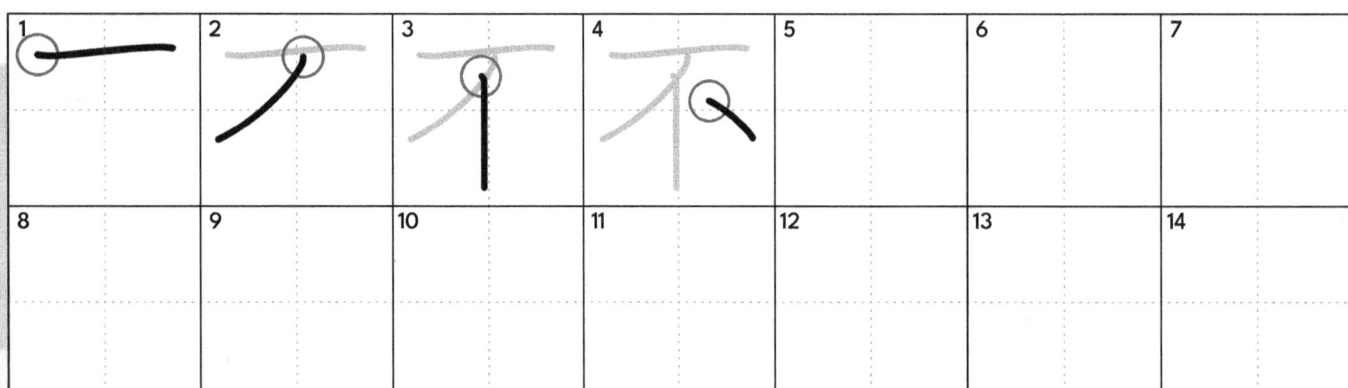

Writing Practice

Meaning(s)	make, prepare, build	**Components**	一 丨 ノ 化 乞
Radical	人 (亻) (human)	**Kun'yomi**	つく(る)
Strokes	7	**On'yomi**	サク、サ

Vocabulary	Meaning	Pronunciation
作る	to make, to produce, to manufacture	つくる
作	work (e.g. of art), production	サク
作業	work, operation, task	サギョウ
作る	to raise, to grow, to cultivate, to train	つくる

Stroke Order

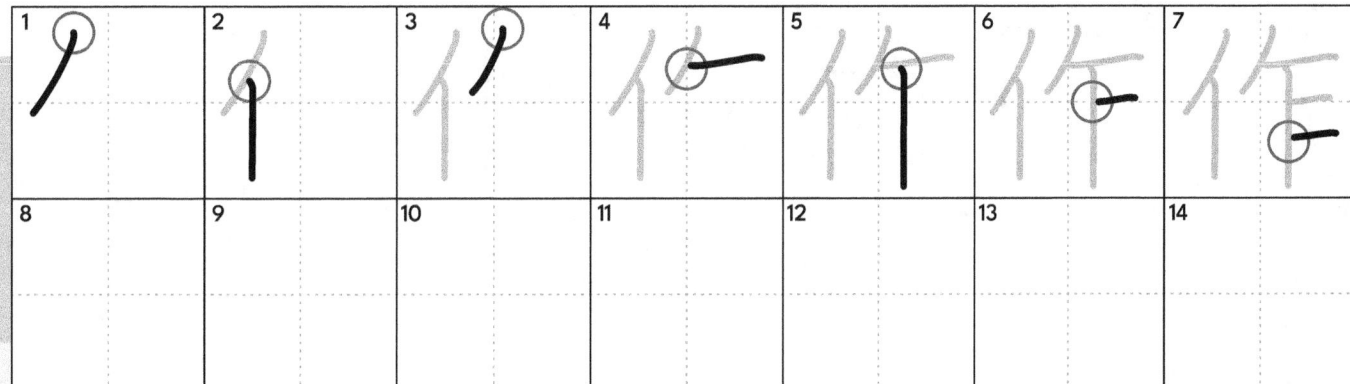

Writing Practice

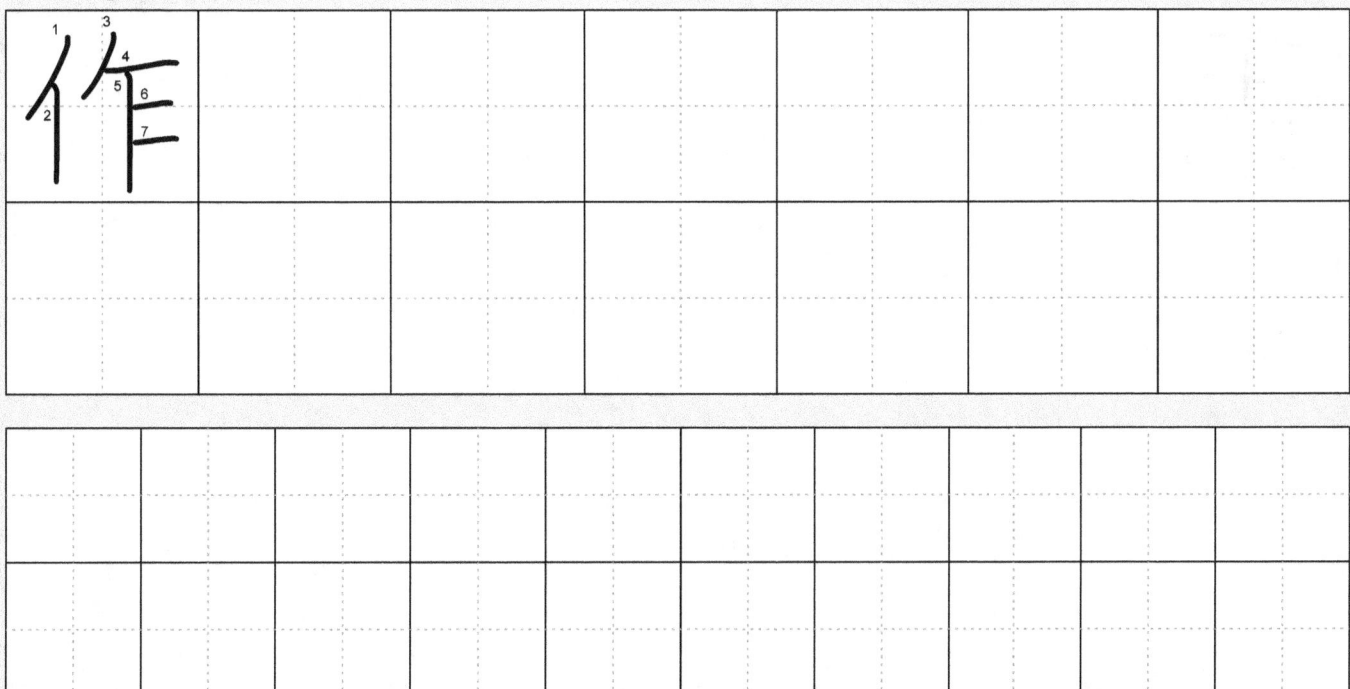

Meaning(s)	business, service, use	Components	用
Radical	用 (甩) (use)	Kun'yomi	もち(いる)
Strokes	5	On'yomi	ヨウ

Vocabulary	Meaning	Pronunciation
用いる	to use, to make use of, to utilize	もちいる
用	business, task, errand, engagement	ヨウ
登用	appointment, assignment, promotion	トウヨウ
用意	preparation, arrangements	ヨウイ

Stroke Order

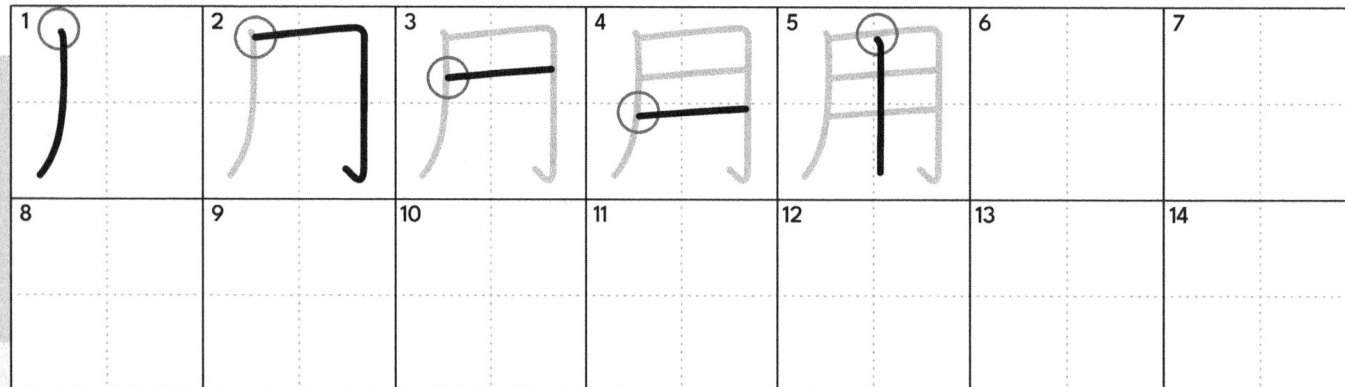

Writing Practice

Meaning(s)	occurrence, time	Components	一 又 广 口
Radical	广 (house on cliff)	Kun'yomi	たび、た(い)
Strokes	9	On'yomi	ド、タク

Vocabulary	Meaning	Pronunciation
度	time (three times, each time, etc.)	たび
度	degree (angle, temperature, etc.), extent	ド
法度	law, ban, prohibition, ordinance	ハット
中度	midway (through), halfway	なかたび

Stroke Order

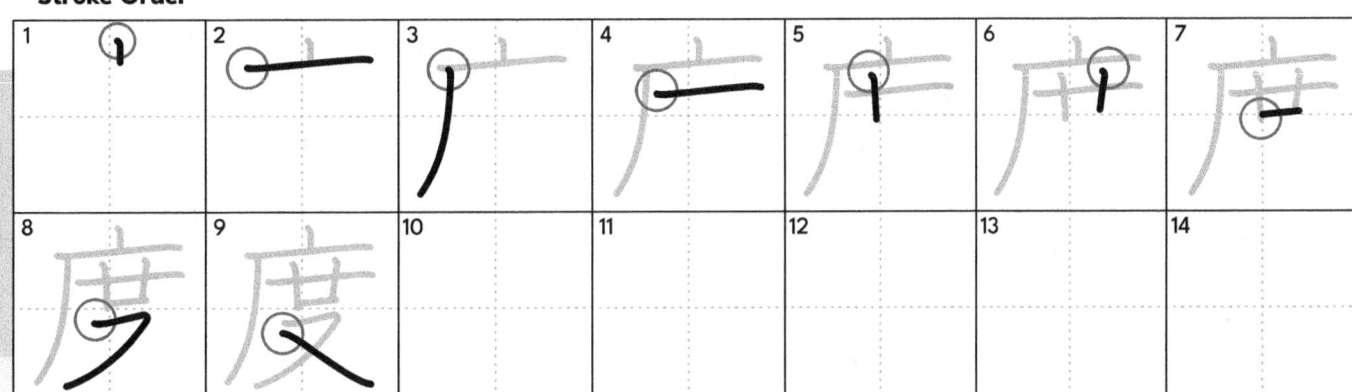

Writing Practice

強

Meaning(s)	strong	Components	ム 弓 虫
Radical	弓 (bow)	Kun'yomi	つよ(い)
Strokes	11	On'yomi	キョウ、ゴウ

Vocabulary	Meaning	Pronunciation
強い	strong, potent, competent, skilled, knowledgeable, being able to handle	つよい
強	a little more than, strength, one of the biggest	キョウ
強盗	robber, mugger, robbery, burglary	ゴウトウ

Stroke Order

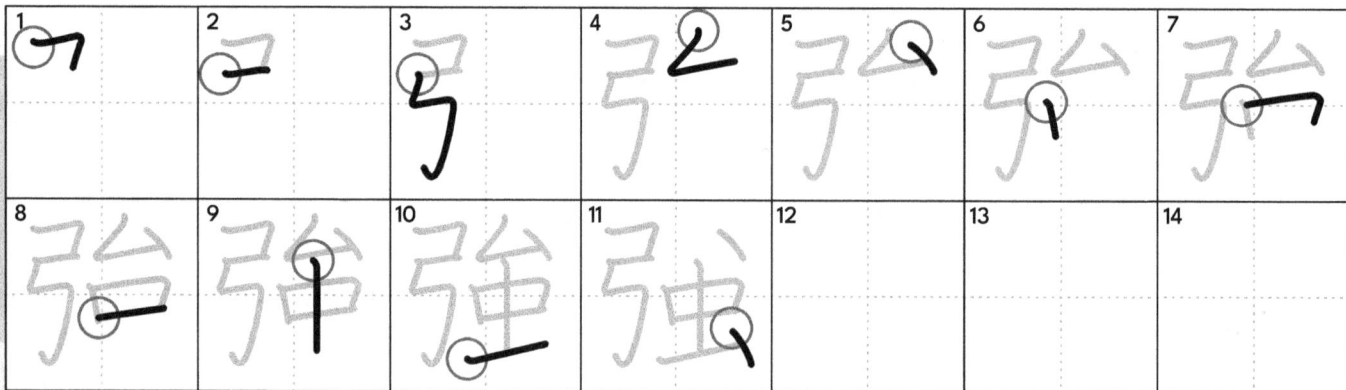

Writing Practice

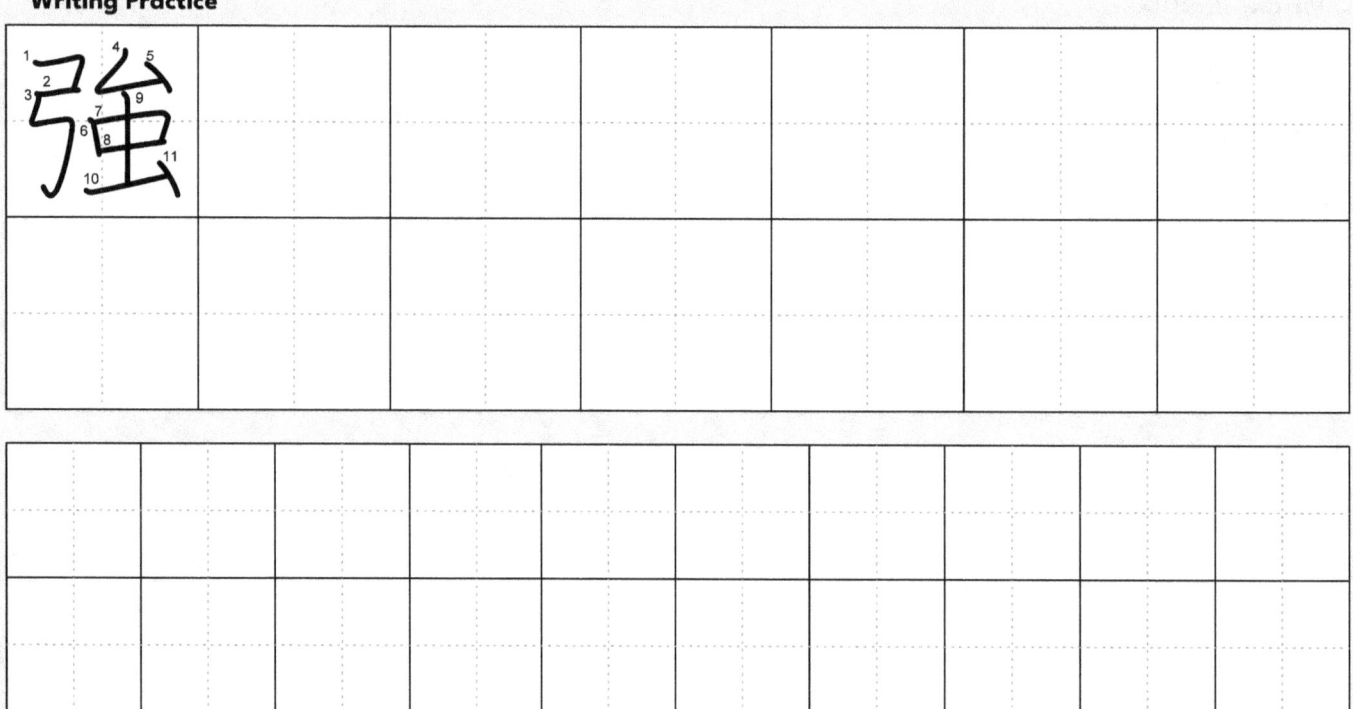

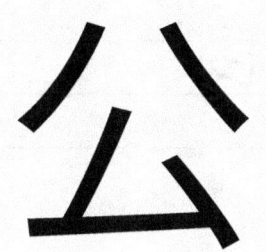

Meaning(s)	public, prince, official	Components	ハ ム
Radical	八 (eight)	Kun'yomi	おおやけ
Strokes	4	On'yomi	コウ

Vocabulary	Meaning		Pronunciation
公	official, formal, public (use, matter, etc.)		おおやけ
公	public affair, government matter		コウ
公廨	government office		クガイ
王侯	king and princes, noble rank		オウコウ

Stroke Order

Writing Practice

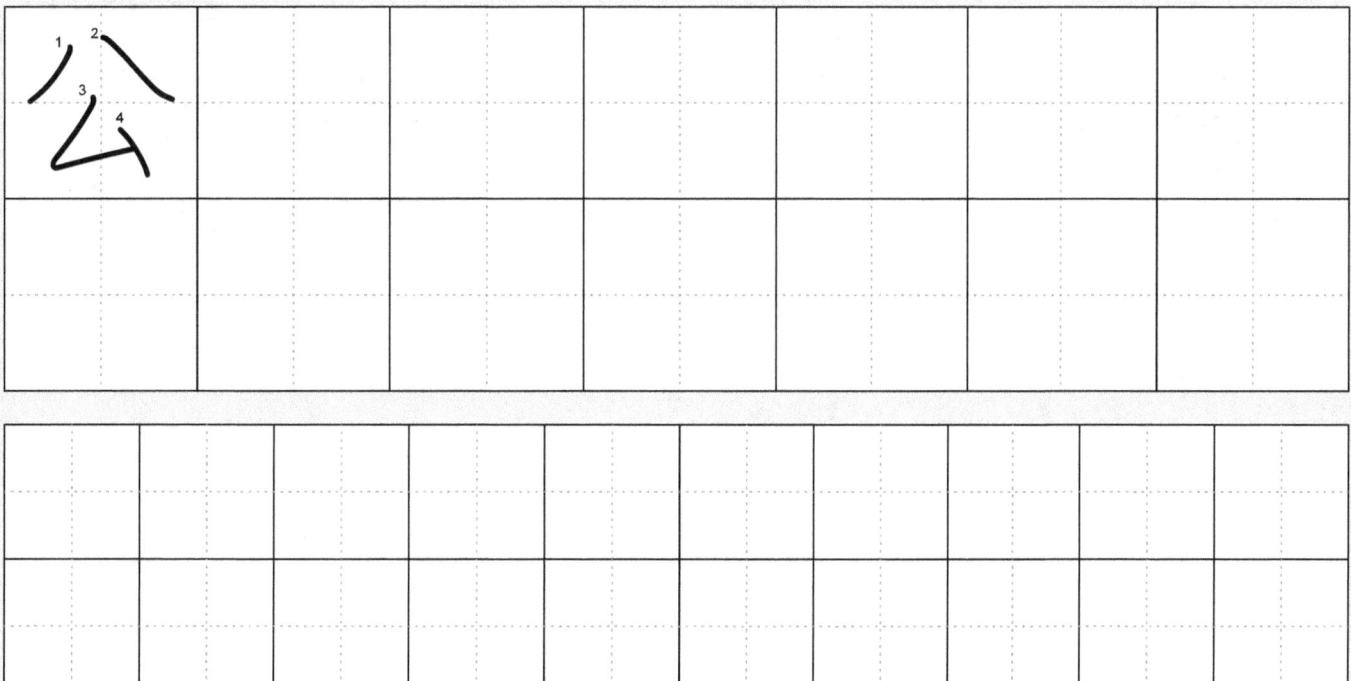

Meaning(s)	hold, have	Components	土寸扎
Radical	手 (扌 ⺘) (hand)	Kun'yomi	も(つ)
Strokes	9	On'yomi	ジ

Vocabulary	Meaning		Pronunciation
持つ	to hold (in one's hand), to take/carry		もつ
持久	endurance, persistence		ジキュウ
持	draw (in a contest), tie		ジ
持てる	to be welcomed, to be popular		もてる

Stroke Order

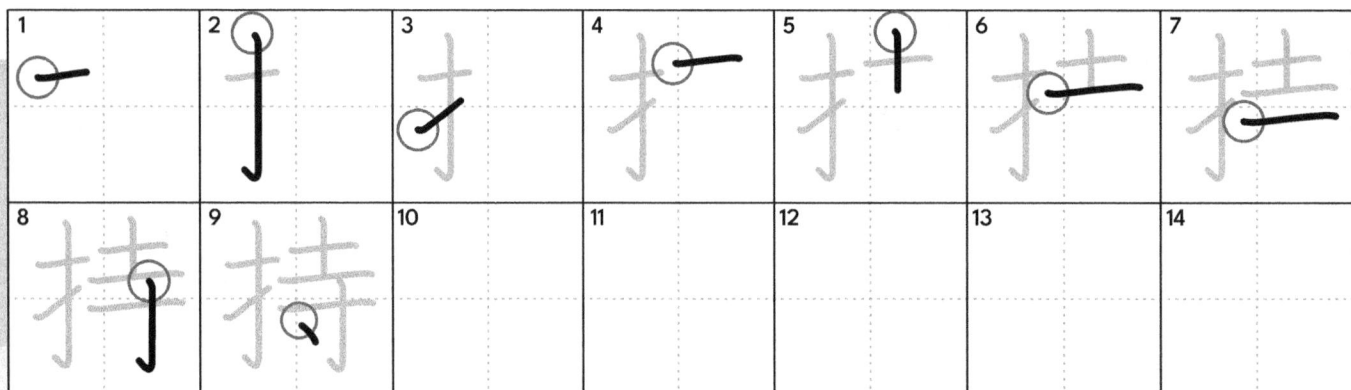

Writing Practice

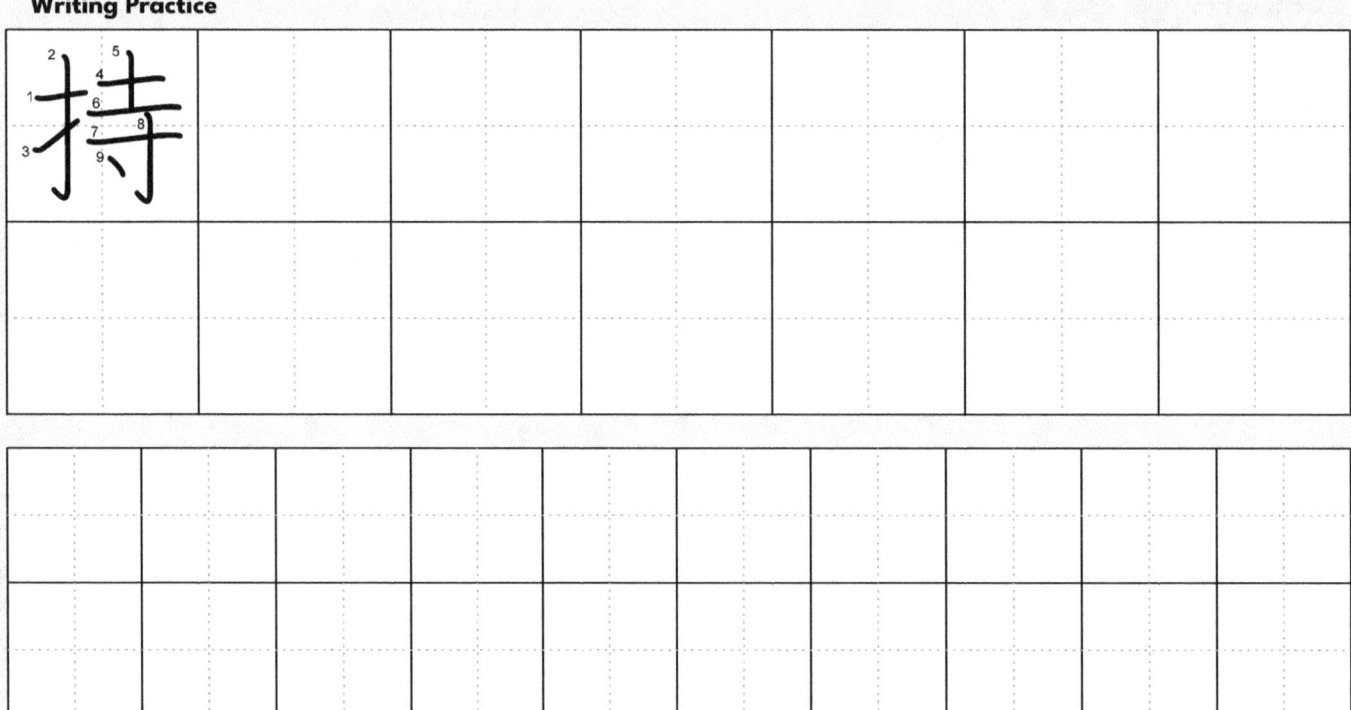

Meaning(s)	plains, field, rustic	Components	乛 矛 里
Radical	里 (village, mile)	Kun'yomi	の
Strokes	11	On'yomi	ヤ

Vocabulary	Meaning	Pronunciation
野	plain, field, wild	の
野	plain, field, hidden (structural) member	ノ
野外	outdoors, outside, open air	ヤガイ
在野	out of office, out of power	ザイヤ

Stroke Order

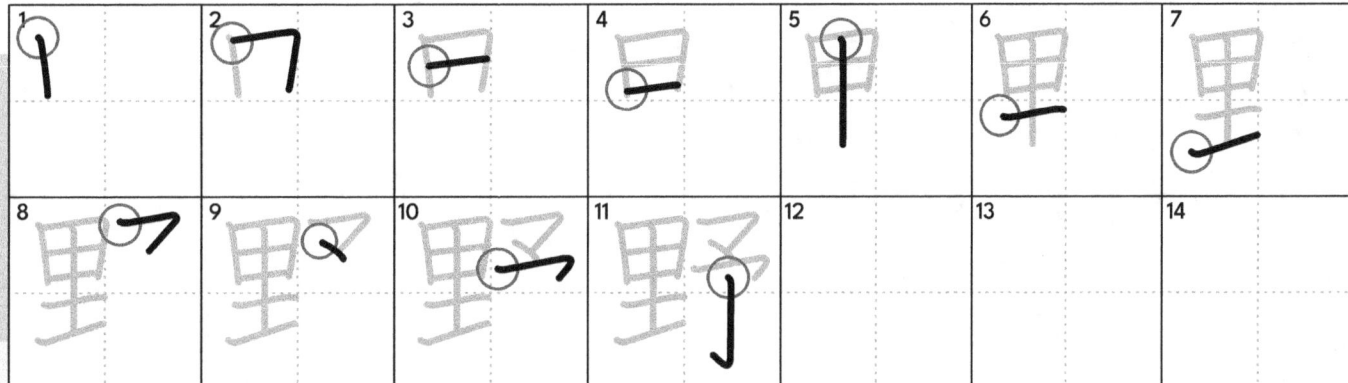

Writing Practice

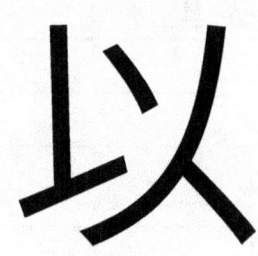

Meaning(s)	by means of, because	Components	｜、人
Radical	人 (亻) (human)	Kun'yomi	もっ(て)
Strokes	5	On'yomi	イ

Vocabulary	Meaning	Pronunciation
以て 以降 以下	with, by, by means of, because of on and after, from ... onward not exceeding ..., not more than ...	もって イコウ イカ

Stroke Order

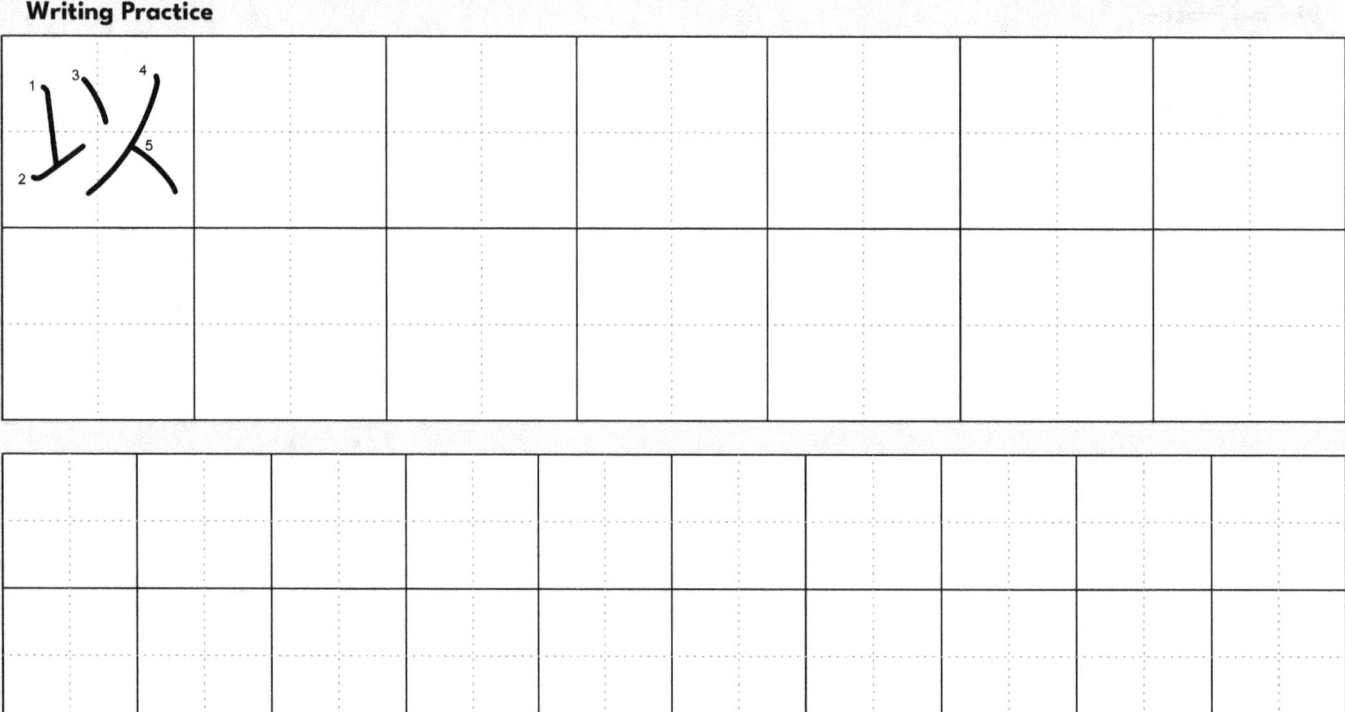

Writing Practice

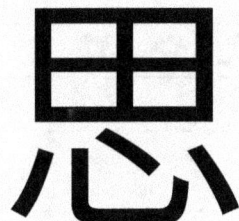

Meaning(s)	think	Components	心 田
Radical	心 (忄, 㣺) (heart)	Kun'yomi	おも(う)
Strokes	9	On'yomi	シ

Vocabulary	Meaning	Pronunciation
思う	to think, to consider, to believe	おもう
思考	thought, consideration, thinking	シコウ
相思	mutual affection, mutual love	ソウシ
哀思	sad feeling	アイシ

Stroke Order

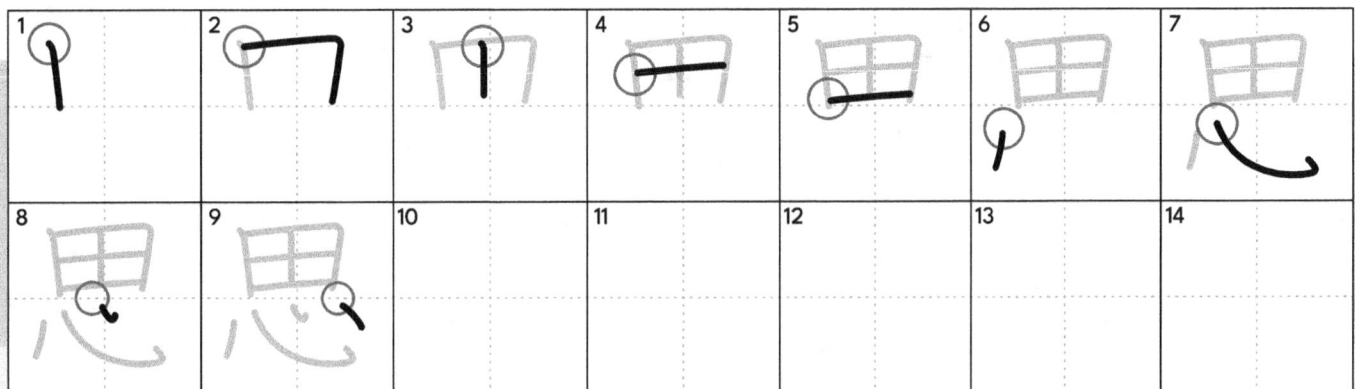

Writing Practice

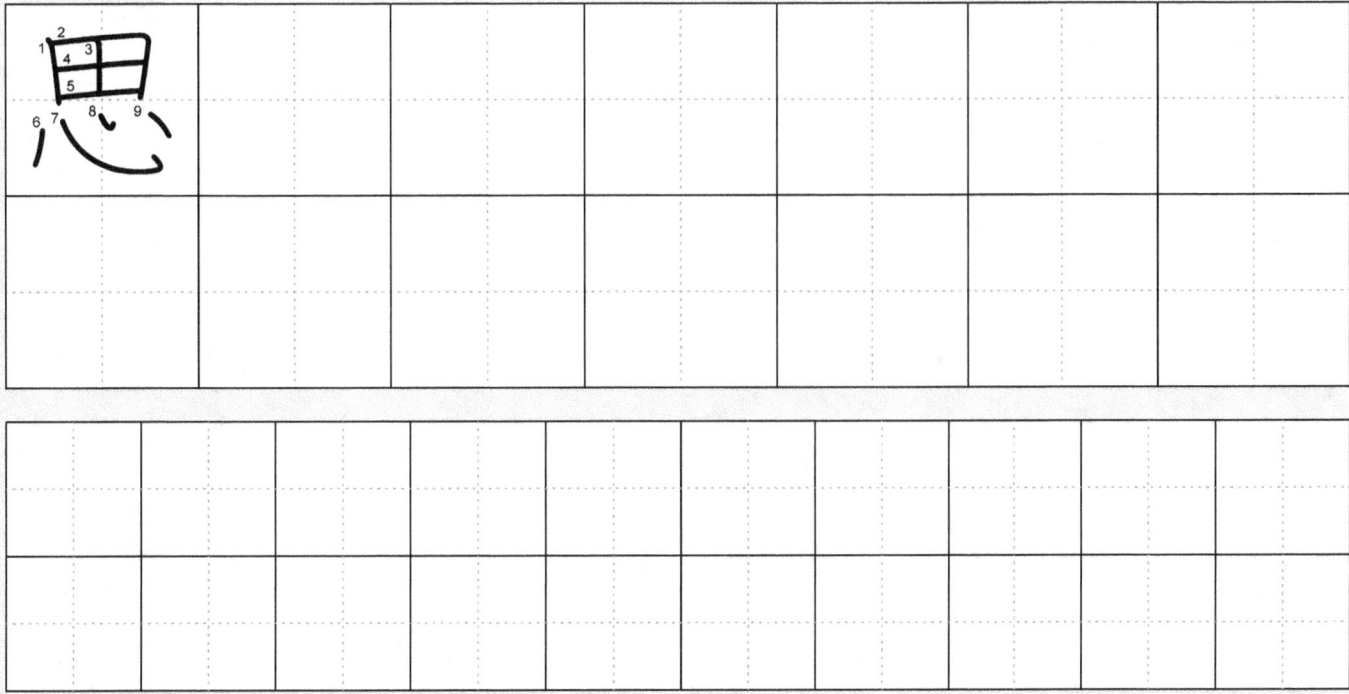

Meaning(s)	house, home, family	Components	人
Radical	宀 (roof)	Kun'yomi	いえ、や、うち
Strokes	10	On'yomi	カ

Vocabulary	Meaning		Pronunciation
家	house, residence, dwelling, family		いえ
家主	landlord, landlady, house owner		やぬし
家	-ist, -er		カ
家	house, one's house/home,, one's family		うち

Stroke Order

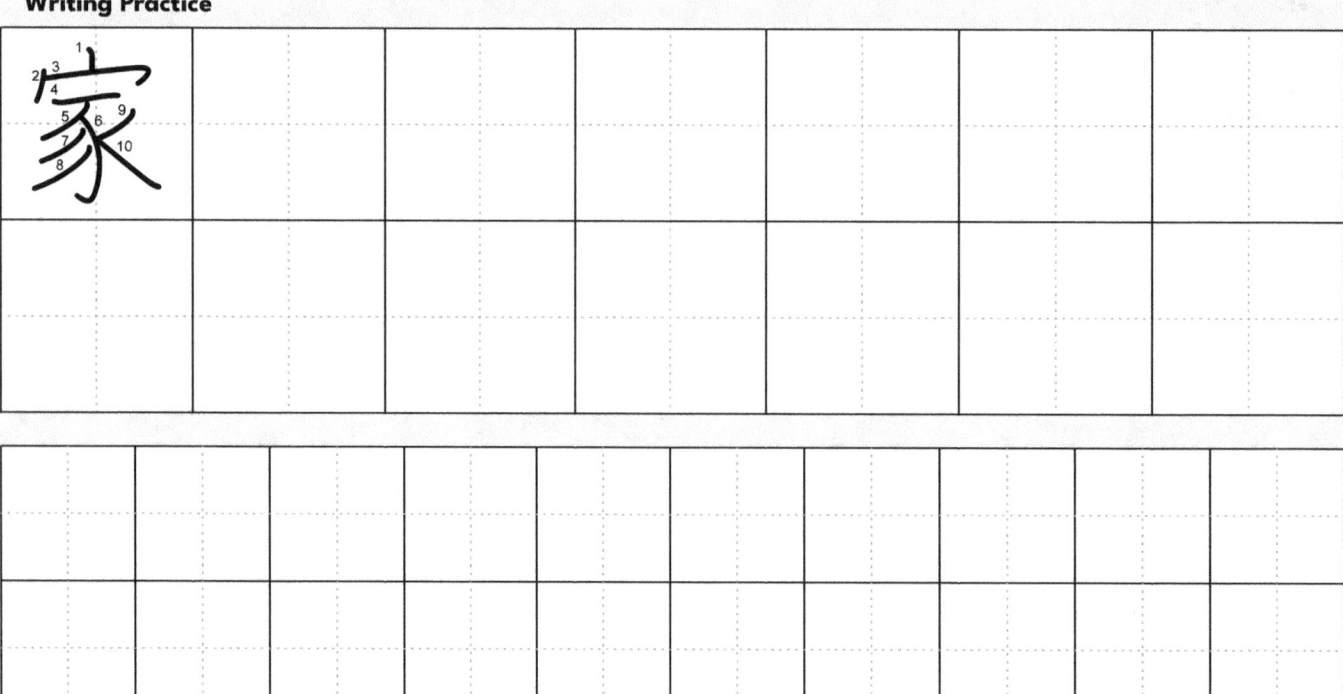

Writing Practice

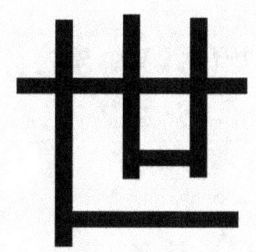

Meaning(s)	society, world, public	**Components**	一 | 世
Radical	一 (one)	**Kun'yomi**	よ
Strokes	5	**On'yomi**	セイ、セ

Vocabulary	Meaning	Pronunciation
世	world, society, public, life, lifetime	よ
世	counter for generations, epoch	セイ
世の中	society, the world, the times	よのなか
夜店	night stall, night shop, night fair	ヨミセ

Stroke Order

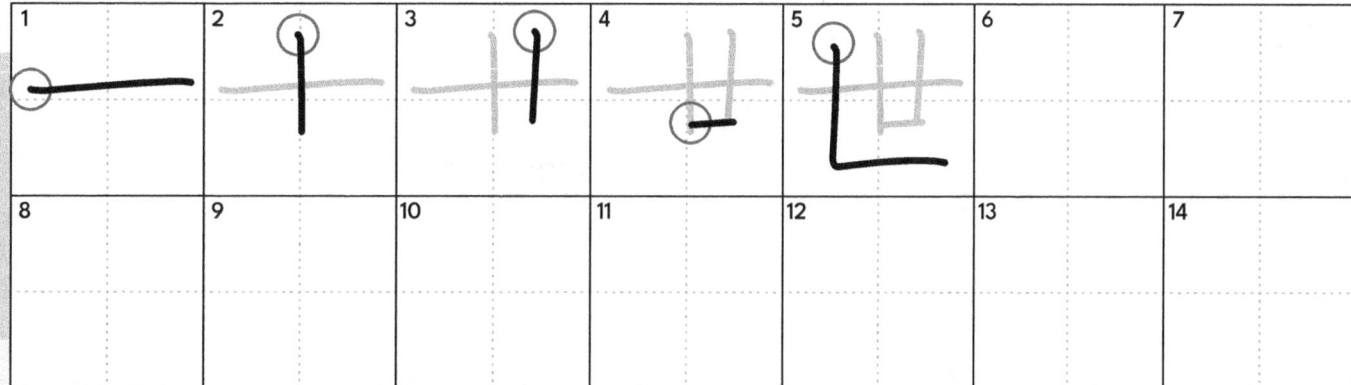

Writing Practice

Meaning(s)	correct, justice, righteous		Components	一 止
Radical	止 (stop)		Kun'yomi	ただ(しい)、まさ(に)
Strokes	5		On'yomi	セイ、ショウ

Vocabulary	Meaning	Pronunciation
正しい	right, correct, proper, honest	ただしい
正	(logical) true, regular	セイ
正解	correct answer, right solution	セイカイ
正(に)	exact(ly), precise(ly)	まさ(に)

Stroke Order

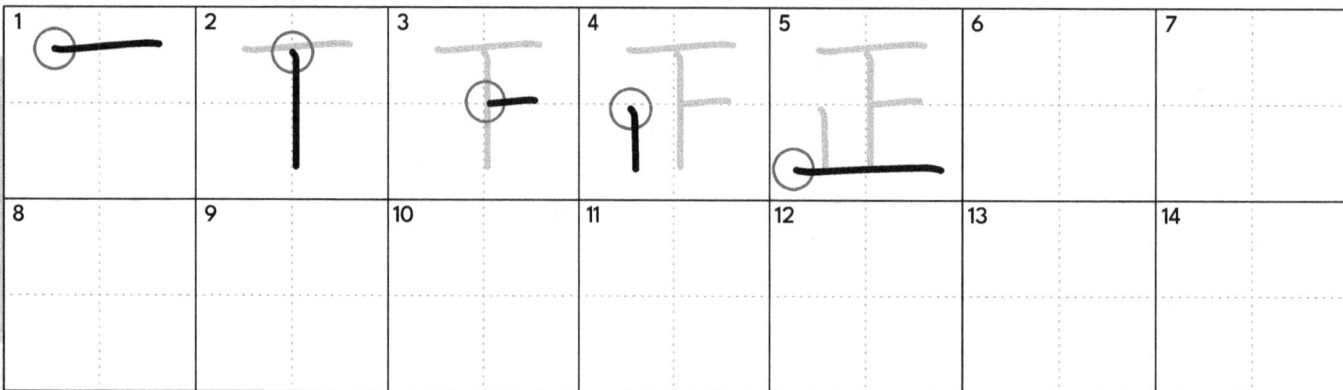

Writing Practice

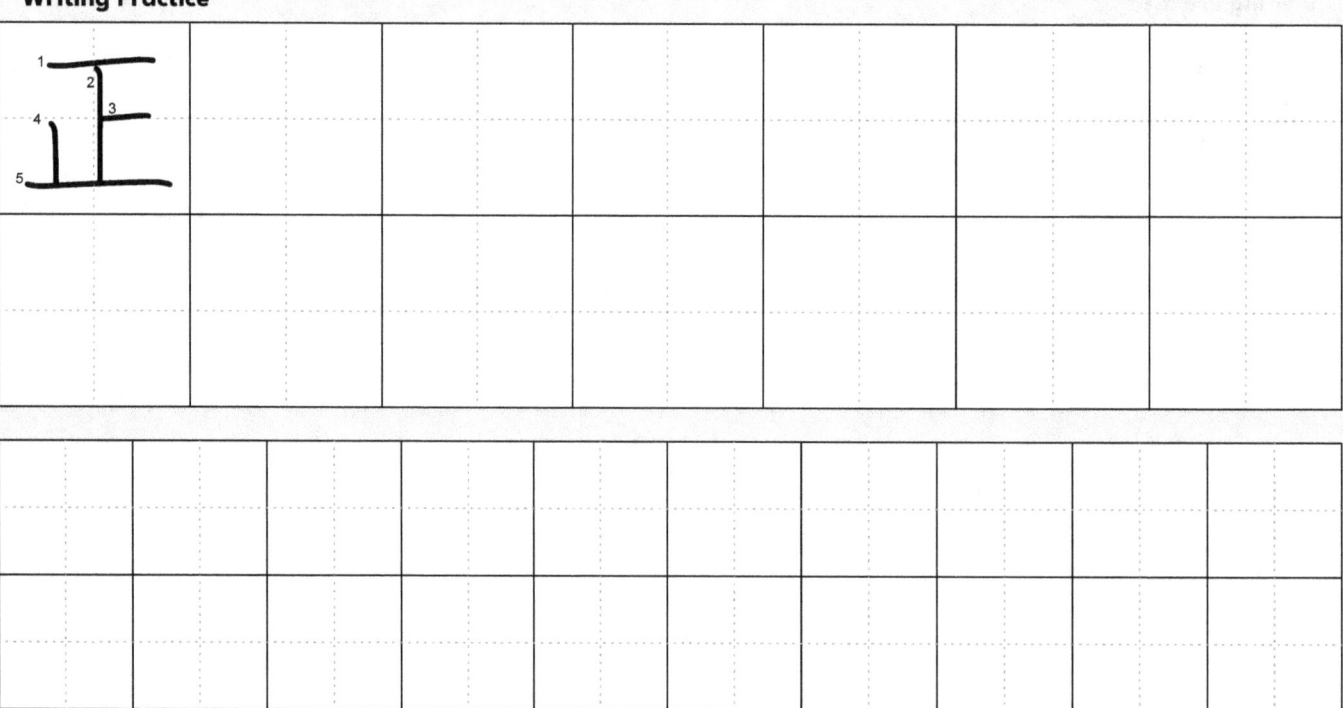

院

Meaning(s)	temple, mansion, school	Components	二儿宀阝元
Radical	阜 (阝)(mound, dam)	Kun'yomi	
Strokes	10	On'yomi	イン

Vocabulary	Meaning	Pronunciation
院	house of parliament (congress, etc.), graduate school, postgraduate school	イン
院長	director (of a hospital, institution, etc.)	インチョウ
棋院	go institution, go club, go hall	キイン

Stroke Order

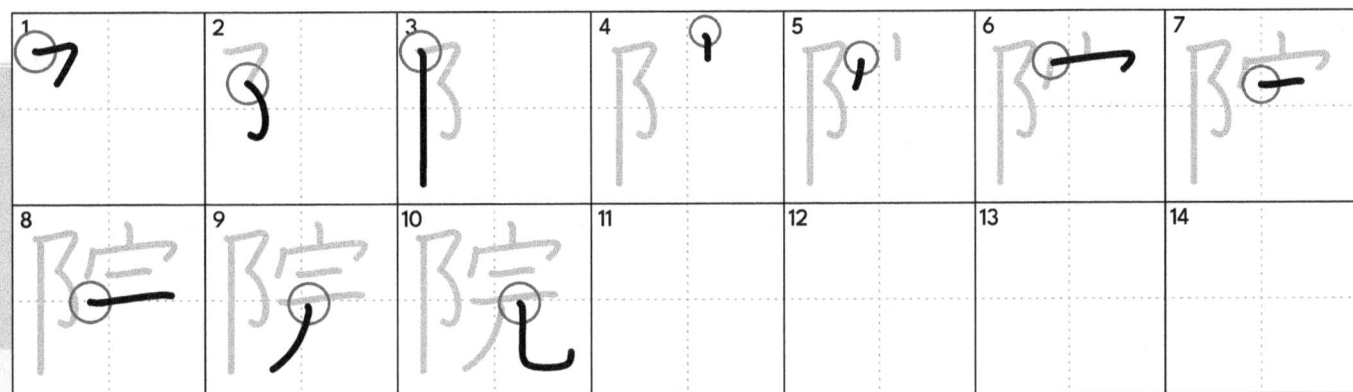

Writing Practice

Meaning(s)	heart, mind, spirit	Components	心	
Radical	心 (忄, 小) (heart)	Kun'yomi	こころ	
Strokes	4	On'yomi	シン	

Vocabulary	Meaning	Pronunciation
心	mind, heart, spirit, the meaning of a phrase	こころ
心	heart, mind, spirit, vitality, inner strength	シン
我が心	my heart	わがこころ
会心	congeniality, satisfaction, gratification	カイシン

Stroke Order

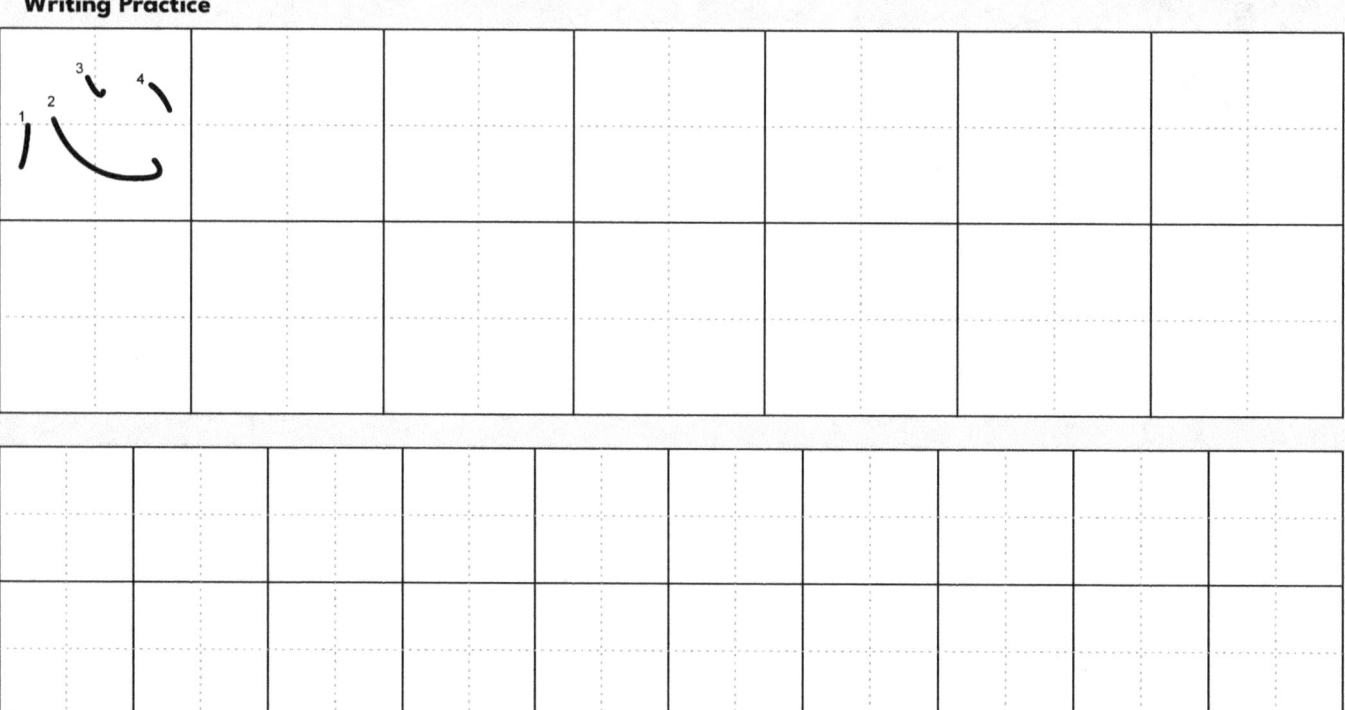

Writing Practice

Meaning(s)	world, boundary	Components	个儿田
Radical	田 (field)	Kun'yomi	
Strokes	9	On'yomi	カイ

Vocabulary	Meaning		Pronunciation
界	community, circles, world, kingdom		カイ
界隈	neighborhood, neighbourhood		カイワイ
球界	the baseball world		キュウカイ
経済界	economic world, financial circles		ケイザイカイ

Stroke Order

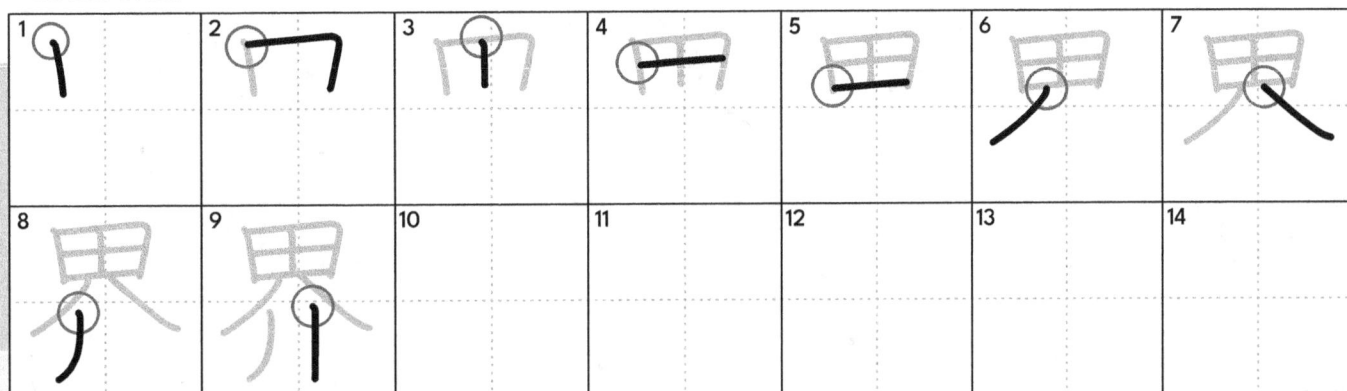

Writing Practice

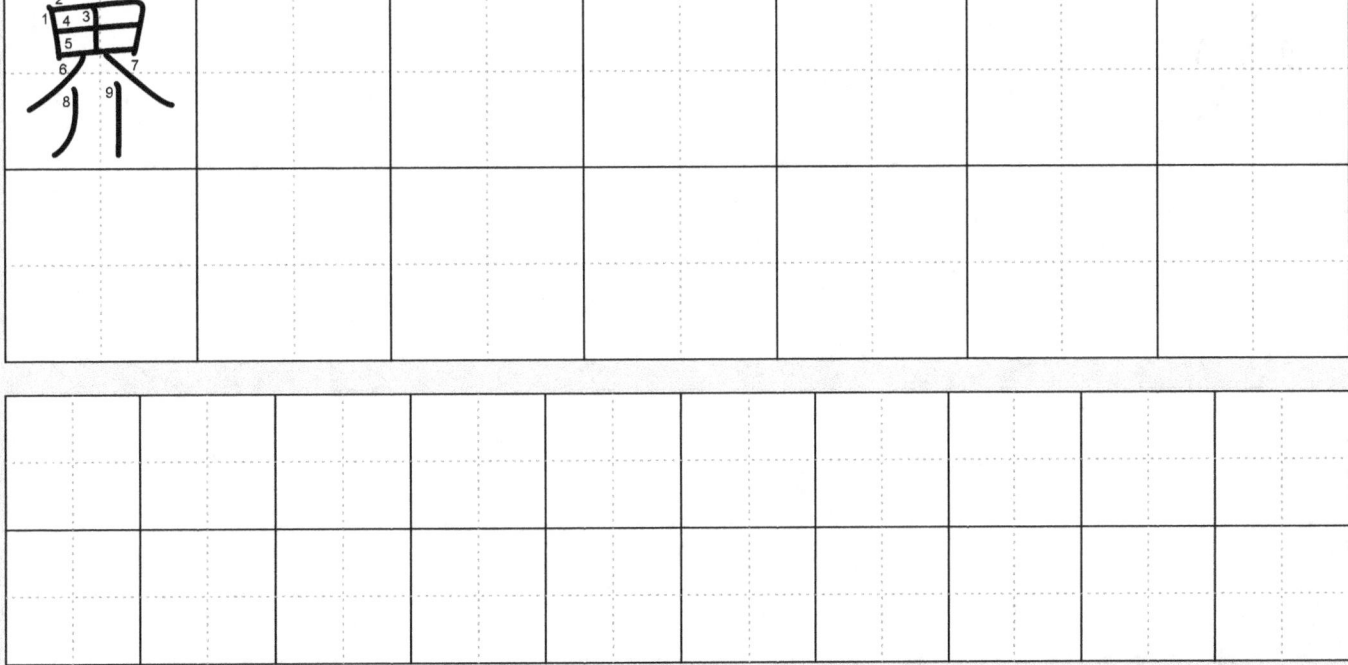

Meaning(s)	teach, faith	Components	子老乞攵
Radical	攴 (攵) (rap)	Kun'yomi	おし(える)、おそ(わる)
Strokes	11	On'yomi	キョウ

Vocabulary	Meaning		Pronunciation
教える	to teach, to instruct, to tell		おしえる
教わる	to be taught, to learn		おそわる
教育	education, schooling, training		キョウイク
政教	religion and politics, church and state		セイキョウ

Stroke Order

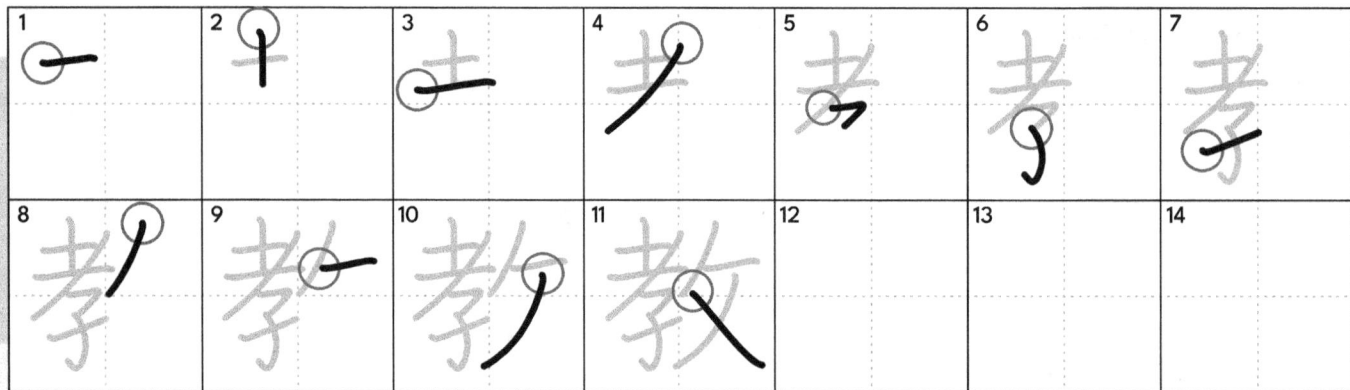

Writing Practice

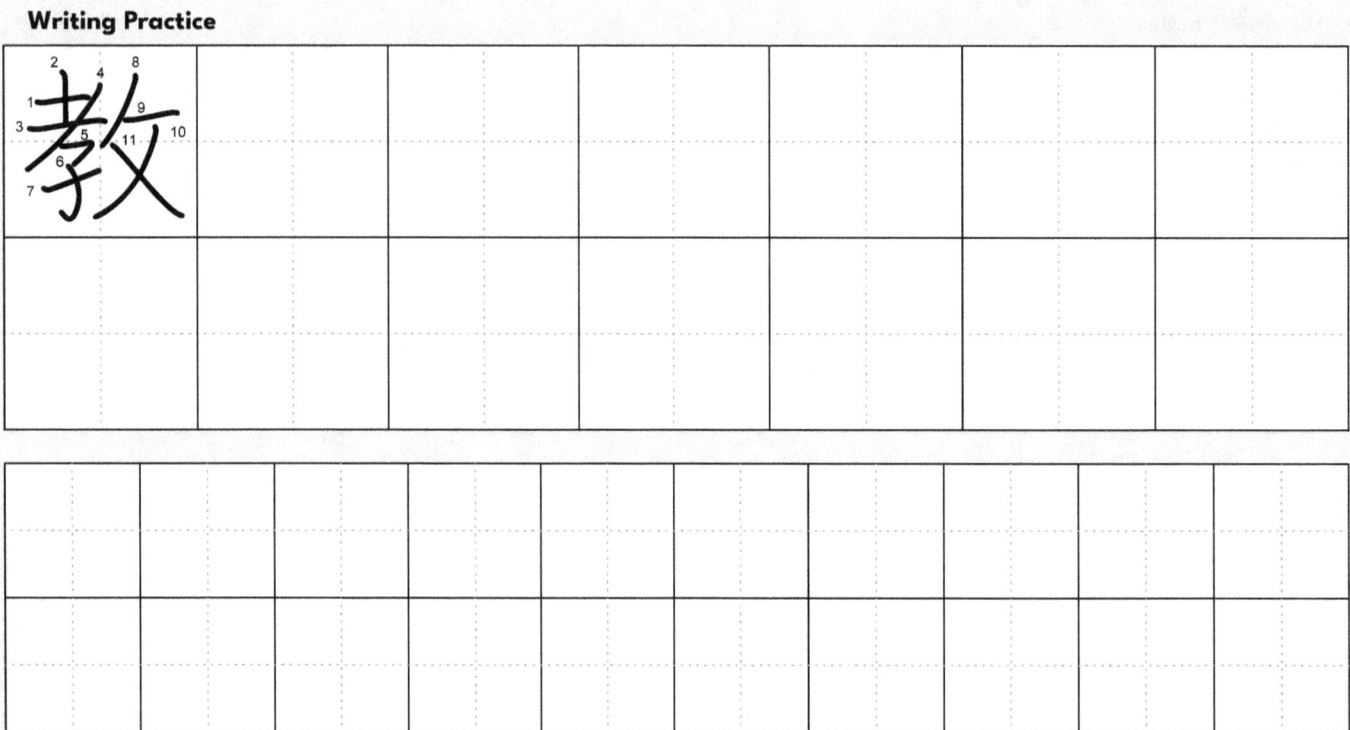

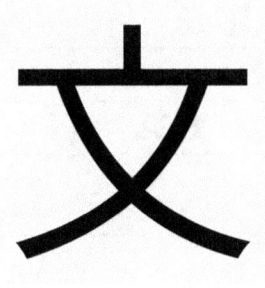

Meaning(s)	sentence, literature		Components	文
Radical	文 (script, literature)		Kun'yomi	ふみ
Strokes	4		On'yomi	ブン、モン

Vocabulary	Meaning	Pronunciation
文	letter, writings	ふみ
文	sentence, composition, text	ブン
文化	culture, civilization, civilisation	ブンカ
文	letter, character, sentence	モン

Stroke Order

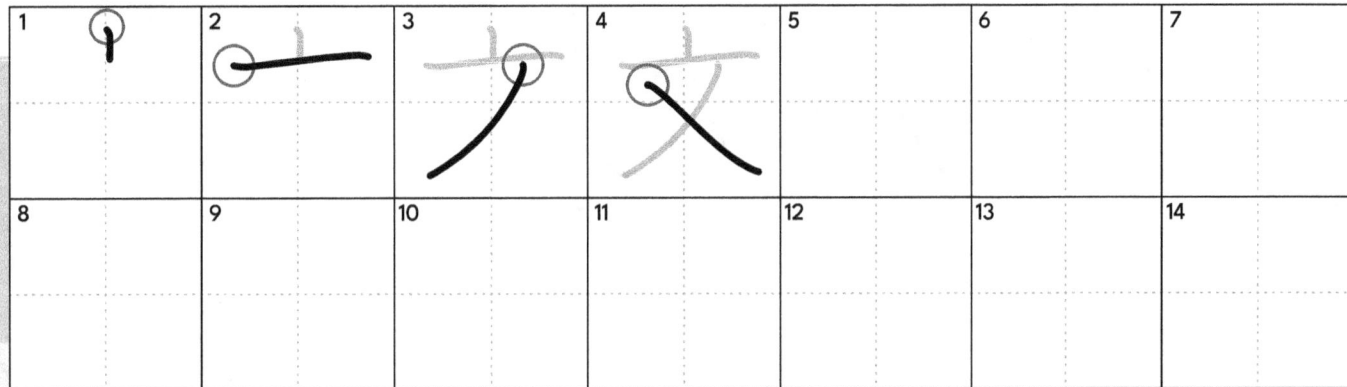

Writing Practice

元

Meaning(s)	beginning, origin	Components	二 儿 元
Radical	儿 (legs)	Kun'yomi	もと
Strokes	4	On'yomi	ゲン、ガン

Vocabulary	Meaning	Pronunciation
元	origin, source, base, basis, foundation	もと
元	unknown (e.g. in an equation)	ゲン
元日	New Year's Day	ガンジツ
元祖	originator, pioneer, inventor	ガンソ

Stroke Order

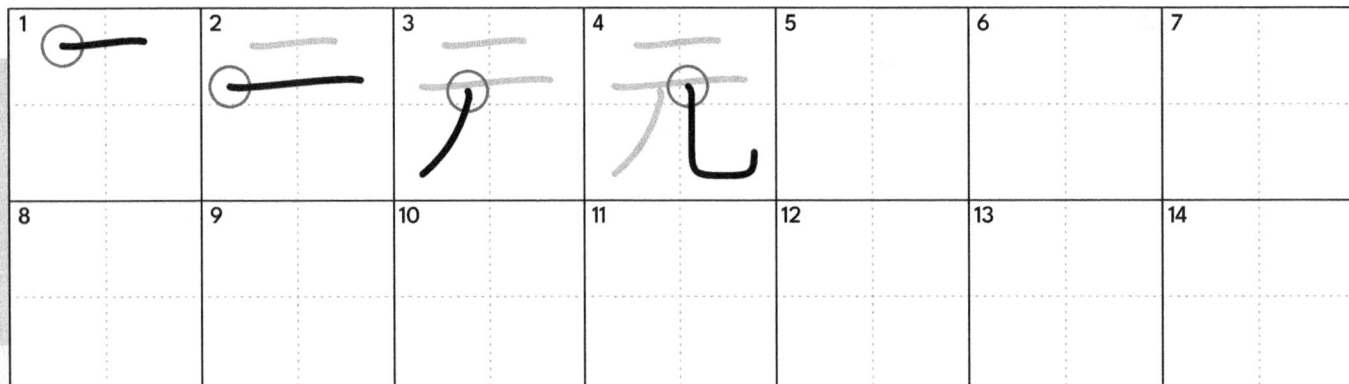

Writing Practice

Meaning(s)	important, respect	Components	一 丨 ノ 日 里
Radical	里 (mile, village)	Kun'yomi	おも(い)、かさ(ねる)
Strokes	9	On'yomi	ジュウ、チョウ

Vocabulary	Meaning		Pronunciation
重複	duplication, repetition		チョウフク
重い	heavy, uneasy, slow, sluggish		おもい
重ねる	to pile up, to heap up, to stack up		かさねる
重	heavy, serious, extreme, -fold, -ply		ジュウ

Stroke Order

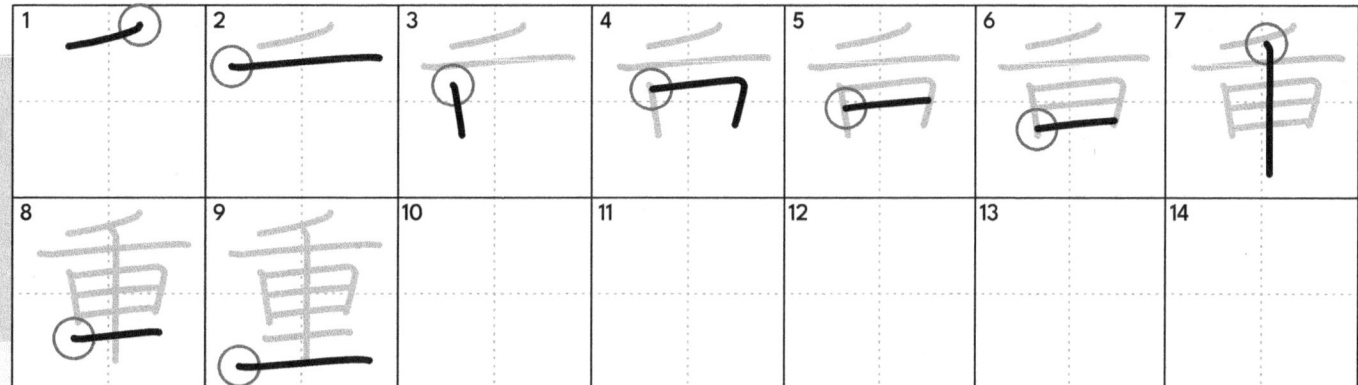

Writing Practice

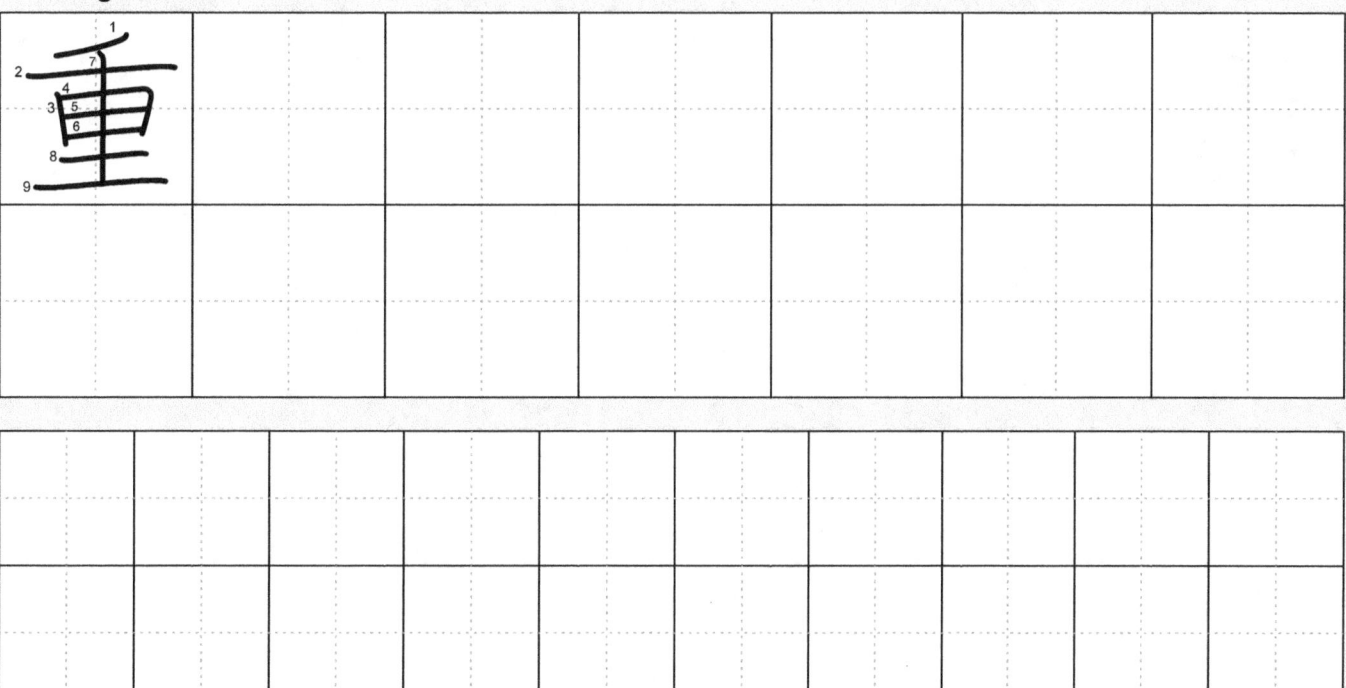

近

Meaning(s)	near, early, akin		Components	込 斤
Radical	辵 (辶, ⻌) (walk)		Kun'yomi	ちか(い)
Strokes	7		On'yomi	キン

Vocabulary	Meaning	Pronunciation
近い	near, close, short (distance), soon, close (relationship), friendly, intimate	ちかい
至近	very near	シキン
近海	coastal waters, adjacent seas	キンカイ

Stroke Order

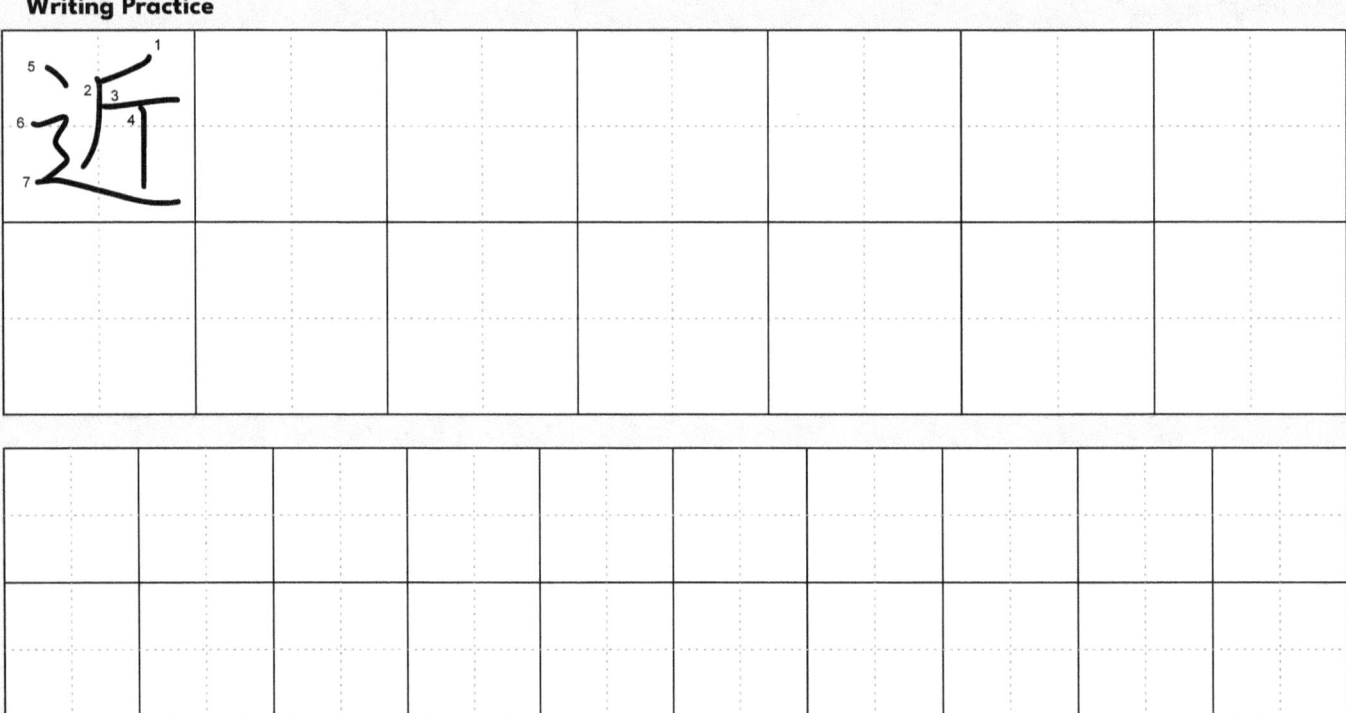

Writing Practice

Meaning(s)	consider, think over	Components	勹 老
Radical	老 (耂) (old)	Kun'yomi	かんが(える)
Strokes	6	On'yomi	コウ

Vocabulary	Meaning	Pronunciation
考える	to think (about, of), to think over, to bear in mind, to allow for, to believe	かんがえる
考え方	way of thinking	かんがえかた
備考	note (for reference), remarks, N.B.	ビコウ

Stroke Order

Writing Practice

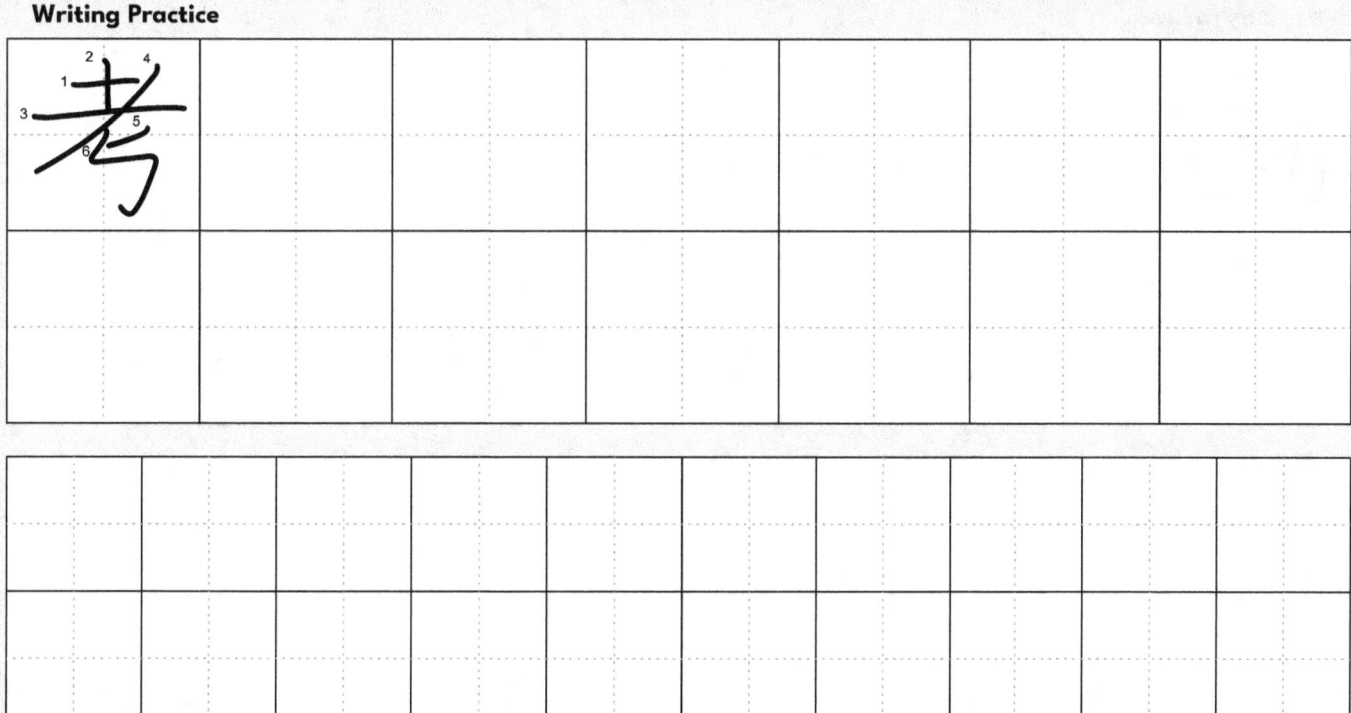

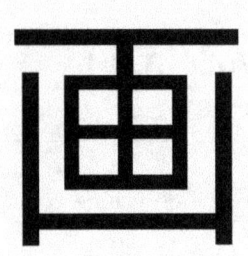

Meaning(s)	brush-stroke, picture	Components	一 凵 田
Radical	田 (field)	Kun'yomi	かく(する)
Strokes	8	On'yomi	ガ、カク

Vocabulary	Meaning	Pronunciation
描く	to draw, to paint, to sketch	えがく
画する	to draw (a line), to mark	かくする
画家	painter, artist	ガカ
画	stroke (of a kanji, etc.)	カク

Stroke Order

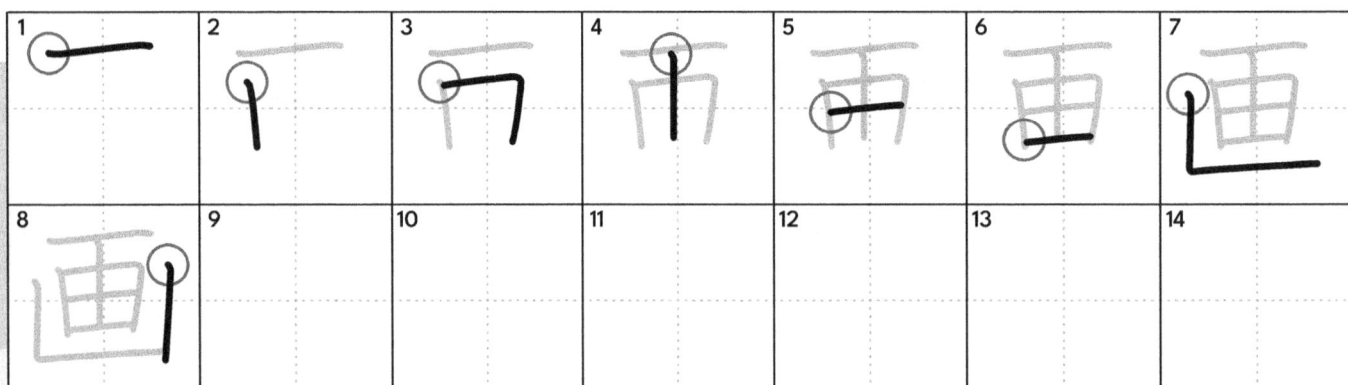

Writing Practice

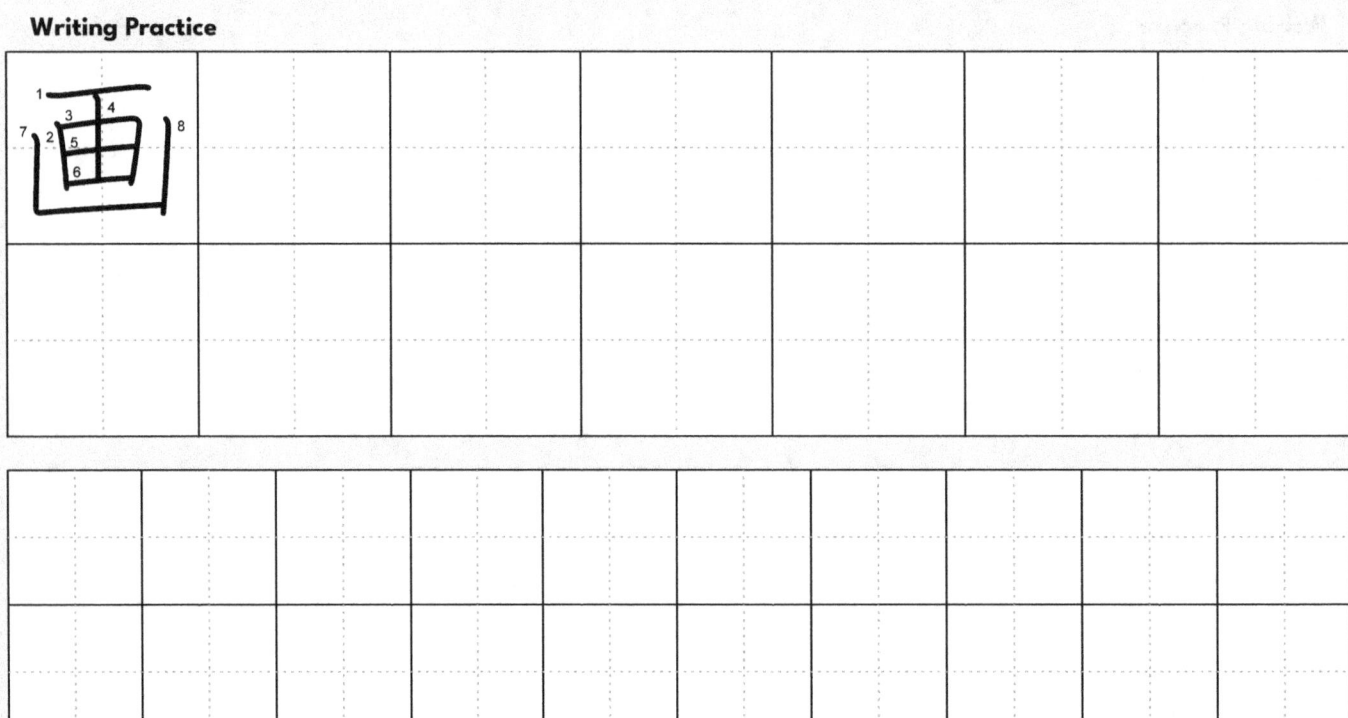

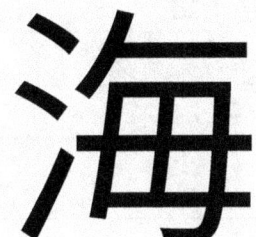

Meaning(s)	sea, ocean	Components	汁母毋乞
Radical	水 (氵, 氺) (water)	Kun'yomi	うみ
Strokes	9	On'yomi	カイ

Vocabulary	Meaning	Pronunciation
海	sea, ocean, waters	うみ
海辺	beach, seashore, seaside	うみべ
公海	high seas, international waters	コウカイ
内海	inlet, gulf, bay, lake	ないかい

Stroke Order

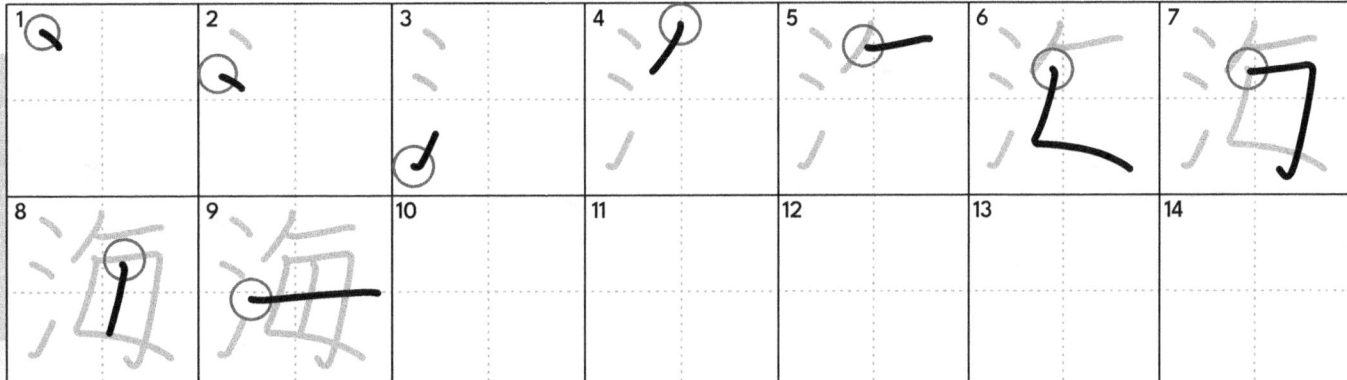

Writing Practice

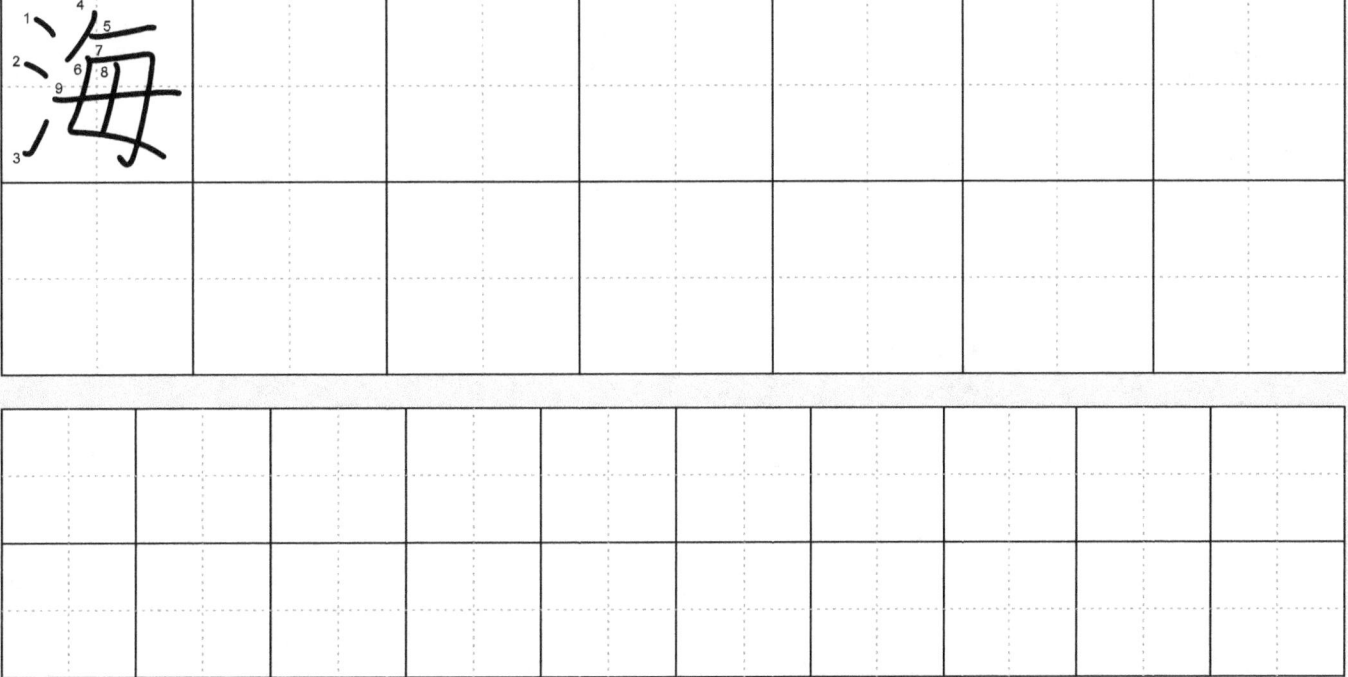

Meaning(s)	sell	Components	ル 冖 士
Radical	士 (scholar)	Kun'yomi	う(る)
Strokes	7	On'yomi	バイ

Vocabulary	Meaning		Pronunciation
売る	to sell		うる
売れる	to sell (well), to be well known		うれる
売却	selling off, disposal by sale		バイキャク
転売	resale		テンバイ

Stroke Order

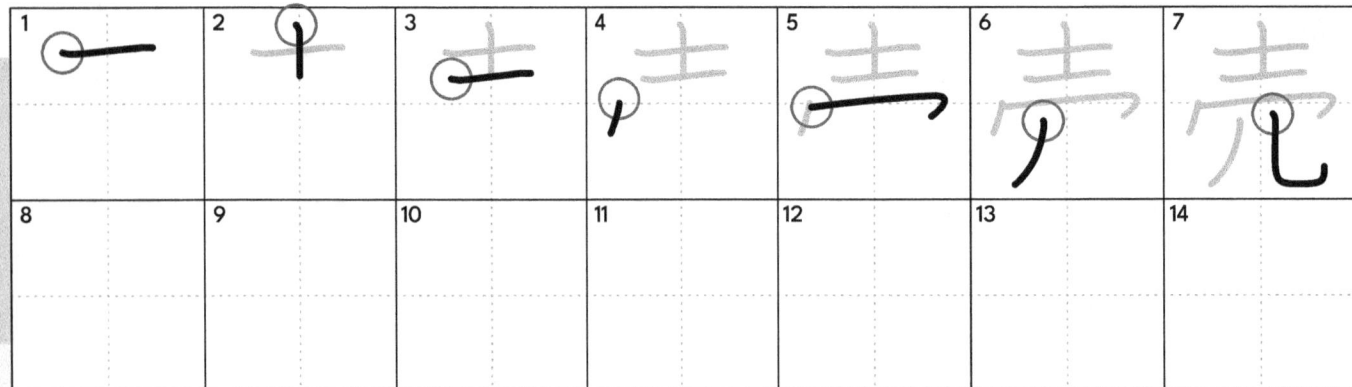

Writing Practice

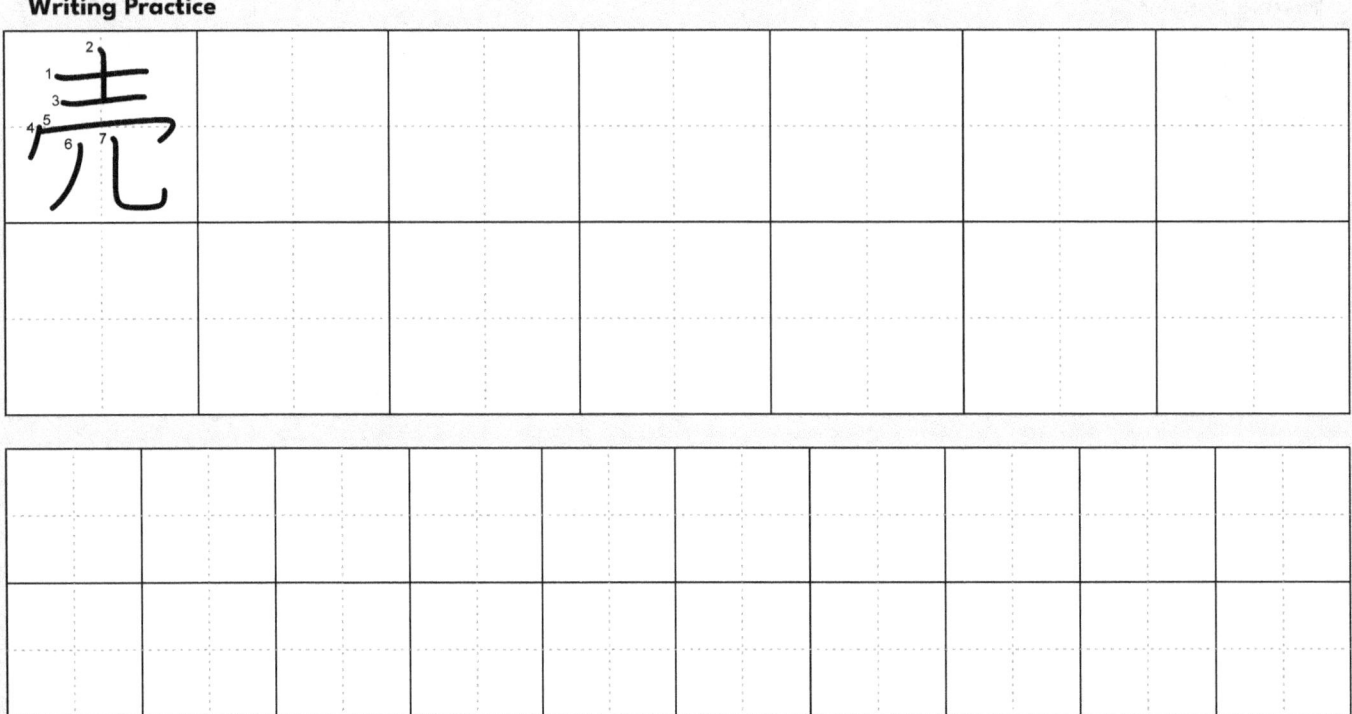

知

Meaning(s)	know, wisdom	Components	口 矢 乞
Radical	矢 (arrow)	Kun'yomi	し(る)
Strokes	8	On'yomi	チ

Vocabulary	Meaning	Pronunciation
知る	to know, to be aware (of), to learn (of), to find out, to discover, to sense, to feel	しる
知恵	wisdom, wit, sagacity, sense, intelligence	チエ
認知	acknowledgement, recognition	ニンチ

Stroke Order

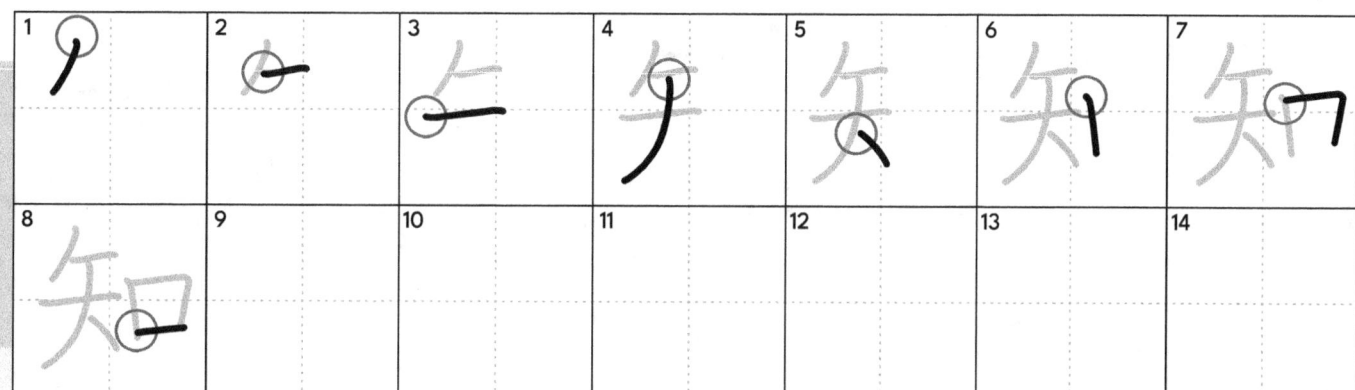

Writing Practice

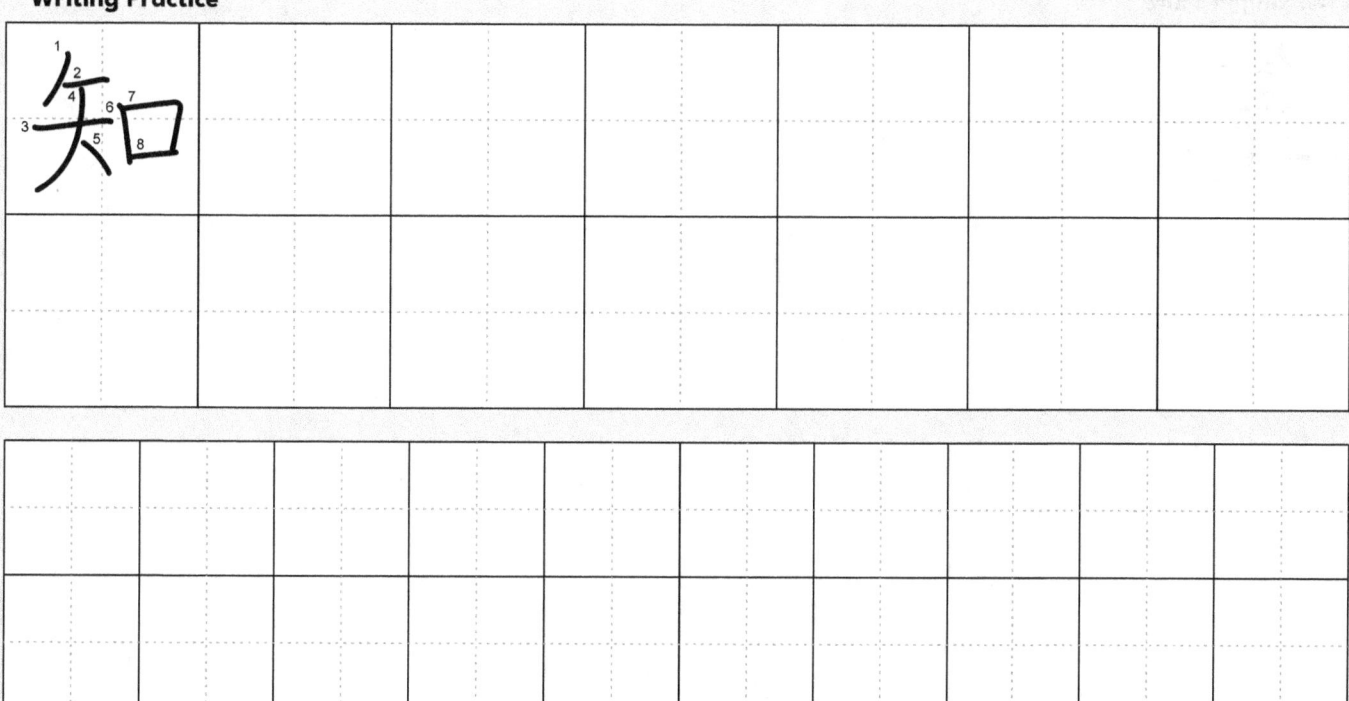

Meaning(s)	gather, meet	Components	木 隹
Radical	隹 (small bird)	Kun'yomi	あつ(める)
Strokes	12	On'yomi	シュウ

Vocabulary	Meaning	Pronunciation
集まる	to gather, to collect, to assemble	あつまる
集	collection, compilation	シュウ
集める	to collect, to assemble, to gather	あつめる
集う	to meet, to assemble	つどう

Stroke Order

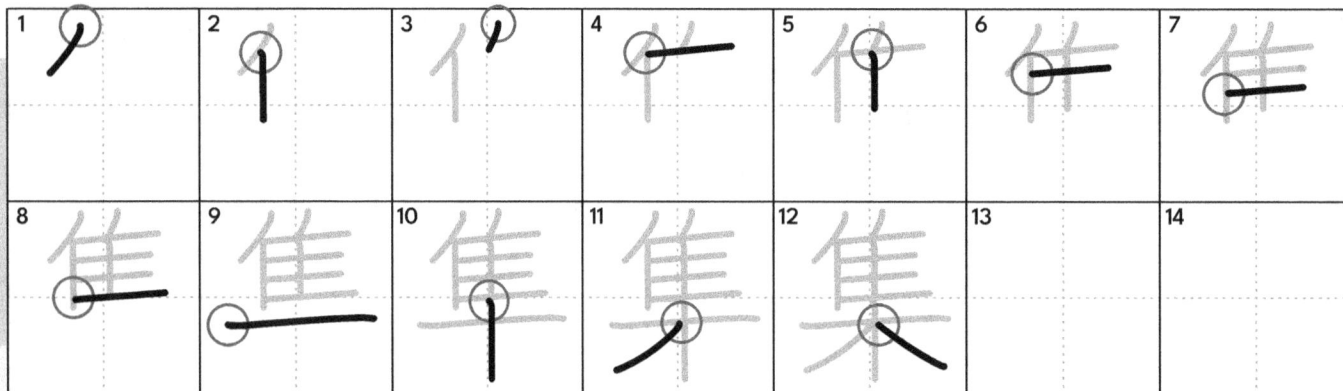

Writing Practice

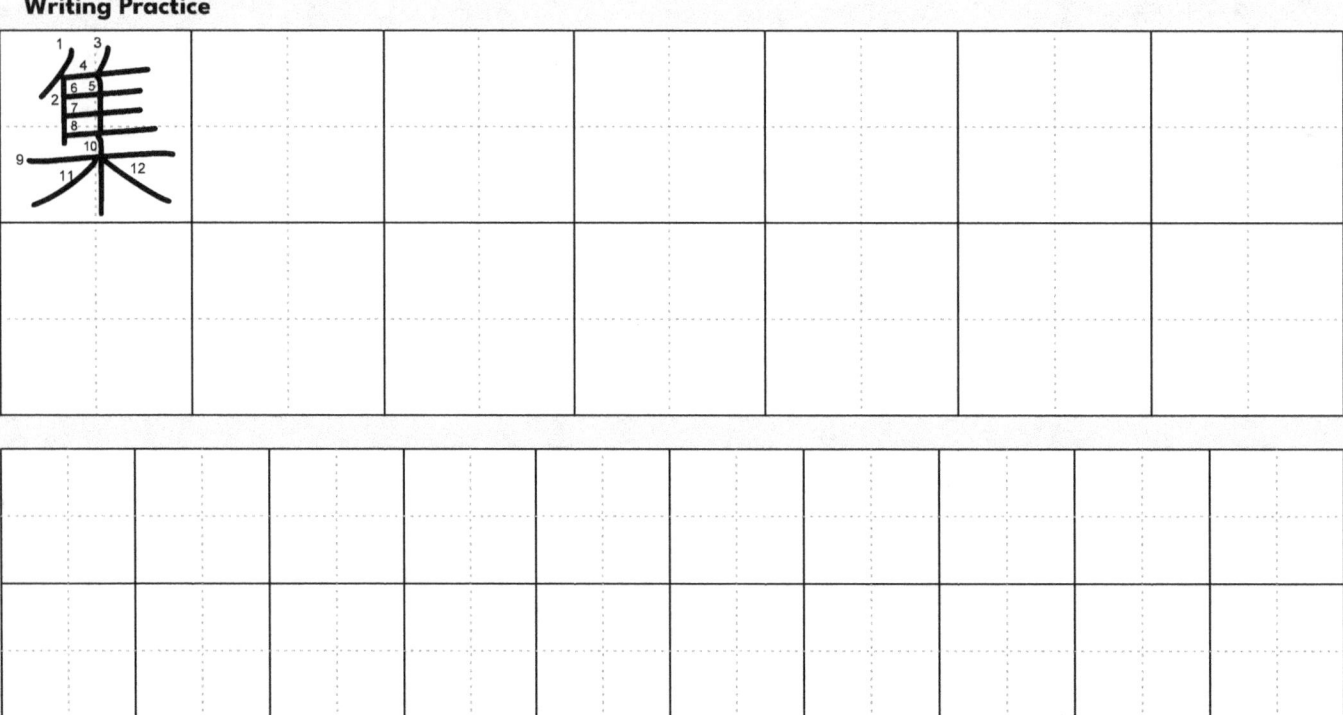

Meaning(s)	separate, branch off	Components	刈カケロ
Radical	刀 (刂) (knife, sword)	Kun'yomi	わか(れる)、わ(ける)
Strokes	7	On'yomi	ベツ

Vocabulary	Meaning	Pronunciation
別れる	to part (usu. of people), to part from/with	わかれる
別	distinction, difference	ベツ
告別	farewell, leave-taking	コクベツ
分ける	to divide (into), to split (into)	わける

Stroke Order

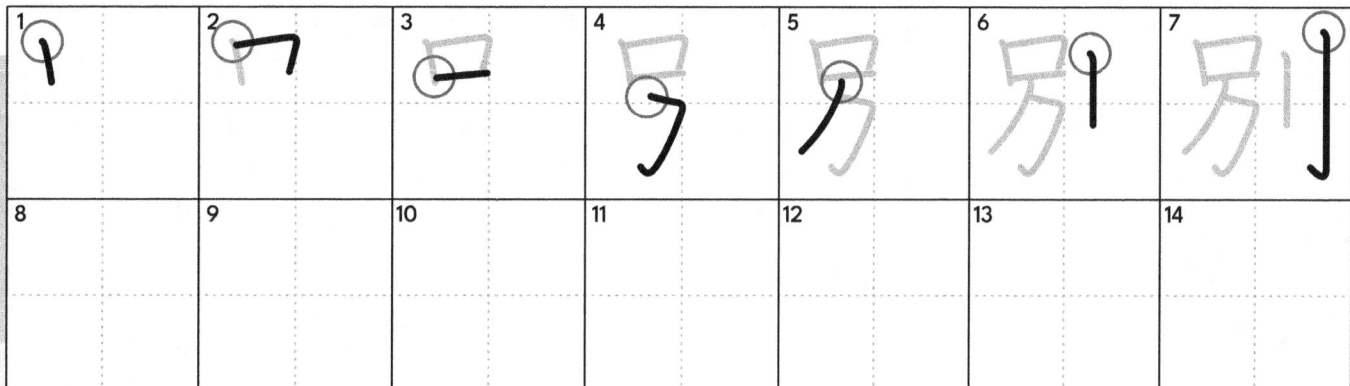

Writing Practice

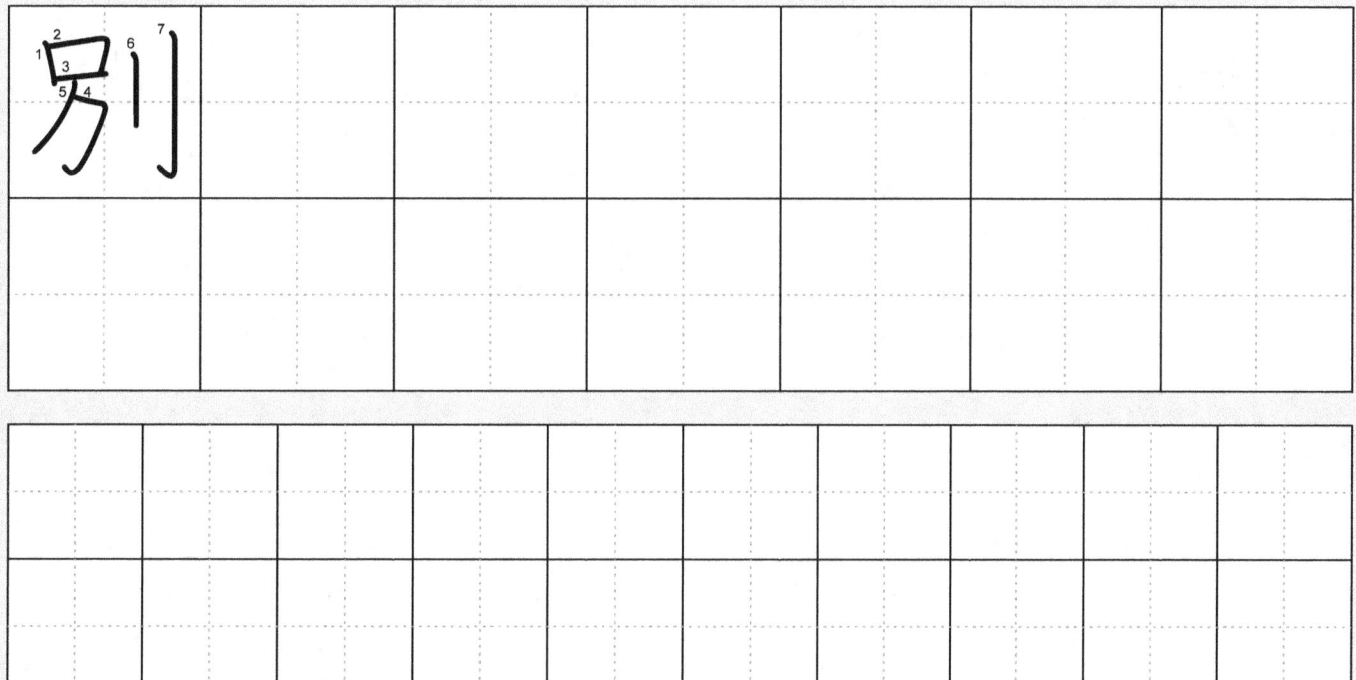

Meaning(s)	thing, object, matter	Components	ノ ク 牛 勿
Radical	牛 (牜) (cow)	Kun'yomi	もの
Strokes	8	On'yomi	ブツ、モツ

Vocabulary	Meaning	Pronunciation
物	thing, object, article, stuff	もの
物	stock, products, stolen goods	ブツ
財物	property	ザイブツ
幣物	Shinto offerings, present to a guest	ヘイモツ

Stroke Order

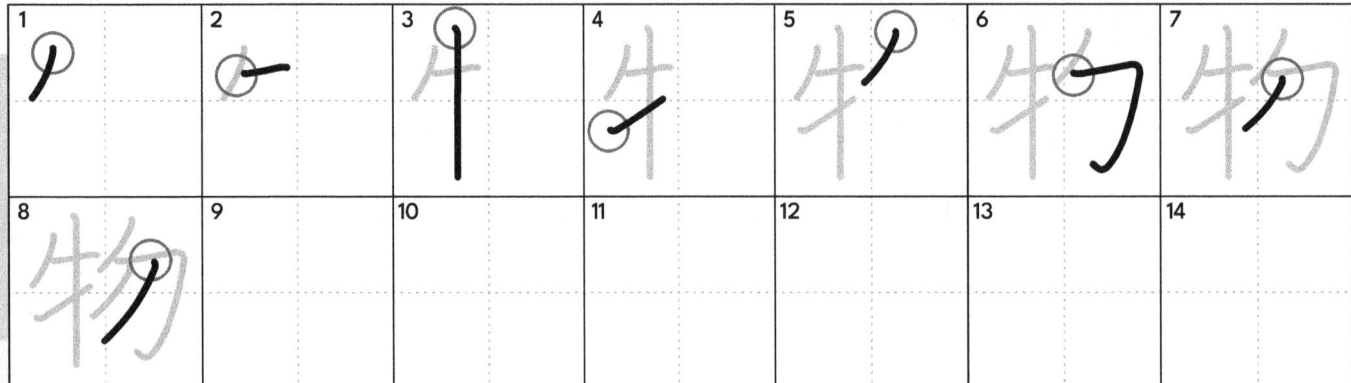

Writing Practice

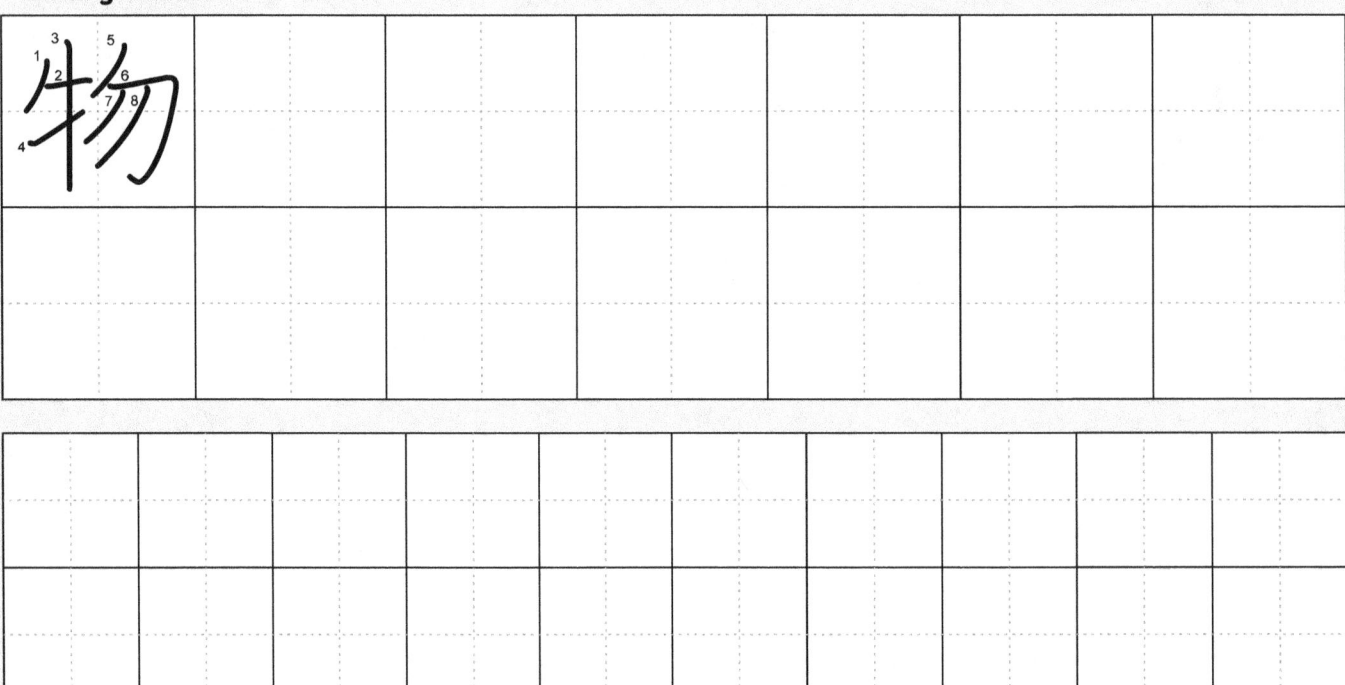

Meaning(s)	use, order, messenger	Components	一ノ化口
Radical	人 (亻) (human)	Kun'yomi	つか(う)
Strokes	8	On'yomi	シ

Vocabulary	Meaning	Pronunciation
使う	to use (a tool, method, etc.), to make use of	つかう
使者	messenger, envoy, emissary	シシャ
使い	errand, mission, going as envoy	つかい
使い方	way of using (something)	つかいかた

Stroke Order

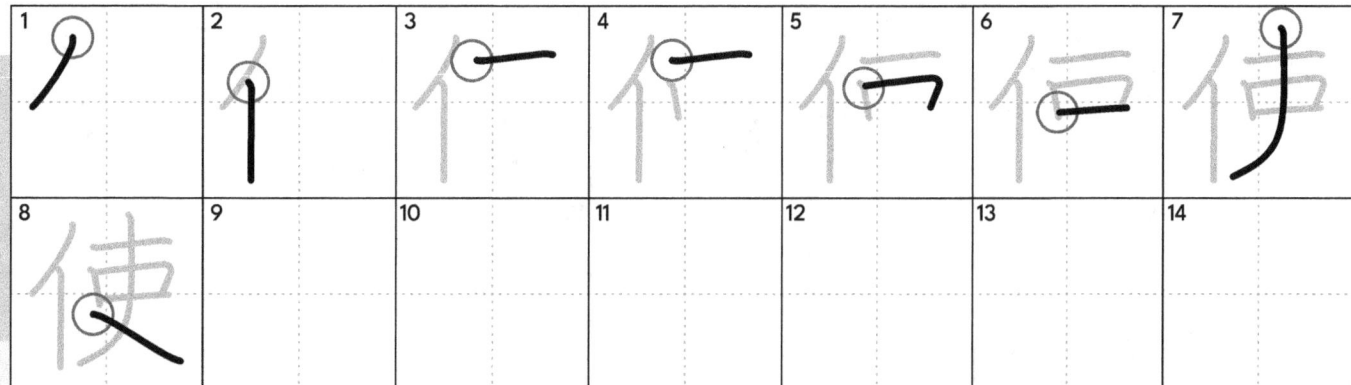

Writing Practice

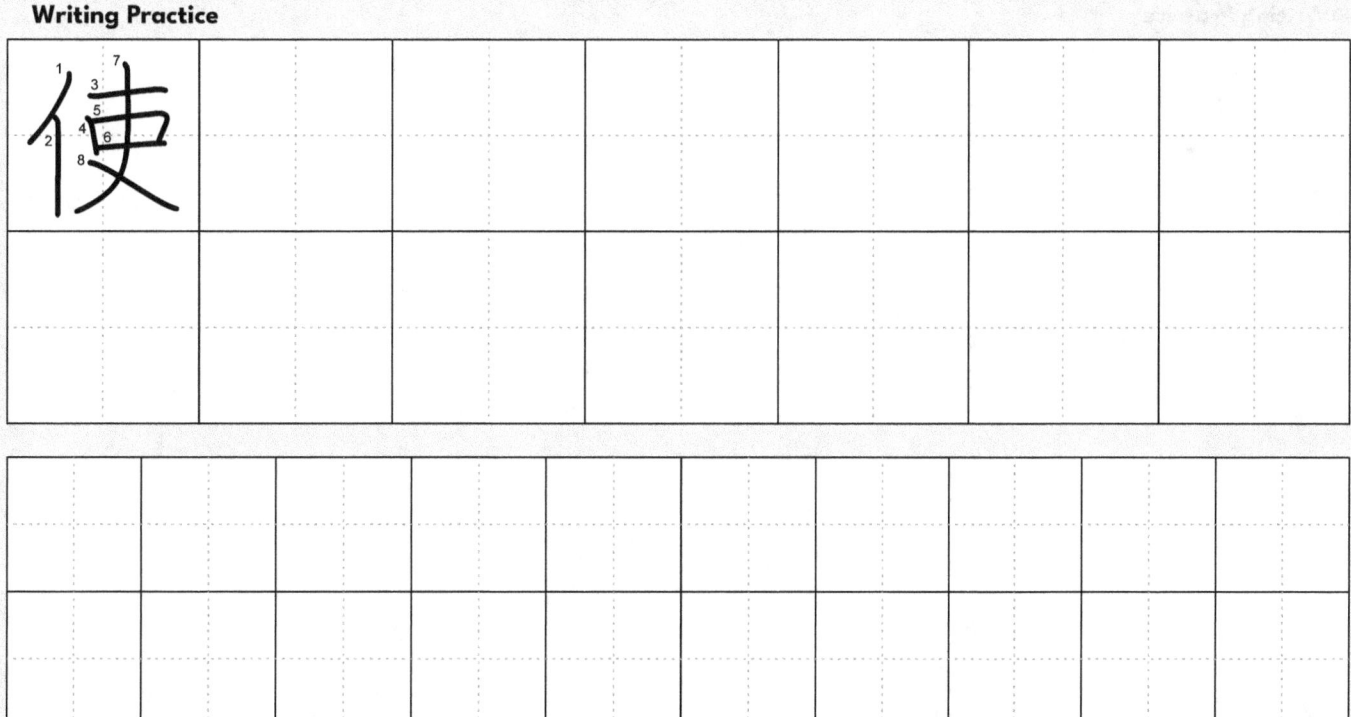

Meaning(s)	goods, refinement		Components	口 品
Radical	口 (mouth)		Kun'yomi	しな
Strokes	9		On'yomi	ヒン

Vocabulary	Meaning	Pronunciation
品	article, item, thing, goods, stock	しな
品	elegance, grace, refinement, class	ヒン
品位	dignity, grace, nobility, grade, quality	ヒンイ
品目	item, commodity, list of articles	ひんもく

Stroke Order

Writing Practice

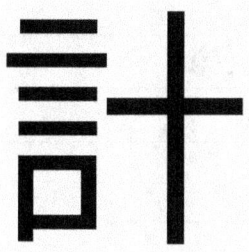

Meaning(s)	plot, plan, scheme	Components	十 言
Radical	言 (訁) (speech)	Kun'yomi	はか(る)
Strokes	9	On'yomi	ケイ

Vocabulary	Meaning	Pronunciation
計る	to measure, to weigh, to survey	はかる
計らう	to manage/arrange, to see to (a matter)	はからう
計画	plan, project, schedule, scheme, program	ケイカク
計	plan, meter, measuring device	ケイ

Stroke Order

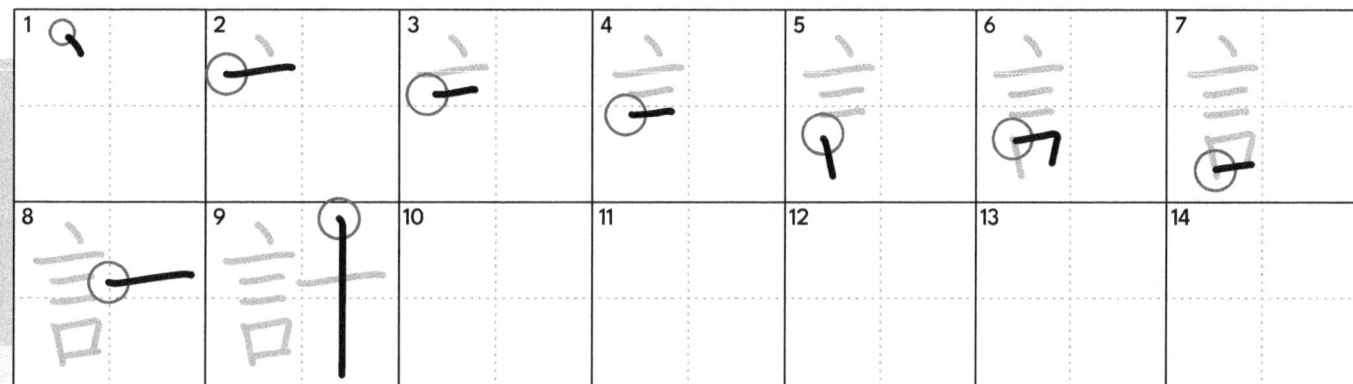

Writing Practice

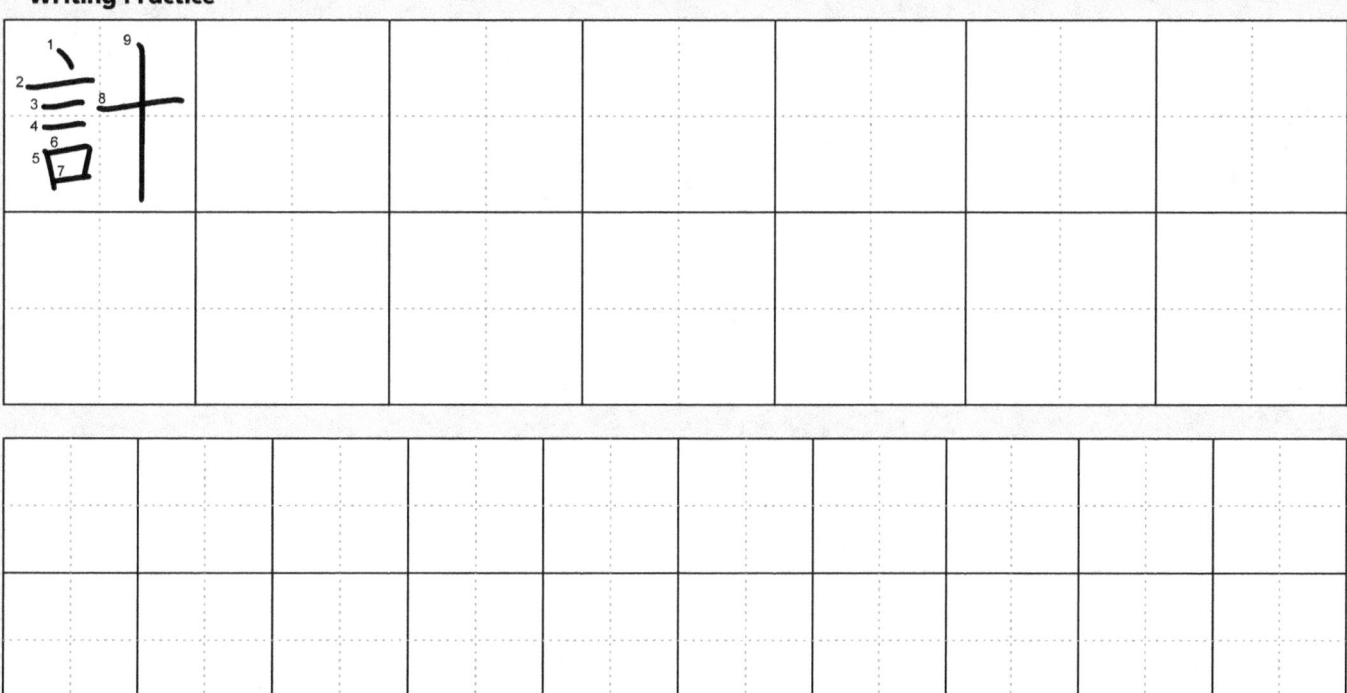

Meaning(s)	death, die	Components	一ヒタ歹
Radical	歹 (歺) (death, decay)	Kun'yomi	し(ぬ)
Strokes	6	On'yomi	シ

Vocabulary	Meaning	Pronunciation
死ぬ	to die, to pass away, to lose spirit	しぬ
死	death, decease, (an) out	シ
死因	cause of death	シイン
死ぬ気で	all out, like hell, like crazy, desperately	しぬきで

Stroke Order

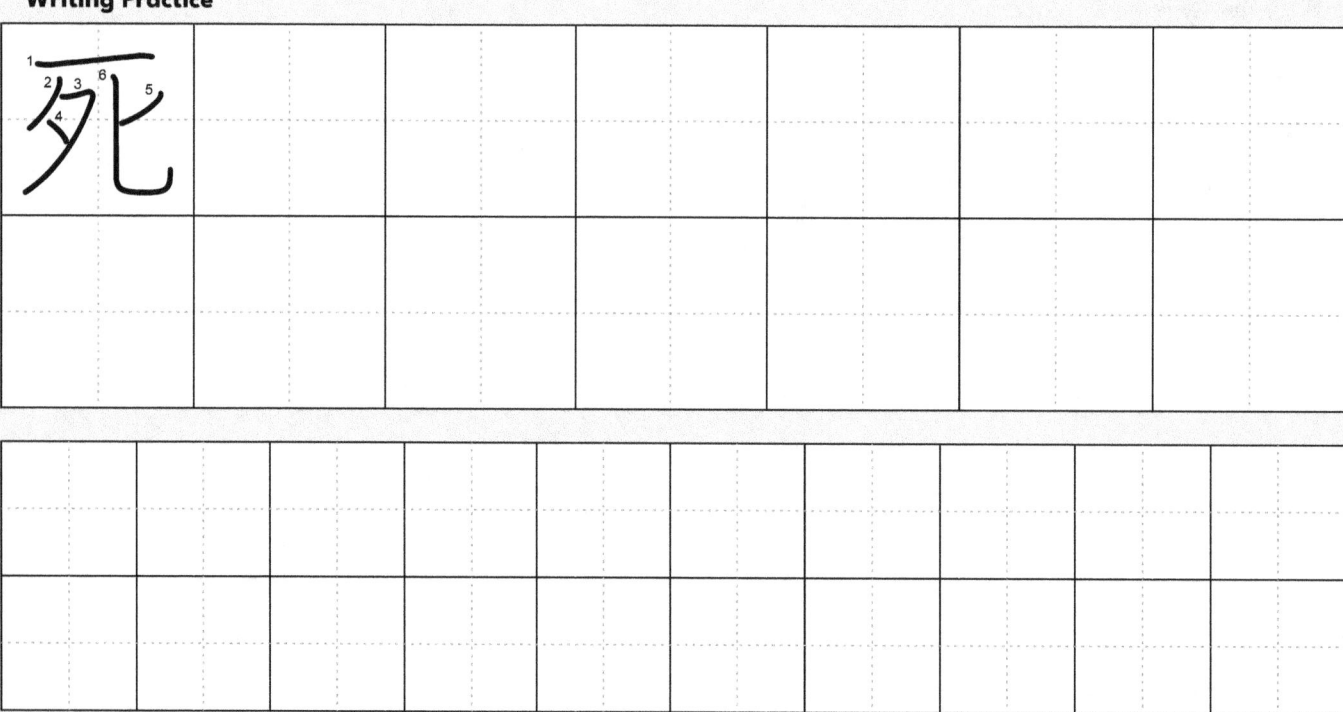

Writing Practice

Meaning(s)	special		Components	土寸牛
Radical	牛 (牛) (cow)		Kun'yomi	
Strokes	10		On'yomi	トク

Vocabulary	Meaning	Pronunciation
特産	local specialty	トクサン
特異	unique, peculiar, singular	トクイ
快特	rapid express (train service)	カイトク
在特	Special Permission to Stay in Japan	ザイトク

Stroke Order

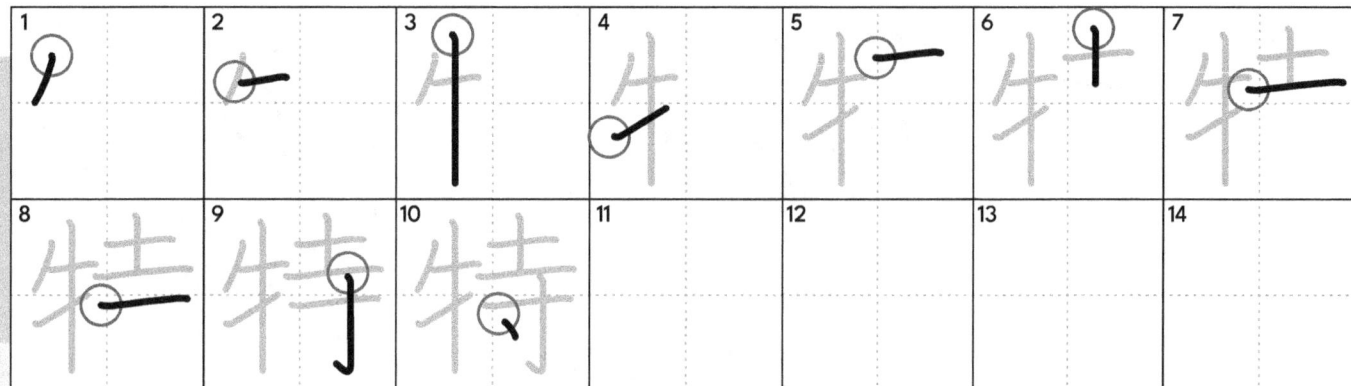

Writing Practice

Meaning(s)	private, I, me	Components	ム 禾
Radical	禾 (grain)	Kun'yomi	わたくし、わたし
Strokes	7	On'yomi	シ

Vocabulary	Meaning		Pronunciation
私	I, me, personal (affairs, etc.), private		わたくし
私私	private affairs, personal matter		シ
私案	private plan, one's own plan		シアン
私	I, me		わたし

Stroke Order

Writing Practice

Meaning(s)	commence, begin	Components	ム 口 女
Radical	女 (woman, female)	Kun'yomi	はじ(める)
Strokes	8	On'yomi	シ

Vocabulary	Meaning	Pronunciation
始める	to start, to begin, to commence	はじめる
始発	first departure (of the day), first train/bus	シハツ
始業	start of work, commencement	シギョウ
創始	creation, founding, initiating	ソウシ

Stroke Order

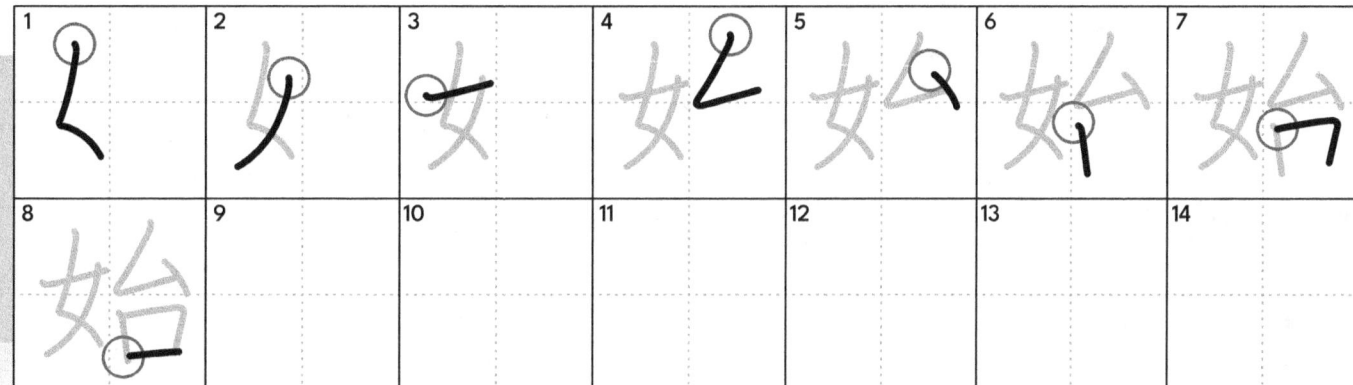

Writing Practice

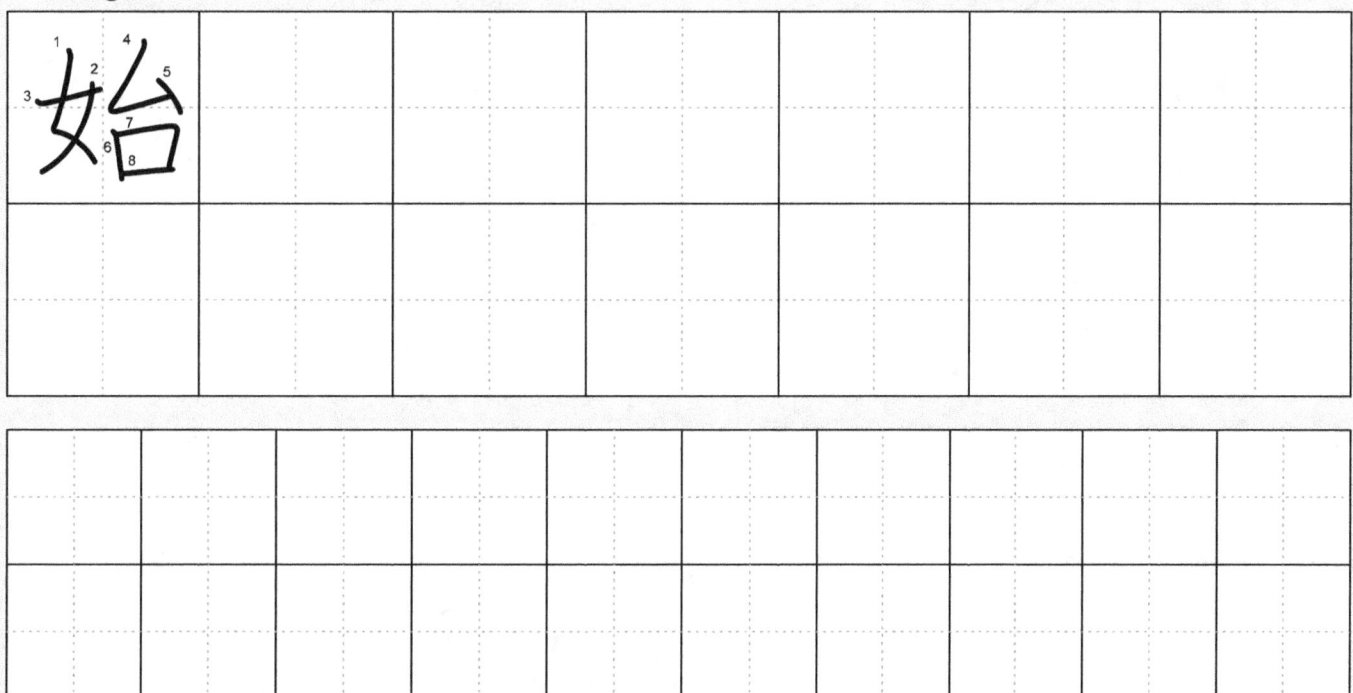

Meaning(s)	morning	Components	十 日 月
Radical	月 (moon, month)	Kun'yomi	あさ
Strokes	12	On'yomi	チョウ

Vocabulary	Meaning	Pronunciation
朝	morning, breakfast, next morning	あさ
朝方	early morning, early hours	あさがた
朝刊	morning newspaper	チョウカン
朝	dynasty, reign, period, epoch, age	チョウ

Stroke Order

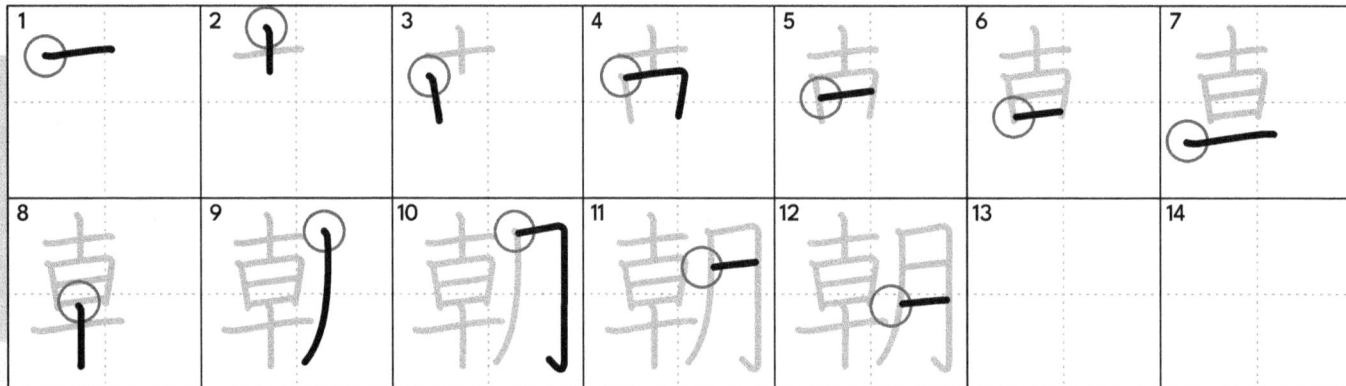

Writing Practice

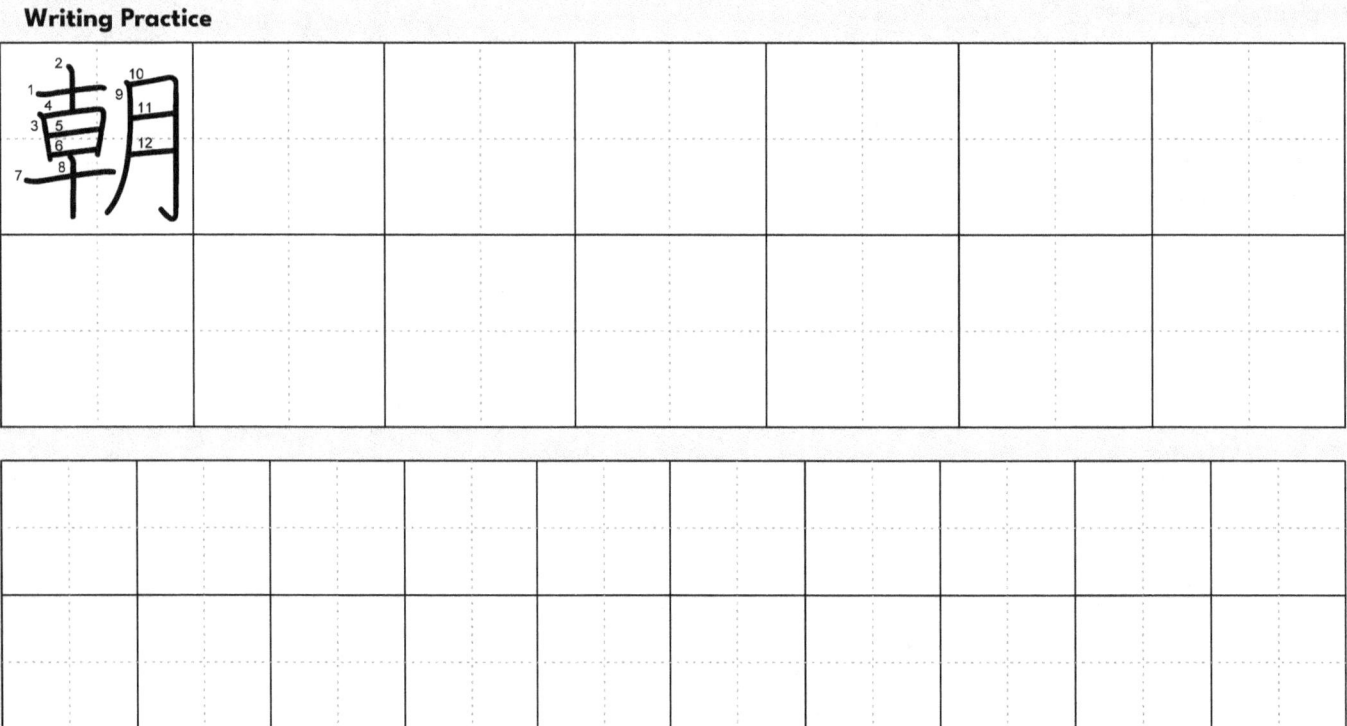

Meaning(s)	carry, luck, fate	Components	冖 込 車
Radical	辵 (辶, ⻌) (walk)	Kun'yomi	はこ(ぶ)
Strokes	12	On'yomi	ウン

Vocabulary	Meaning	Pronunciation
運ぶ	to carry, to transport, to move	はこぶ
運	fortune, luck	ウン
運営	management, administration	ウンエイ
機運	opportunity, chance, good time (to do)	キウン

Stroke Order

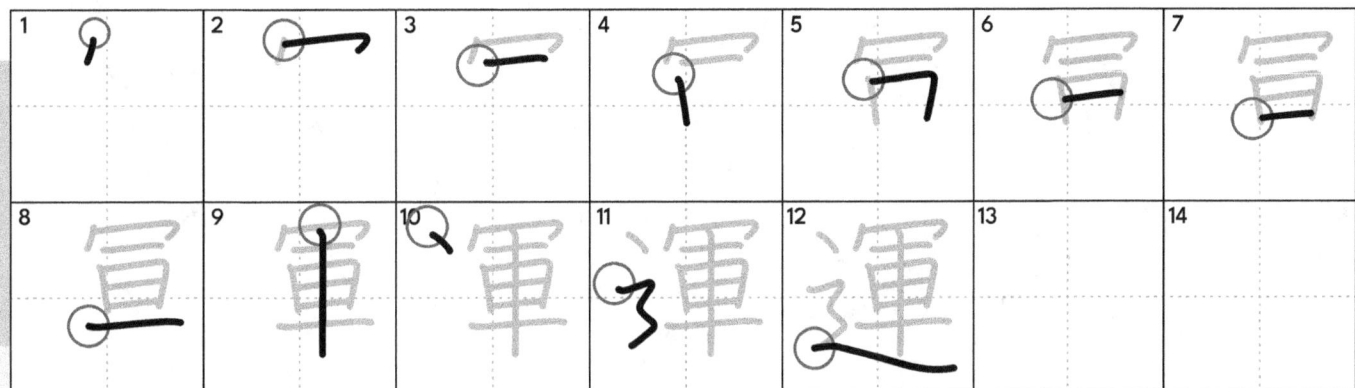

Writing Practice

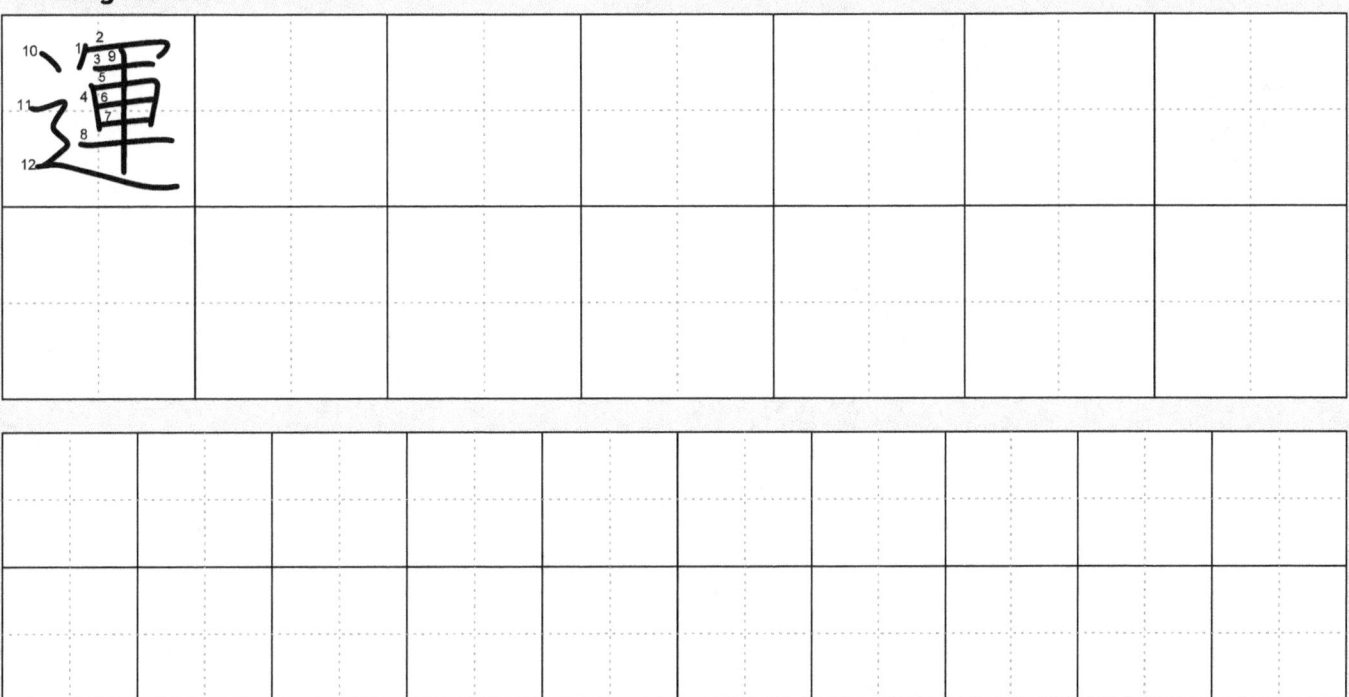

Meaning(s)	end, finish	Components	夂 小 幺 糸
Radical	糸 (糸) (silk)	Kun'yomi	お(わる)
Strokes	11	On'yomi	シュウ

Vocabulary	Meaning	Pronunciation
終わる	to end, to come to an end	終わる
終局	end, close, conclusion	シュウキョク
終える	to finish, to graduate	おえる
終	end, final, end of life, death, never	つい

Stroke Order

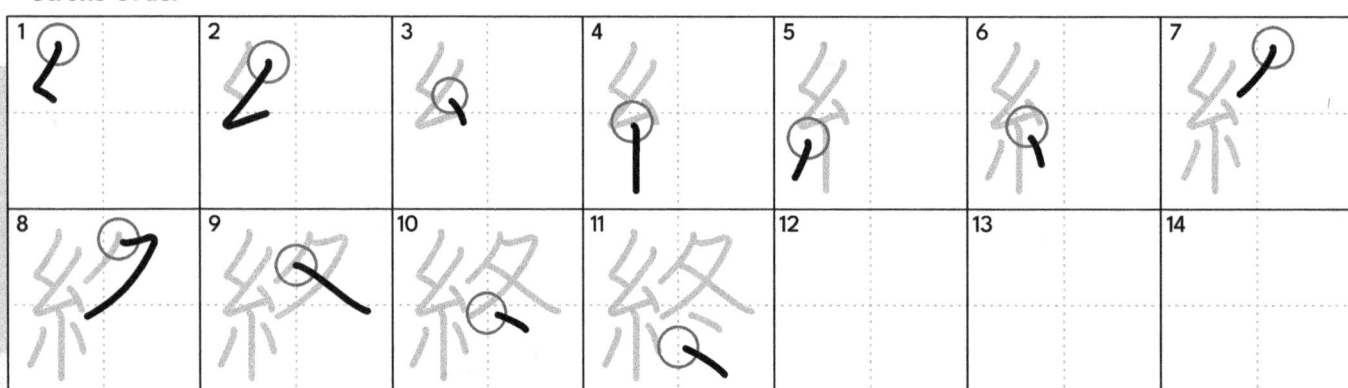

Writing Practice

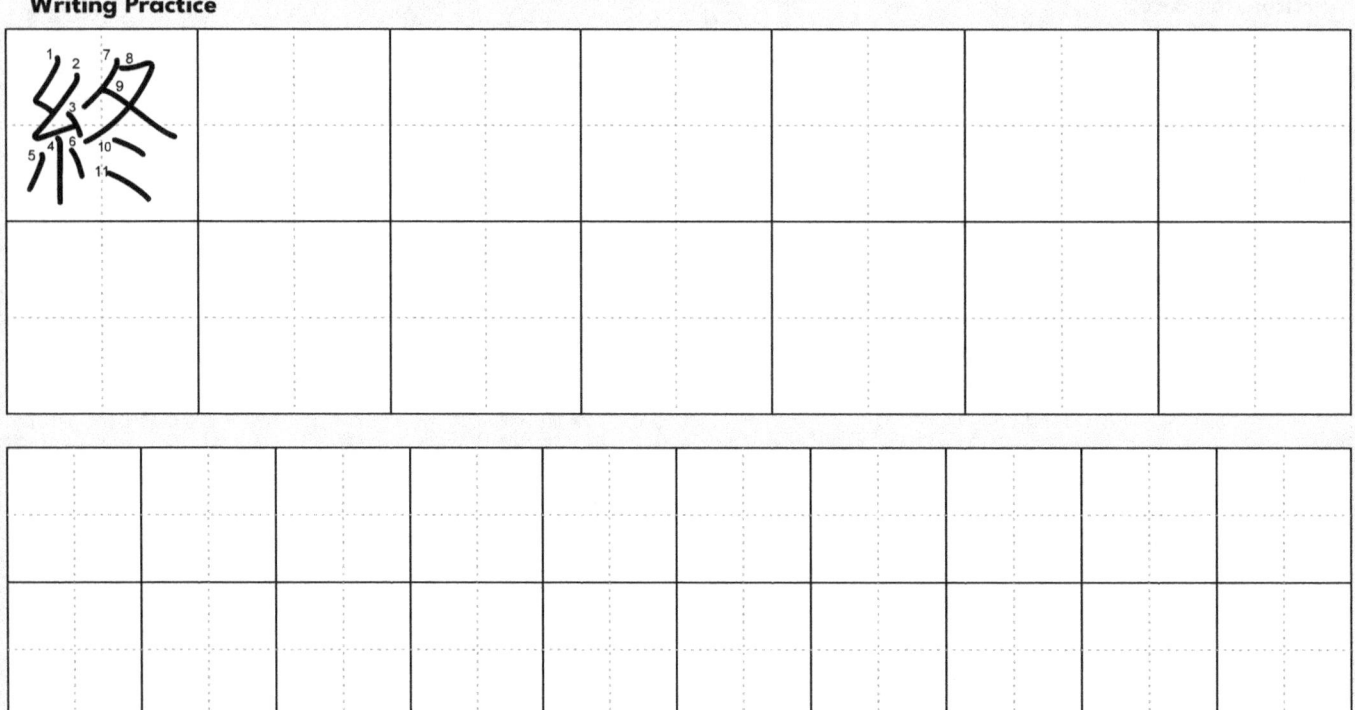

Meaning(s)	pedestal, a stand	**Components** ム口女
Radical	口 (mouth)	**Kun'yomi** うてな
Strokes	5	**On'yomi** ダイ、タイ

Vocabulary	Meaning	Pronunciation
台	stand, rack, table, bench, podium, pedestal, platform, stage, holder, rack	ダイ
台	tower, stand, pedestal	うてな
台	Taiwan	タイ

Stroke Order

Writing Practice

Meaning(s)	wide, broad, spacious	**Components**	ム 广
Radical	广 (house on cliff)	**Kun'yomi**	ひろ(い)
Strokes	5	**On'yomi**	コウ

Vocabulary	Meaning	Pronunciation
広い	spacious, vast, wide	ひろい
広告	advertisement, advertising	コウコク
広域	wide area, wide view, zoomed-out view	コウイキ
広がる	to spread (out), to extend, to stretch	ひろがる

Stroke Order

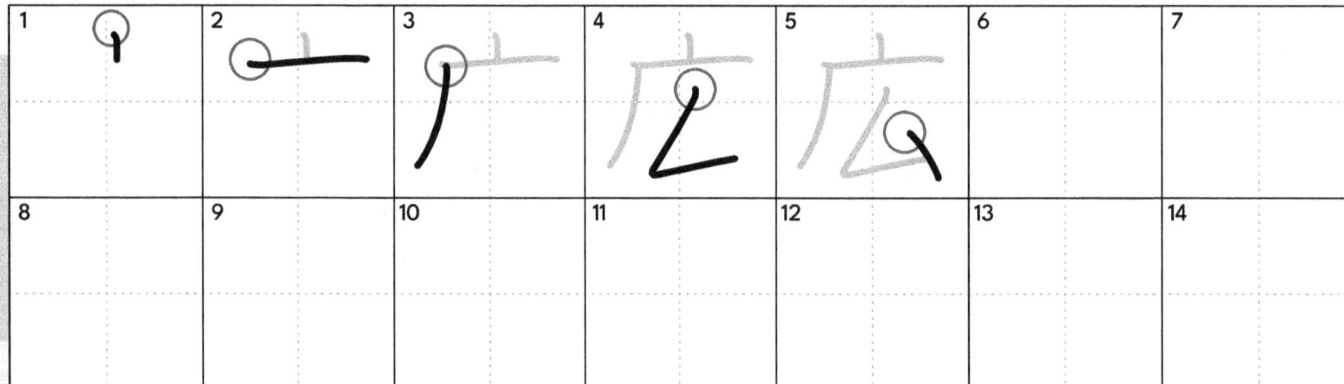

Writing Practice

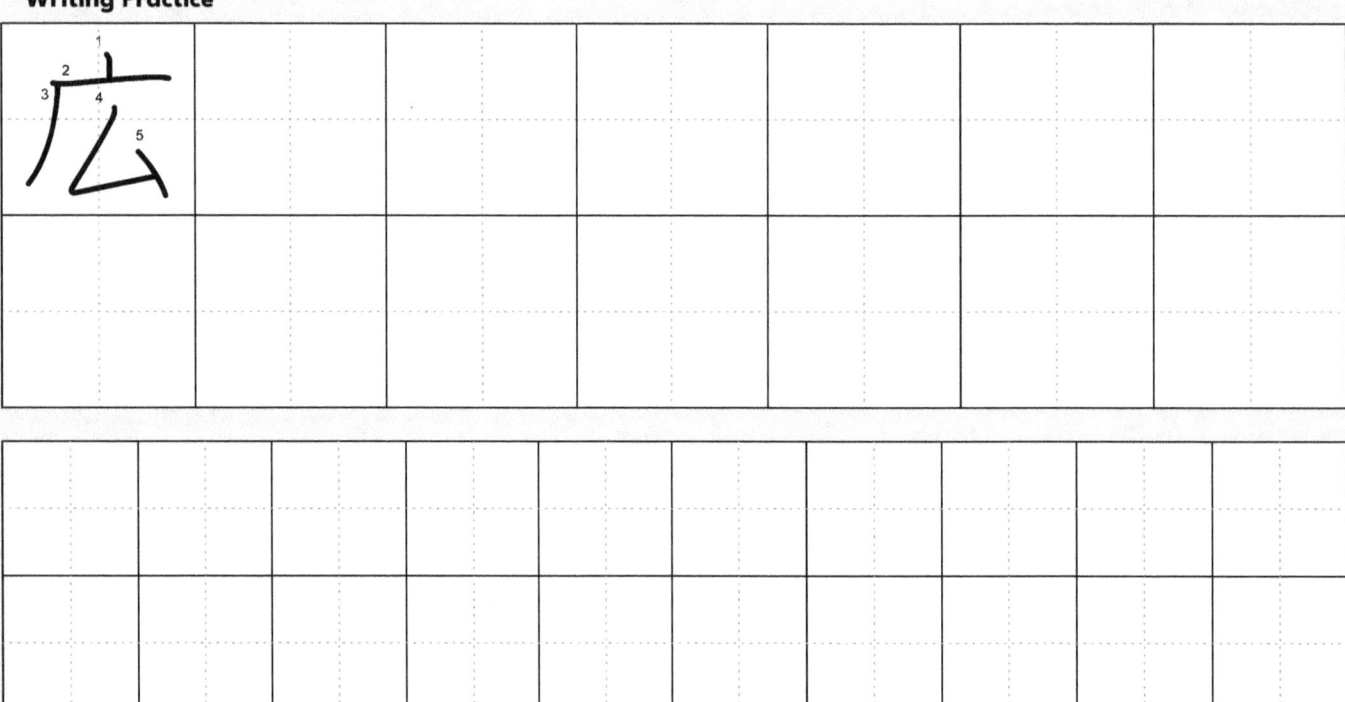

Meaning(s)	dwell, reside, live	**Components**	、化王
Radical	人(イ) (human)	**Kun'yomi**	す(む)
Strokes	7	**On'yomi**	ジュウ、チュウ

Vocabulary	Meaning	Pronunciation
住む	to live (of humans), to reside	すむ
住	dwelling, living	ジュウ
住居	dwelling, house, residence, address	ジュウキョ
住まう	to live, to reside, to inhabit	すまう

Stroke Order

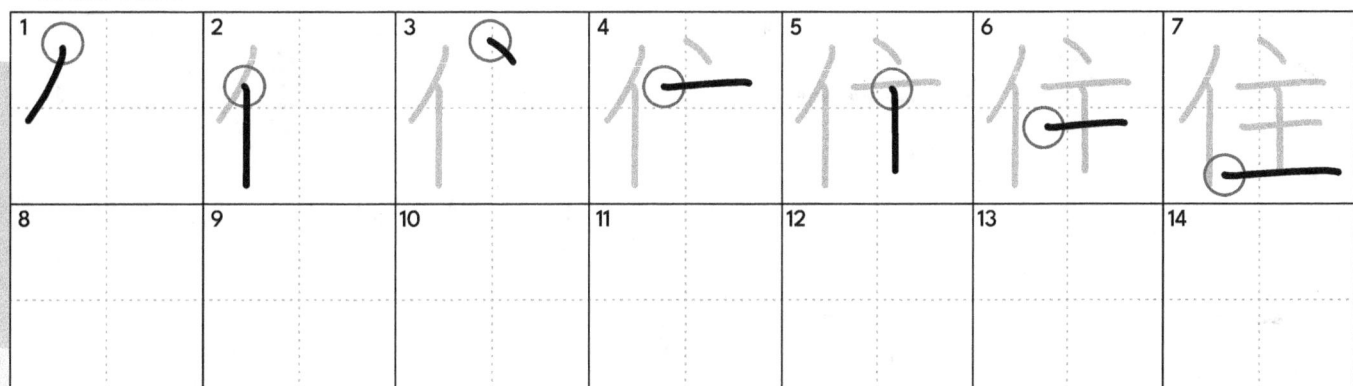

Writing Practice

Meaning(s)	nothingness, none	Components	一丨ノ杰無乞
Radical	火 (灬) (fire)	Kun'yomi	な(い)
Strokes	12	On'yomi	ム、ブ

Vocabulary	Meaning	Pronunciation
無い	nonexistent, not being (there)	ない
無	nothing, naught, nought, nil, zero, un-, non-, un-, non-, bad ..., poor ...	ム、ブ
皆無	nonexistent, nil, none	カイム

Stroke Order

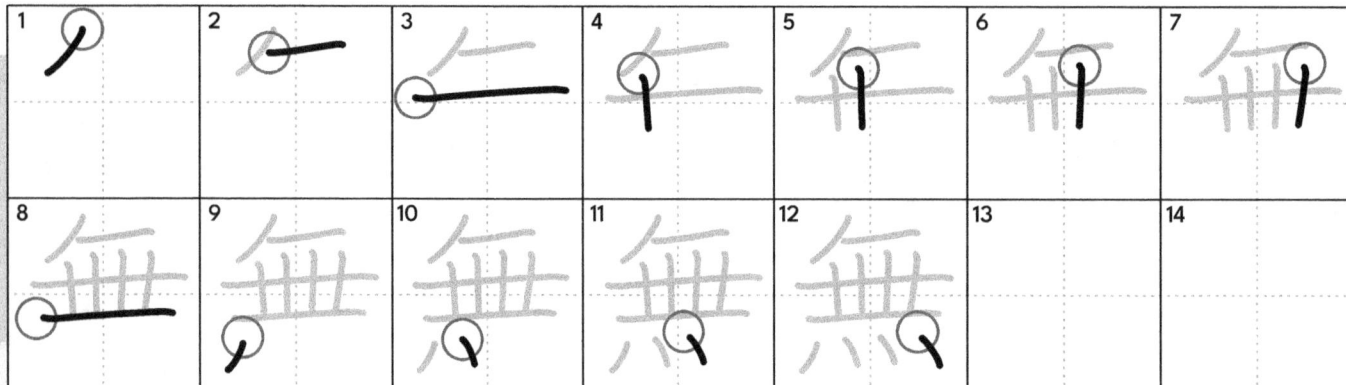

Writing Practice

Meaning(s)	true, reality	Components	一 ハ 十 目
Radical	目 (eye)	Kun'yomi	ま、まこと
Strokes	10	On'yomi	シン

Vocabulary	Meaning	Pronunciation
真	just, right, due (east), pure, genuine	ま
真	truth, reality, genuineness	シン
迫真	realistic, true to life	ハクシン
実しやか	plausible (but untrue), credible (lie)	まことしやか

Stroke Order

Writing Practice

Meaning(s)	possess, have, exist		Components	一ノ月
Radical	月 (moon, month)		Kun'yomi	あ(る)
Strokes	6		On'yomi	ユウ、ウ

Vocabulary	Meaning	Pronunciation
有る	to be, to exist, to live, to have	ある
有	existence, possession, having	ユウ
有無	existence or nonexistence	ウム
有意義	significant, useful, meaningful	ユウイギ

Stroke Order

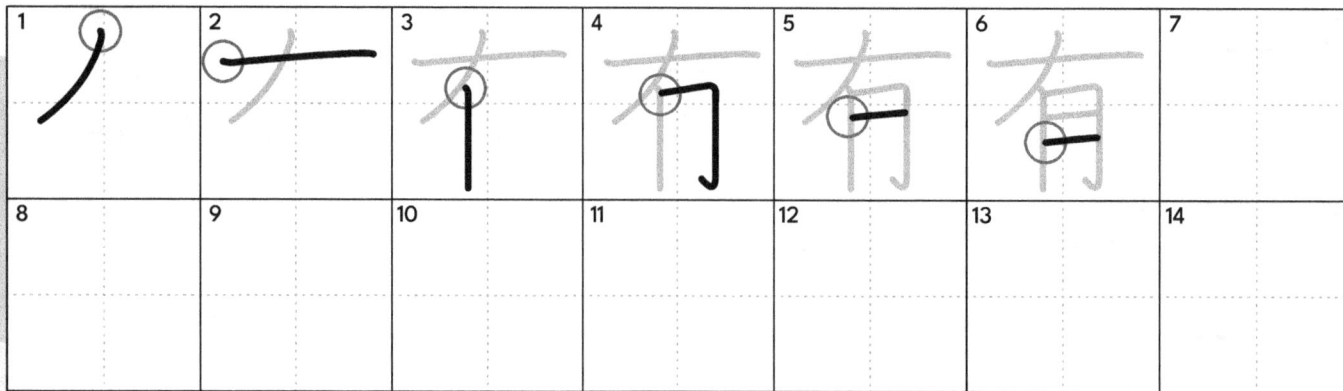

Writing Practice

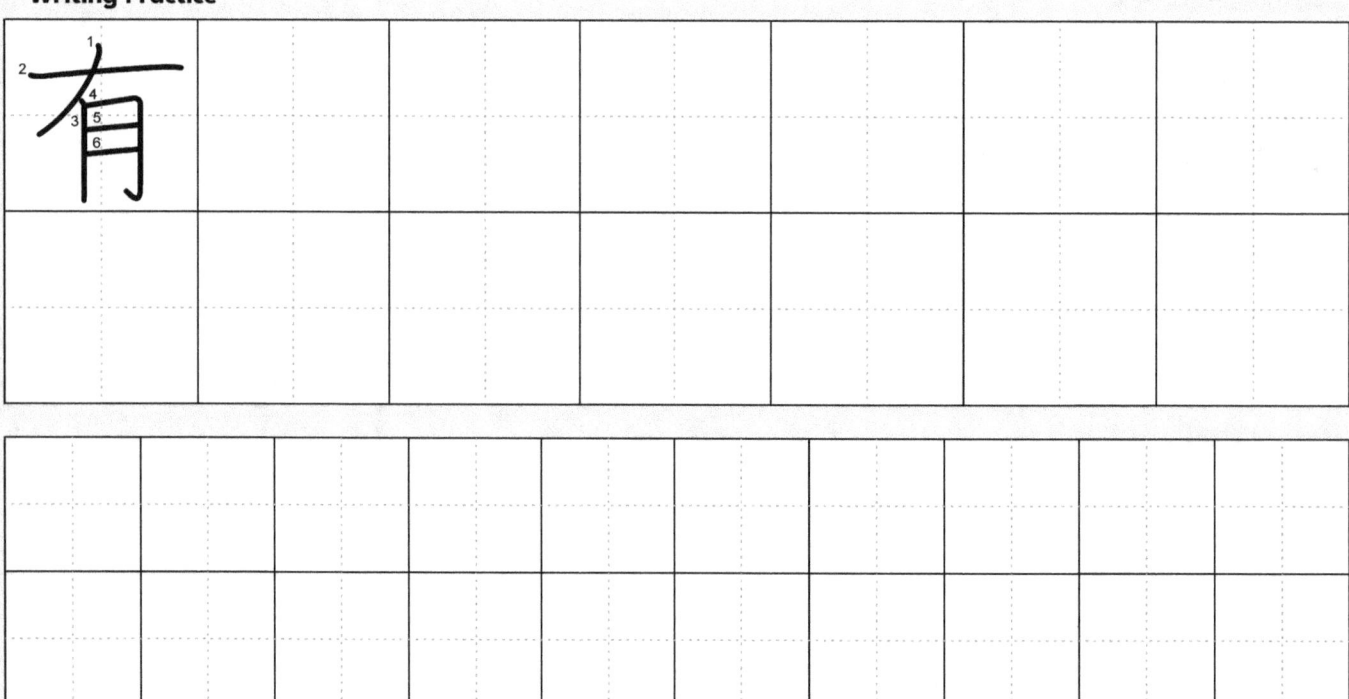

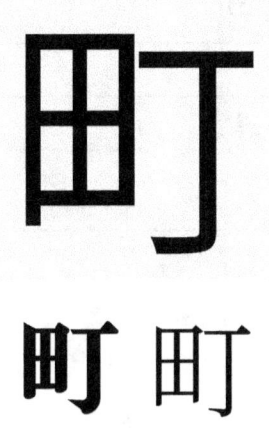

Meaning(s)	town, village, street	Components	一 亅 田
Radical	田 (field)	Kun'yomi	まち
Strokes	7	On'yomi	チョウ

Vocabulary	Meaning	Pronunciation
町	town, block, neighborhood, main street	まち
町	town, block, neighborhood	チョウ
町議会	town council	チョウギカイ
街角	street corner	まちかど

Stroke Order

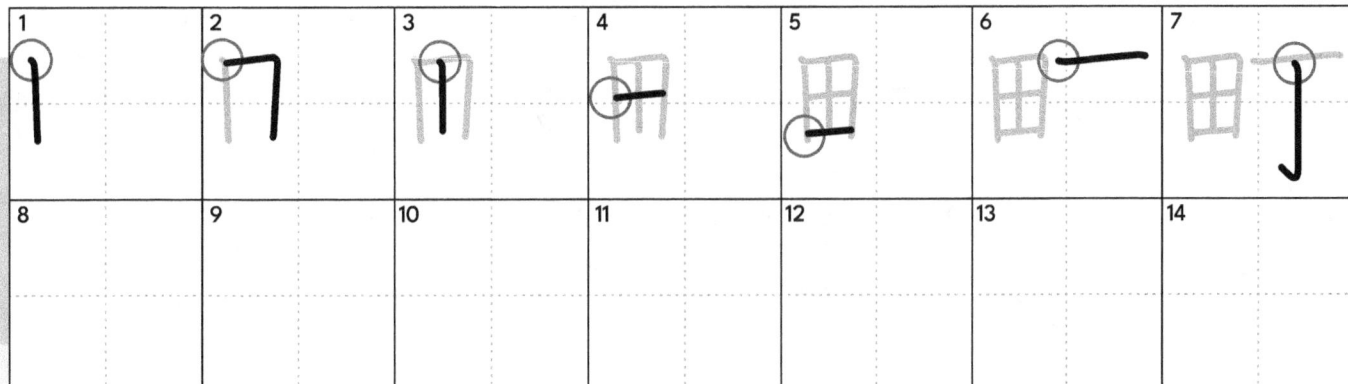

Writing Practice

Meaning(s)	fee, materials	Components	斗 米
Radical	斗 (dipper)	Kun'yomi	
Strokes	10	On'yomi	リョウ

Vocabulary	Meaning		Pronunciation
料	fee, charge, rate, material		リョウ
料金	fee, charge, fare		リョウキン
史料	historical materials, historical records		シリョウ
使用料	use fee, rent		ショウリョウ

Stroke Order

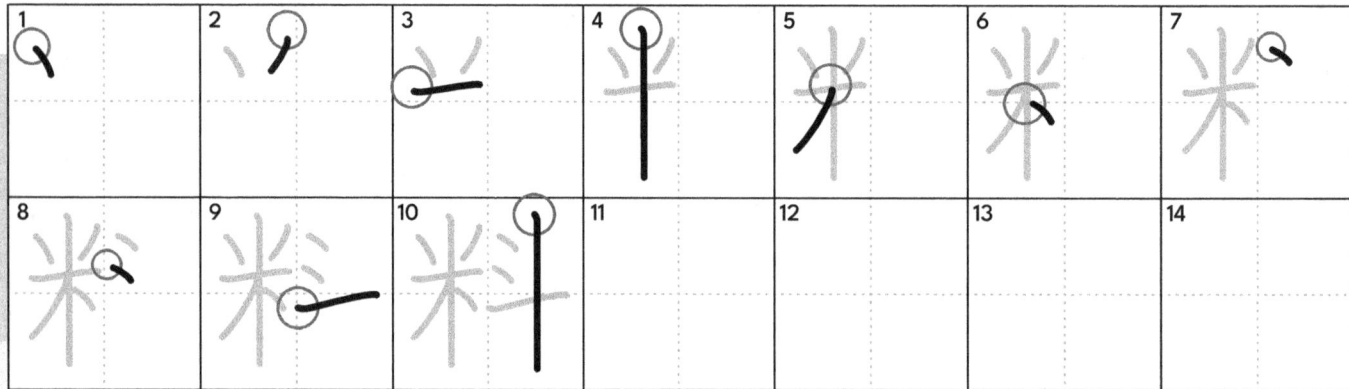

Writing Practice

Meaning(s)	craft, construction	**Components**	工	
Radical	工 (work)	**Kun'yomi**		
Strokes	3	**On'yomi**	コウ、ク、グ	

Vocabulary	Meaning	Pronunciation
工	(factory) worker	コウ
商工	commerce and industry	ショウコウ
工夫	inventing, thinking up, figuring out	クフウ
竹細工	bamboo work, bamboo ware	タケザイク

Stroke Order

Writing Practice

建

Meaning(s)	build	Components	廴 聿
Radical	廴 (long stride)	Kun'yomi	た(てる)
Strokes	9	On'yomi	ケン、コン

Vocabulary	Meaning	Pronunciation
建てる	to build, to construct	たてる
建て	contract, commitment	たて
建立	(act of) building (monument, etc.)	コンリュウ
建議	proposition, motion, proposal	ケンギ

Stroke Order

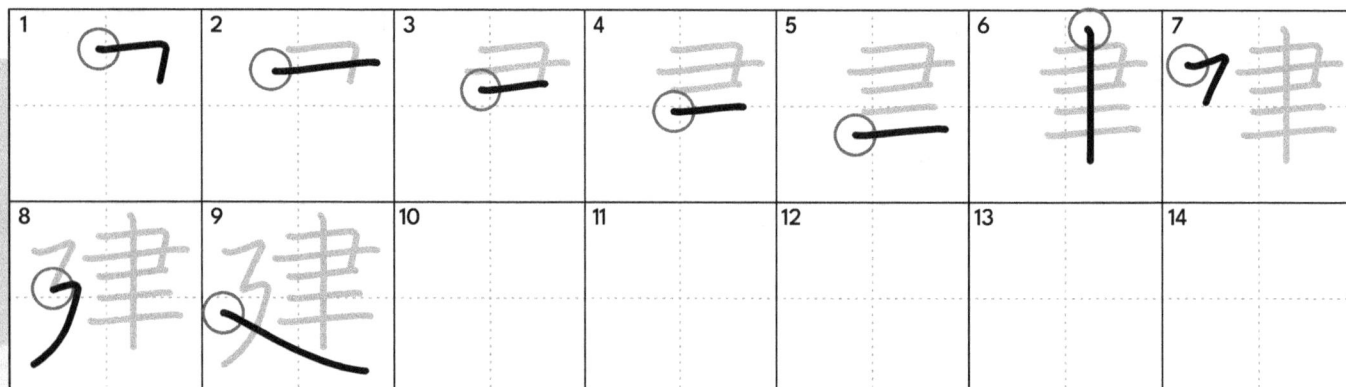

Writing Practice

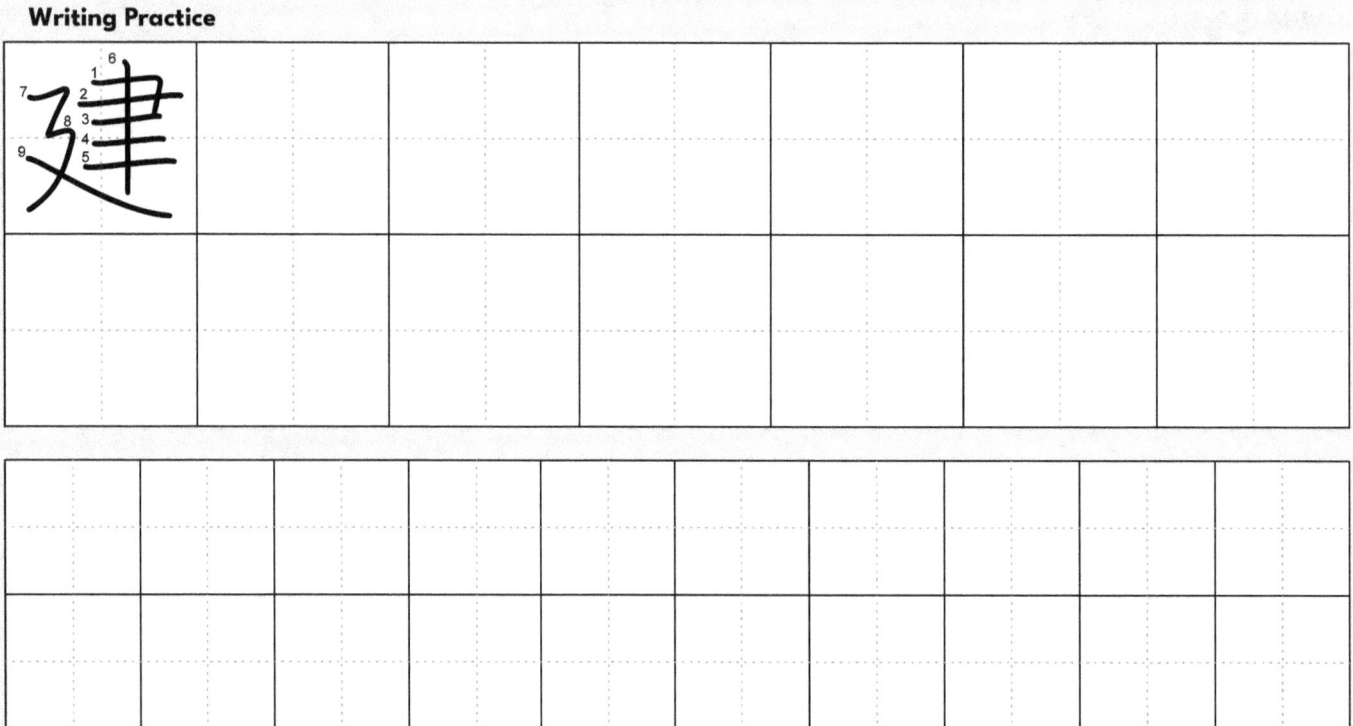

Meaning(s)	hurry, sudden, steep	Components	ク ヨ 心
Radical	心 (忄, 小) (heart)	Kun'yomi	いそ(ぐ)
Strokes	9	On'yomi	キュウ

Vocabulary	Meaning		Pronunciation
急ぐ	to hurry, to rush, to hasten		いそぐ
急	sudden, abrupt, unexpected		キュウ
急ぎ	haste, hurry, expedition		いそぎ
快急	rapid express (train)		カイキュウ

Stroke Order

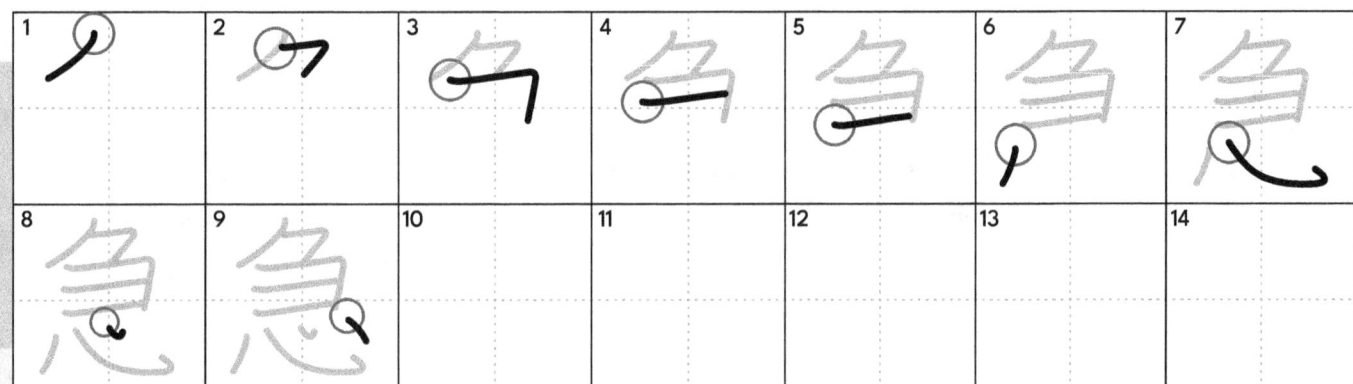

Writing Practice

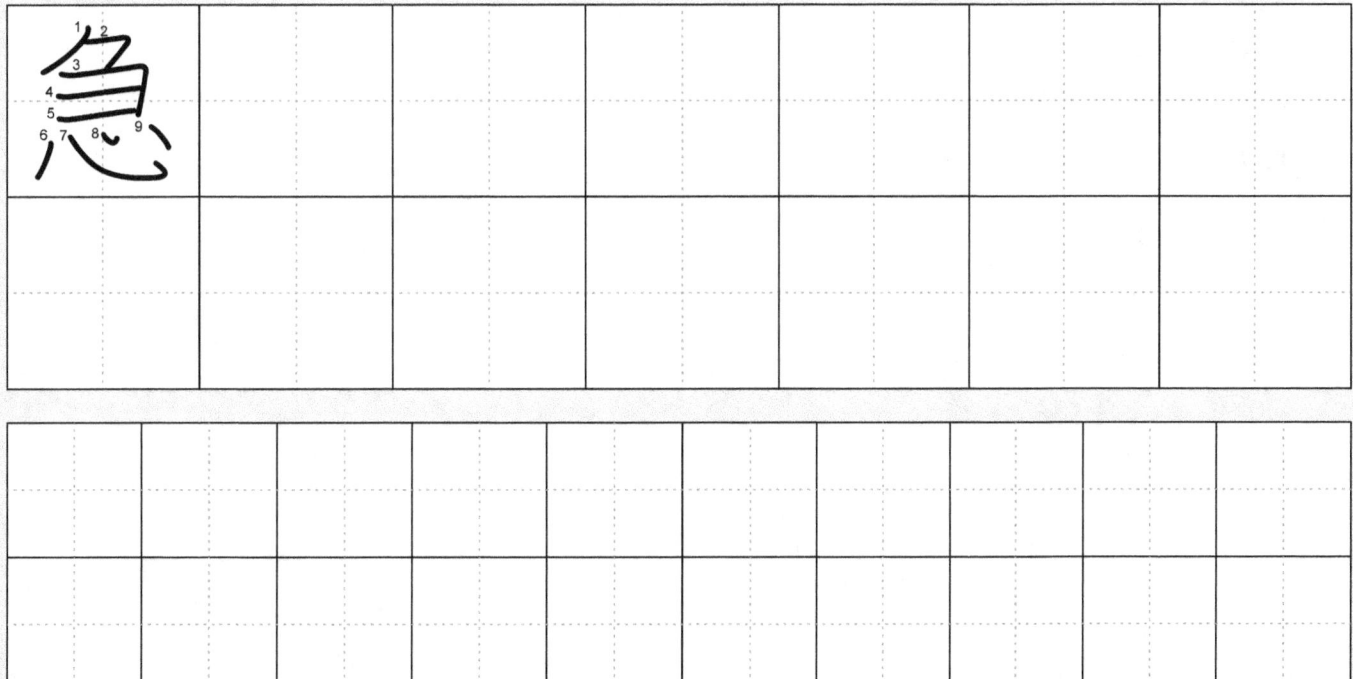

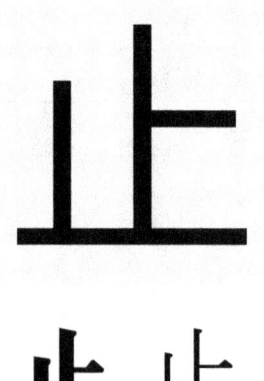

Meaning(s)	stop, halt	Components	止
Radical	止 (stop)	Kun'yomi	と(まる)、とど(まる)、よ(す)
Strokes	4	On'yomi	シ

Vocabulary	Meaning	Pronunciation
止まる	to stop (moving), to come to a stop	とまる
止まる	to remain, to abide, to stay (in the one place)	とどまる
止める	to stop, to turn off, to park, to prevent	とめる
解止	termination	カイシ

Stroke Order

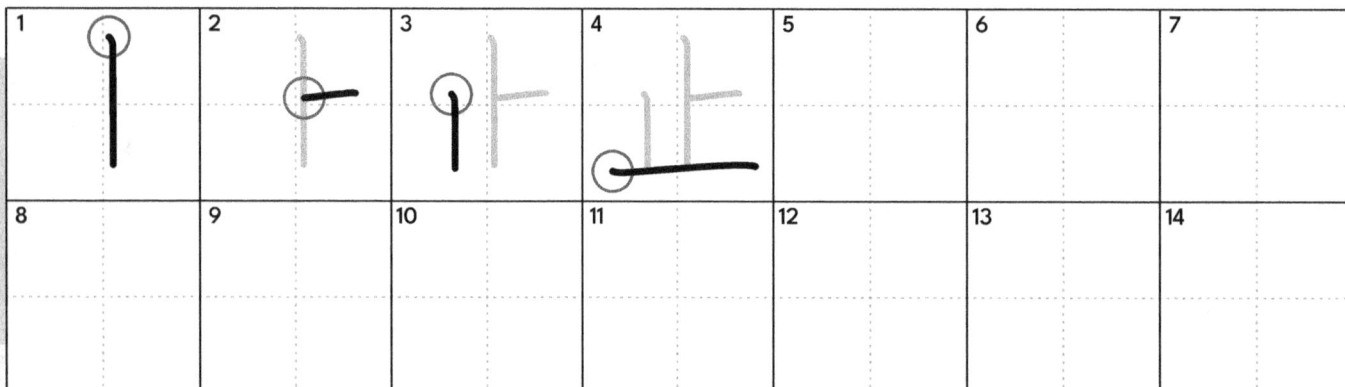

Writing Practice

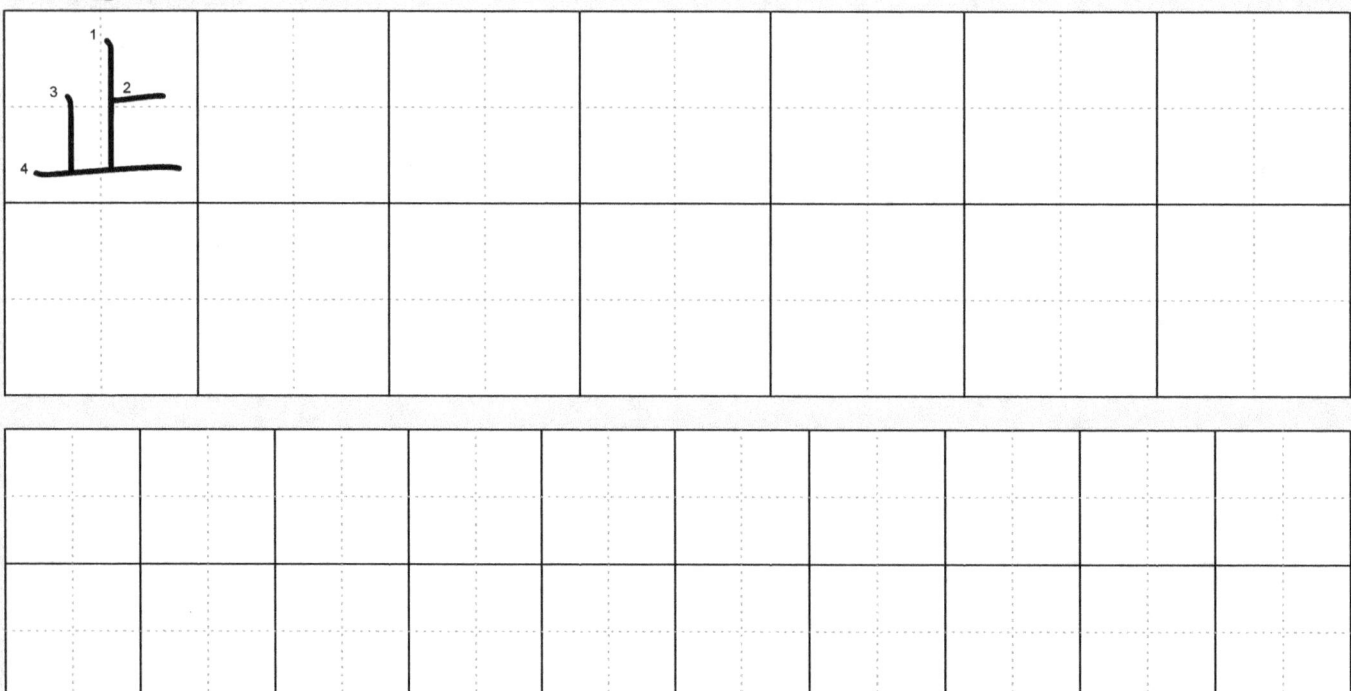

Meaning(s)	escort, send	Components	一 二 丼 込 大
Radical	辵 (辶, ⻌) (walk)	Kun'yomi	おく(る)
Strokes	9	On'yomi	ソウ

Vocabulary	Meaning		Pronunciation
送る	to send/transmit (a thing), to despatch, to see off (a person), to spend (time)		おくる
送球	throwing a ball, handball		ソウキュウ
移送	transfer, transport, transportation		イソウ

Stroke Order

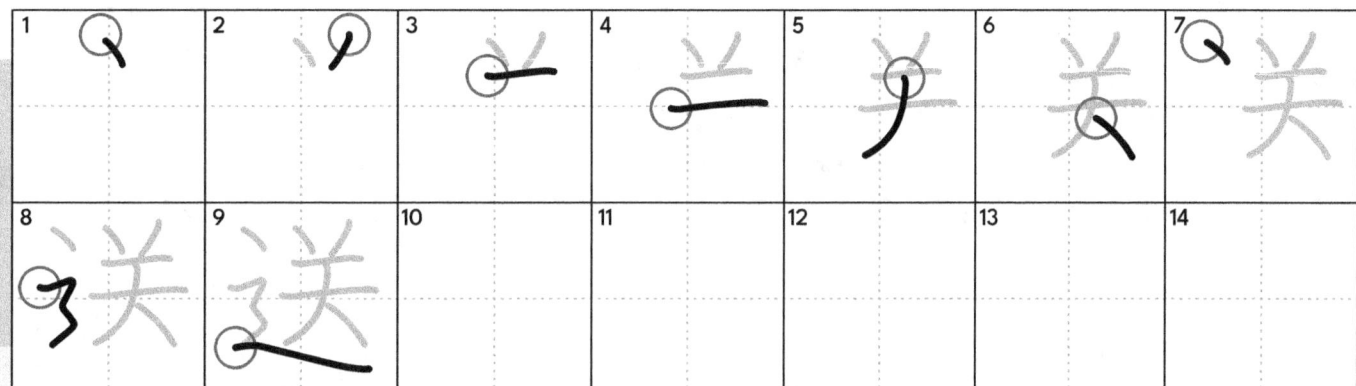

Writing Practice

切

Meaning(s)	cut, cutoff, be sharp	Components	刀 ヒ
Radical	刀 (刂) (knife, sword)	Kun'yomi	き(る)
Strokes	4	On'yomi	セツ、サイ

Vocabulary	Meaning	Pronunciation
切る	to cut, to cut through, to disconnect, to open (something sealed), to start,	きる
切	eager, earnest, ardent, kind	セツ
家財一切	complete set of household goods	カザイイッサイ

Stroke Order

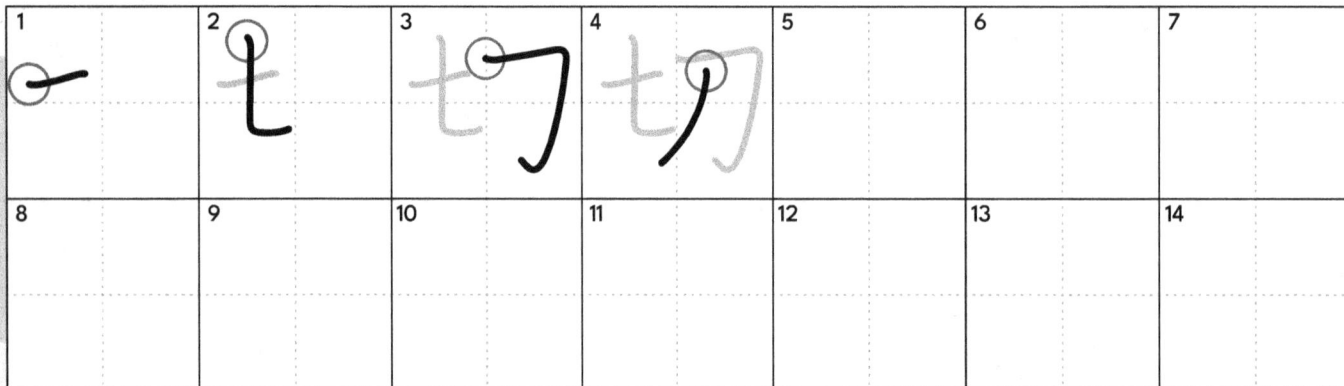

Writing Practice

Meaning(s)	turn around, change	Components	ニ ム 車
Radical	車 (car, cart)	Kun'yomi	ころ(がる)
Strokes	11	On'yomi	テン

Vocabulary	Meaning	Pronunciation
転がる	to roll, to tumble, to fall over, to roll over	ころがる
転	change in pronunciation or meaning of word	テン
転移	change, transition, moving (location)	テンイ
転ぶ	to fall down, to fall over, to turn out	ころぶ

Stroke Order

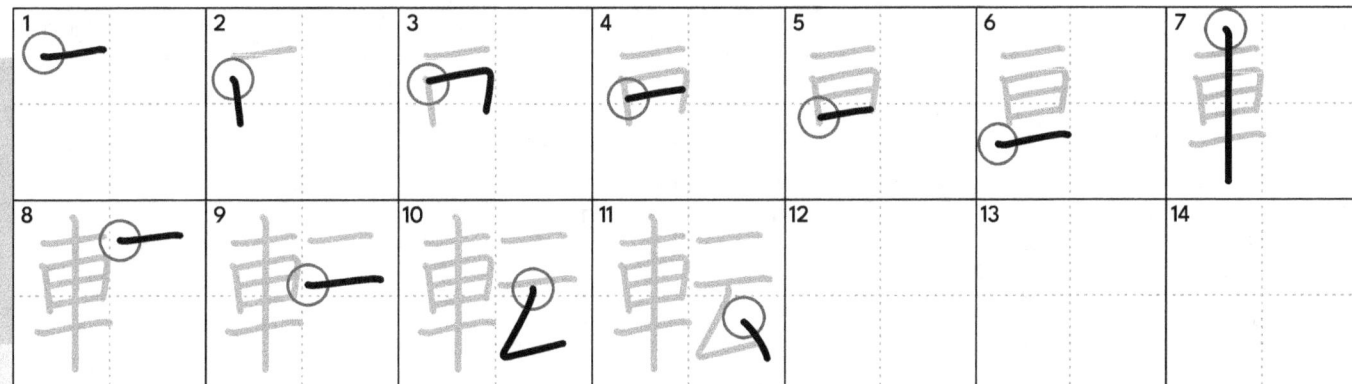

Writing Practice

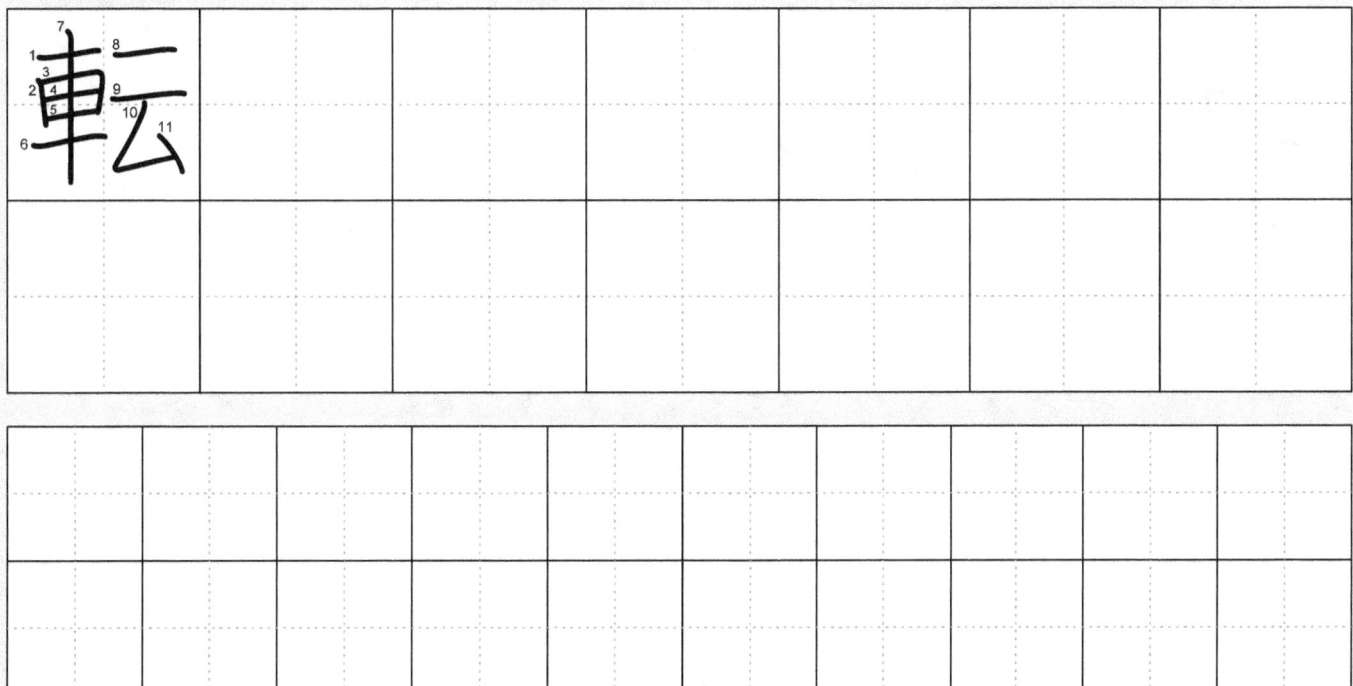

研

Meaning(s)	polish, study of, sharpen	Components	一 丨 ノ 亅 二 口 开 石
Radical	石 (stone)	Kun'yomi	と(ぐ)
Strokes	9	On'yomi	ケン

Vocabulary	Meaning	Pronunciation
研ぐ	to sharpen, to hone, to whet, to polish	とぐ
研究	study, research, investigation	ケンキュウ
予研	National Institute of Health	ヨケン
研究員	researcher, lab worker	ケンキュウイン

Stroke Order

Writing Practice

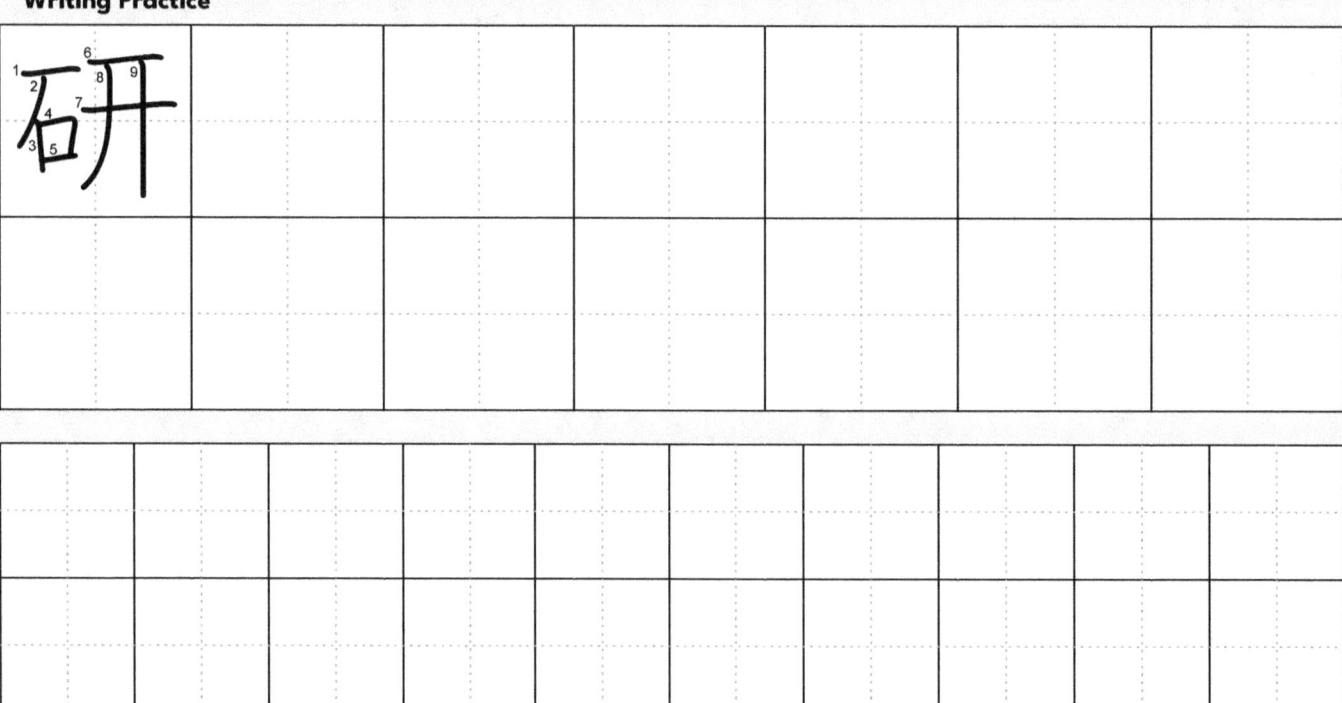

Meaning(s)	research, study	Components	儿 九 宀 穴
Radical	穴 (cave)	Kun'yomi	きわめる
Strokes	7	On'yomi	キュウ

Vocabulary	Meaning		Pronunciation
極める	to carry to extremes, to master		きわめる
究明	investigation (esp. academic or scientific)		キュウメイ
究竟	culmination, conclusion		クキョウ
究竟	after all, in the end, finally, excellent, ideal		クッキョウ

Stroke Order

Writing Practice

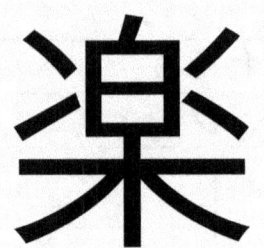

Meaning(s)	music, comfort, ease	Components	冫 木 白
Radical	木 (tree)	Kun'yomi	たの(しい)
Strokes	13	On'yomi	ガク、ラク

Vocabulary	Meaning		Pronunciation
楽しい	enjoyable, fun, pleasant, happy		たのしい
楽	music, old Japanese court music		ガク
楽	comfort, ease, relief, (at) peace, easy		ラク
行楽	outing, excursion, pleasure trip		コウラク

Stroke Order

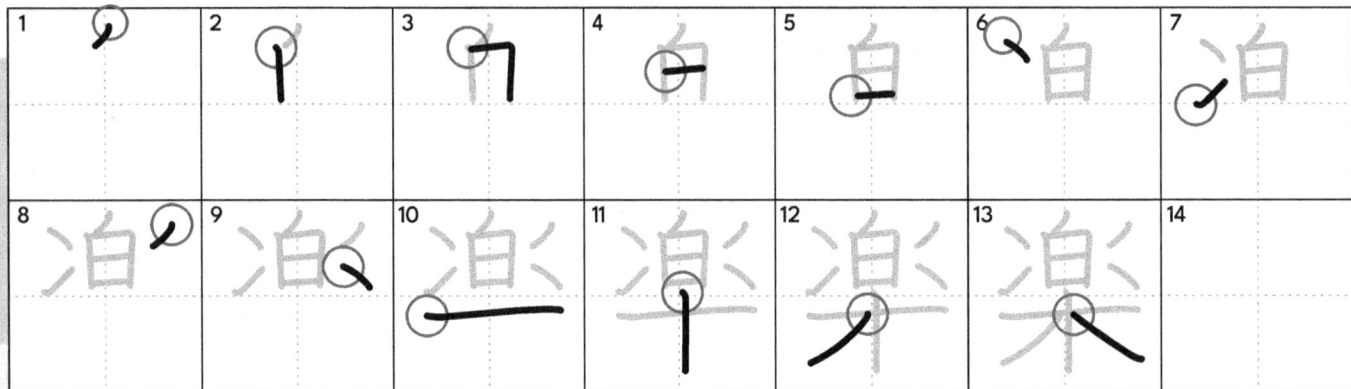

Writing Practice

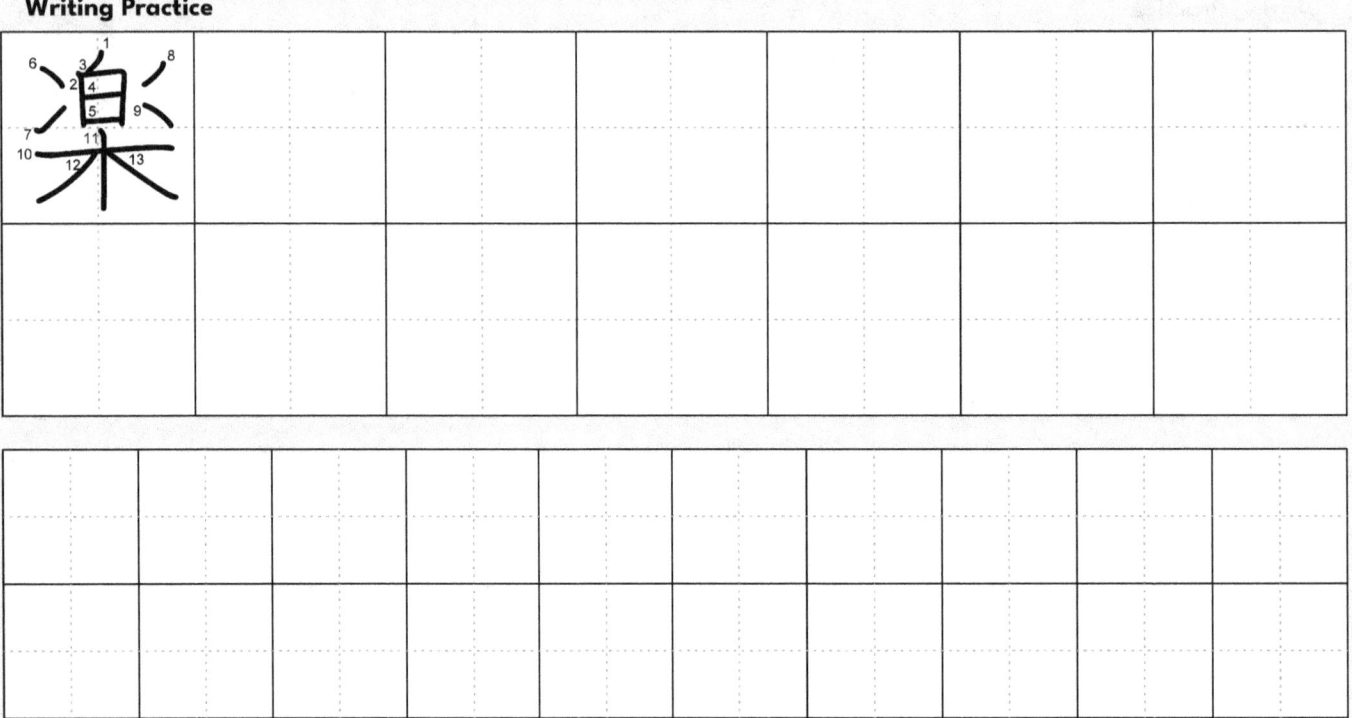

Meaning(s)	wake up, get up; rouse	Components	土 巳 走
Radical	走 (辵) (run)	Kun'yomi	お(きる)、おこ(す)
Strokes	10	On'yomi	キ

Vocabulary	Meaning	Pronunciation
起きる	to get up, to rise, to wake or wake up	おきる
起源	origin, beginning, source, rise	キゲン
起こる	to occur, to happen	おこる
起こす	to raise, to raise up, to set up, to pick up	おこす

Stroke Order

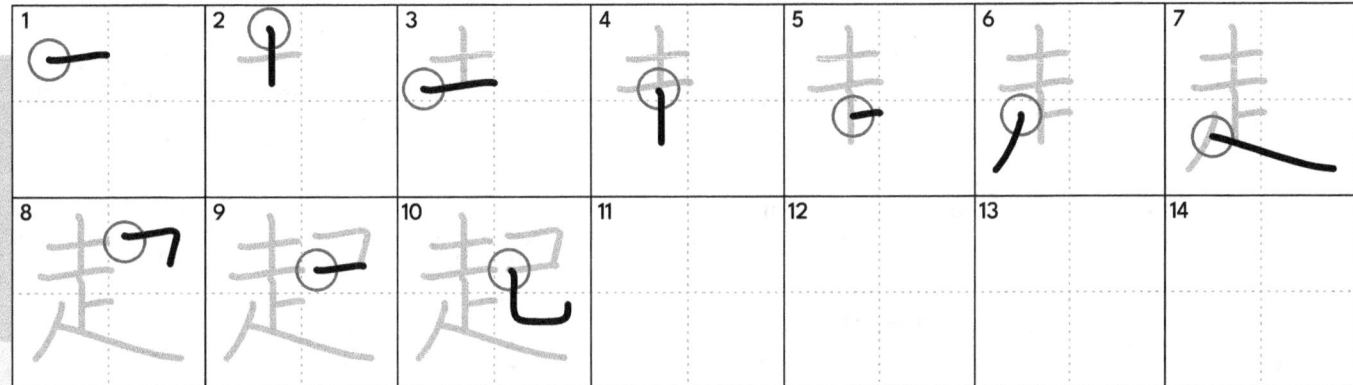

Writing Practice

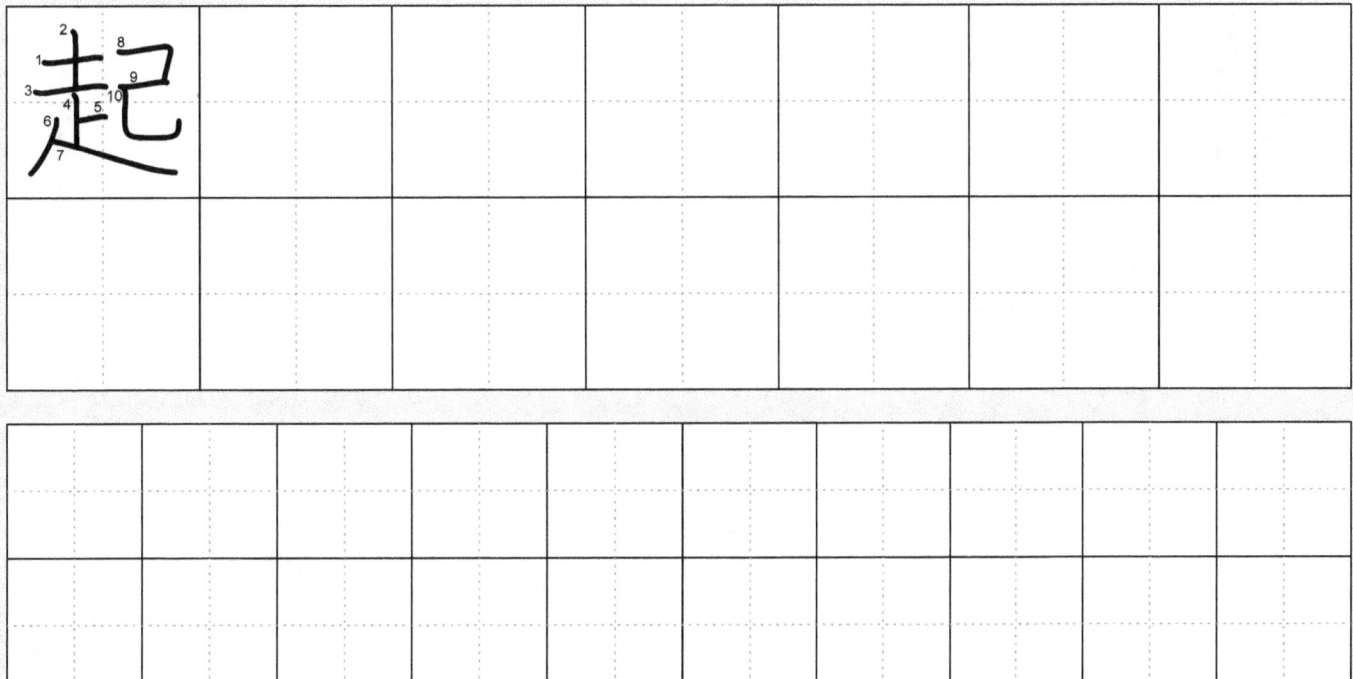

Meaning(s)	arrive, wear	Components	ノ丼王目羊
Radical	目 (eye)	Kun'yomi	き(る)、つ(く)
Strokes	12	On'yomi	チャク

Vocabulary	Meaning		Pronunciation
着る	to wear, to put on, to bear		きる
着く	to arrive at, to reach, to sit on		つく
着	arrival, arriving at ...		チャク
決着	conclusion, decision, end		ケッチャク

Stroke Order

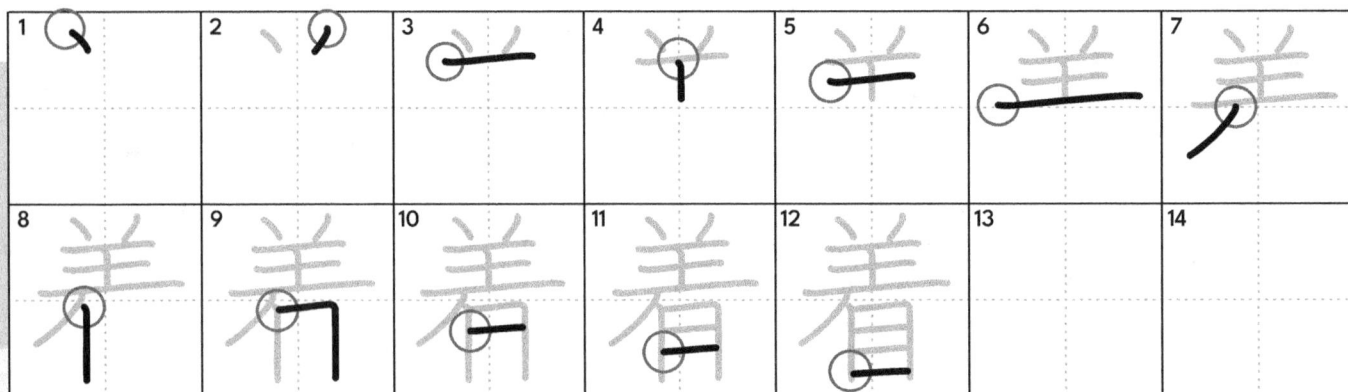

Writing Practice

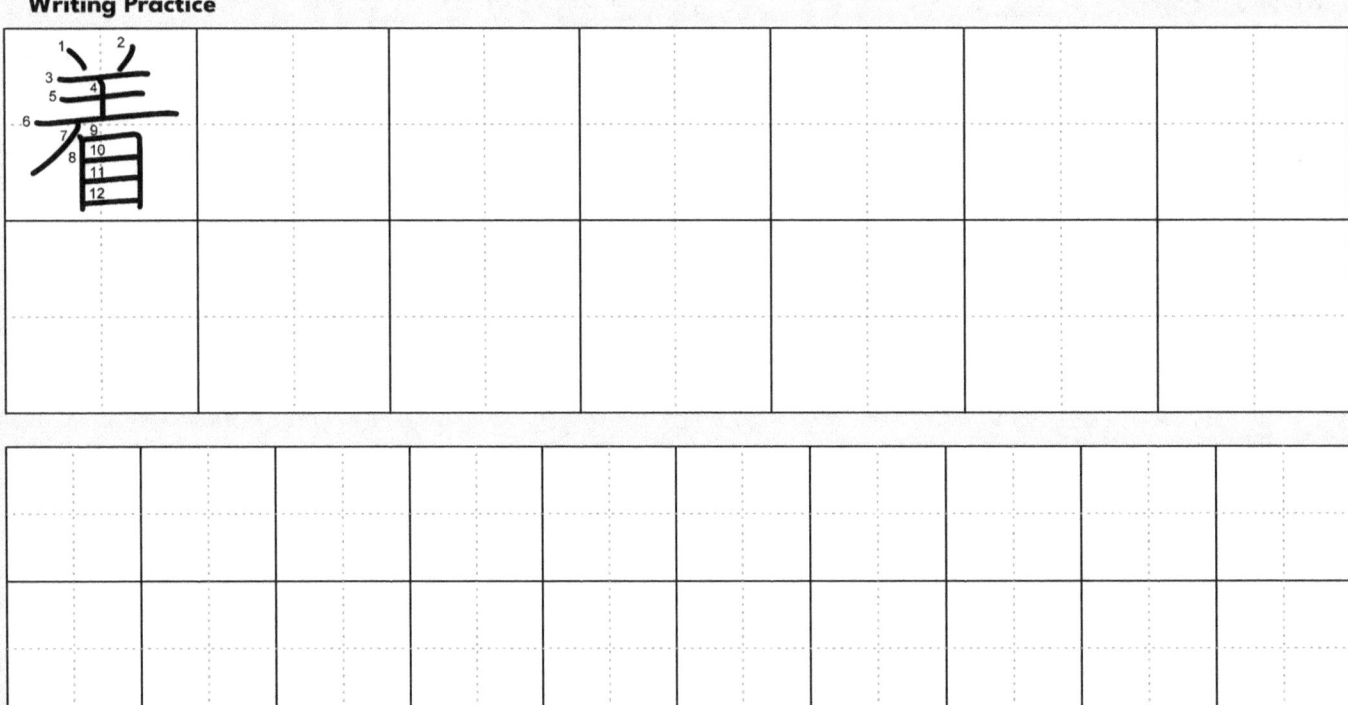

Meaning(s)	ill, sick	Components	一 人 冂 疒
Radical	疒 (sickness)	Kun'yomi	や(む)
Strokes	10	On'yomi	ビョウ

Vocabulary	Meaning	Pronunciation
病む	to fall ill, to suffer from (e.g. a disease)	やむ
病	illness, disease, bad habit, weakness	やまい
病	disease, -pathy	ビョウ
病院	hospital, clinic, doctor's surgery, infirmary	ビョウイン

Stroke Order

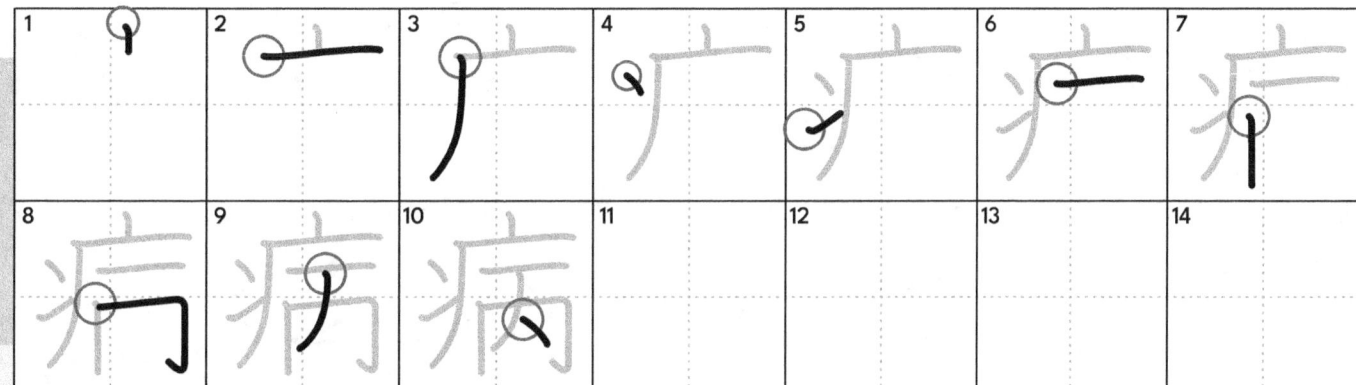

Writing Practice

Meaning(s)	substance, quality	Components	八 斤 目 貝
Radical	貝 (shell)	Kun'yomi	たち、ただ(す)
Strokes	15	On'yomi	シツ、シチ

Vocabulary	Meaning		Pronunciation
質	nature (of a person), disposition		たち
質	quality, value, nature, character		シツ
質	pawn, pawned article, pledge		シチ
質す	to ask (about), to inquire		ただす

Stroke Order

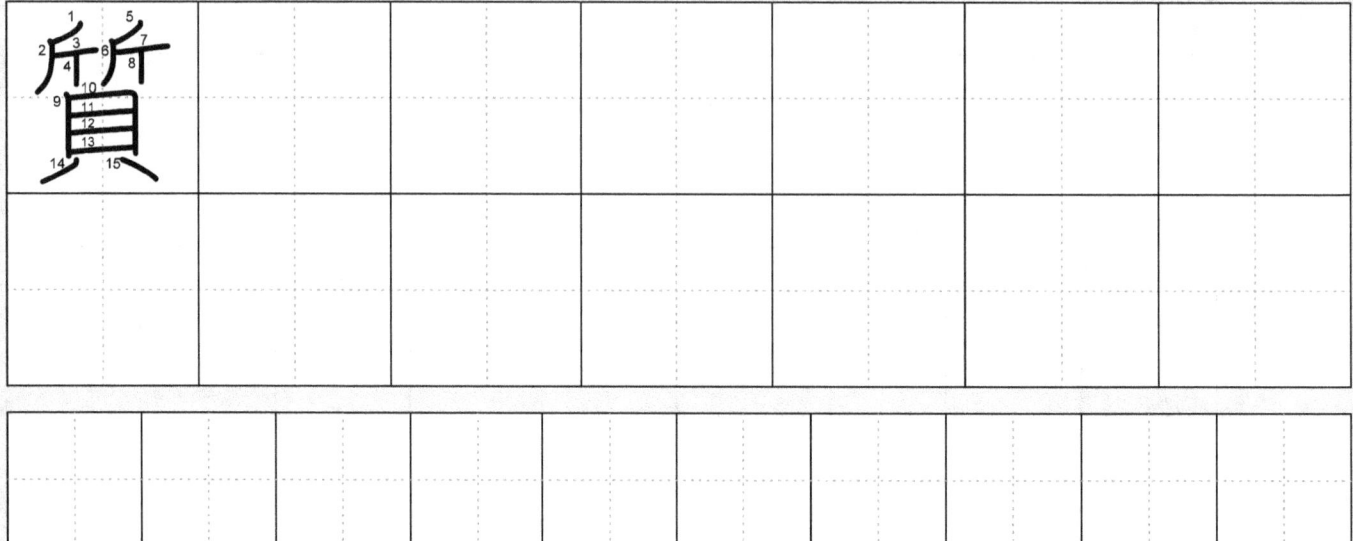

Writing Practice

Meaning(s)	wait, depend on	Components	土寸彳
Radical	彳 (step)	Kun'yomi	ま(つ)
Strokes	9	On'yomi	タイ

Vocabulary	Meaning		Pronunciation
待つ	to wait, to await, to look forward to		まつ
待遇	treatment, reception, service		タイグウ
歓待	warm welcome, friendly reception		カンタイ
待機	standing by, awaiting an opportunity		タイキ

Stroke Order

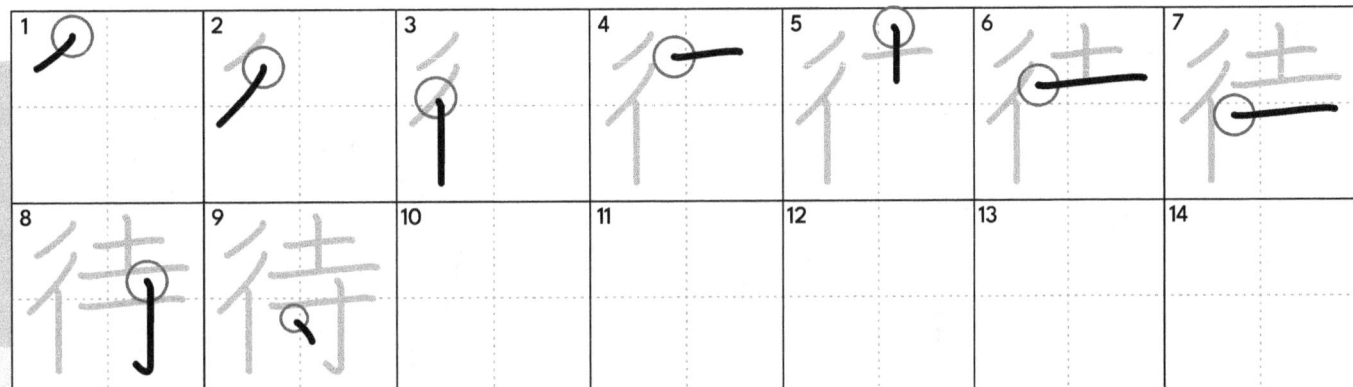

Writing Practice

Meaning(s)	test, try, attempt	Components	工 弋 言
Radical	言 (言) (speech)	Kun'yomi	こころ(みる)、ため(す)
Strokes	13	On'yomi	シ

Vocabulary	Meaning		Pronunciation
試みる	to try, to attempt, to have a go (at)		こころみる
試	testing, experiment, test, examination		シ
試す	to try (out), to have a try (at)		ためす
考試	test, exam		コウシ

Stroke Order

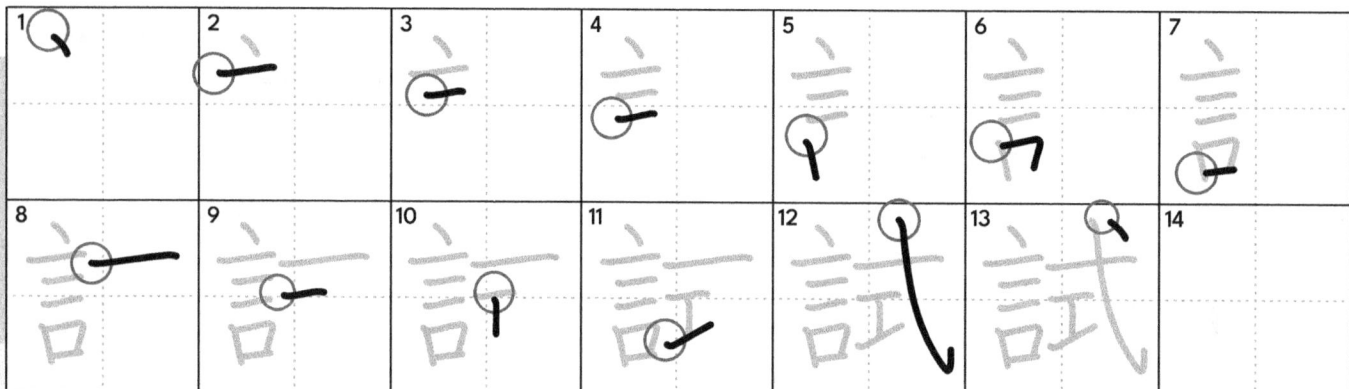

Writing Practice

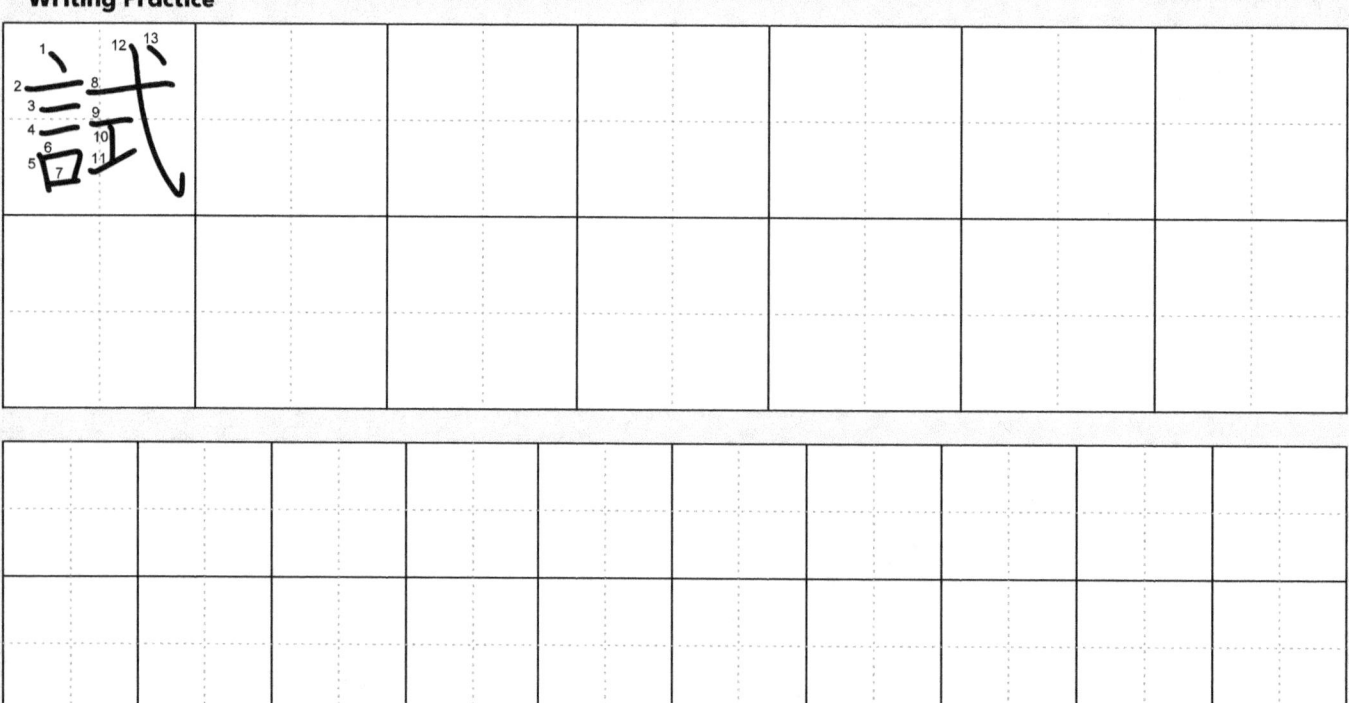

族

Meaning(s)	tribe, family	Components	方矢乞
Radical	方 (square)	Kun'yomi	
Strokes	11	On'yomi	ゾク

Vocabulary	Meaning	Pronunciation
族	tribe, clan, band, family	ゾク
族長	patriarch, head of a family	ゾクチョウ
皇族	imperial family, royalty	コウゾク
王族	royalty	オウゾク

Stroke Order

Writing Practice

Meaning(s)	silver		Components	艮 金
Radical	金 (金) (metal, gold)		Kun'yomi	
Strokes	14		On'yomi	ギン

Vocabulary	Meaning	Pronunciation
銀	silver (Ag), silver coin, money, silver medal, silver colour/color, bank, silver general	ぎん / ギン
銀色	silver (color, colour)	ギンイロ
世銀	World Bank	セギン

Stroke Order

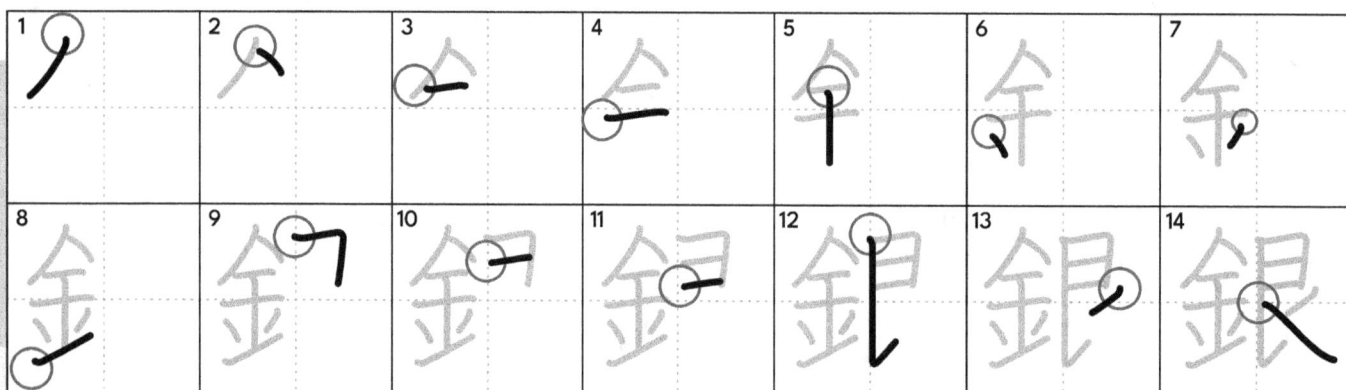

Writing Practice

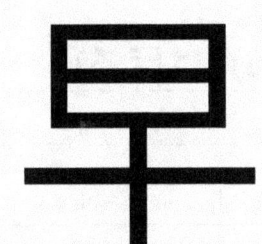

Meaning(s)	early, fast	**Components**	十 日
Radical	日 (sun, day)	**Kun'yomi**	はや(い)
Strokes	6	**On'yomi**	ソウ、サッ

Vocabulary	Meaning	Pronunciation
早い	fast, quick, rapid, swift, speedy, prompt	はやい
早	already, now, by this time, quick	はや
早急	immediate, prompt, quick, rapid, urgent	ソウキュウ
早速	at once, immediately, without delay	サッソク

Stroke Order

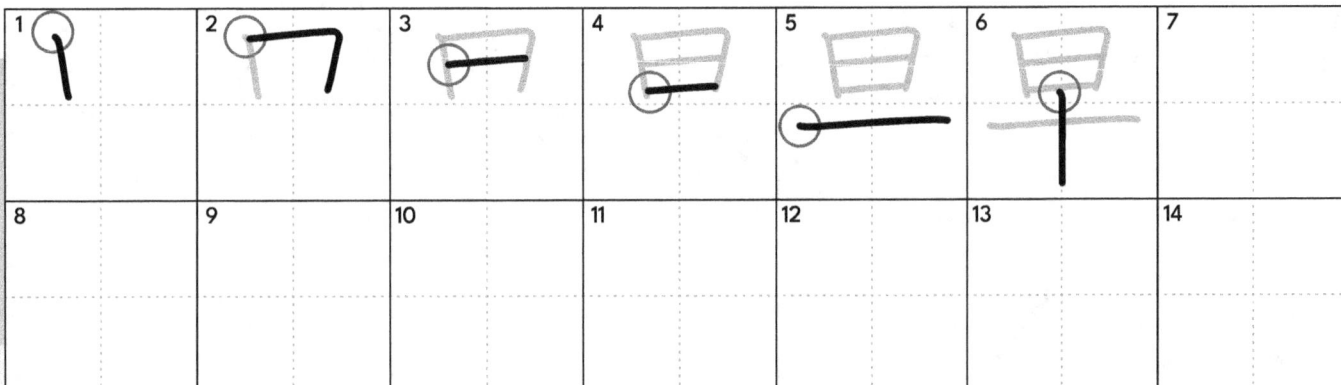

Writing Practice

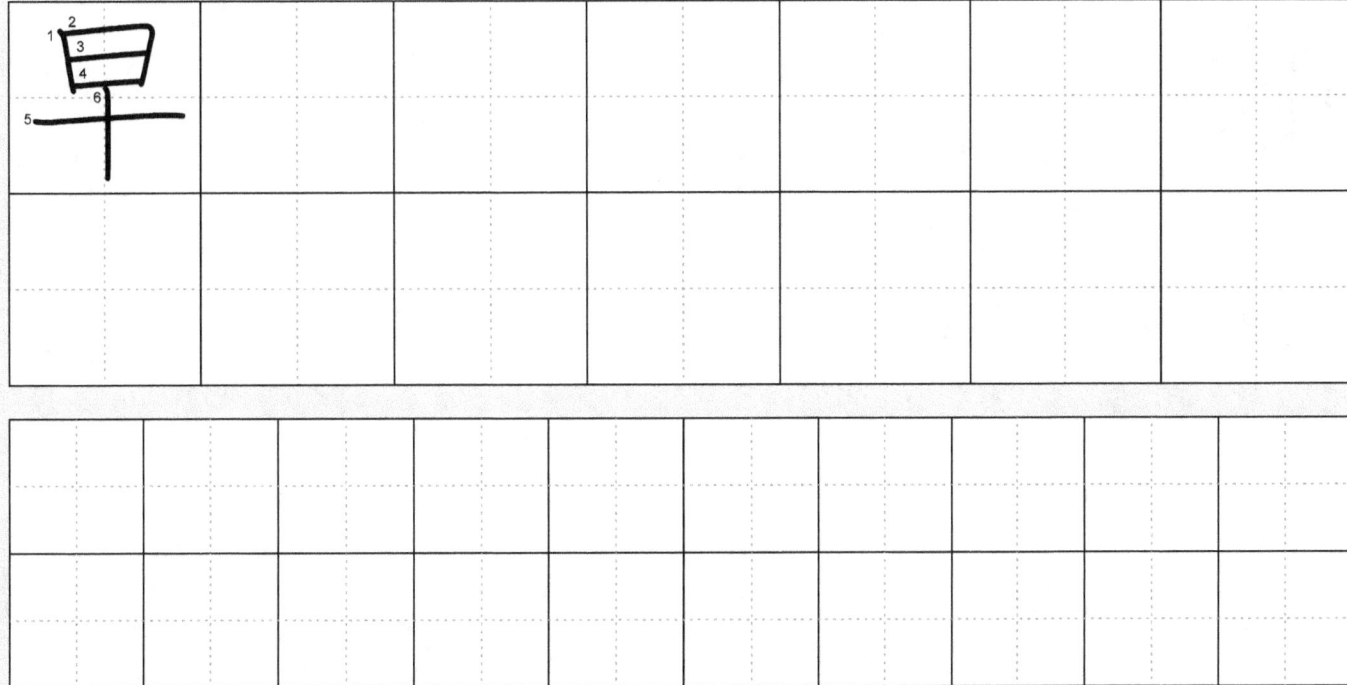

Meaning(s)	reflect, reflection	Components	ノ冂大日
Radical	日 (sun, day)	Kun'yomi	うつ(る)、は(える)
Strokes	9	On'yomi	エイ

Vocabulary	Meaning	Pronunciation
映る	to be reflected, to harmonize with	うつる
映す	to project, to reflect, to cast (shadow)	うつす
映える	to shine, to glow, to look attractive	はえる
映画	movie, film, motion picture	エイガ

Stroke Order

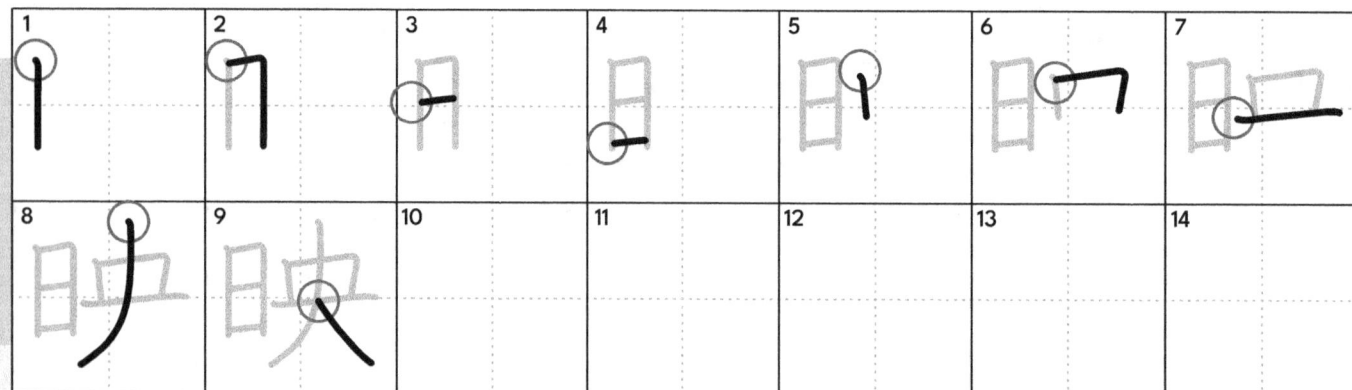

Writing Practice

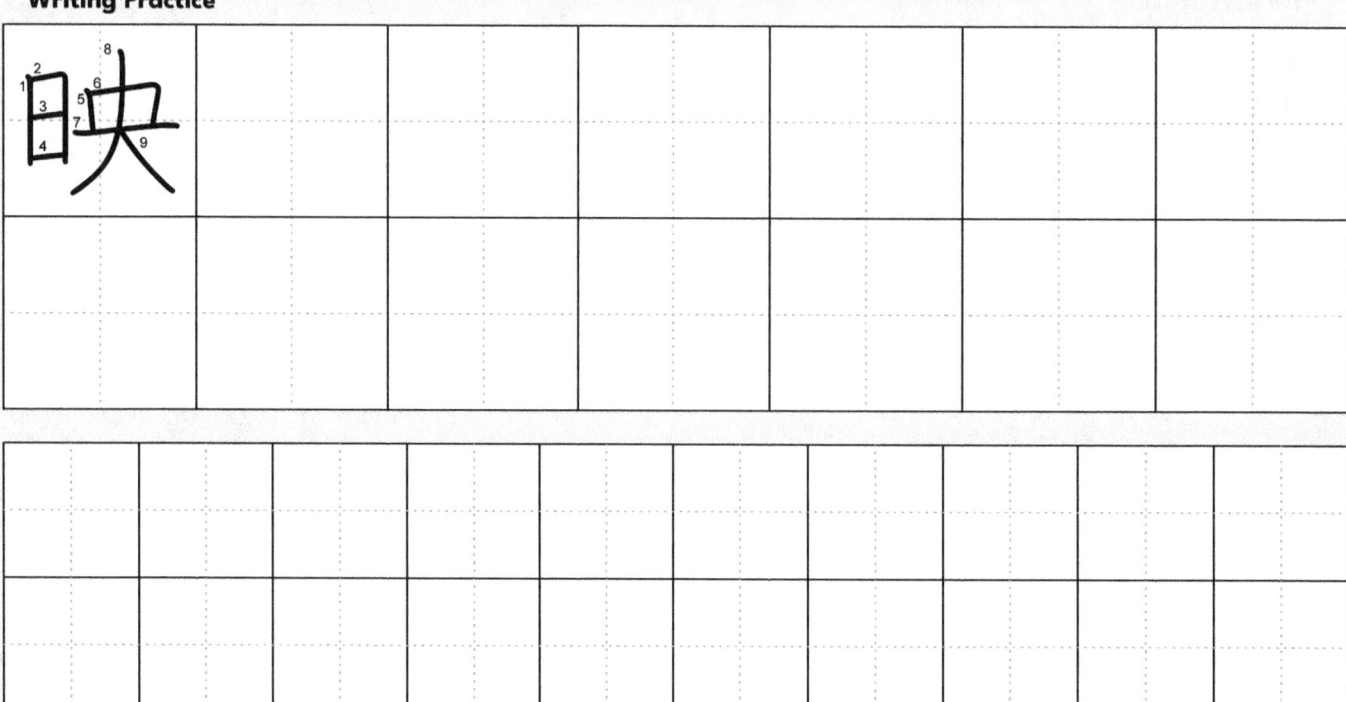

Meaning(s)	relative, familiarity	Components	亠 井 木 立 見 辛
Radical	見 (see)	Kun'yomi	おや、した(しい)
Strokes	16	On'yomi	シン

Vocabulary	Meaning	Pronunciation
親	parent, parents, mother and father, banker	おや
親しい	close (e.g. friend), familiar, friendly, intimate	したしい
親	intimacy/closeness, friendliness, close relative	シン
親方	master, boss, chief, foreman, supervisor	おやかた

Stroke Order

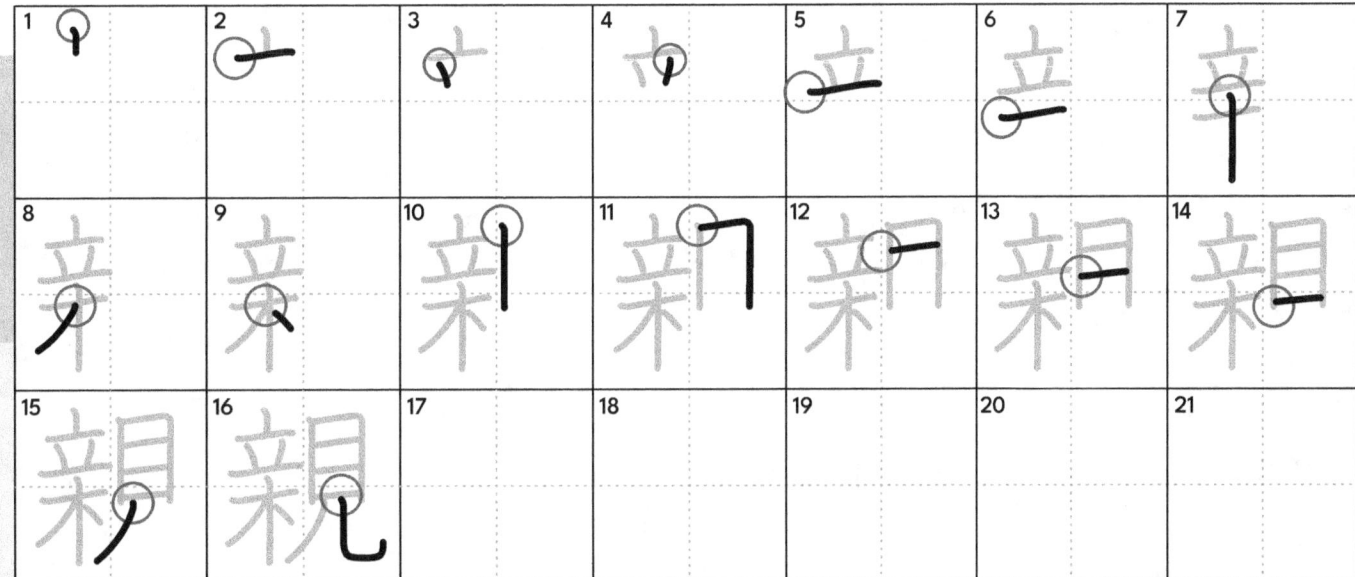

Writing Practice

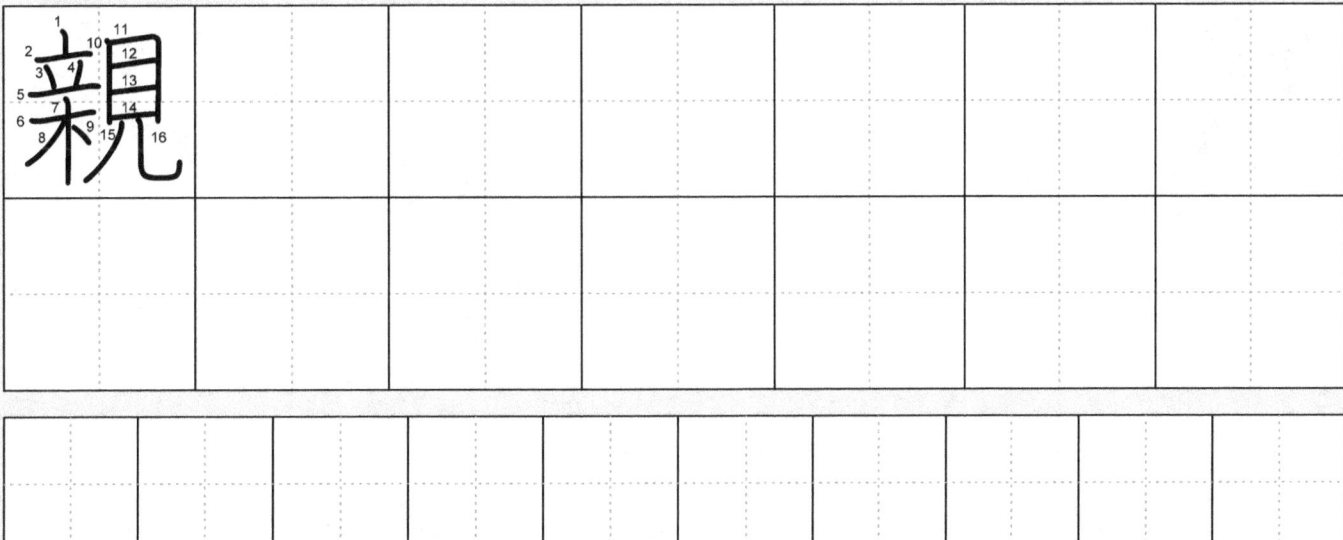

験

Meaning(s)	effect, testing, verification	Components	人 亻 口 杰 馬
Radical	馬 (horse)	Kun'yomi	
Strokes	18	On'yomi	ケン

Vocabulary	Meaning		Pronunciation
徴験	sign, indication, omen		しるし
験	effect, efficacy, omen		ゲン
霊験	miraculous efficacy, miracle		レイゲン
筆記試験	written examination		ヒッキシケン

Stroke Order

Writing Practice

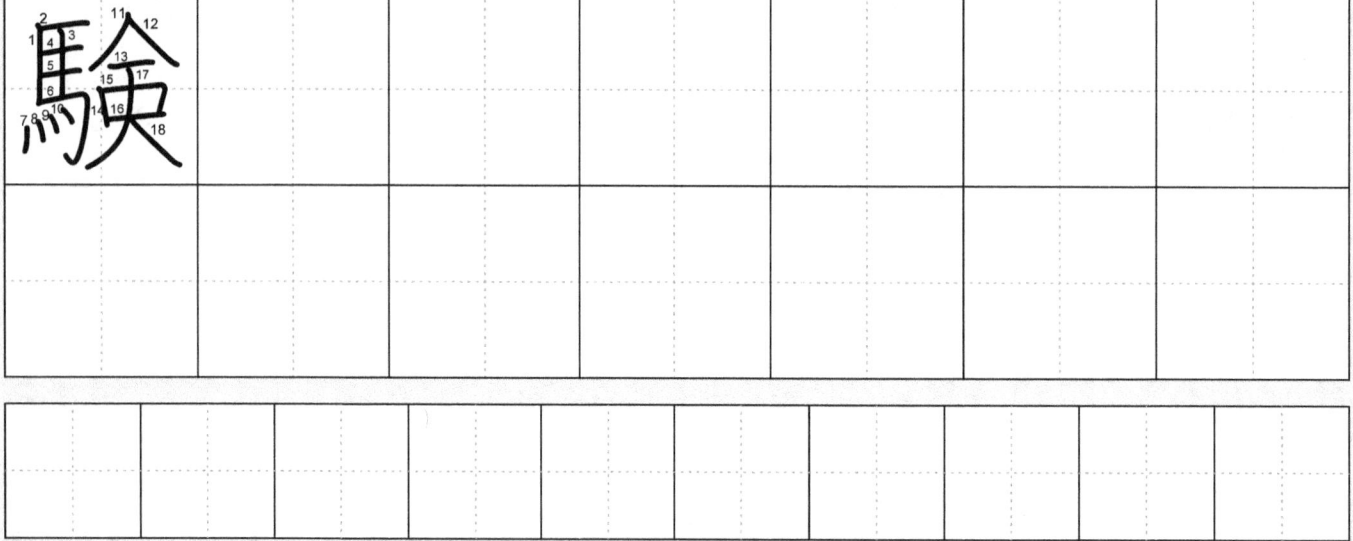

Meaning(s)	England, English, hero	Components	ノ一大艾
Radical	艸 (艹) (grass)	Kun'yomi	
Strokes	8	On'yomi	エイ

Vocabulary	Meaning	Pronunciation
英	United Kingdom, Britain, English (language)	エイ
英語	English (language)	エイゴ
和英	Japanese-English (dictionary)	ワエイ

Stroke Order

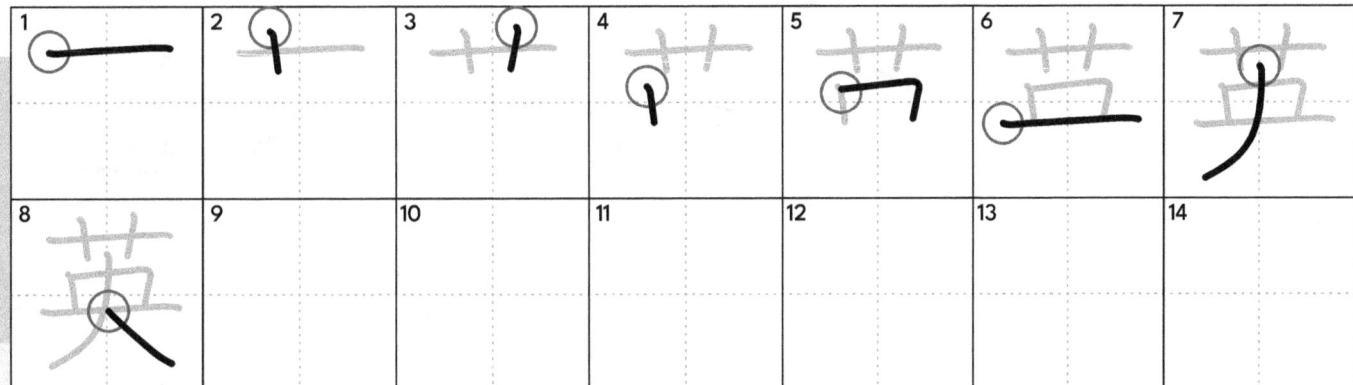

Writing Practice

Meaning(s)	doctor, medicine		Components	匚矢乞
Radical	匚 (enclosure (hiding))		Kun'yomi	
Strokes	7		On'yomi	イ

Vocabulary	Meaning	Pronunciation
医	medicine, healing art, healing, curing, doctor	イ
医院	doctor's office, doctor's surgery, clinic	イイン
軍医	military physician or surgeon	グンイ
校医	school doctor	コウイ

Stroke Order

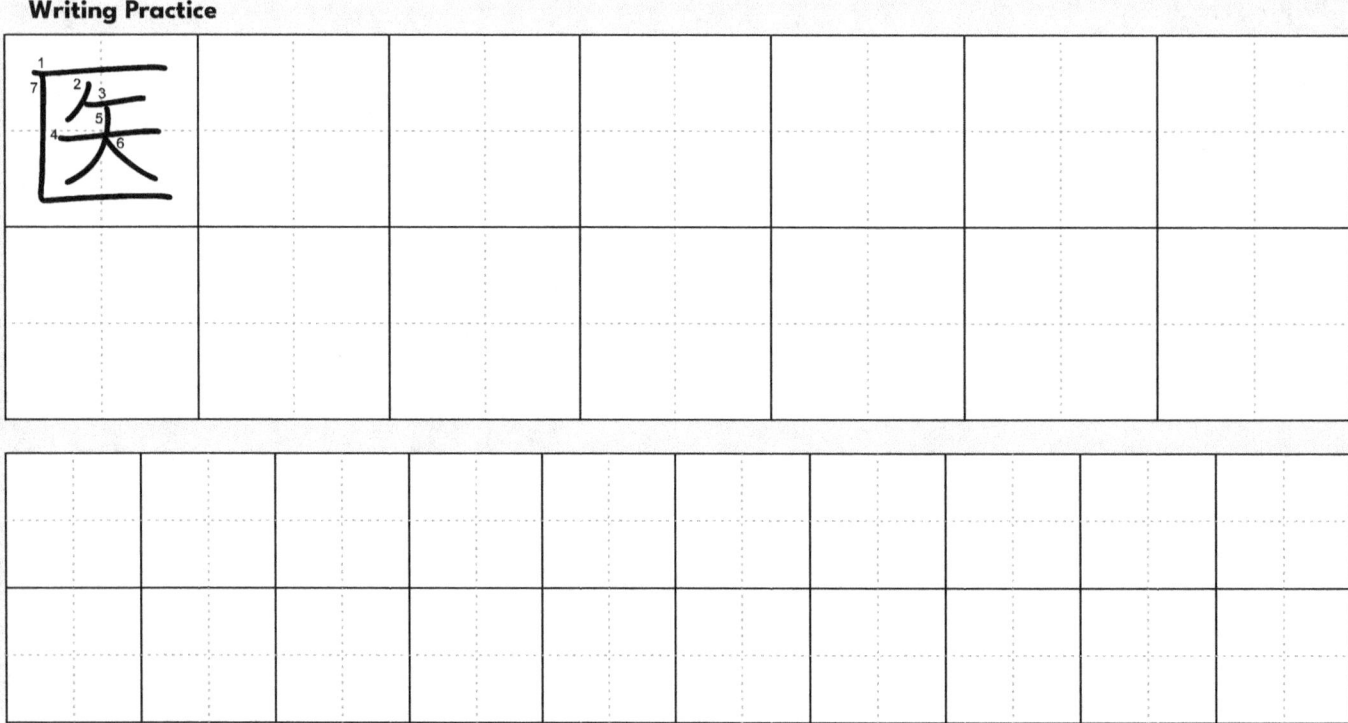

Writing Practice

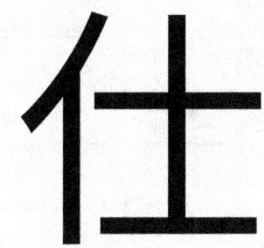

Meaning(s)	attend, doing, official	Components	化士
Radical	人 (亻) (human)	Kun'yomi	
Strokes	5	On'yomi	シ

Vocabulary	Meaning		Pronunciation
仕	official, civil service		シ
社会奉仕	voluntary social service		シャカイホウシ
致仕	resignation, seventy years of age		チシ
仕込み	learned at ..., acquired at ...		ジコミ

Stroke Order

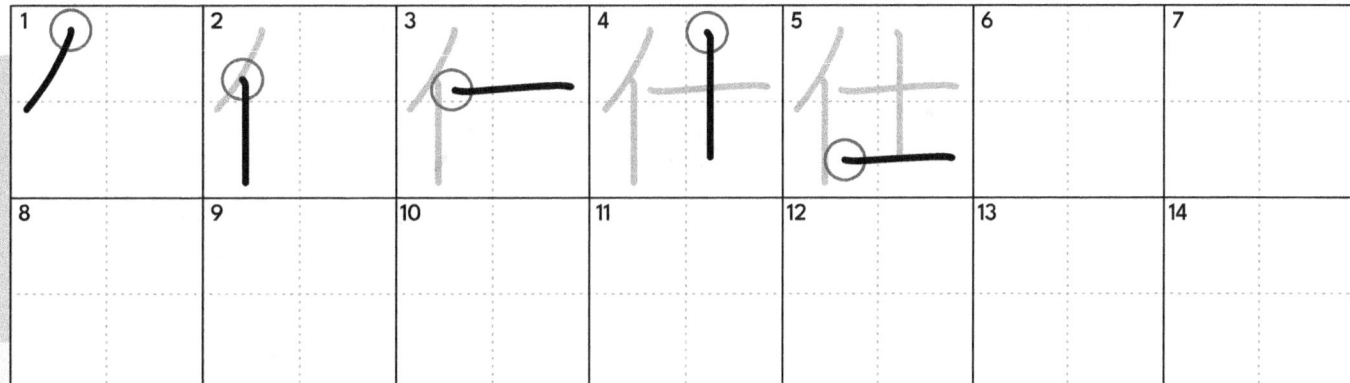

Writing Practice

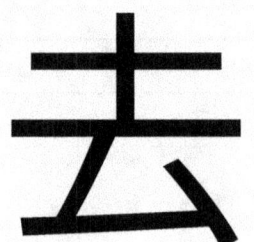

Meaning(s)	gone, past, quit, leave	Components	ム 土
Radical	ム (private)	Kun'yomi	さ(る)
Strokes	5	On'yomi	キョ、コ

Vocabulary	Meaning	Pronunciation
去る	to leave, to go away, to pass, to elapse	ぎんこう
去年	last year	キョネン
大過去	past perfect tense, pluperfect	ダイカコ
去就	leaving or staying, (one's) course of action	キョシュウ

Stroke Order

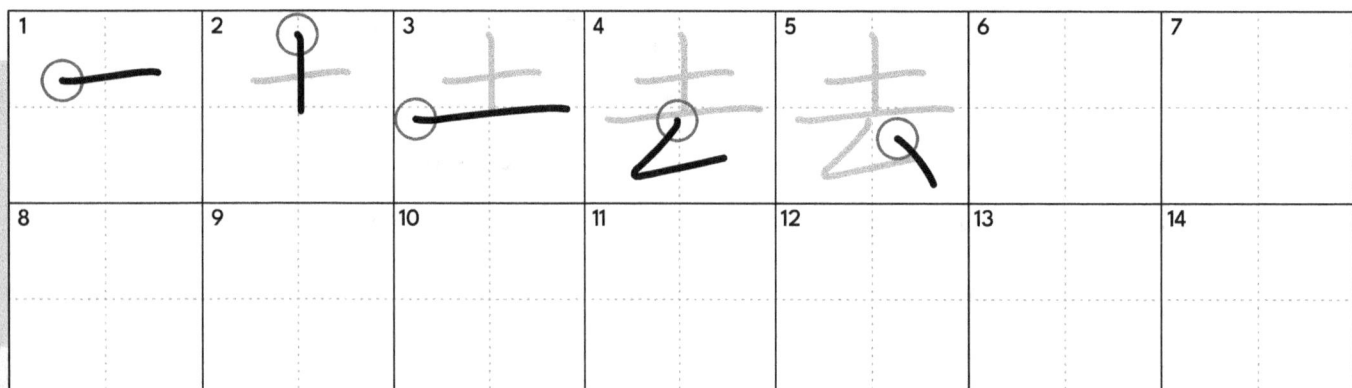

Writing Practice

味

Meaning(s)	flavor, taste	Components	丨 二 ㄍ ハ 口 木
Radical	口 (mouth)	Kun'yomi	あじ
Strokes	8	On'yomi	ミ

Vocabulary	Meaning	Pronunciation
味	flavor, flavour, taste, charm, appeal	あじ
味	(sense of) taste, counter for food and drink	ミ
味覚	taste, palate, sense of taste	ミカク
味付け	seasoning, flavour, flavor	あじつけ

Stroke Order

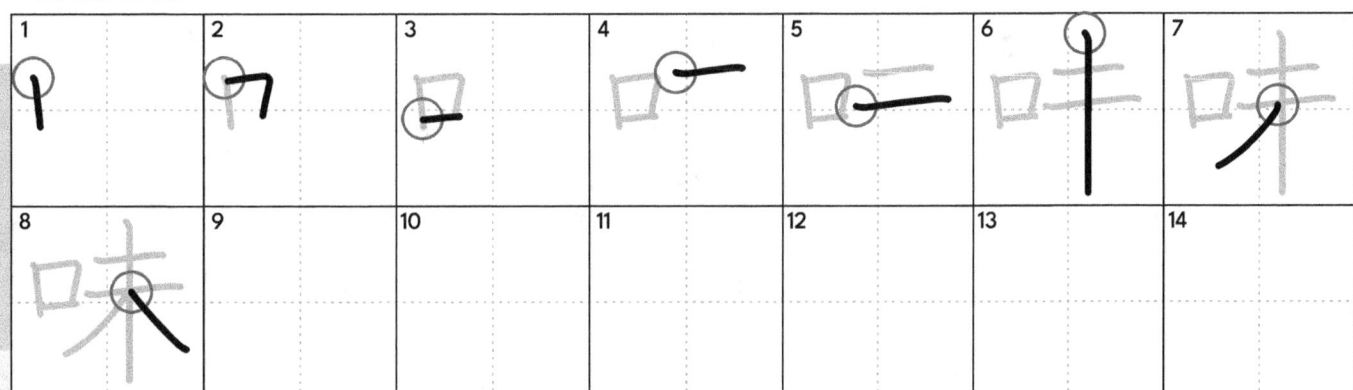

Writing Practice

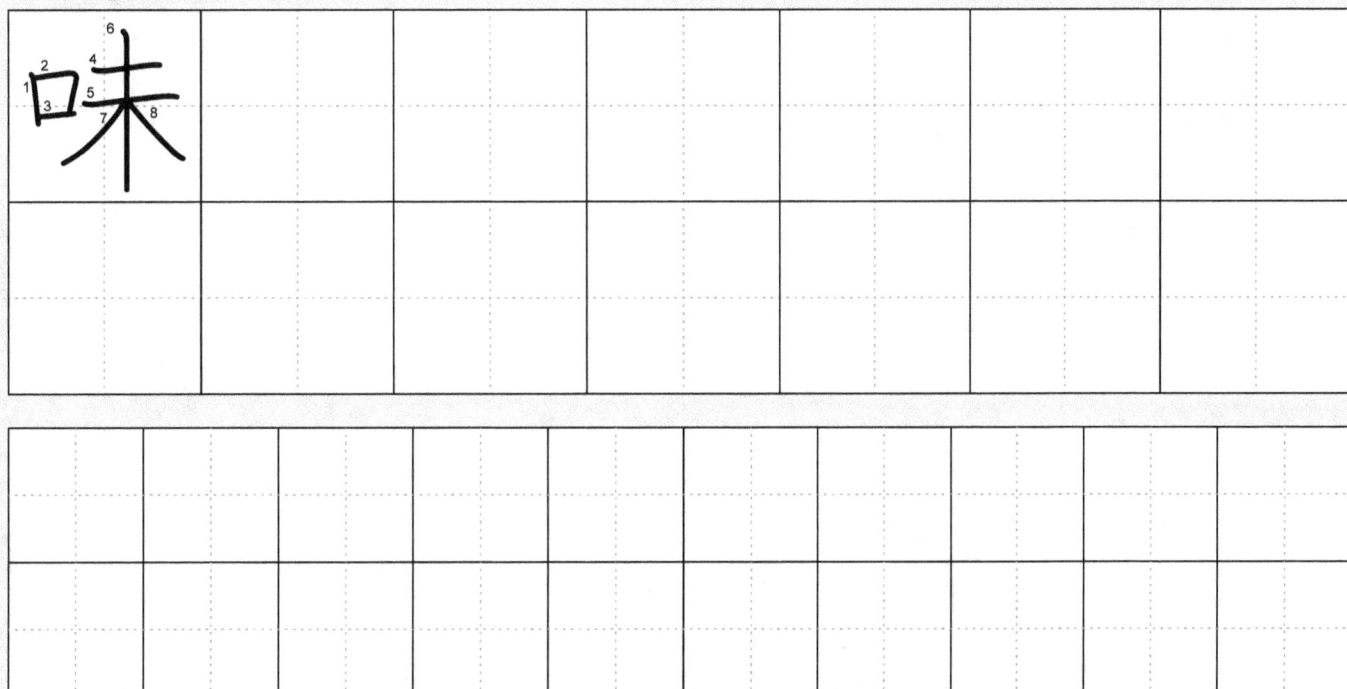

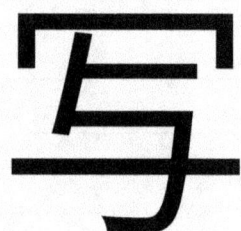

写写

Meaning(s)	copy, describe, be photographed	Components	一冖ク
Radical	冖 (cover)	Kun'yomi	うつ(る)
Strokes	5	On'yomi	シャ

Vocabulary	Meaning	Pronunciation
写す	to transcribe, to duplicate, to reproduce	うつす
写る	to be photographed, to be projected	うつる
写真	photograph, photo, picture, snapshot	シャシン
活写	vivid description, painting a lively picture (of)	カッシャ

Stroke Order

Writing Practice

Meaning(s)	character, letter, word	**Components**	子 宀	
Radical	子 (child, seed)	**Kun'yomi**		
Strokes	6	**On'yomi**	ジ	

Vocabulary	Meaning	Pronunciation
字	character (esp. kanji), letter, written text, handwriting, penmanship	ジ
字形	character style, character form	ジケイ
英字	English letter, alphabetic character	エイジ

Stroke Order

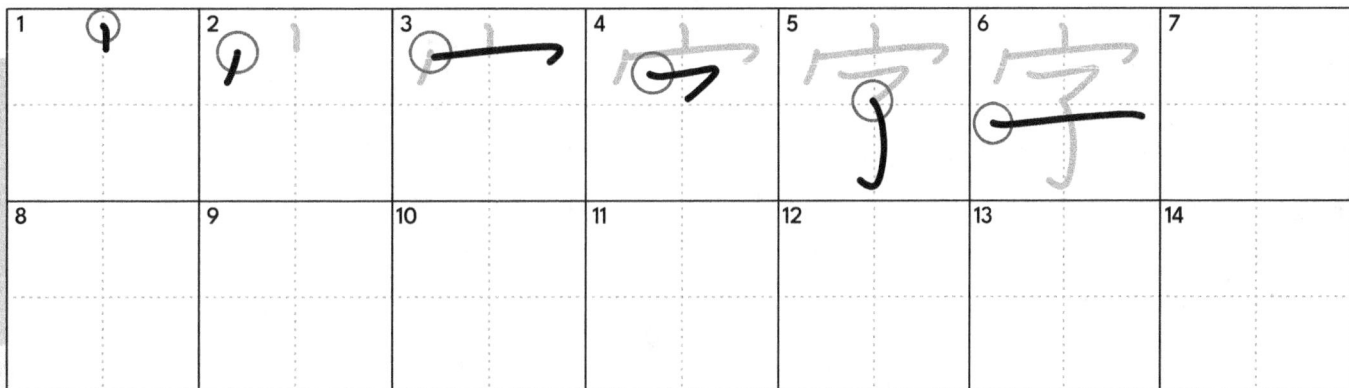

Writing Practice

Meaning(s)	solution, answer	Components	一个口竹乞
Radical	竹 (⺮) (bamboo)	Kun'yomi	こた(える)
Strokes	12	On'yomi	トウ

Vocabulary	Meaning		Pronunciation
答える	to answer, to reply		こたえる
答申	report, reply, findings		トウシン
答え	answer, reply, response, answer, solution		こたえ
正答	correct answer		セイトウ

Stroke Order

Writing Practice

Meaning(s)	night, evening	Components	亠化夕
Radical	夕 (evening, sunset)	Kun'yomi	よ、よる
Strokes	8	On'yomi	ヤ

Vocabulary	Meaning	Pronunciation
夜	evening, night, dinner	よる
夜明け	dawn, daybreak	よあけ
夜	counter for nights	ヤ
同夜	the same night, that night	ドウヤ

Stroke Order

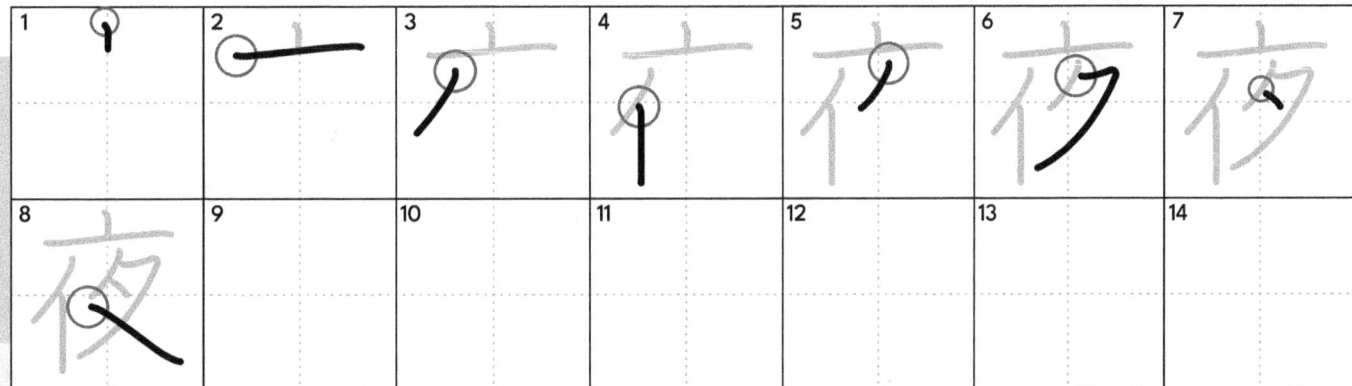

Writing Practice

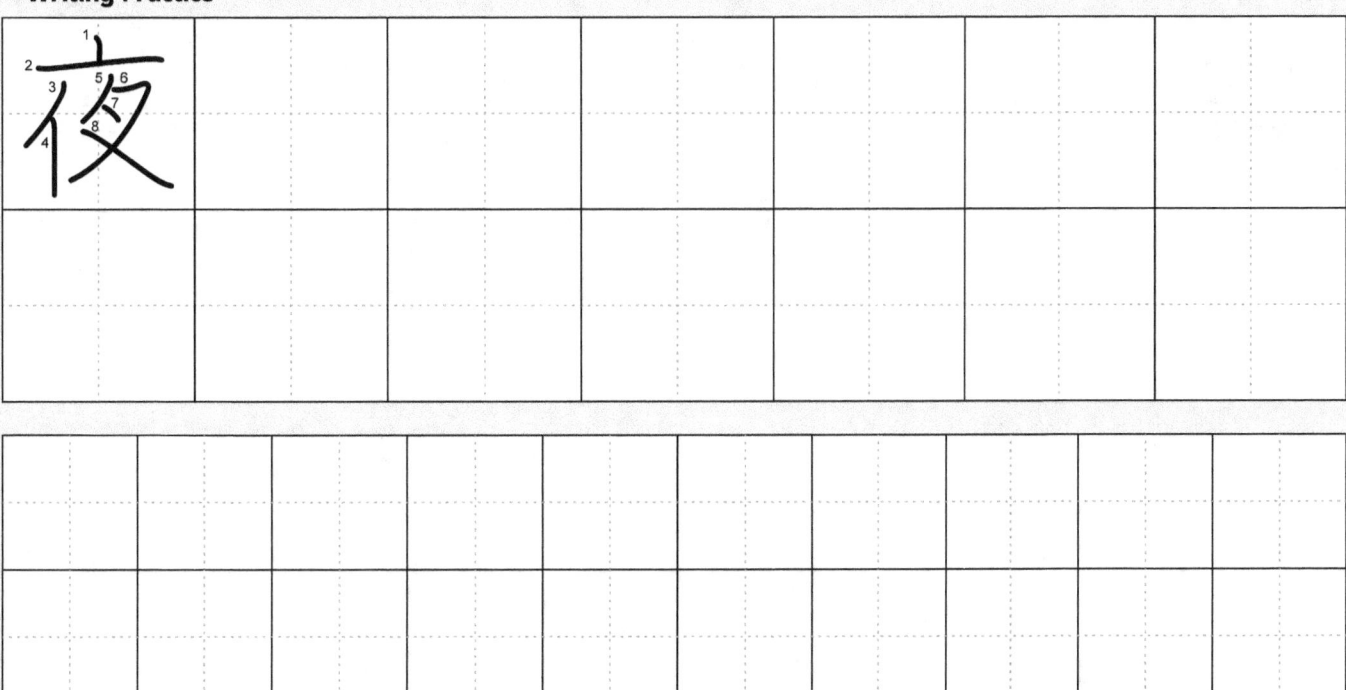

音

Meaning(s)	sound, noise
Radical	音 (sound)
Strokes	9
Components	日 立 音
Kun'yomi	おと、ね
On'yomi	オン

Vocabulary	Meaning	Pronunciation
音	sound, noise, report, note, fame	おと/オト
弱音	feeble complaint, whine	よわね
音楽	music	オンガク
音信	correspondence, news, letter, tidings	オンシン

Stroke Order

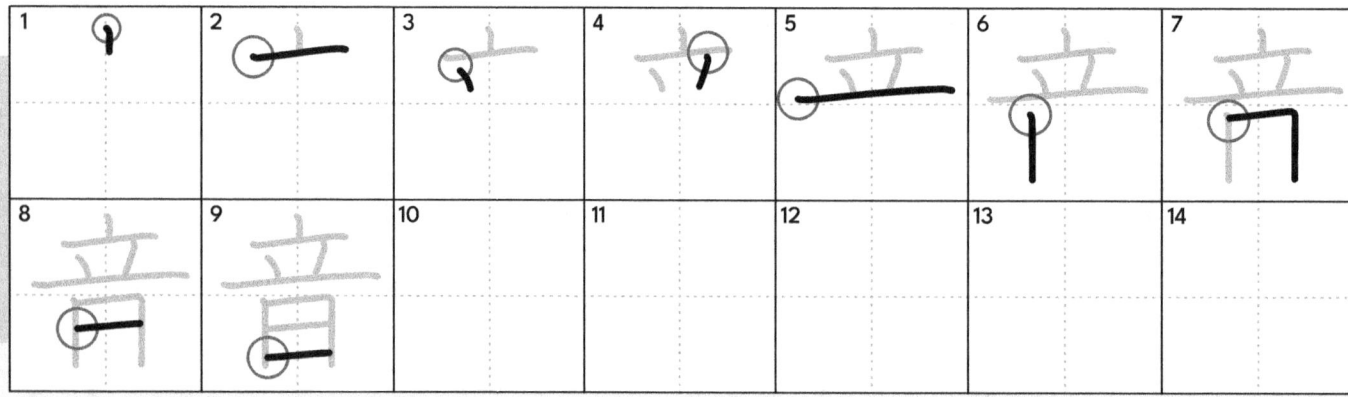

Writing Practice

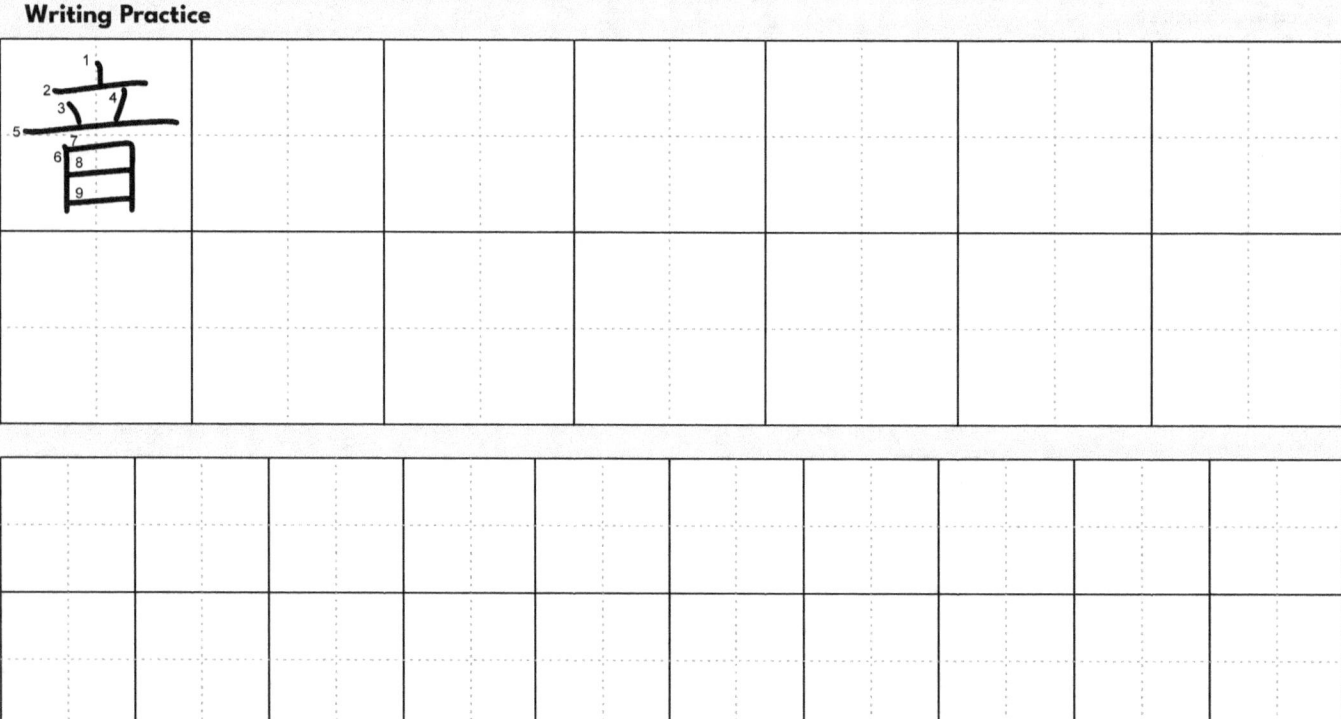

Meaning(s)	pour, irrigate	Components	丶 汁 王
Radical	水 (氵, 氺) (water)	Kun'yomi	そそ(ぐ)、さ(す)、つ(ぐ)
Strokes	8	On'yomi	チュウ

Vocabulary	Meaning	Pronunciation
注ぐ	to pour (into), to sprinkle on (from above)	そそぐ
注す	to pour, to add (liquid), to serve (drinks)	さす
注	annotation, explanatory note, comment	チュウ
注意	attention, notice, heed, care, caution	チュウイ

Stroke Order

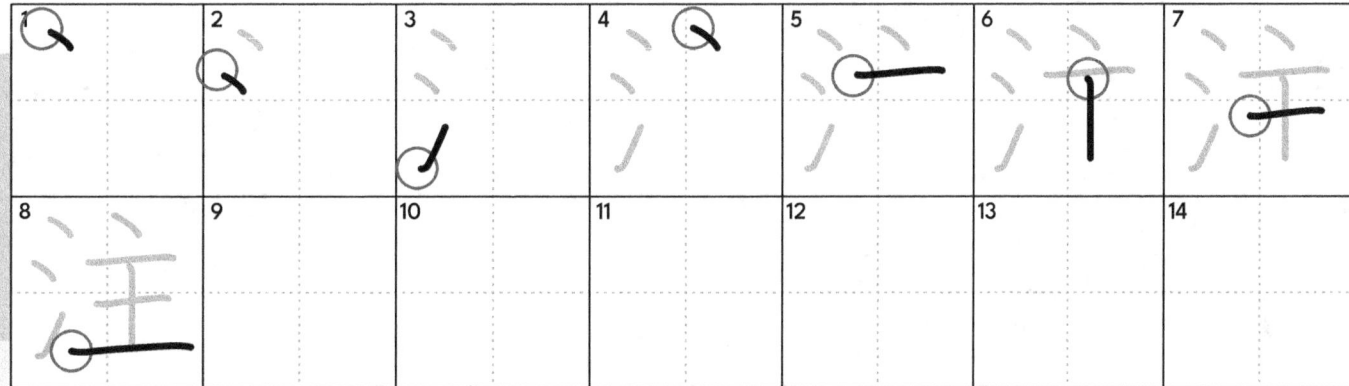

Writing Practice

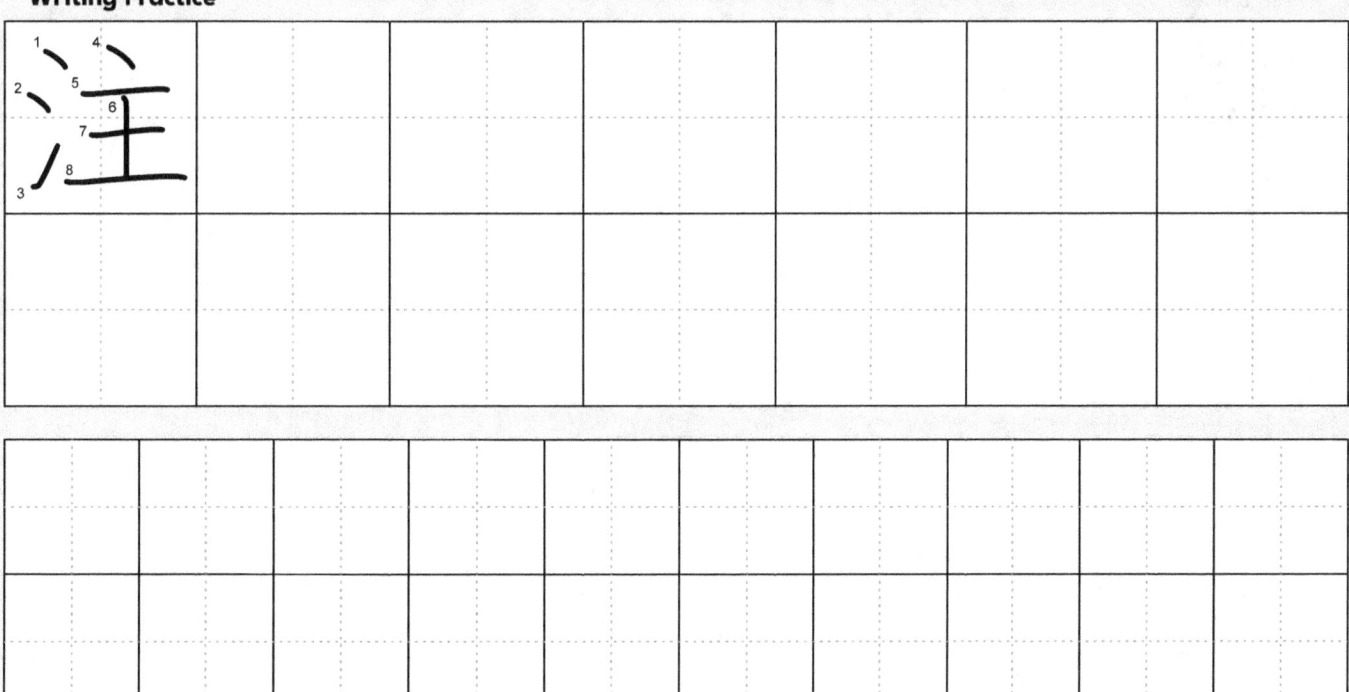

Meaning(s)	lead to, result in	Components	冖 刈 巾 ヨ	
Radical	巾 (scarf, turban)	Kun'yomi	かえ(る)、かえ(す)	
Strokes	10	On'yomi	キ	

Vocabulary	Meaning	Pronunciation
帰る	to return, to come home, to go home	かえる
帰還	return (home), repatriation	キカン
帰す	to send (someone) back / home	かえす
回帰	return (to), revolution, recurrence	カイキ

Stroke Order

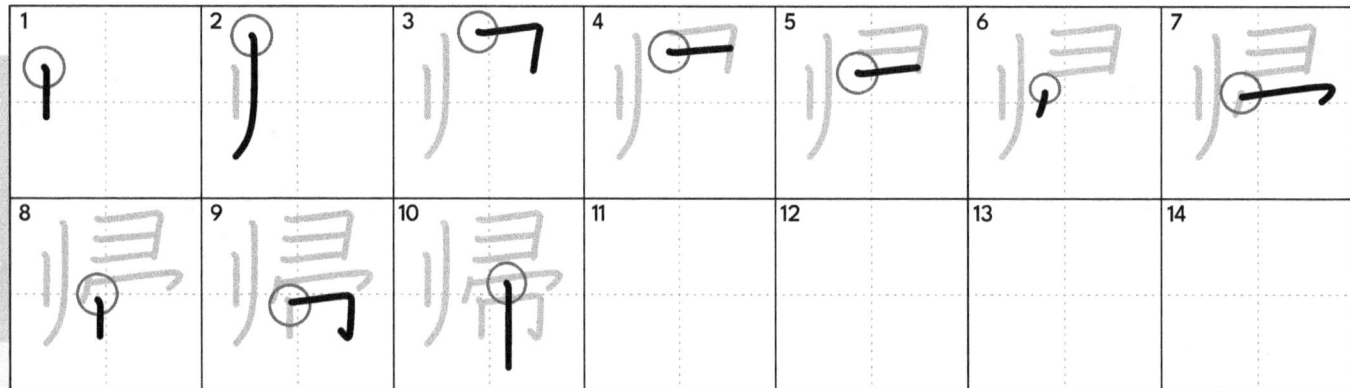

Writing Practice

Meaning(s)	song, sing	Components	一 亅 口 欠
Radical	欠 (lack, yawn)	Kun'yomi	うた、うた(う)
Strokes	14	On'yomi	カ

Vocabulary	Meaning	Pronunciation
歌	song, singing, classical Japanese poem	うた
歌劇	opera	カゲキ
歌曲	melody, tune, song	カキョク
歌う	to sing, to sing of (love, etc.) in a poem	うたう

Stroke Order

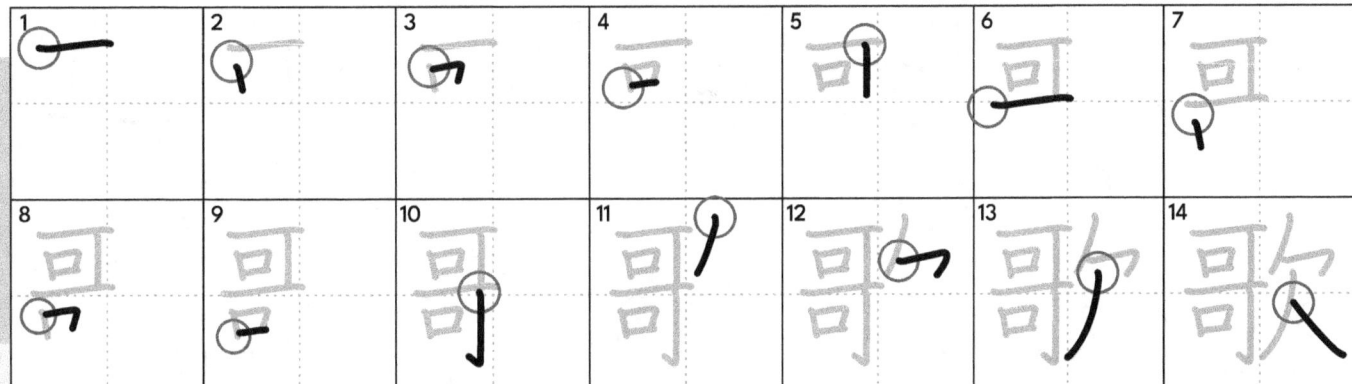

Writing Practice

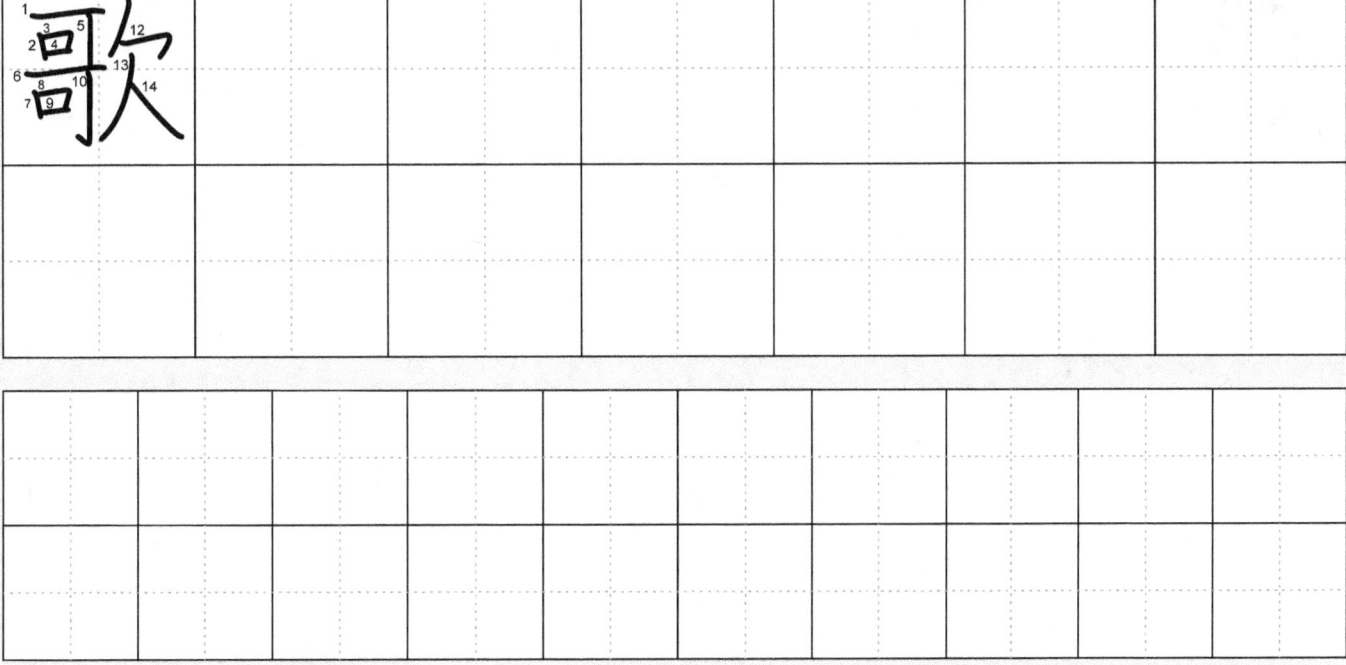

Meaning(s)	bad, evil, wrong	Components	一 丨 口 心
Radical	心 (忄, 小) (heart)	Kun'yomi	わる(い)
Strokes	11	On'yomi	アク

Vocabulary	Meaning	Pronunciation
悪い	bad, poor, undesirable, poor (quality), inferior	わるい
悪	evil, wickedness	アク
好悪	likes and dislikes	コウオ
悪し	bad, evil	あし

Stroke Order

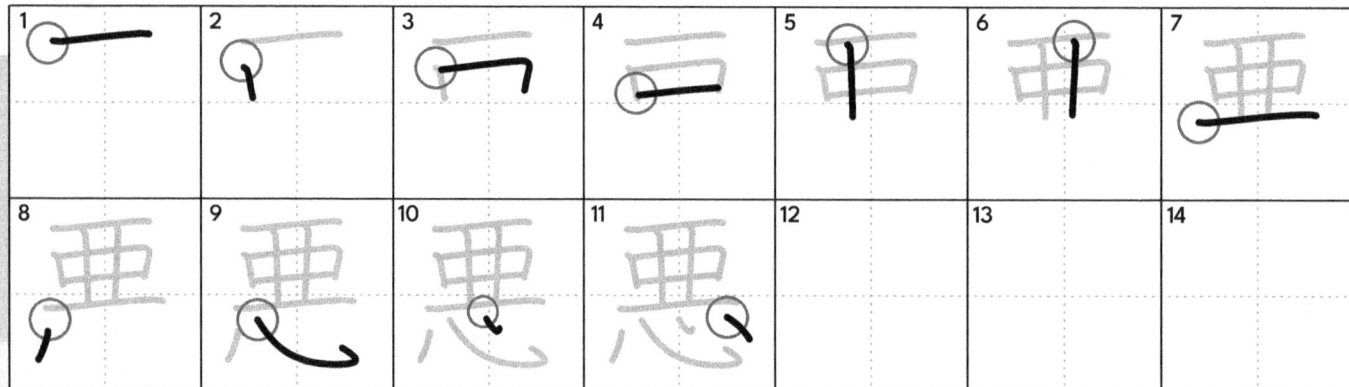

Writing Practice

Meaning(s)	map, drawing, plan	Components	口 斗
Radical	囗 (enclosure)	Kun'yomi	はか(る)
Strokes	7	On'yomi	ズ、ト

Vocabulary	Meaning	Pronunciation
図る	to plan, to attempt, to devise, to plot, to conspire, to scheme, to aim for, to strive for	はかる
図	drawing, picture, diagram, figure, illustration	ズ
図書	books	トショ

Stroke Order

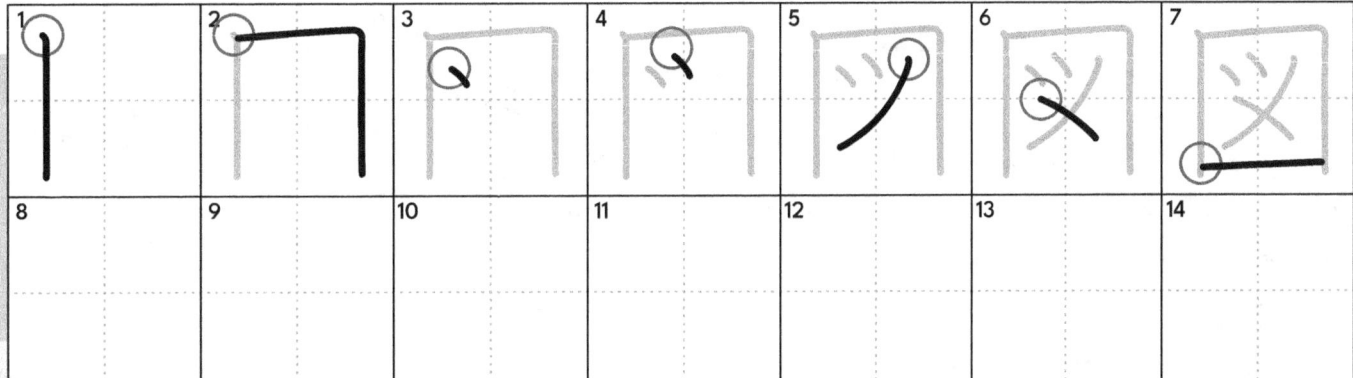

Writing Practice

Meaning(s)	room, apartment		Components	ム 土 宀 至
Radical	宀 (roof)		Kun'yomi	むろ
Strokes	9		On'yomi	シツ

Vocabulary	Meaning	Pronunciation
室	greenhouse, icehouse, cellar	むろ
室	room, wife (of someone of high rank)	シツ
同室	same room, sharing a room	ドウシツ

Stroke Order

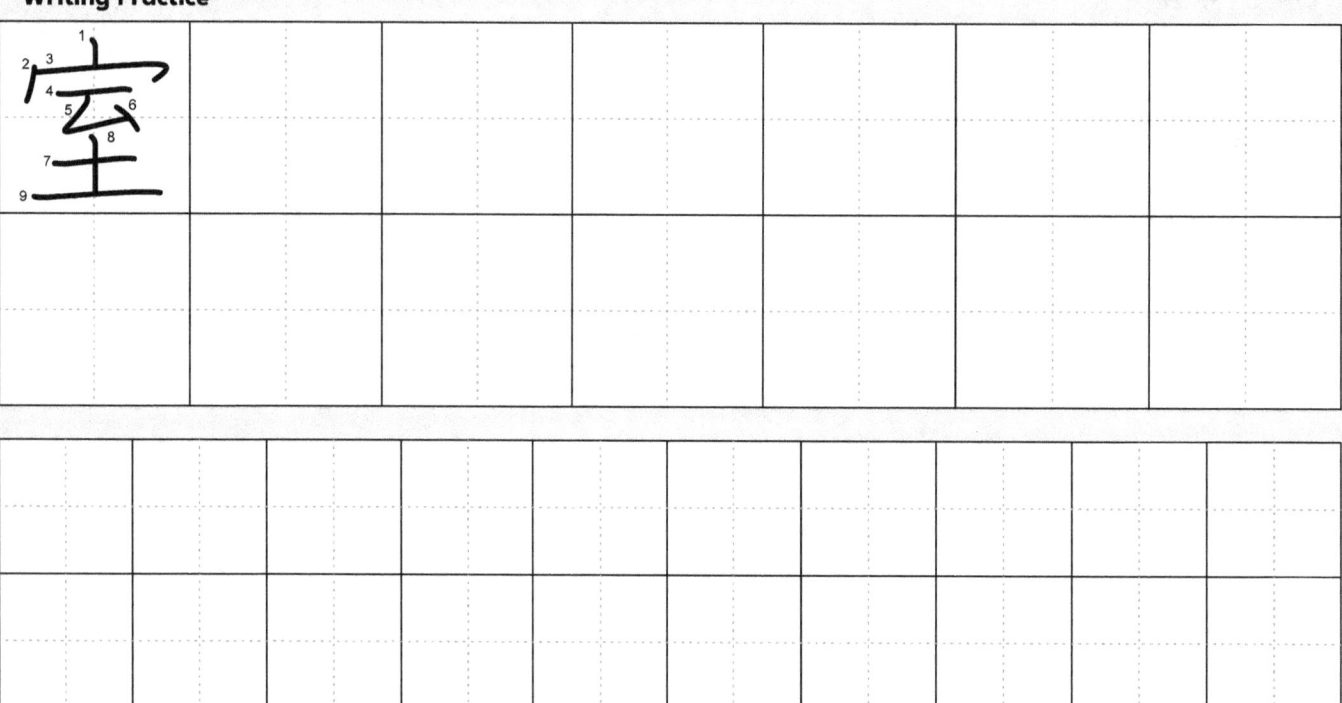

Writing Practice

Meaning(s)	walk, counter for steps	Components	ノ 小 止
Radical	止 (stop)	Kun'yomi	ある(く)、あゆ(む)
Strokes	8	On'yomi	ホ、ブ

Vocabulary	Meaning	Pronunciation
歩く	to walk	あるく
歩む	to walk, to go on foot, to follow	あゆむ
歩	step, stride, counter for steps	ホ
歩合	rate, ratio, percentage, commission	ブアイ

Stroke Order

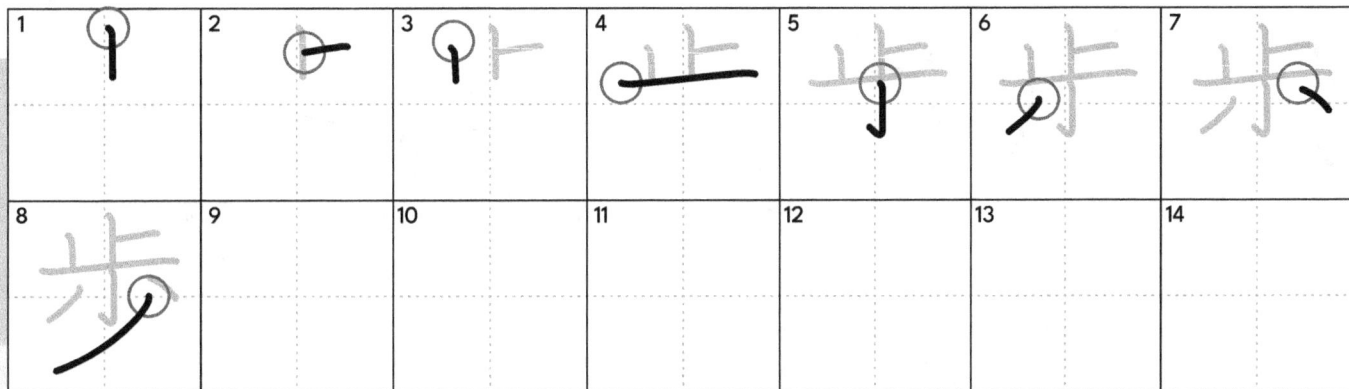

Writing Practice

Meaning(s)	wind, air, style		Components	ノ 几 虫 風
Radical	風 (wind)		Kun'yomi	かぜ、かざ-
Strokes	9		On'yomi	フウ、フ

Vocabulary	Meaning	Pronunciation
風	wind, breeze, draught, manner, behaviour	かぜ
風	method, manner, way, style, appearance	フウ
風格	personality, style, appearance	フウカク
涼風	cool breeze, refreshing breeze	りょうふう

Stroke Order

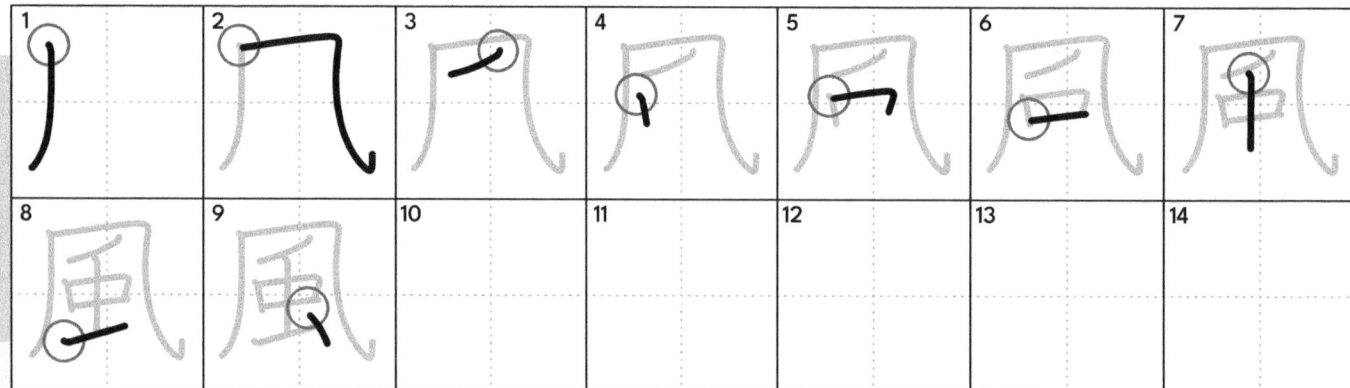

Writing Practice

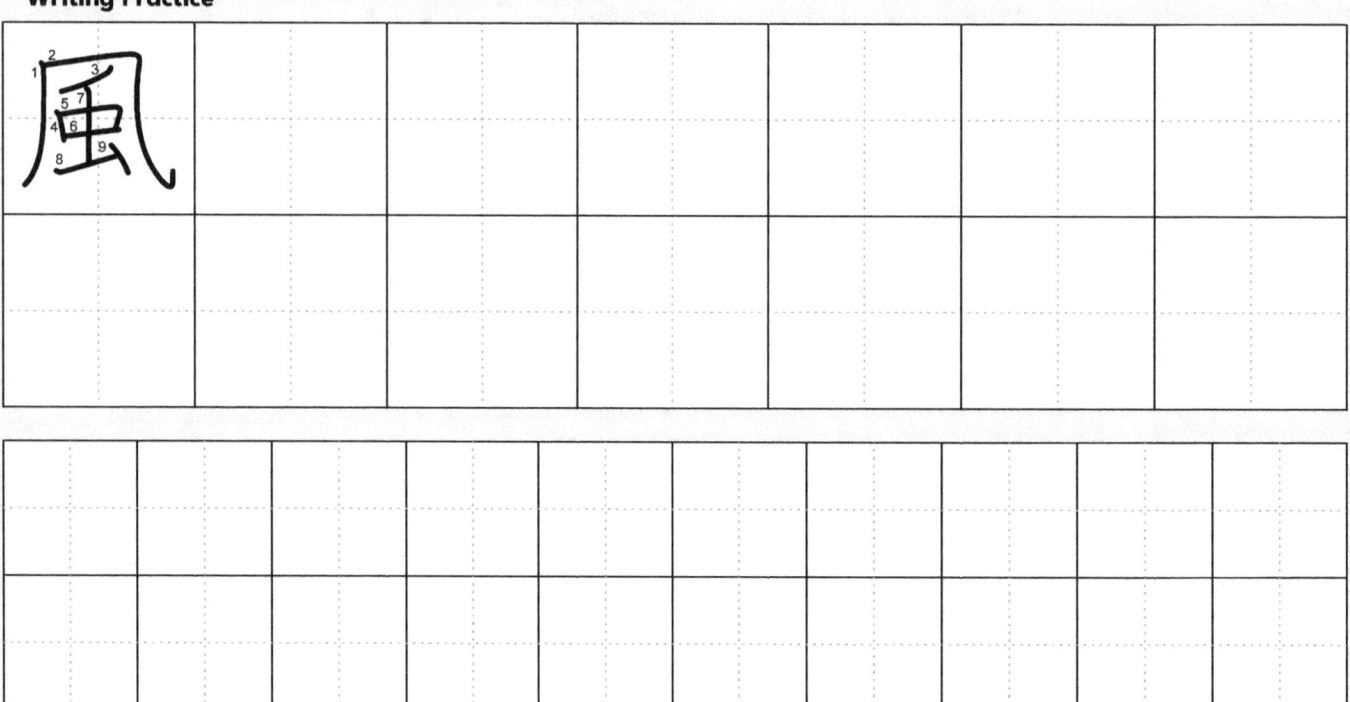

紙

Meaning(s)	paper	Components	小 幺 氏 糸
Radical	糸 (糸) (silk)	Kun'yomi	かみ
Strokes	10	On'yomi	シ

Vocabulary	Meaning	Pronunciation
紙	paper	かみ
紙	newspaper	シ
紙上	on paper, in the newspapers, in a letter	シジョウ
製紙	papermaking, paper manufacture	セイシ

Stroke Order

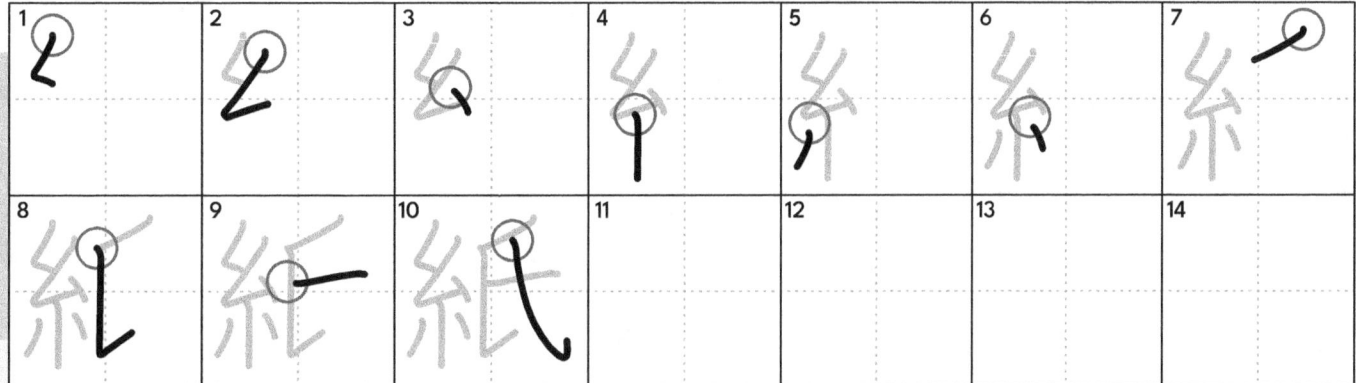

Writing Practice

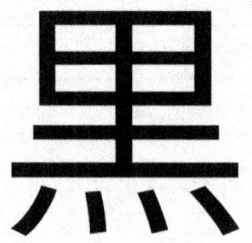

Meaning(s)	black	Components	杰 里 黒	
Radical	黒 (black)	Kun'yomi	くろ	
Strokes	11	On'yomi	コク	

Vocabulary	Meaning	Pronunciation
黒	black, black go stone, guilt	くろ
黒煙	black smoke	コクエン
黒衣	black clothes	コクイ
黒い	black, dark, blackish, sun-tanned (skin)	くろい

Stroke Order

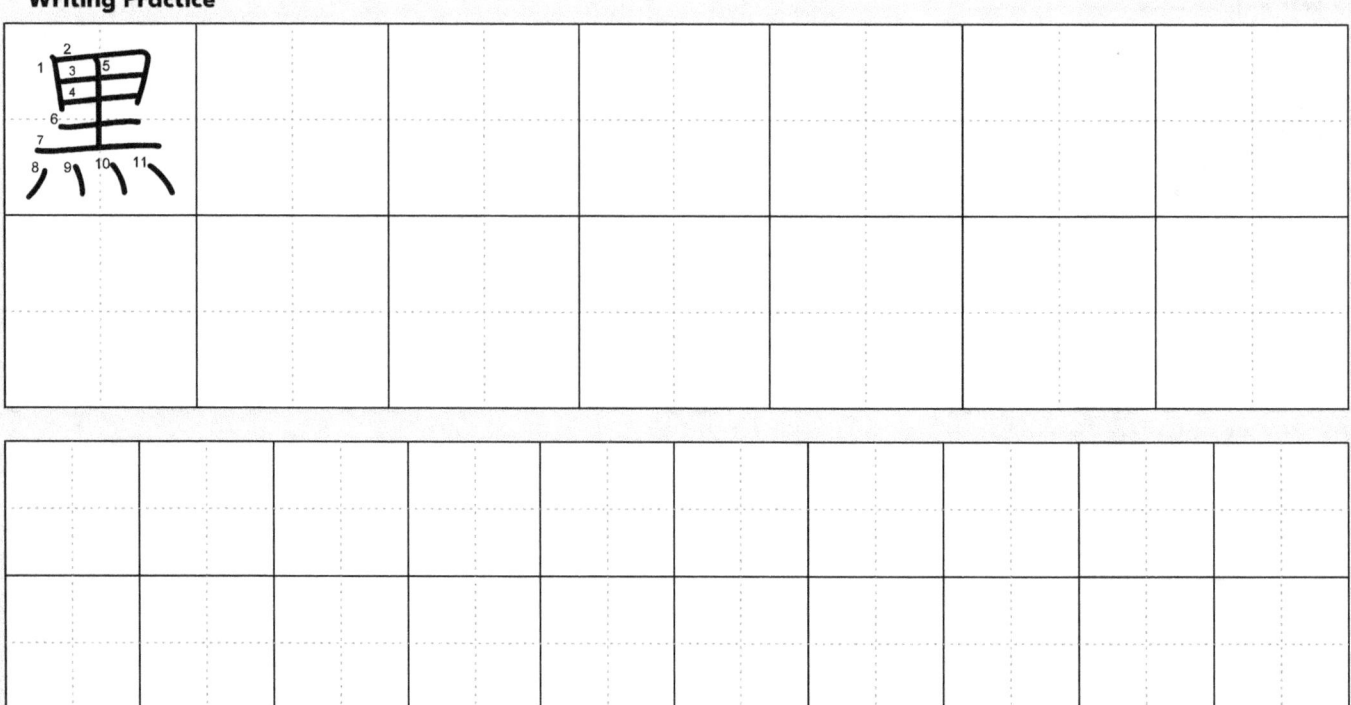

Writing Practice

Meaning(s)	spring	Components	一 二 人 大 日
Radical	日 (sun, day)	Kun'yomi	はる
Strokes	9	On'yomi	シュン

Vocabulary	Meaning	Pronunciation
春	spring, springtime, New Year, prime (of life)	はる
春秋	spring and autumn, spring and fall	シュンジュウ
春季	spring season	シュンキ
毎春	every spring	まいしゅん

Stroke Order

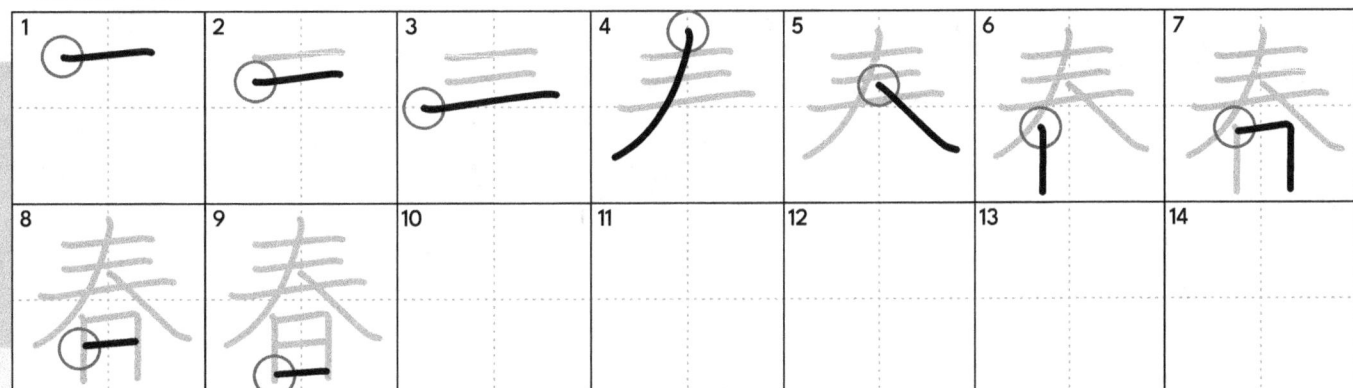

Writing Practice

Meaning(s)	red	Components	土 赤
Radical	赤 (red, naked)	Kun'yomi	あか(い)
Strokes	7	On'yomi	セキ、シャク

Vocabulary	Meaning	Pronunciation
赤	red, crimson, scarlet, copper, perfect	あか
真赤	bright red, deep red	まあか
赤らむ	to redden, to blush	あからむ
赤銅色	brown, tan	シャクドウイロ

Stroke Order

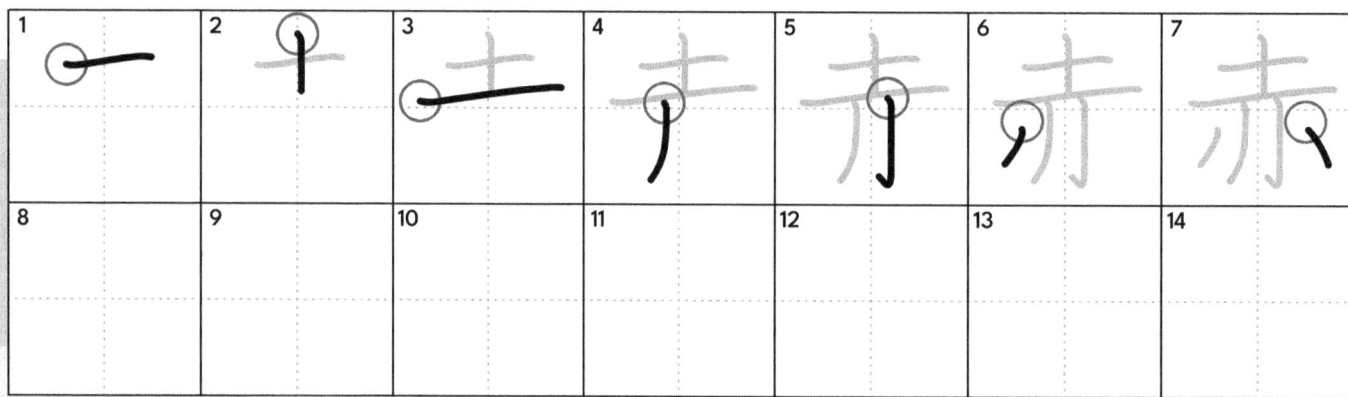

Writing Practice

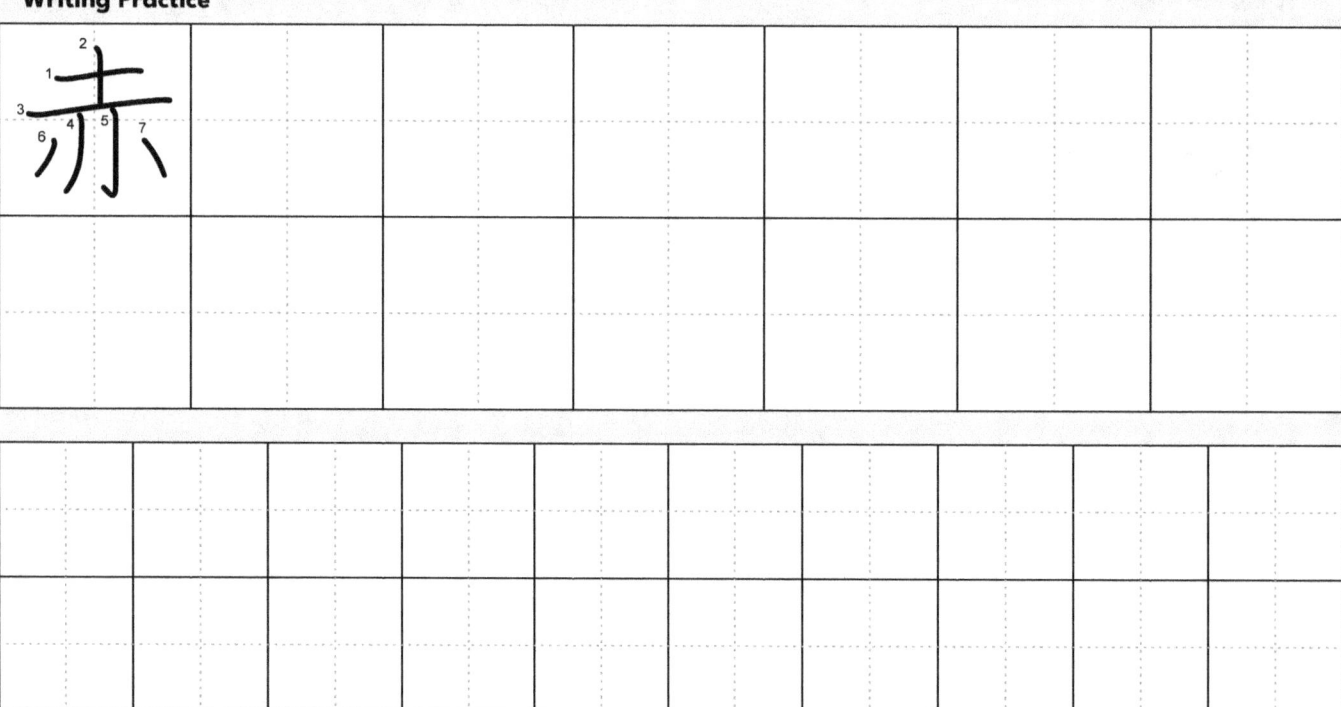

Meaning(s)	blue	Components	二 十 土 月 青
Radical	青 (青) (blue)	Kun'yomi	あお(い)
Strokes	8	On'yomi	セイ、ショウ

Vocabulary	Meaning	Pronunciation
青	blue, azure, green, green light (traffic)	あお
青い	blue, azure, green, pale, gray, grey	あおい
青果	fruit(s) and vegetables, produce	セイカ
緑青	verdigris, green rust, copper rust	ロクショウ

Stroke Order

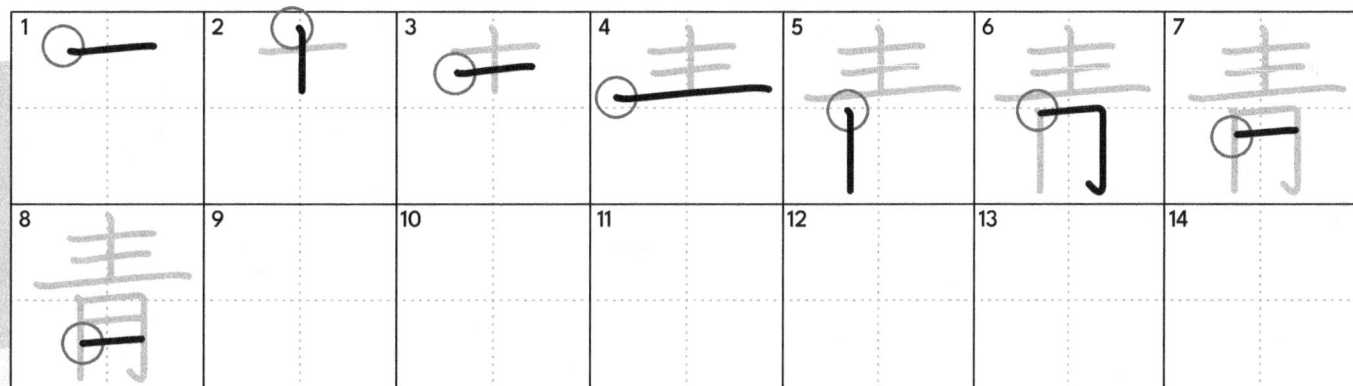

Writing Practice

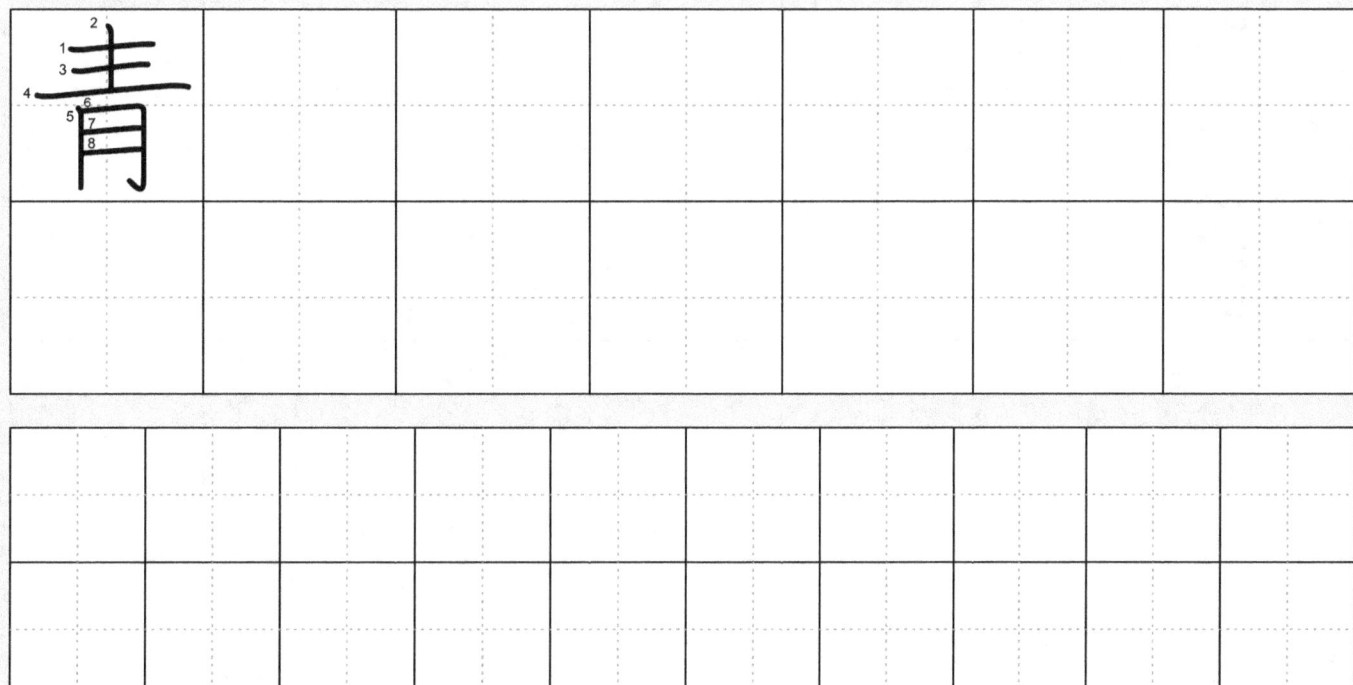

Meaning(s)	building, mansion	Components	丨 口 宀 食
Radical	食 (𩙿) (eat, food)	Kun'yomi	やかた
Strokes	16	On'yomi	カン

Vocabulary	Meaning	Pronunciation
館	mansion, palace, manor house, castle	やかた
館	(large) building, public building, hall	カン
公館	official residence	コウカン
館長	superintendent, director, curator	カンチョウ

Stroke Order

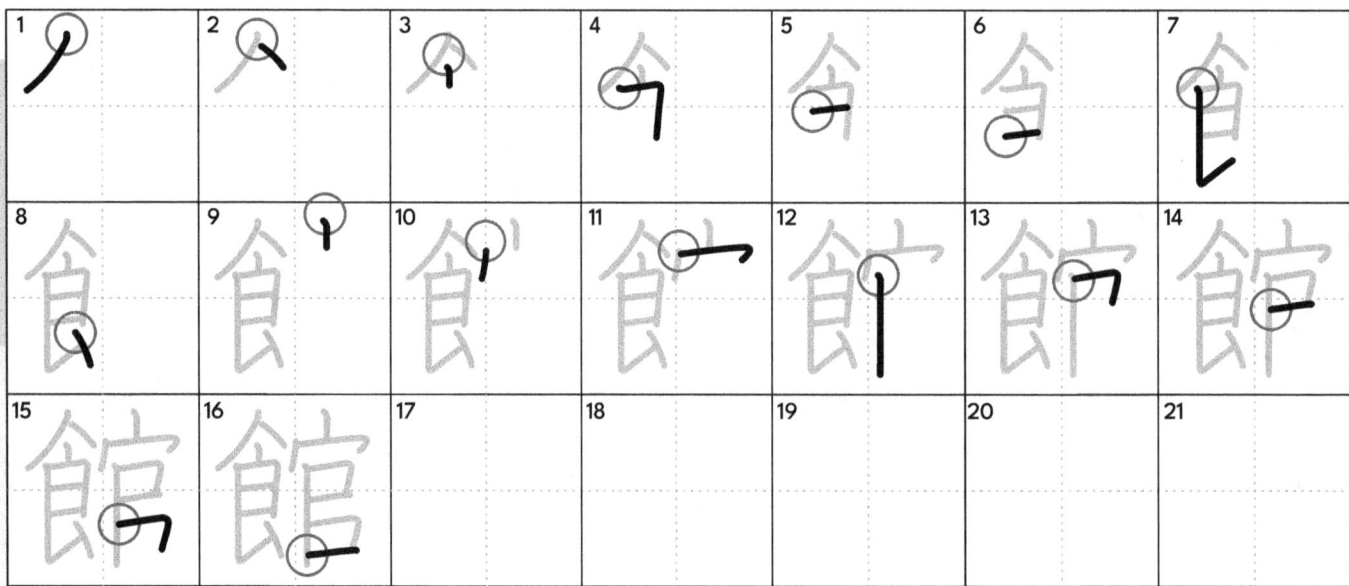

Writing Practice

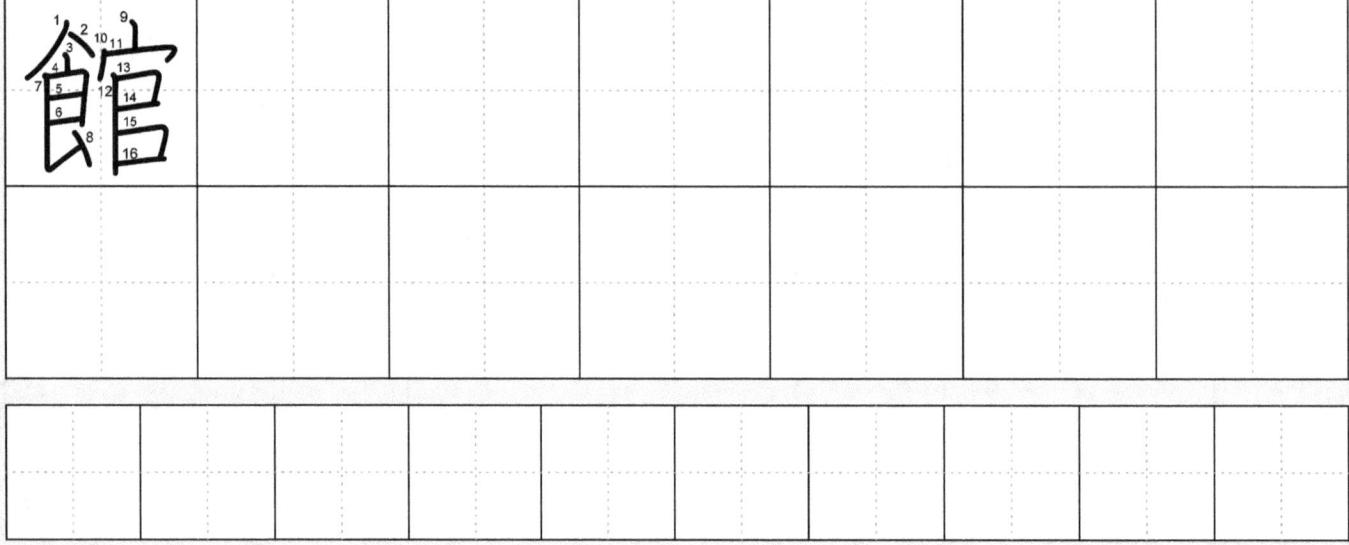

Meaning(s)	roof, house, shop	Components	ム 土 尸 至
Radical	尸 (corpse)	Kun'yomi	や
Strokes	9	On'yomi	オク

Vocabulary	Meaning	Pronunciation
屋	shop, store, restaurant, someone who sells or works as (something), roof, house	や
屋	house, building, roof	オク
屋外	outdoors, outside	オクガイ

Stroke Order

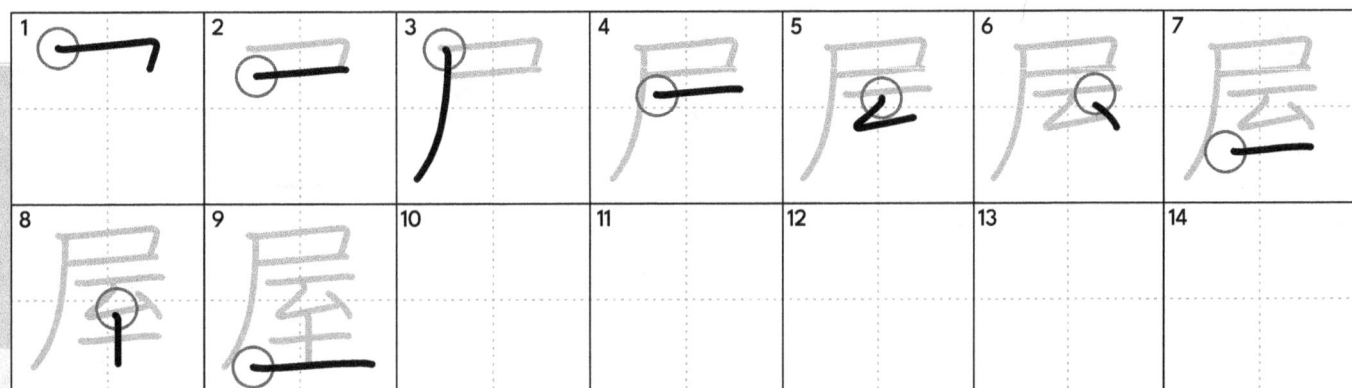

Writing Practice

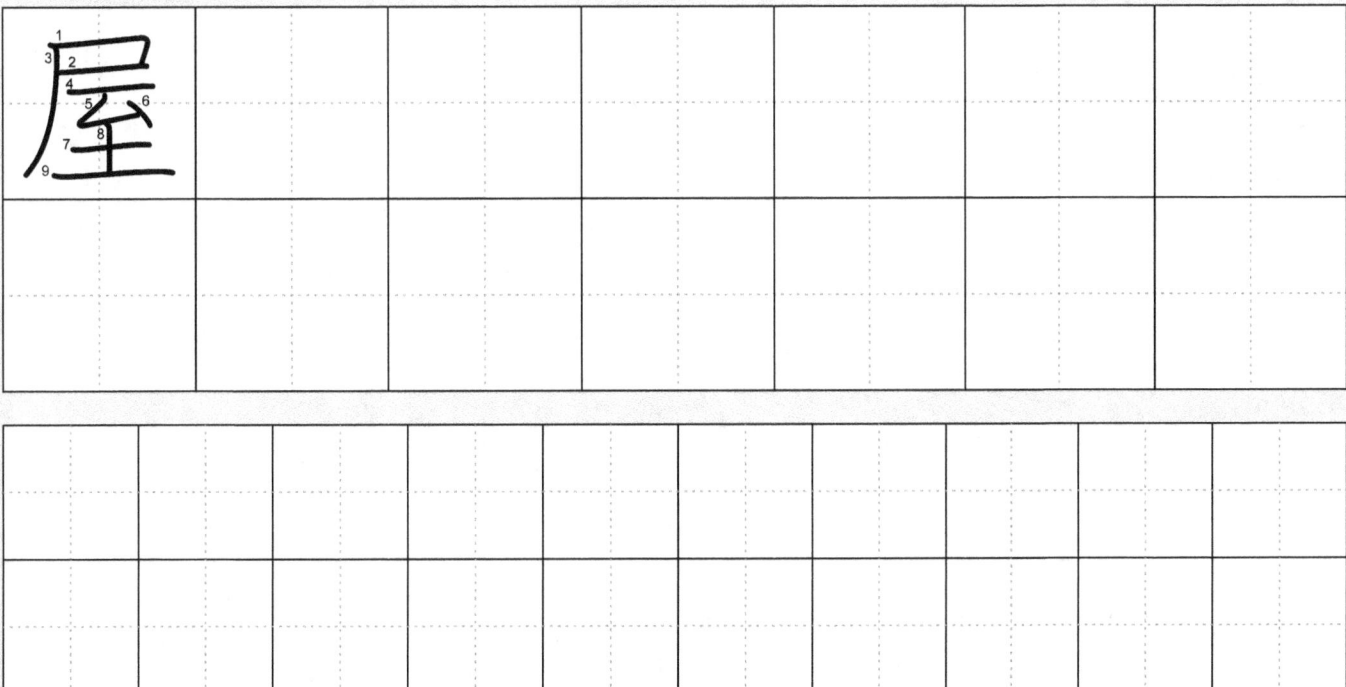

Meaning(s)	color	Components	ク巴色
Radical	色 (color)	Kun'yomi	いろ
Strokes	6	On'yomi	ショク、シキ

Vocabulary	Meaning	Pronunciation
色	colour, color, hue, tint, tinge, shade	いろ
色	counter for colours	ショク
色彩	colour, color, hue, tints	シキサイ
色合い	colouring, coloring, shade (of colour), hue	いろあい

Stroke Order

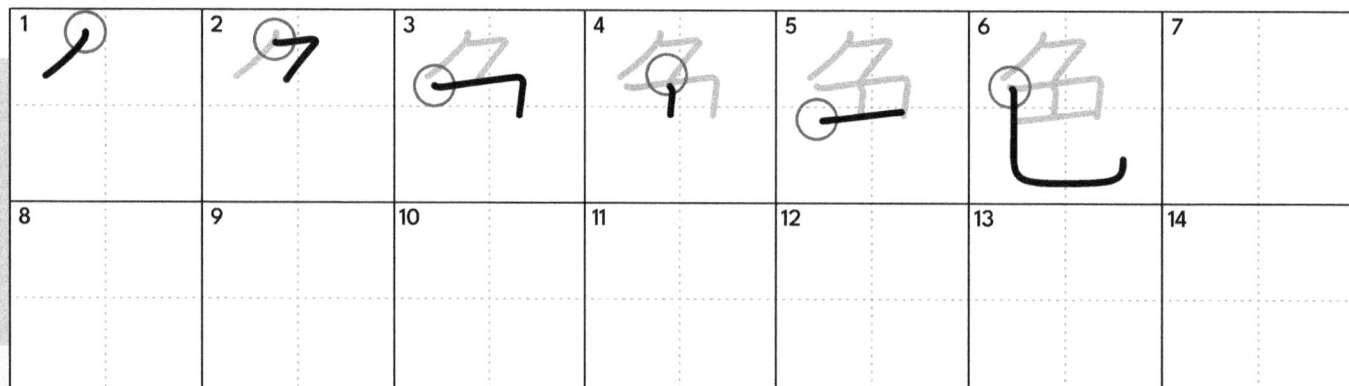

Writing Practice

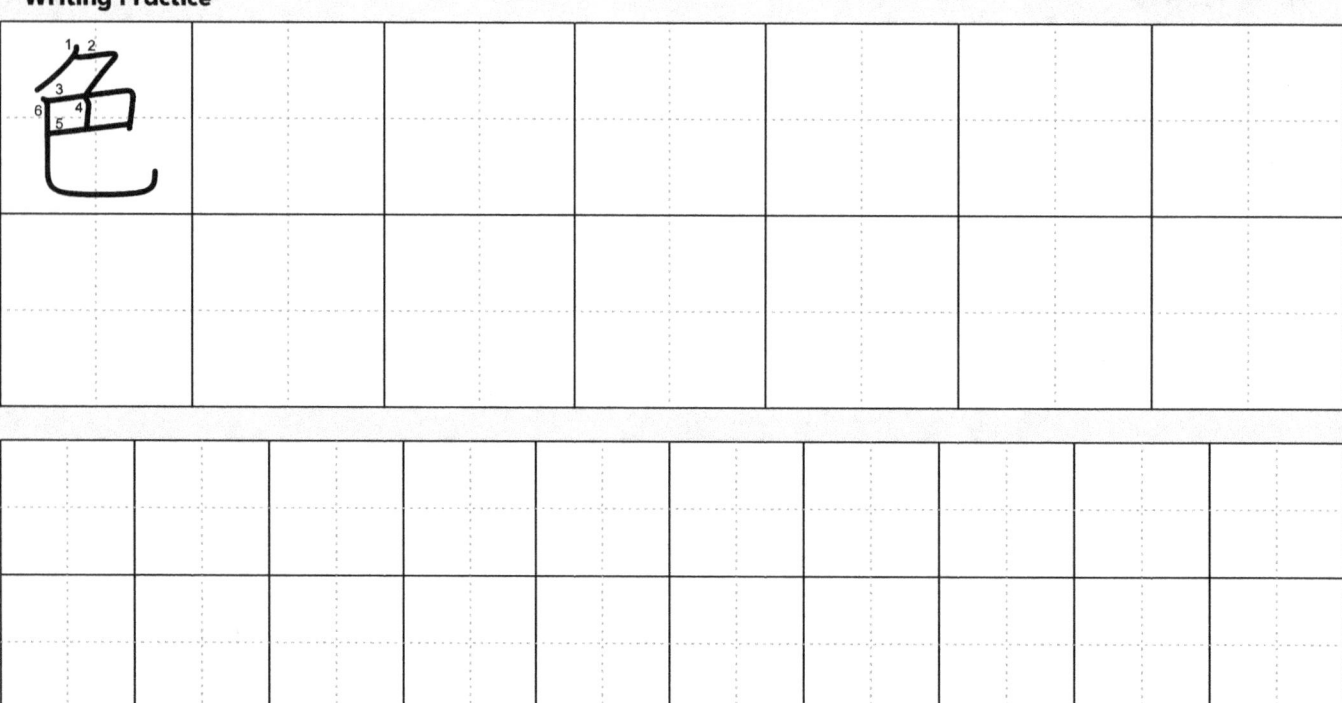

Meaning(s)	run	Components	土 走
Radical	走 (赱) (run)	Kun'yomi	はし(る)
Strokes	7	On'yomi	ソウ

Vocabulary	Meaning		Pronunciation
走	to run, to run (of a vehicle), to drive, to travel, to move, to sail, to dash/race		はしる
快走	run, race fast moving, fast running, fast sailing		ソウ カイソウ

Stroke Order

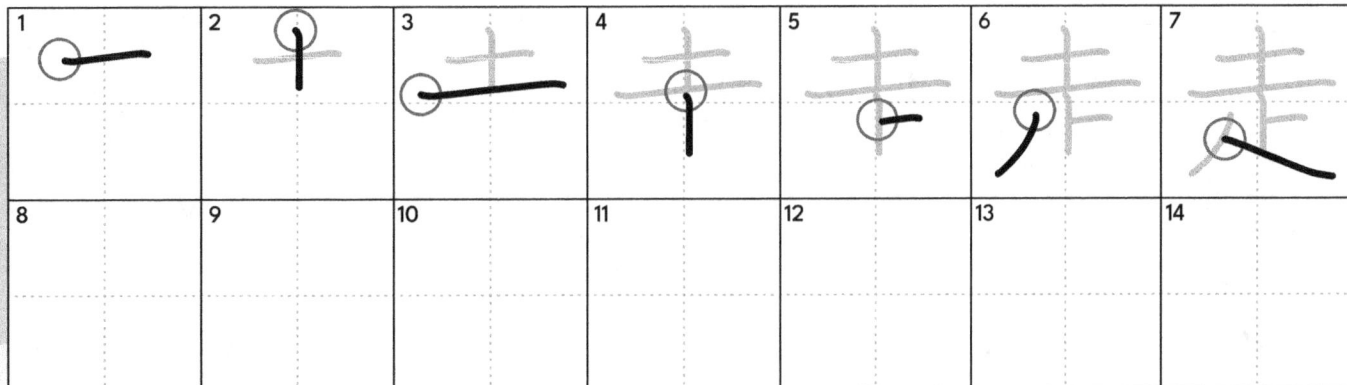

Writing Practice

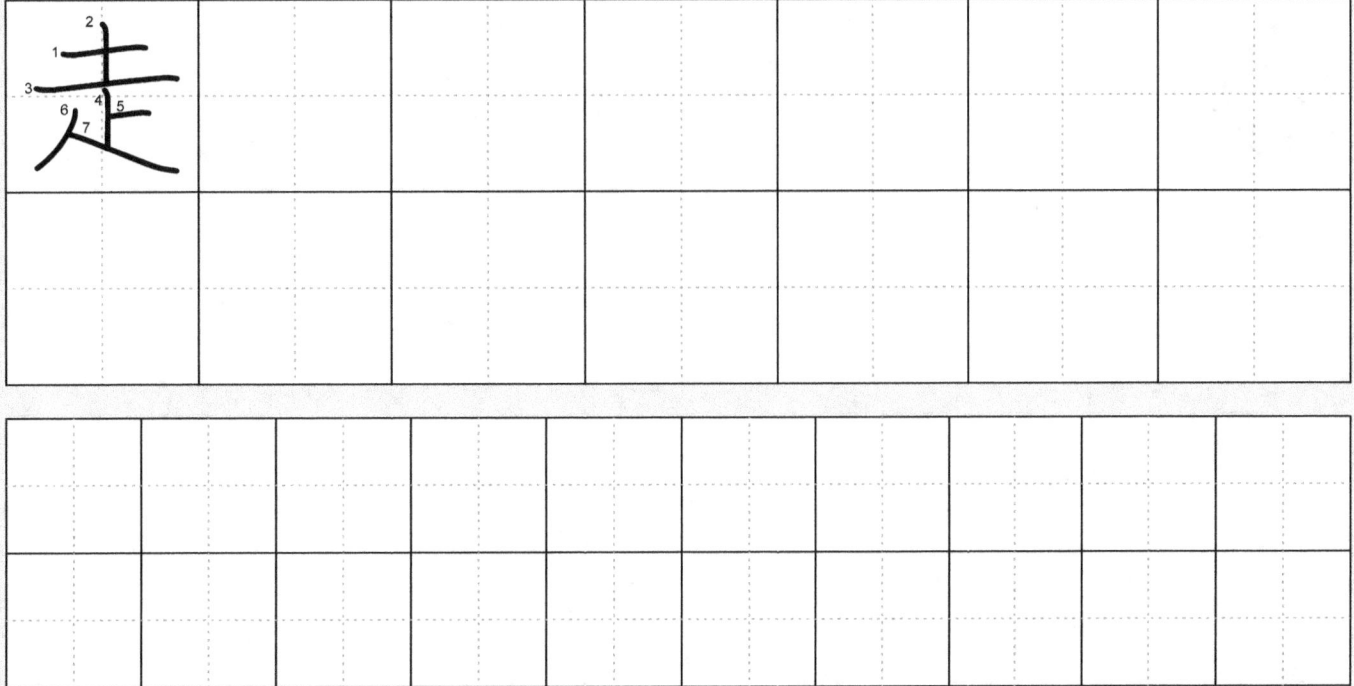

Meaning(s)	autumn, fall	Components	火 禾
Radical	禾 (grain)	Kun'yomi	あき
Strokes	9	On'yomi	シュウ

Vocabulary	Meaning	Pronunciation
秋	autumn, fall	あき
秋季	fall season, autumn season	シュウキ
秋風	autumn breeze, fall breeze	アキカゼ
秋口	beginning of autumn/fall	あきぐち

Stroke Order

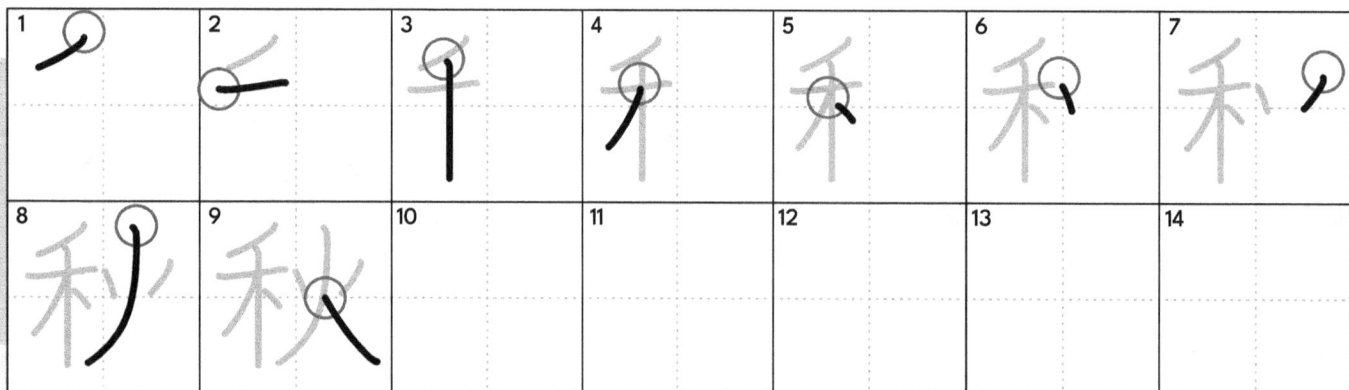

Writing Practice

Meaning(s)	summer	Components	一夂目自
Radical	夂 (go slowly)	Kun'yomi	なつ
Strokes	10	On'yomi	カ、ゲ

Vocabulary	Meaning		Pronunciation
夏	summer		なつ
夏季	summer season		カキ
夏至	summer solstice		ゲシ
初夏	early summer, fourth month (lunar calendar)		しょか

Stroke Order

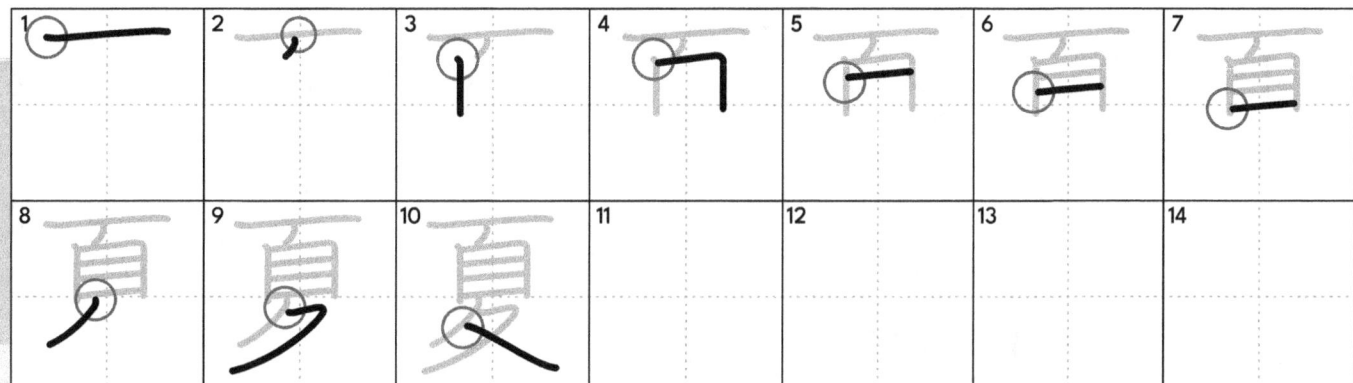

Writing Practice

Meaning(s)	learn	Components	冫 白 羽
Radical	羽 (feather)	Kun'yomi	なら(う)
Strokes	11	On'yomi	シュウ

Vocabulary	Meaning		Pronunciation
習う	to take lessons in, to be taught, to learn		ならう
習性	habit, behavior, trait, nature		シュウセイ
演習	practice, exercise, drill, military exercise		エンシュウ
見習い	apprenticeship, probation, apprentice/trainee		みならい

Stroke Order

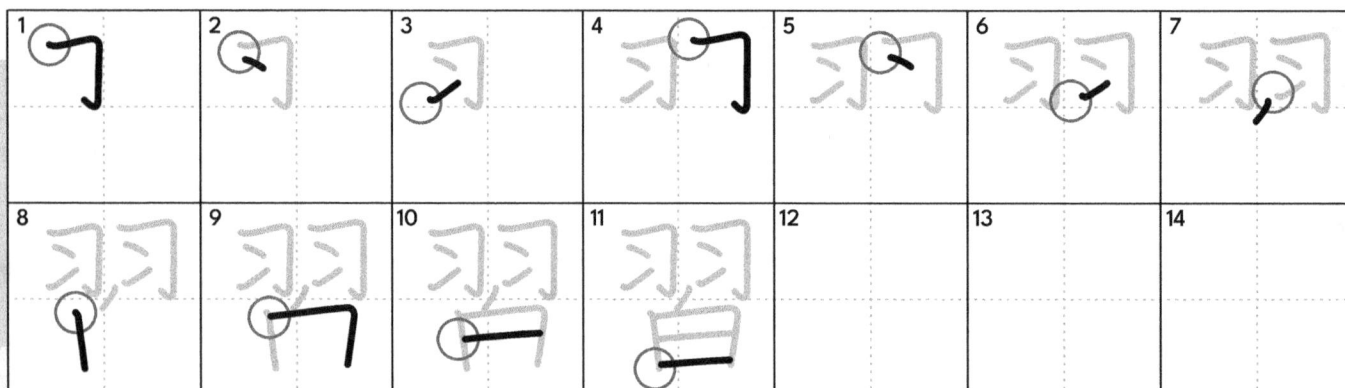

Writing Practice

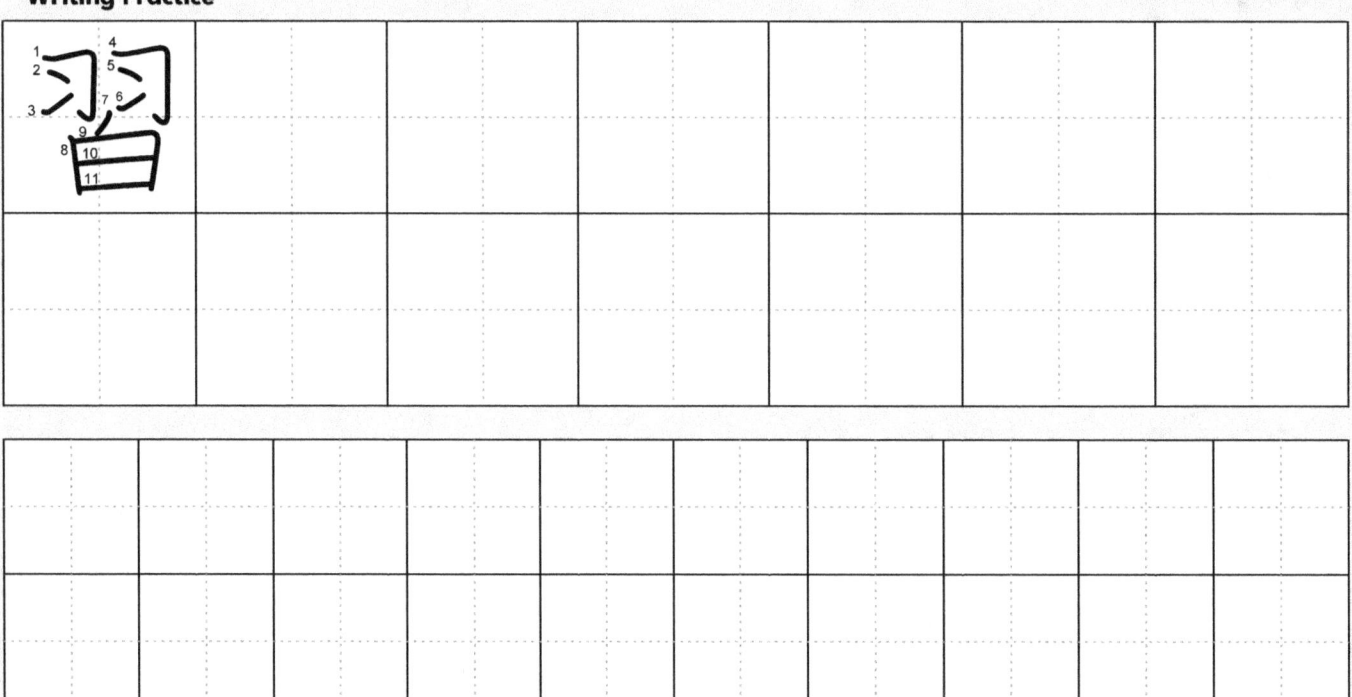

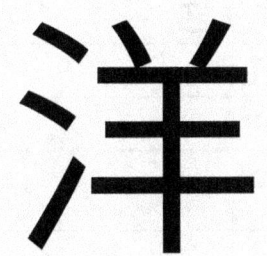

Meaning(s)	ocean, sea, foreign	Components	井 汁 王 羊
Radical	水 (氵, 氺) (water)	Kun'yomi	
Strokes	9	On'yomi	ヨウ

Vocabulary	Meaning	Pronunciation
洋	Occident and Orient (esp. the Occident), ocean, sea, foreign, Western, European	ヨウ
洋画	Western painting, Western film/movie	ヨウガ
南氷洋	Antarctic Ocean	ナンヒョウヨウ

Stroke Order

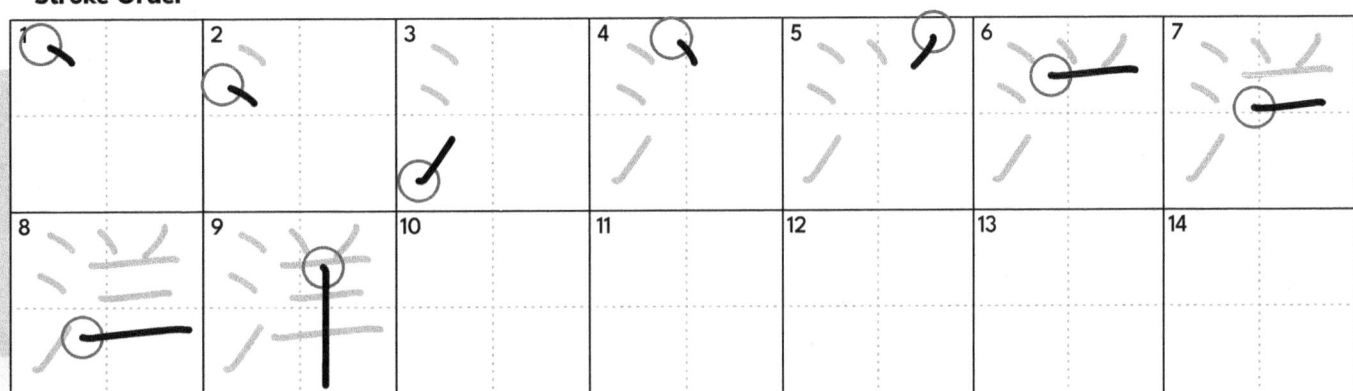

Writing Practice

Meaning(s)	trip, travel		Components	ノ 方 乞
Radical	方 (square)		Kun'yomi	たび
Strokes	10		On'yomi	リョ

Vocabulary	Meaning	Pronunciation
旅	travel, trip, journey	たび
旅客	passenger, traveller, traveler, tourist	リョカク
旅先	destination, place one stays during a trip	たびさき
修旅	excursion, field trip, school trip	シュウリョ

Stroke Order

Writing Practice

Meaning(s)	clothing, admit, obey	Components	卩 又 月
Radical	月 (moon, month)	Kun'yomi	
Strokes	8	On'yomi	フク

Vocabulary	Meaning	Pronunciation
服	clothes (esp. Western clothes), gulps of tea	フク
服役	penal servitude, serving time in prison	フクエキ
私服	civilian clothes, plain clothes	シフク
呉服	cloth (for Japanese clothes), kimono fabrics	ゴフク

Stroke Order

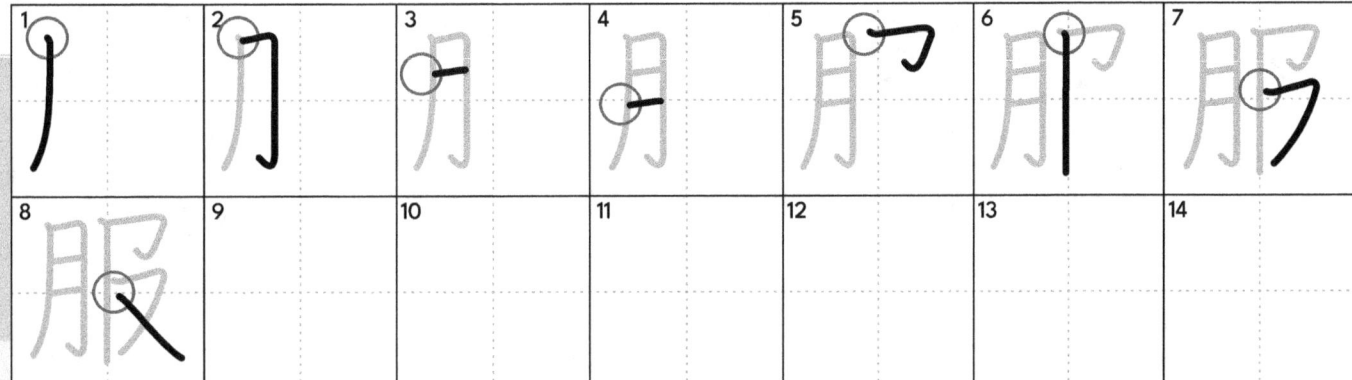

Writing Practice

Meaning(s)	evening		Components	夕
Radical	夕 (evening, sunset)		Kun'yomi	ゆう
Strokes	3		On'yomi	

Vocabulary	Meaning	Pronunciation
夕	evening	ゆう
夕刊	evening paper	ゆうかん
昨夕	yesterday evening, last night	さくゆう
春の夕	spring evening	はるのゆう

Stroke Order

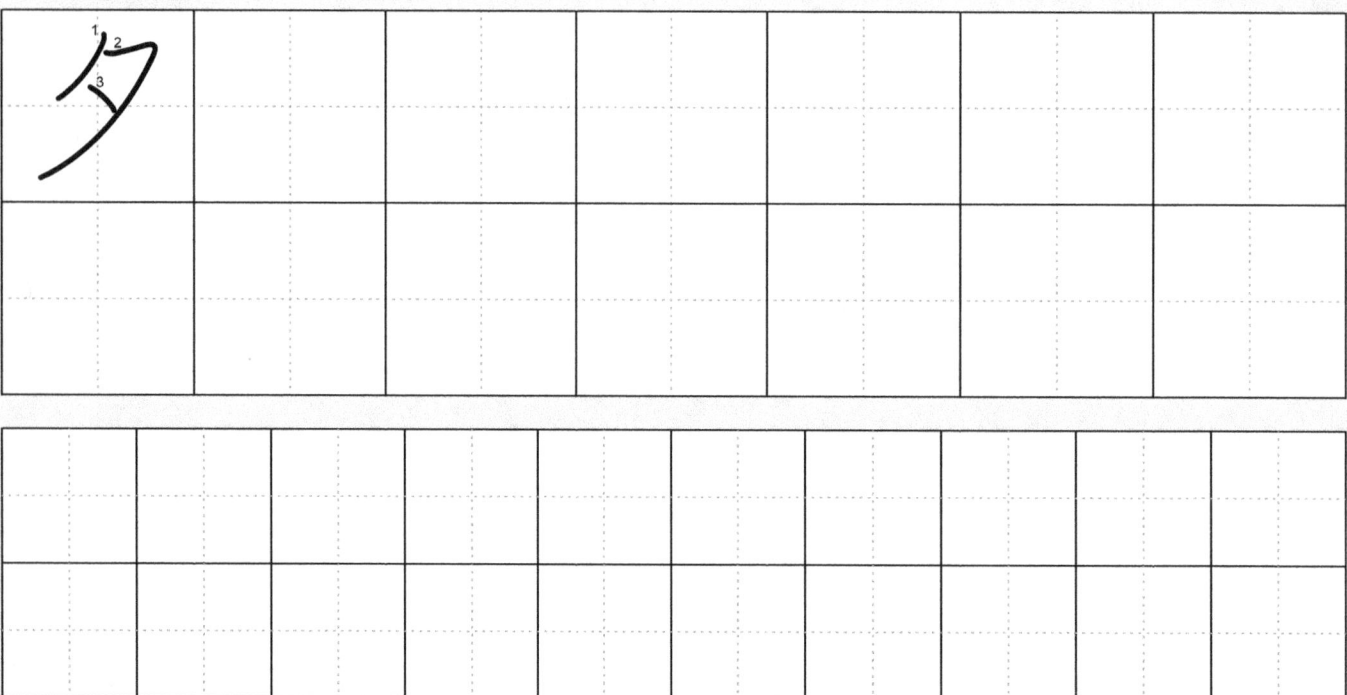

Writing Practice

Meaning(s)	borrow, rent	Components	二 化 卄 日
Radical	人 (亻) (human)	Kun'yomi	か(りる)
Strokes	10	On'yomi	シャク

Vocabulary	Meaning	Pronunciation
借りる	to borrow, to have a loan, to rent/hire	かりる
借家	rented house, house for rent	シャクヤ
賃借	hiring, renting, leasing	チンシャク
借地	leased land	シャクチ

Stroke Order

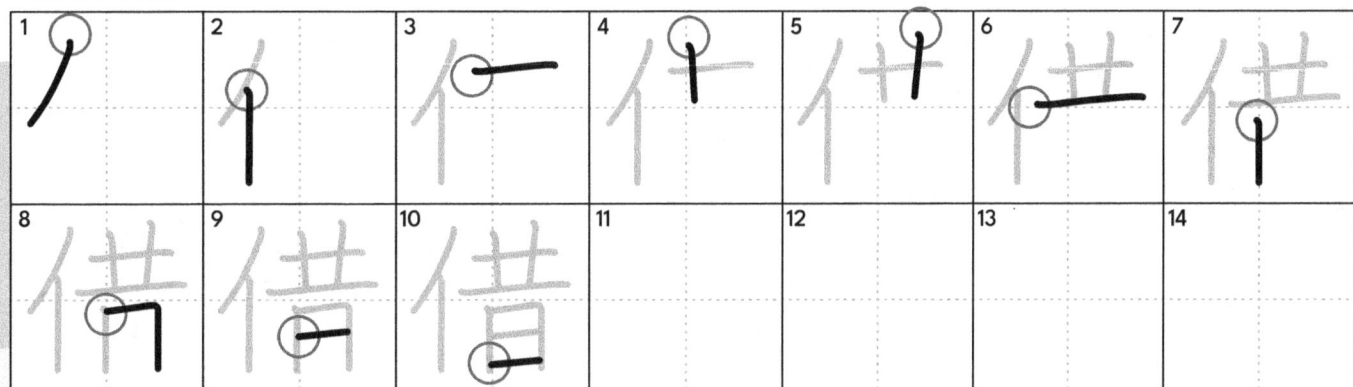

Writing Practice

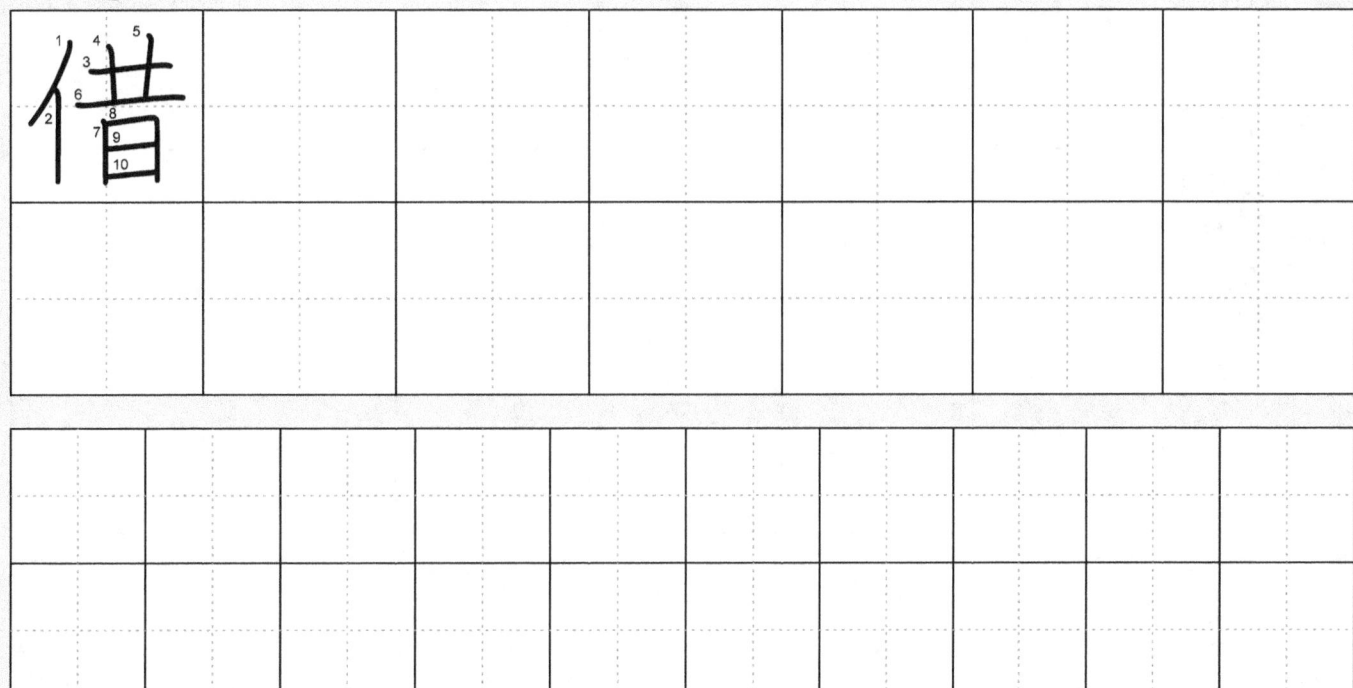

曜

Meaning(s)	weekday	Components	ヨ 日 隹
Radical	日 (sun, day)	Kun'yomi	
Strokes	18	On'yomi	ヨウ

Vocabulary	Meaning		Pronunciation
曜日	day of the week		ヨウビ
曜霊	the sun		ヨウレイ
晃曜	dazzling brightness		コウヨウ

Stroke Order

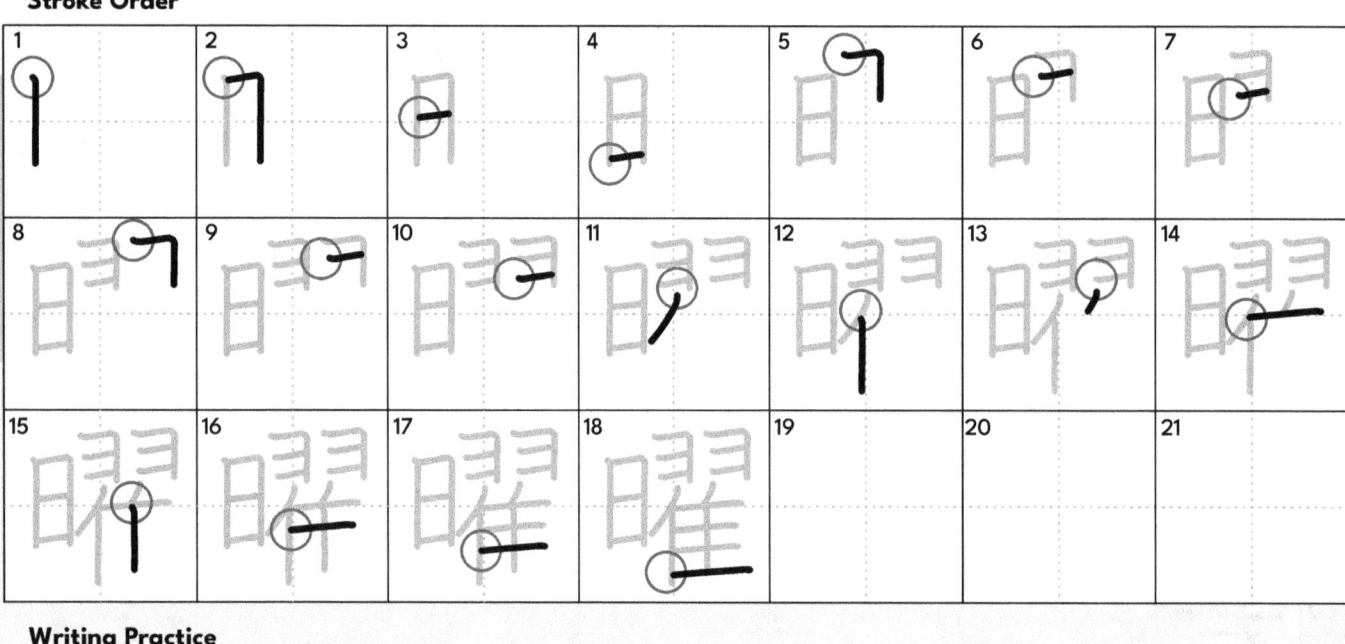

Writing Practice

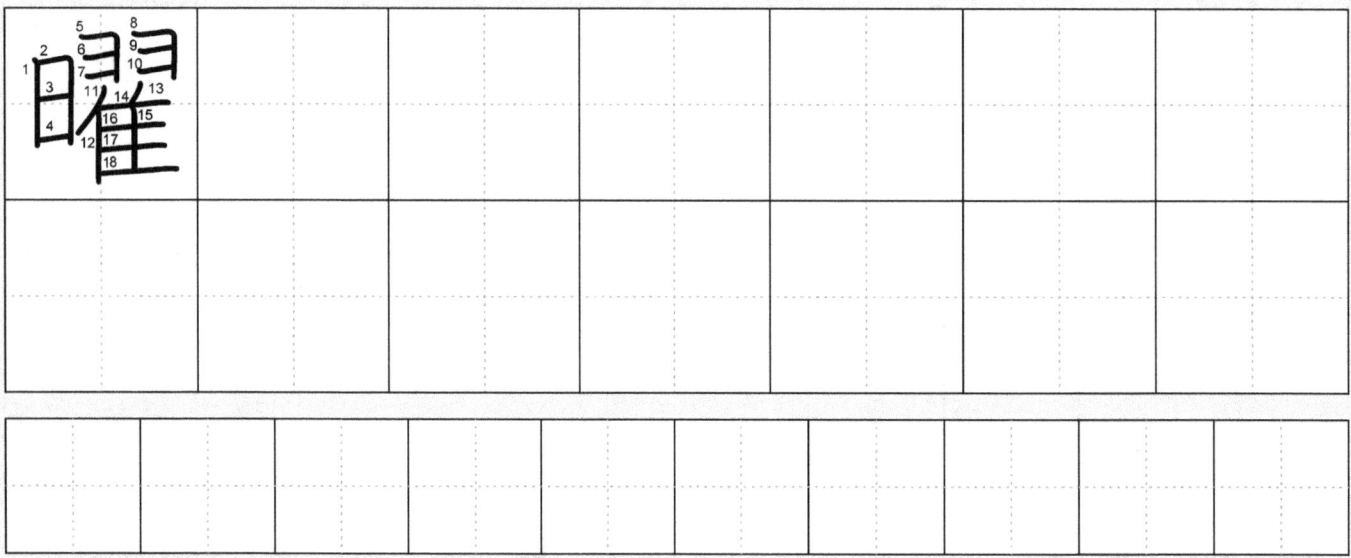

Meaning(s)	meat	Components	人 冂 肉
Radical	肉 (月) (meat)	Kun'yomi	
Strokes	6	On'yomi	ニク

Vocabulary	Meaning	Pronunciation
肉	flesh, meat, flesh (of a fruit), pulp, thickness, content, substance, flesh, ink pad	ニク
食肉	meat (for consumption)	ショクニク
中肉	medium build, meat of medium quality	チュウニク

Stroke Order

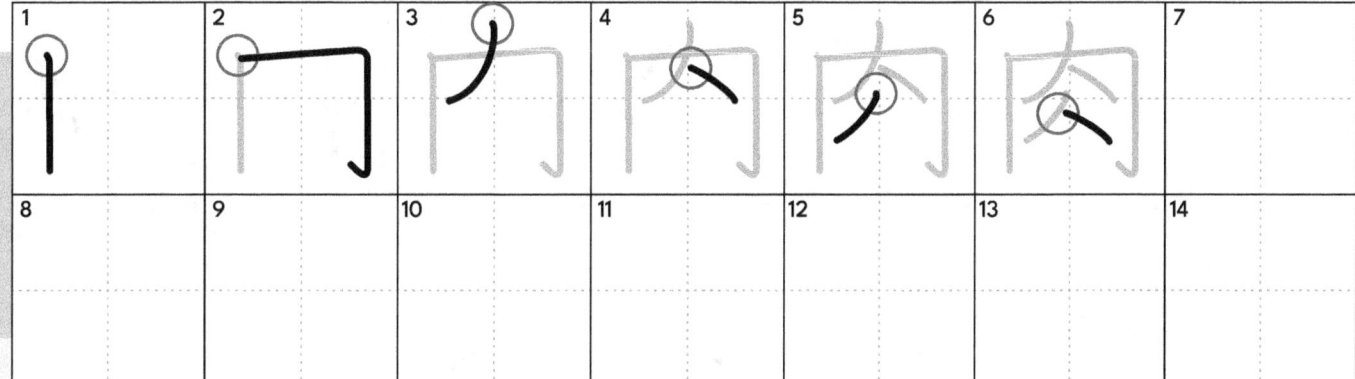

Writing Practice

Meaning(s)	lend		Components	化 ハ 弋 目 貝
Radical	貝 (shell)		Kun'yomi	か(す)、かし
Strokes	12		On'yomi	タイ

Vocabulary	Meaning	Pronunciation
貸す	to lend, to loan, to rent out, to hire out	かす
貸与	loan, lending	タイヨ
貸借	loan, debit and credit, lending & borrowing	タイシャク
転貸	subleasing	テンタイ

Stroke Order

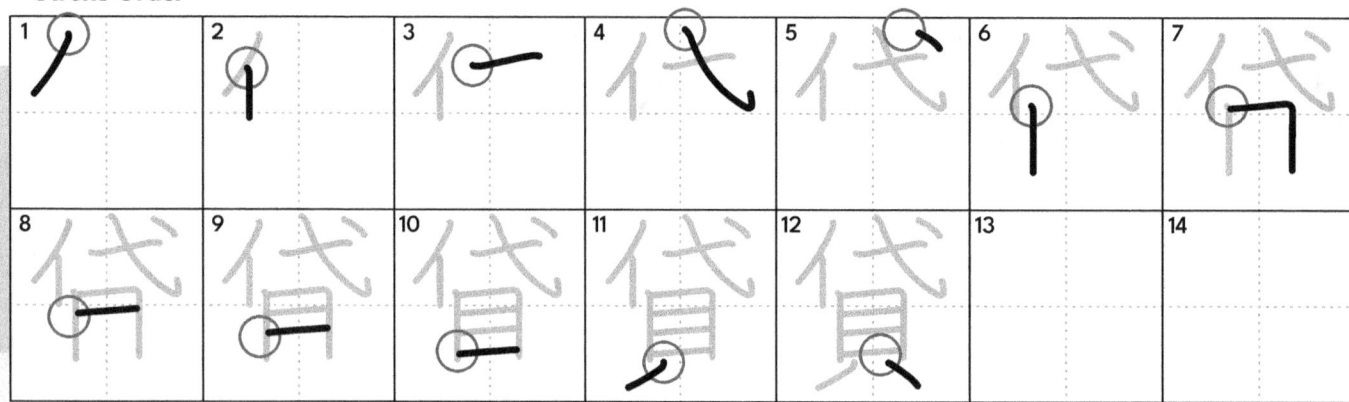

Writing Practice

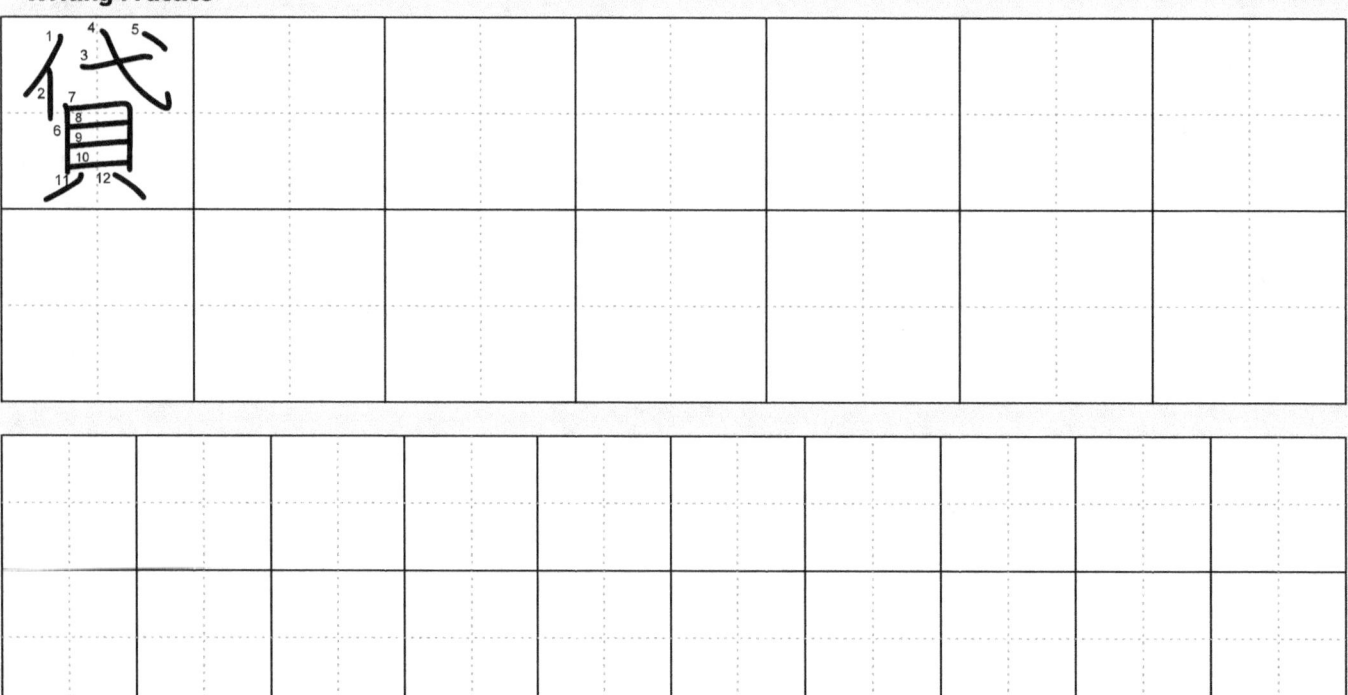

Meaning(s)	public chamber, hall	Components	冖 口 土 尚
Radical	土 (earth)	Kun'yomi	
Strokes	11	On'yomi	ドウ

Vocabulary	Meaning		Pronunciation
堂	temple, shrine, chapel, hall, company		ドウ
堂々	magnificent, grand, impressive, dignified majestic, imposing, stately, fair, square		ドウドウ
殿堂	palace, hall, shrine, temple, sanctuary		デンドウ

Stroke Order

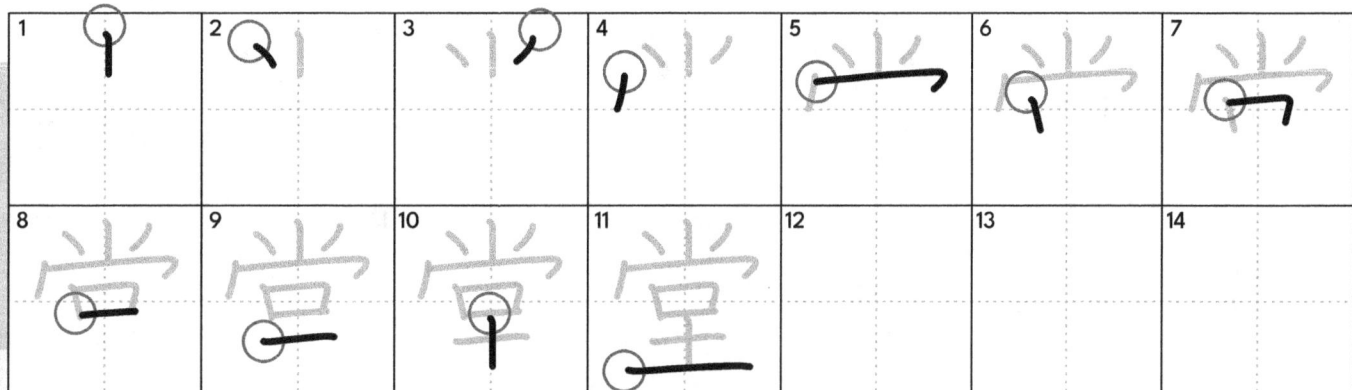

Writing Practice

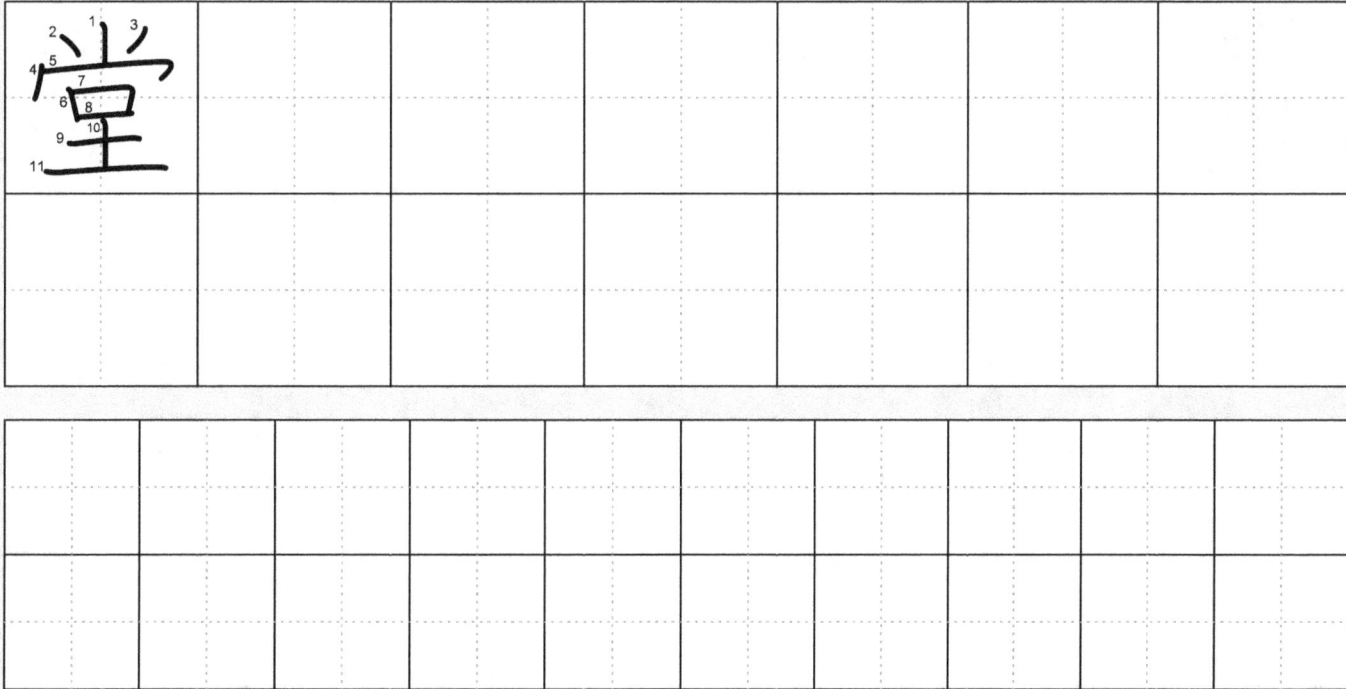

Meaning(s)	bird, chicken	Components	杰 鳥
Radical	鳥 (bird)	Kun'yomi	とり
Strokes	11	On'yomi	チョウ

Vocabulary	Meaning		Pronunciation
鳥	bird, bird meat (esp. chicken), fowl, poultry		とり
鳥居	torii, Shinto shrine archway		とりい
鶏肉	chicken meat, fowl, poultry, bird meat		トリニク
鳥獣	birds and wild animals, wildlife		チョウジュウ

Stroke Order

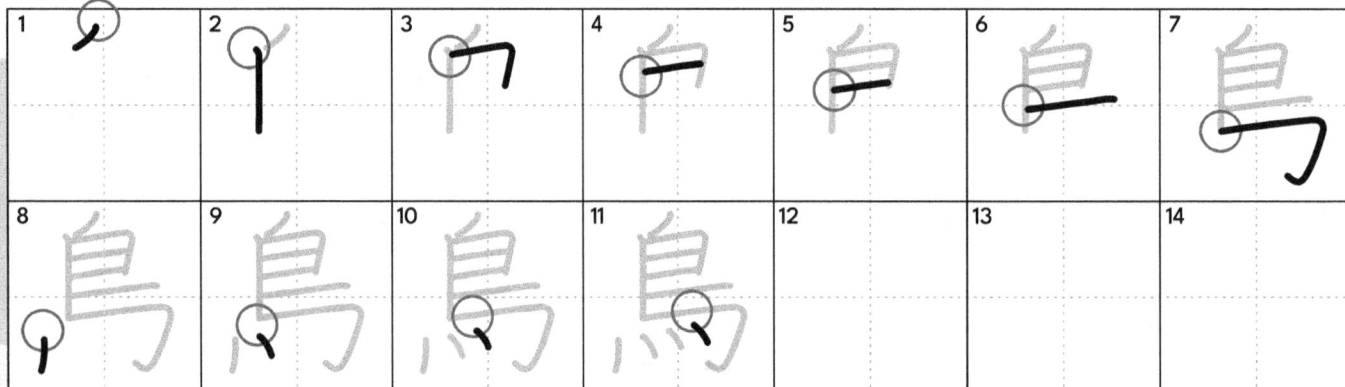

Writing Practice

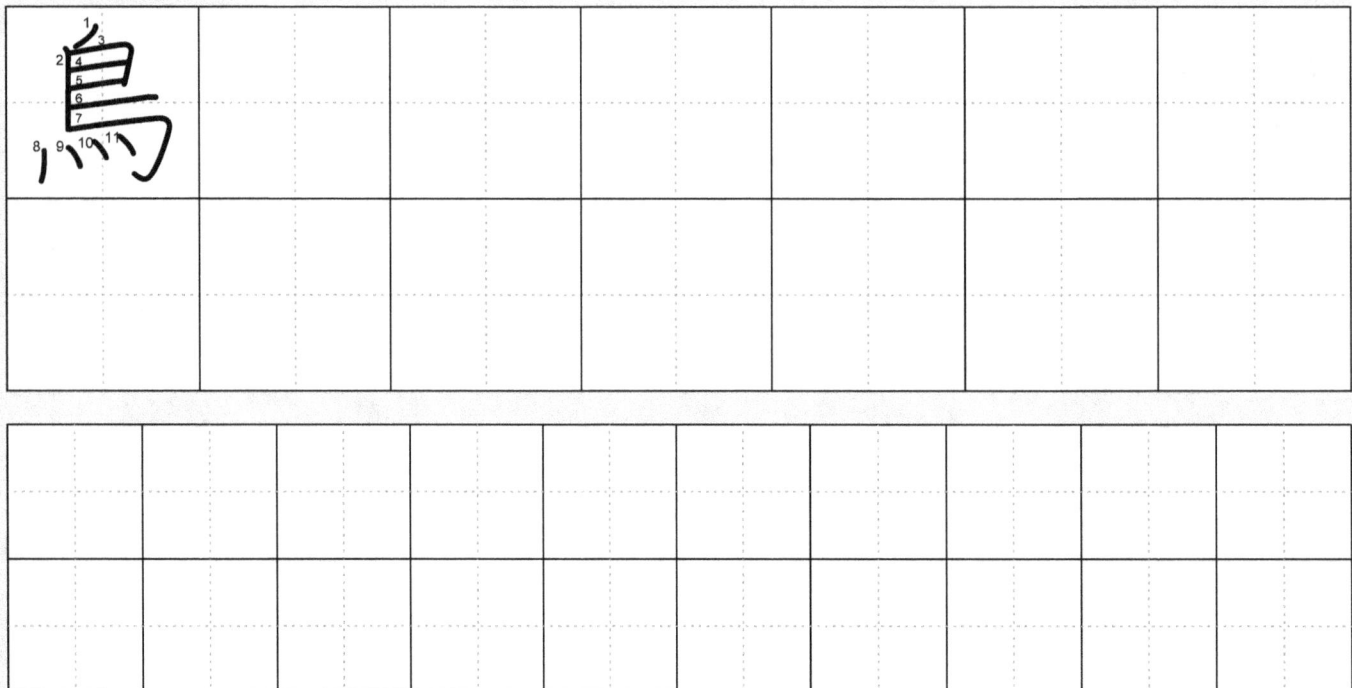

Meaning(s)	meal, rice	Components	厂又食
Radical	食 (飠) (eat, food)	Kun'yomi	めし
Strokes	12	On'yomi	ハン

Vocabulary	Meaning		Pronunciation
飯	cooked rice, meal/food, one's living/livelihood		めし
飯店	Chinese restaurant		ハンテン
米飯	cooked rice		ベイハン
握り飯	rice ball		にぎりめし

Stroke Order

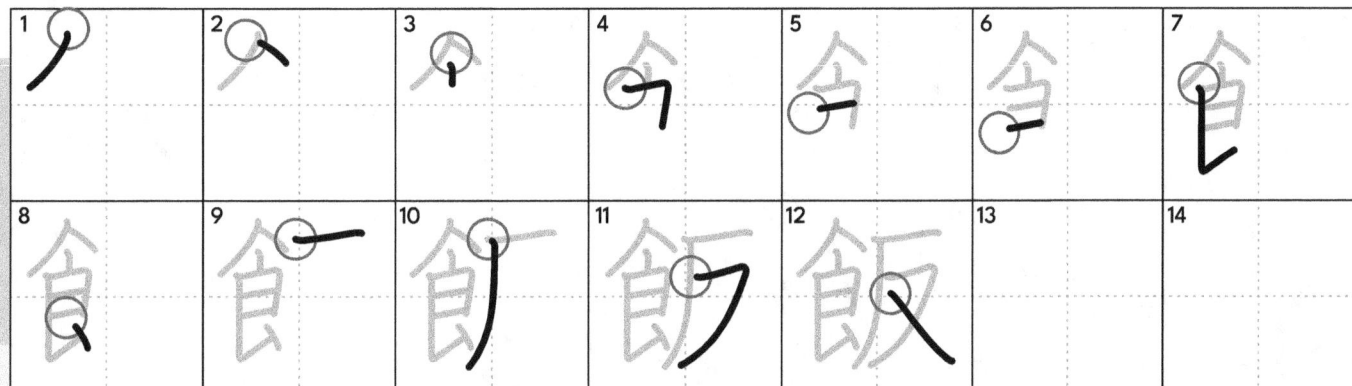

Writing Practice

Meaning(s)	exertion, endeavor, effort	Components	ノカク免
Radical	力 (power, force)	Kun'yomi	つと(める)
Strokes	10	On'yomi	ベン

Vocabulary	Meaning	Pronunciation
勉強	study, diligence, working hard, experience	ベンキョウ
勉学	study, pursuit of knowledge	ベンガク
猛勉	studying hard, cramming	モウベン
努める	to endeavor (to do), to endeavour/try hard	つとめる

Stroke Order

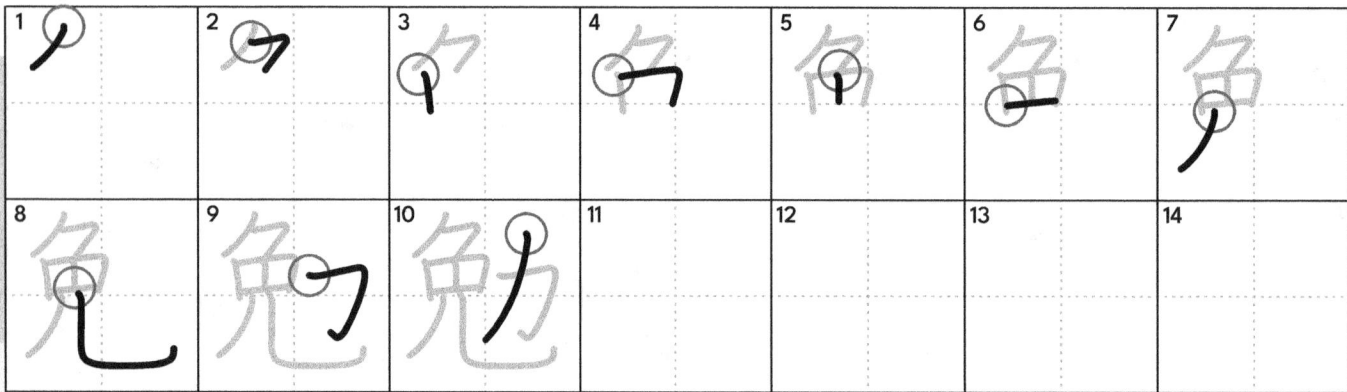

Writing Practice

Meaning(s)	winter		Components	丶 夂 冬
Radical	冫 (ice)		Kun'yomi	ふゆ
Strokes	5		On'yomi	トウ

Vocabulary	Meaning	Pronunciation
冬	winter	ふゆ
冬季	(season of) winter	トウキ
冬場	wintertime, winter season	ふゆば
毎冬	every winter	まいふゆ

Stroke Order

Writing Practice

Meaning(s)	daytime, noon		Components	一、尸日
Radical	日 (sun, day)		Kun'yomi	ひる
Strokes	9		On'yomi	チュウ

Vocabulary	Meaning	Pronunciation
昼	noon, midday, daytime, lunch	ひる
昼食	lunch, midday meal, food served at tea party	チュウショク
夜昼	daytime/during the day, time from sunrise-set	よるひる
昼間	left hand	ヒルマ

Stroke Order

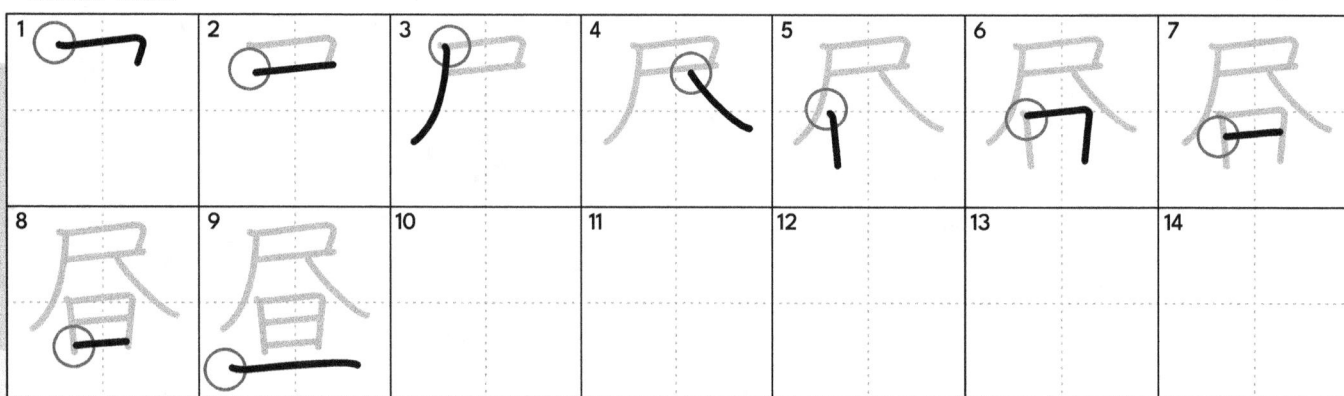

Writing Practice

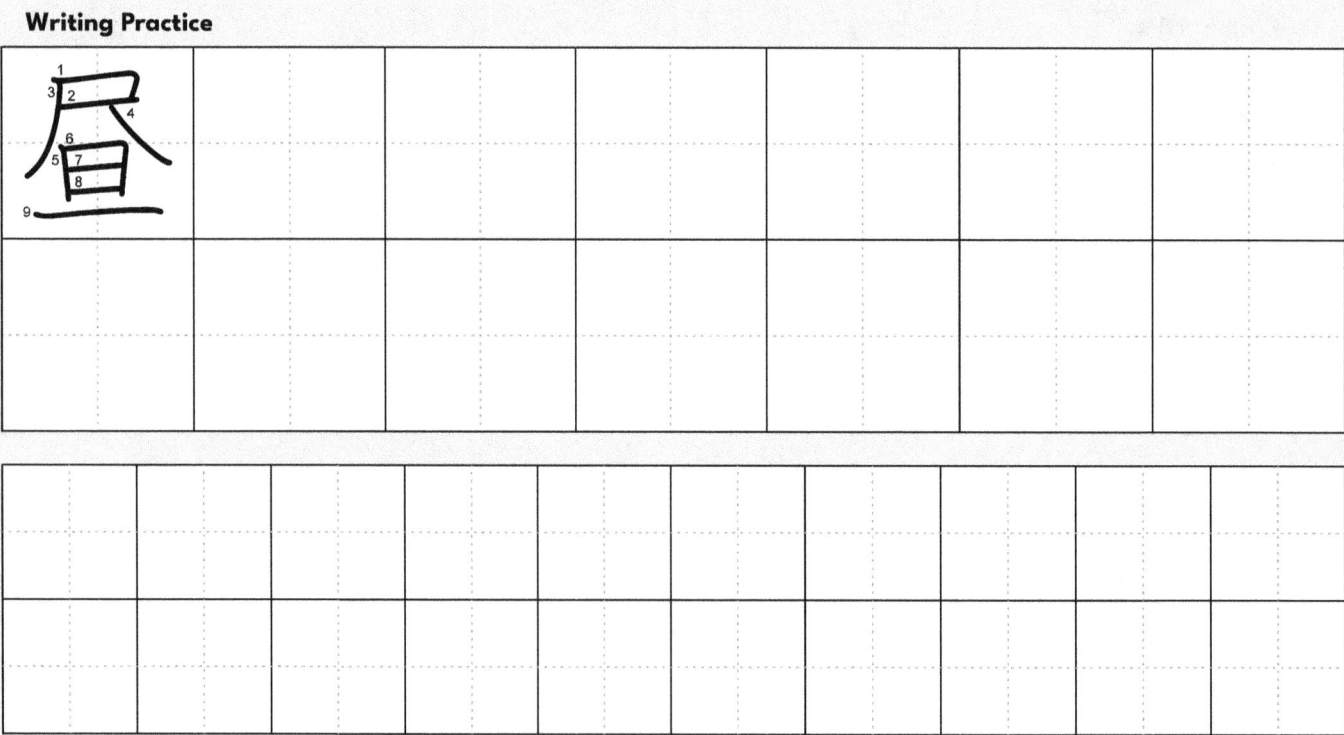

Meaning(s)	tea		Components	个艾木
Radical	艸 (⺾) (grass)		Kun'yomi	
Strokes	9		On'yomi	チャ、サ

Vocabulary	Meaning	Pronunciation
茶	tea, tea preparation, making tea, brown	チャ
茶色	brown, light brown, tawny	チャイロ
煎茶	green tea, green leaf tea	センチャ
喫茶	tea drinking, teahouse, coffee lounge/shop	キッサ

Stroke Order

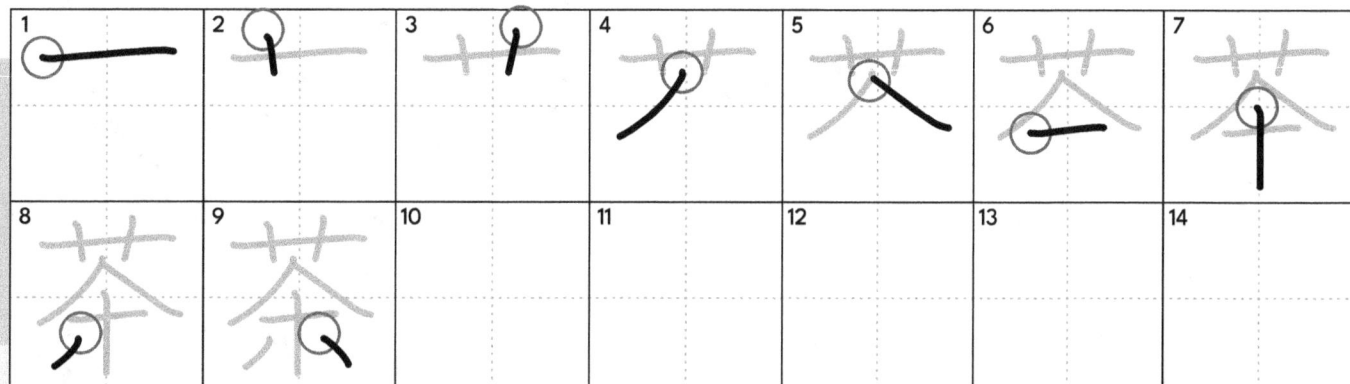

Writing Practice

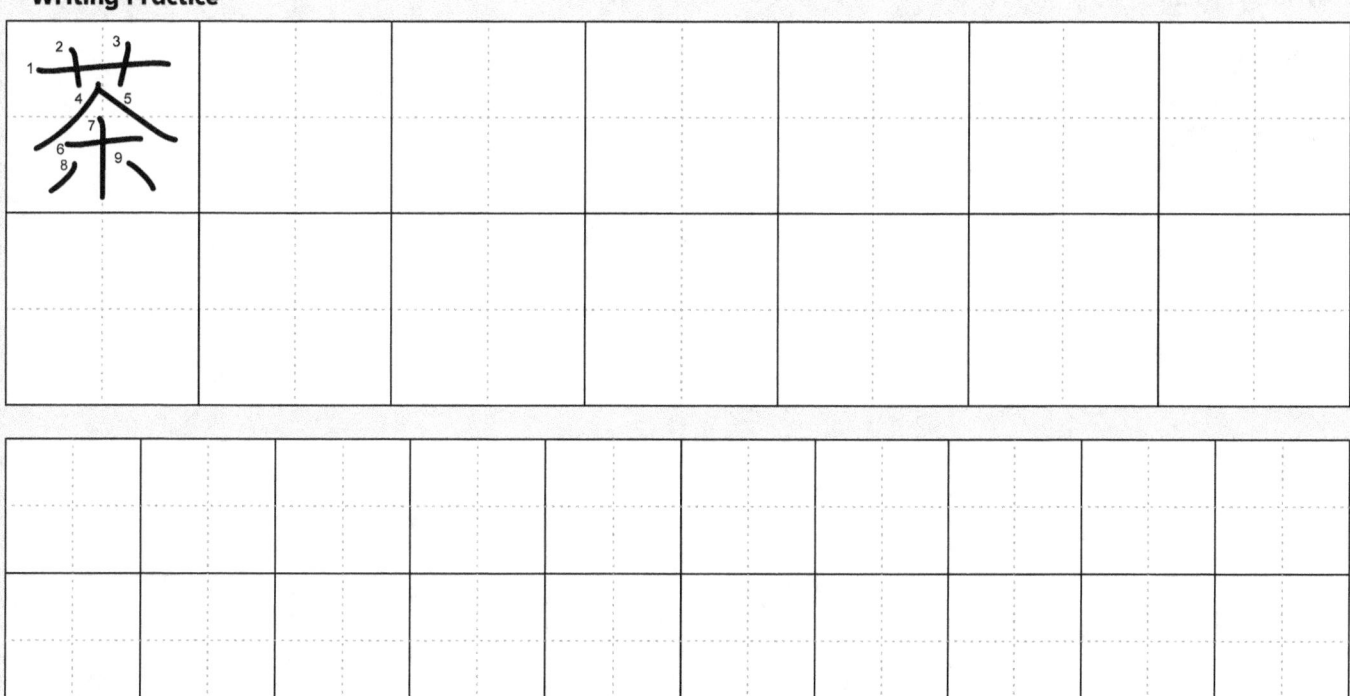

Meaning(s)	younger brother	Components	丨ノ并弓
Radical	弓 (bow)	Kun'yomi	おとうと
Strokes	7	On'yomi	テイ、ダイ、デ

Vocabulary	Meaning	Pronunciation
弟	younger brother, little brother, kid brother	オトウト
弟子	pupil, disciple, adherent, follower, apprentice	デシ
弟	younger brother, little brother, brother-in-law	おとうと
兄弟	siblings, brothers and sisters	キョウダイ

Stroke Order

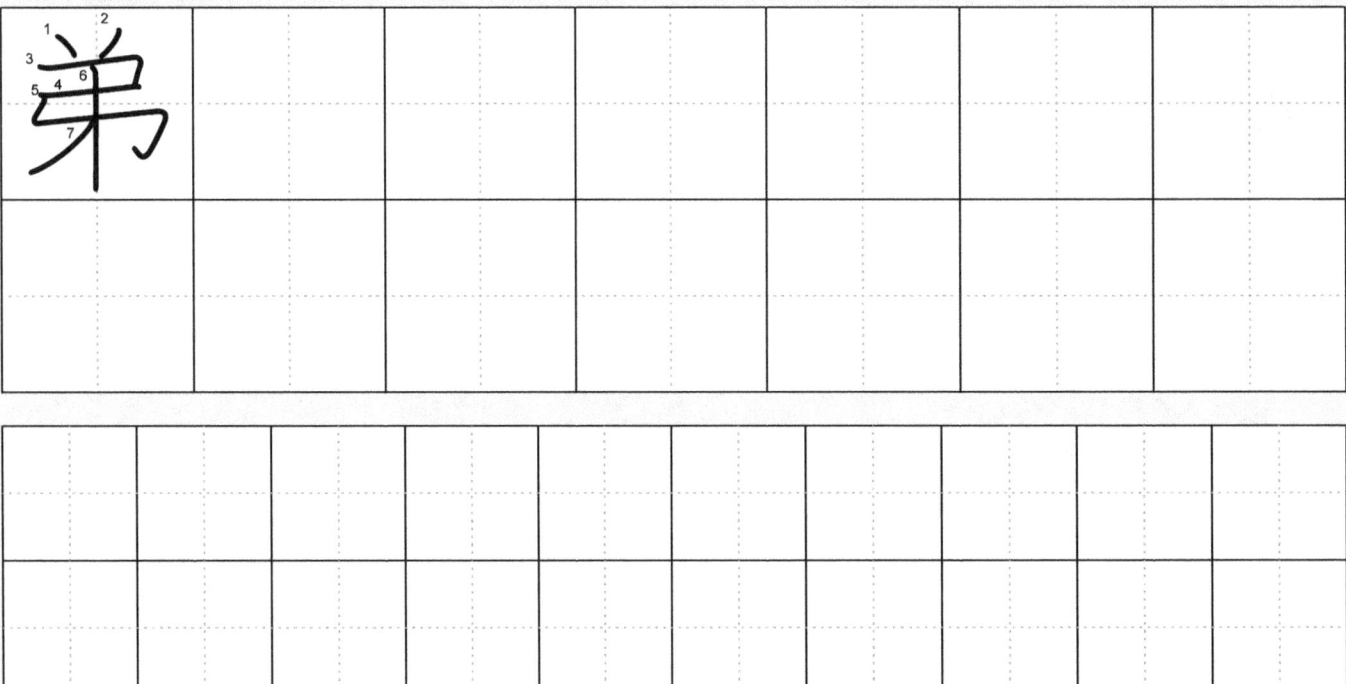

Writing Practice

牛
牛 牛

Meaning(s)	COW		Components	牛
Radical	牛 (牜) (COW)		Kun'yomi	うし
Strokes	4		On'yomi	ギュウ

Vocabulary	Meaning	Pronunciation
牛	cattle, cow, bull, ox, calf, beef	うし
特牛	strong bull	こというし
肉牛	beef cattle	ニクギュウ
去勢牛	ox, bullock	きょせいうし

Stroke Order

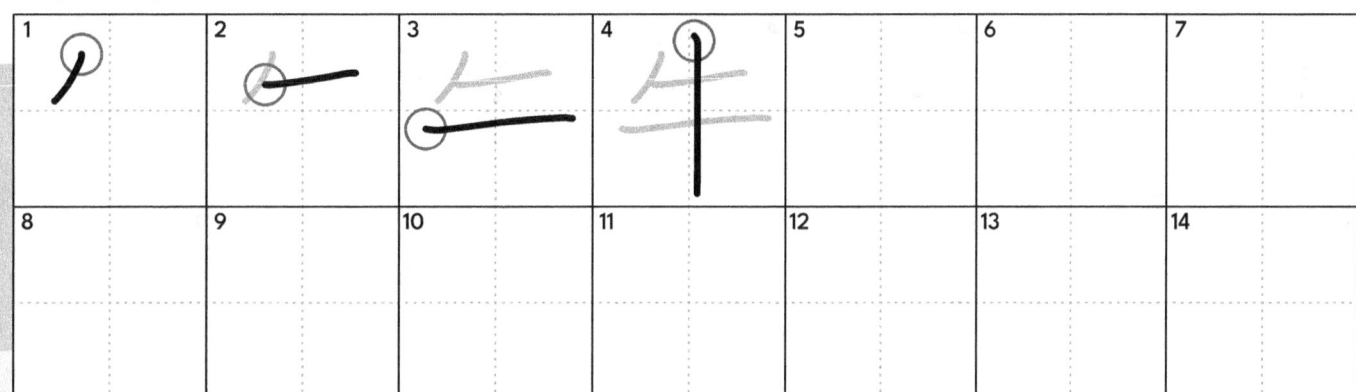

Writing Practice

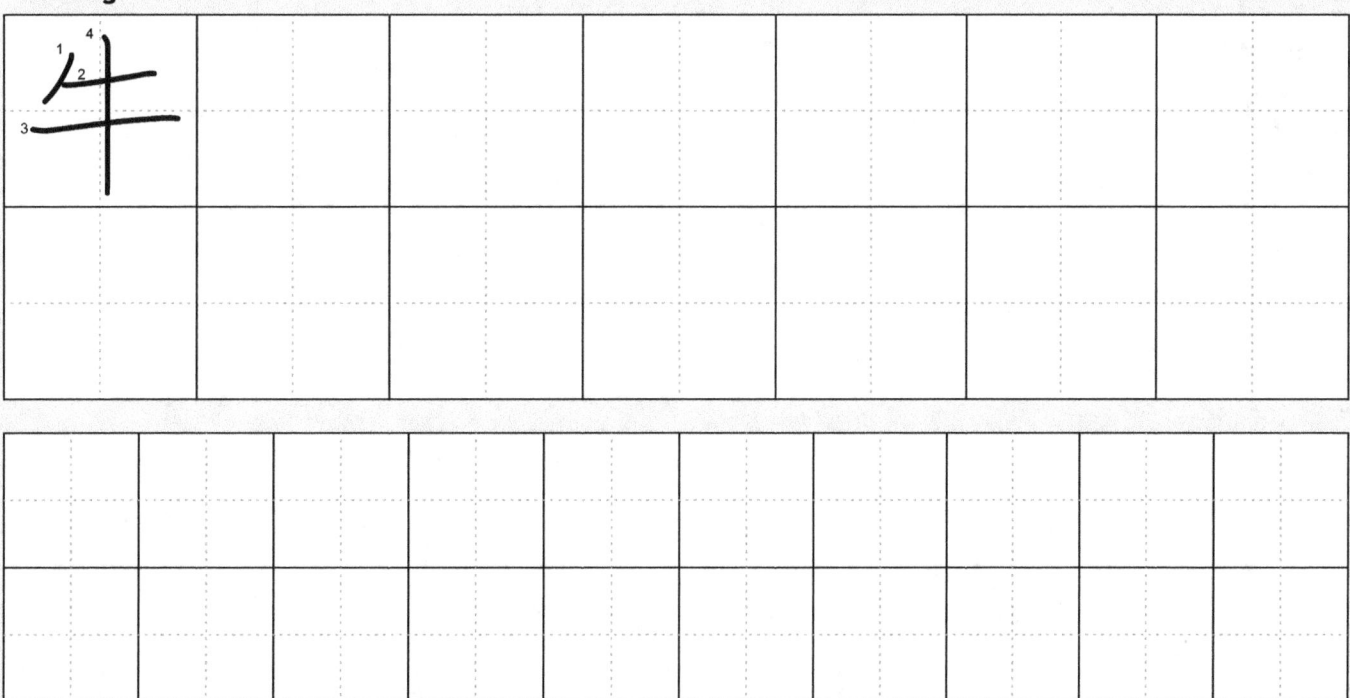

兄

Meaning(s)	elder brother	Components	ルロ
Radical	ル (legs)	Kun'yomi	あに
Strokes	5	On'yomi	キョウ、ケイ

Vocabulary	Meaning	Pronunciation
兄	older brother, elder brother	あに
兄	you, Mr, Mister, older brother, elder brother	ケイ
兄弟	siblings, brothers and sisters	キョウダイ
父兄	guardians, parents	フケイ

Stroke Order

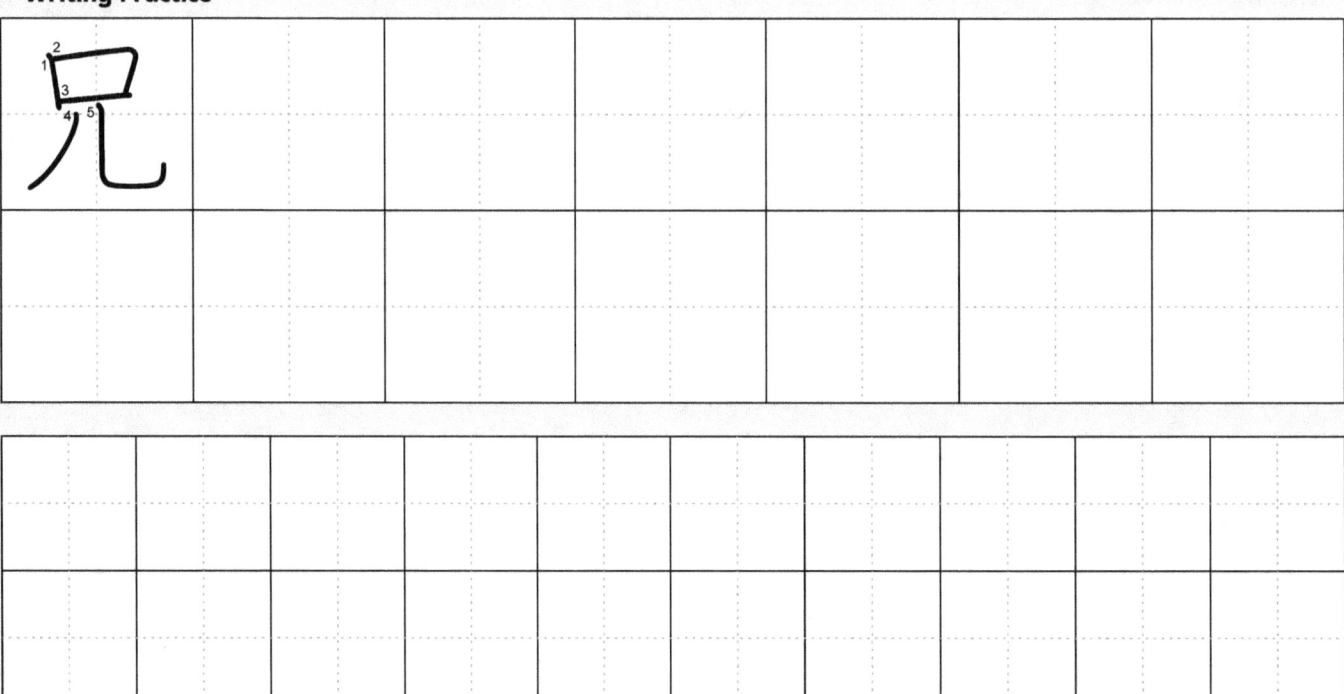

Writing Practice

Meaning(s)	dog		Components	、大犬
Radical	犬 (犭) (dog)		Kun'yomi	いぬ
Strokes	4		On'yomi	ケン

Vocabulary	Meaning	Pronunciation
犬	dog, informer, informant, spy, loser, useless	いぬ
野良犬	stray dog	のらいぬ
柴犬	shiba inu (dog breed), shiba	シバイヌ
柴犬	shiba inu (dog breed), shiba	しばいぬ

Stroke Order

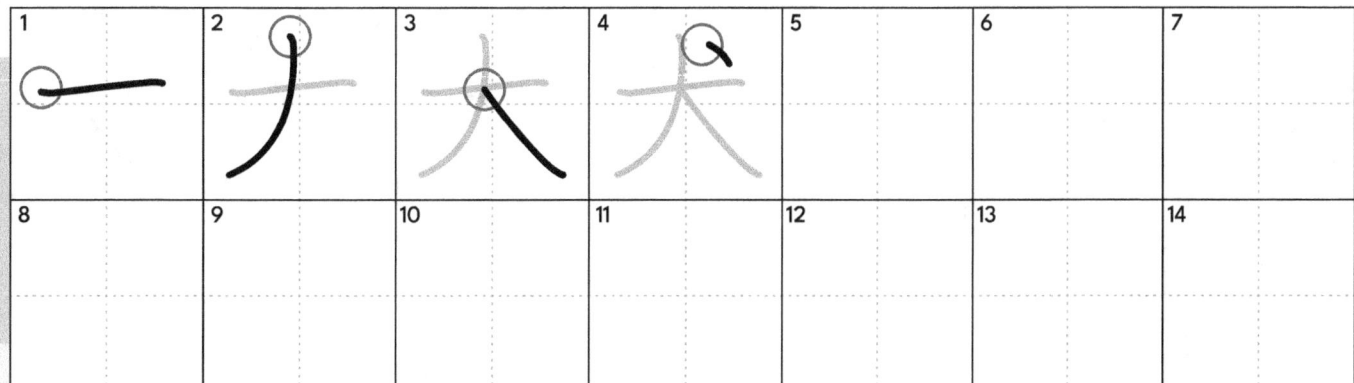

Writing Practice

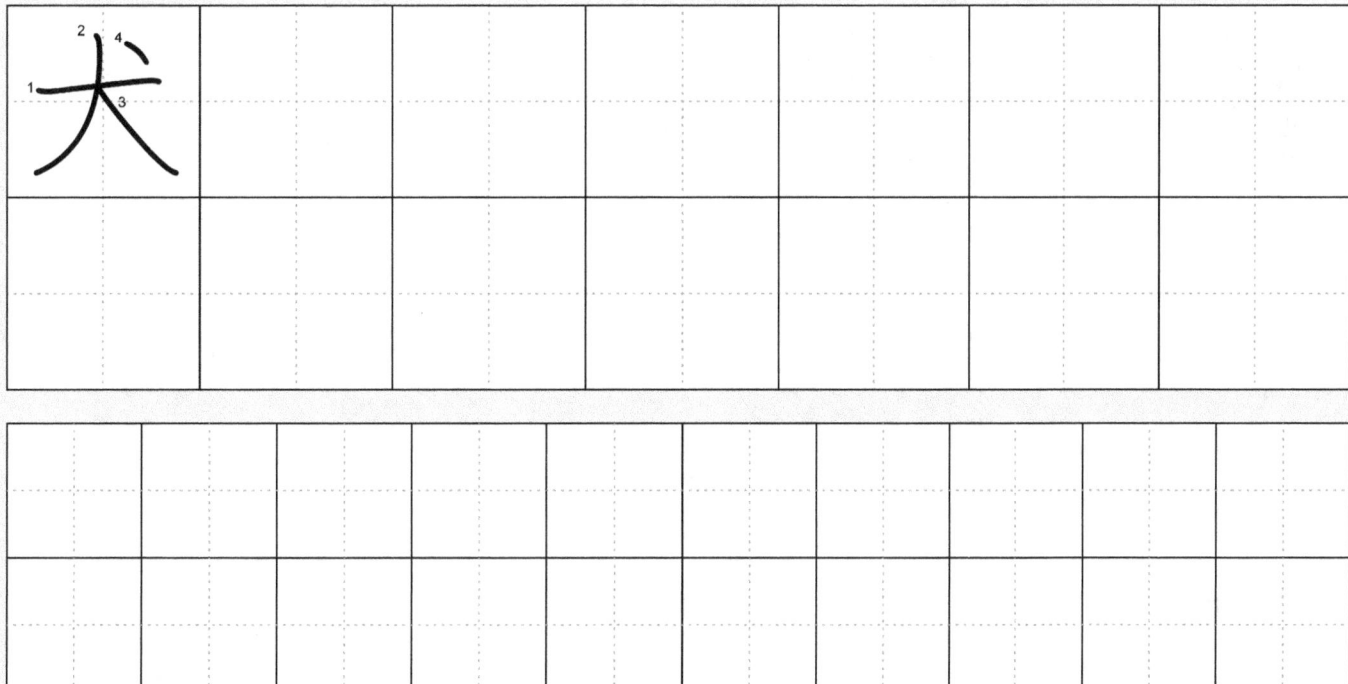

Meaning(s)	younger sister	Components	丨 ニ 亠 ハ 女 木
Radical	女 (woman, female)	Kun'yomi	いもうと
Strokes	8	On'yomi	マイ

Vocabulary	Meaning	Pronunciation
妹	younger sister	いもうと
妹君	(younger) sister	イモウトギミ
弟妹	younger brother and sister	テイマイ
妹君	(younger) sister	いもうとぎみ

Stroke Order

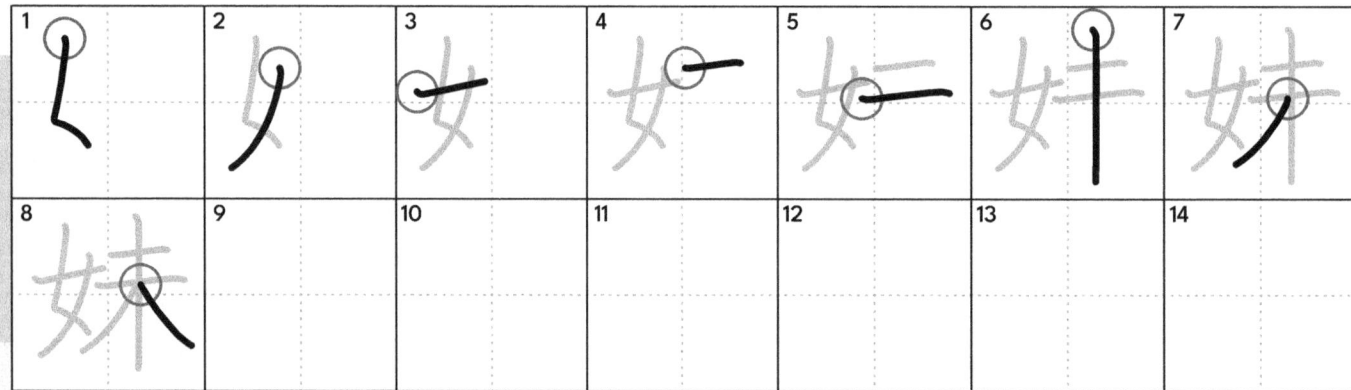

Writing Practice

姉

Meaning(s)	elder sister	Components	亠女巾
Radical	女 (woman, female)	Kun'yomi	あね
Strokes	8	On'yomi	シ

Vocabulary	Meaning	Pronunciation
姉	older sister, elder sister	あね
姉妹	sisters	シマイ
大姉	eldest sister	おおあね
姉さん	older sister, young lady, miss, ma'am	ねえさん

Stroke Order

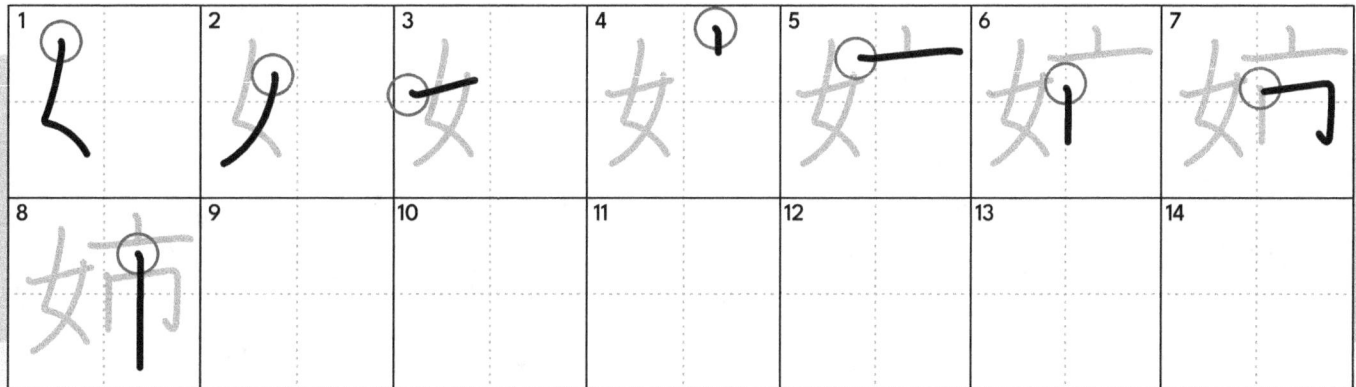

Writing Practice

漢

Meaning(s)	China, Sino-	**Components**	一二口大汁艾
Radical	水 (氵, 氺) (water)	**Kun'yomi**	
Strokes	13	**On'yomi**	カン

Vocabulary	Meaning	Pronunciation
漢	China, Han (dynasty, of China), man	カン
漢字	kanji, Chinese character	カンジ
門外漢	outsider, layman, amateur	モンガイカン

Stroke Order

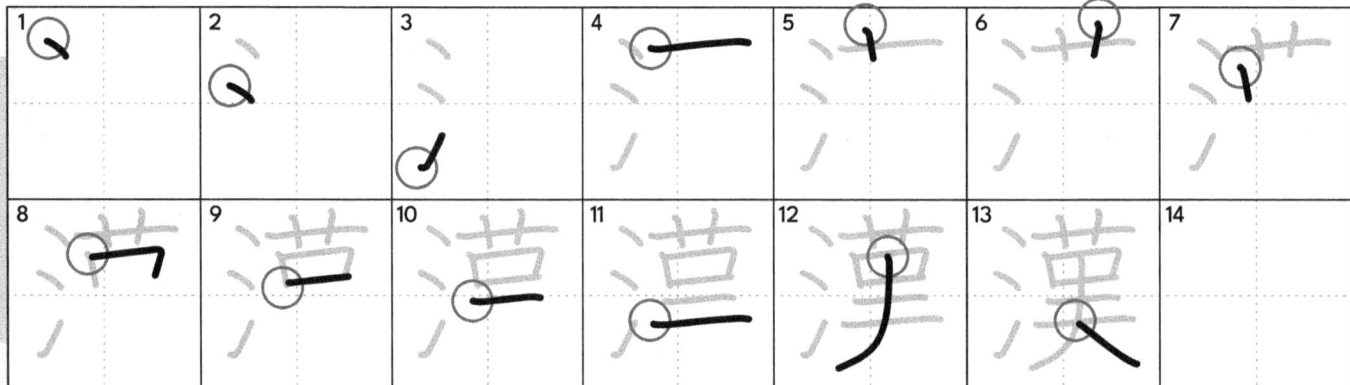

Writing Practice

PART 3
EXTRA STUDY TOOLS

Writing Practice Template

(1-inch grid with guides)

Writing Practice Template

(1-inch grid with guides)

Writing Practice Template

(1-inch grid without guides)

Writing Practice Template

(1-inch grid without guides)

Writing Practice Template

(0.7-inch grid with guides)

Writing Practice Template

(0.7-inch grid with guides)

Writing Practice Template

(0.7-inch grid without guides)

Writing Practice Template

(0.7-inch grid without guides)

Writing Practice Template

(0.7-inch grid without guides)

Writing Practice Template

(0.7-inch grid without guides)

N5 N4 N3 N2 N1

ON'YOMI _____ KUN'YOMI _____

RADICAL(S) VOCAB VOCAB

SENTENCE / MNEMONIC / NOTES

KANJI DETAILS

KANJI STROKE ORDER

KANJI WRITING PRACTICE

Kanji Study Template

N5 N4 N3 N2 N1

KANJI DETAILS

ON'YOMI

KUN'YOMI

RADICAL(S) VOCAB

VOCAB

SENTENCE / MNEMONIC / NOTES

KANJI STROKE ORDER

KANJI WRITING PRACTICE

N5 N4 N3 N2 N1

Kanji Study Template

N5 N4 N3 N2 N1

ON'YOMI

KUN'YOMI

RADICAL(S) VOCAB

VOCAB

SENTENCE / MNEMONIC / NOTES

KANJI DETAILS

KANJI STROKE ORDER

KANJI WRITING PRACTICE

Kanji Study Template

N5 N4 N3 N2 N1

KANJI DETAILS

ON'YOMI

KUN'YOMI

RADICAL(S) VOCAB

VOCAB

SENTENCE / MNEMONIC / NOTES

KANJI STROKE ORDER

KANJI WRITING PRACTICE

N5 N4 N3 N2 N1

Kanji Study Template

N5 N4 N3 N2 N1

KANJI DETAILS

ON'YOMI _____   KUN'YOMI _____

RADICAL(S) | VOCAB | VOCAB

SENTENCE / MNEMONIC / NOTES

KANJI STROKE ORDER

KANJI WRITING PRACTICE

Kanji Study Template

N5 N4 N3 N2 N1

KANJI DETAILS

ON'YOMI

KUN'YOMI

RADICAL(S) | VOCAB | VOCAB

SENTENCE / MNEMONIC / NOTES

KANJI STROKE ORDER

KANJI WRITING PRACTICE

N5 N4 N3 N2 N1

Kanji Study Template

N5 N4 N3 N2 N1

ON'YOMI _____   KUN'YOMI _____

RADICAL(S) VOCAB   VOCAB

KANJI DETAILS

SENTENCE / MNEMONIC / NOTES

KANJI STROKE ORDER

KANJI WRITING PRACTICE

Kanji Study Template

N5　N4　N3　N2　N1

KANJI DETAILS

ON'YOMI

KUN'YOMI

RADICAL(S)　VOCAB

VOCAB

SENTENCE / MNEMONIC / NOTES

KANJI STROKE ORDER

KANJI WRITING PRACTICE

Kanji Study Template

N5 N4 N3 N2 N1

KANJI DETAILS

ON'YOMI

KUN'YOMI

RADICAL(S) VOCAB

VOCAB

SENTENCE / MNEMONIC / NOTES

KANJI STROKE ORDER

KANJI WRITING PRACTICE

Kanji Study Template

自

N4 Level Kanji

Radical	自
Strokes	6
Parts	目自
Kun	みずか.ら
On	ジ、シ

事

N4 Level Kanji

Radical	亅
Strokes	8
Parts	一亅口ヨ
Kun	こと、つか.う
On	ジ、ズ

同

N4 Level Kanji

Radical	口
Strokes	6
Parts	一冂口
Kun	おな.じ
On	ドウ

地

N4 Level Kanji

Radical	土
Strokes	6
Parts	土也
Kun	
On	チ、ジ

者

N4 Level Kanji

Radical	老(耂)
Strokes	8
Parts	老日
Kun	もの
On	シャ

発

N4 Level Kanji

Radical	癶
Strokes	9
Parts	二儿癶
Kun	た.つ、あば.く
On	ハツ、ホツ

場

N4 Level Kanji

Radical	土
Strokes	12
Parts	一土日勿
Kun	ば
On	ジョウ、チョウ

方

N4 Level Kanji

Radical	方
Strokes	4
Parts	方
Kun	かた、-がた
On	ホウ

業

N4 Level Kanji

Radical	木
Strokes	13
Parts	一丨井木王羊未
Kun	わざ
On	ギョウ、ゴウ

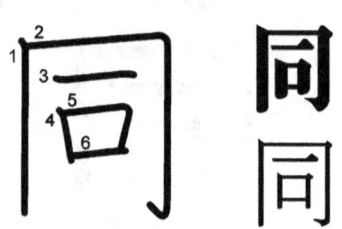

Meaning(s): **same, agree, equal**

同じ	おなじ same, equal
同	ドウ the same, likewise
合同	ゴウドウ combination
同じく	おなじく in the same way

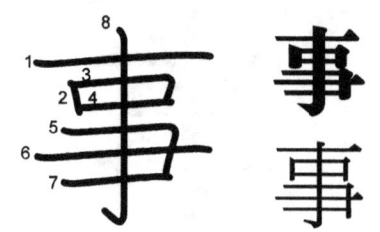

Meaning(s): **matter, thing, fact**

事	こと thing, matter, incident
神事	しんじ Shinto ritual
有事	ユウジ emergency
事業	ジギョウ project, business

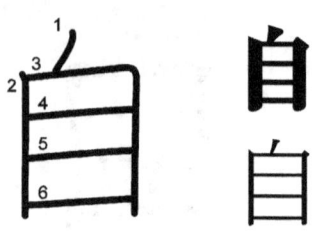

Meaning(s): **oneself**

自然	シゼン natural, spontaneous
出自	シュツジ origin, birthplace
自ら	みずから personally
自ずから	おのずから in due course

Meaning(s): **departure**

発	ハツ departing from ...
発熱	ハツネツ generation of heat
偶発	グウハツ accidental
暴く	あばく to disclose/expose

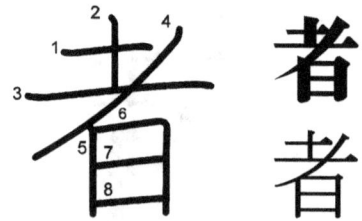

Meaning(s): **someone, person**

者	もの person
芸者	ゲイシャ geisha
者ども	ものども you, people
若い者	わかいもの young person, youth

地 地

Meaning(s): **ground, earth**

地	チ earth, ground, land
地位	チイ (social) position
地	ジ land, earth, soil
下地	シタジ groundwork, foundation

Meaning(s): **business, performance**

業	ギョウ work, company
業	わざ act, work, deed
業界	ギョウカイ (the) industry
業因	ゴウ karma

方 方

Meaning(s): **direction, person**

方	ホウ direction, way, side
途方	トホウ destination, reason
方々	かたがた people, everyone
親方	おやかた master, supervisor

場 場

Meaning(s): **location, place**

場	ば place, space
場	ジョウ grounds, stadium
場合	ばあい case, situation
場外	ジョウガイ outside the (place)

力

N4 Level Kanji

Radical	力
Strokes	2
Parts	力
Kun	ちから
On	リョク、リキ

開

N4 Level Kanji

Radical	門
Strokes	12
Parts	一ノ二开門
Kun	ひら(く)、あ(ける)
On	カイ

員

N4 Level Kanji

Radical	口
Strokes	10
Parts	ハ口目貝
Kun	
On	イン

明

N4 Level Kanji

Radical	日
Strokes	8
Parts	日月
Kun	あか(るい)
On	メイ、ミョウ

代

N4 Level Kanji

Radical	人（イ）
Strokes	5
Parts	化弋
Kun	か(わり)
On	ダイ

問

N4 Level Kanji

Radical	口
Strokes	11
Parts	口門
Kun	と(う)
On	モン

通

N4 Level Kanji

Radical	辵（⻌,⻍）
Strokes	10
Parts	マ込用
Kun	とお(る)、かよ(う)
On	ツウ

京

N4 Level Kanji

Radical	亠
Strokes	8
Parts	亠口小
Kun	みやこ
On	キョウ、ケイ、キン

動

N4 Level Kanji

Radical	力
Strokes	11
Parts	一｜ノ力日里
Kun	うご.く、うご.かす
On	ドウ

員

Meaning(s): **employee, member**

員	イン member
員数	インズウ (total) number
随員	ズイン attendant
執行委員	シッコウイイン exec. committee

開

Meaning(s): **open, unfold, unseal**

開く	ひらく to open, to unpack
開花	カイカ bloom/blossoming
開ける	ひらける to open out (a view)
ひらける	あける to open (a door)

力

Meaning(s): **power, strength**

力	ちから strength, capability
力	リョク power, ability
力強い	ちからづよい powerful, forceful
力学	リキガク mechanics, dynamics

問

Meaning(s): **question, problem**

問	モン counter for questions
問う	とう to inquire, to accuse of
更問	さらとい follow-up question
設問	セツモン posing a question

代

Meaning(s): **substitute, change**

代	ダイ cost, price, age
代わり	かわり substitute, proxy
大時代	オオジダイ old-fashioned
希代	キタイ rare, extraordinary

明

Meaning(s): **bright, light**

明かり	あかり light, glow, gleam
明るい	あかるい well-lit, bright (color)
明	メイ brightness, insight
光明	コウミョウ bright light, hope

動

Meaning(s): **motion, change**

動く	うごく to move, to stir
動かす	うごかす to move, shift/budge
動	ドウ motion
異動	イドウ (personnel) change

京

Meaning(s): **capital**

都	みやこ capital (esp. Kyoto)
京	キョウ imperial capital
京都	キョウト Kyoto (city, prefecture)
英京	エイキョウ British capital, London

通

Meaning(s): **traffic, commute**

通る	とおる to go by/past/along
通り	とおり street, way, road
通	ツウ authority, expert
通う	かよう to go back and forth

田

N4 Level Kanji

Radical	田
Strokes	5
Parts	田
Kun	た
On	デン

体

N4 Level Kanji

Radical	人 (亻)
Strokes	7
Parts	一 化 木
Kun	からだ
On	タイ

理

N4 Level Kanji

Radical	玉 (王)
Strokes	11
Parts	王 里
Kun	ことわり
On	リ

意

N4 Level Kanji

Radical	心 (忄, 小)
Strokes	13
Parts	心 日 立 音
Kun	
On	イ

題

N4 Level Kanji

Radical	頁
Strokes	18
Parts	八 日 疋 目 貝 頁
Kun	
On	ダイ

主

N4 Level Kanji

Radical	丶
Strokes	5
Parts	一 ノ 干 乞
Kun	ぬし、おも
On	シュ

用

N4 Level Kanji

Radical	用 (甩)
Strokes	5
Parts	用
Kun	もち(いる)
On	ヨウ

作

N4 Level Kanji

Radical	人 (亻)
Strokes	7
Parts	一 丨 ノ 化 乞
Kun	つく(る)
On	サク、サ

不

N4 Level Kanji

Radical	一
Strokes	4
Parts	一 丨 丶 ノ
Kun	
On	フ、ブ

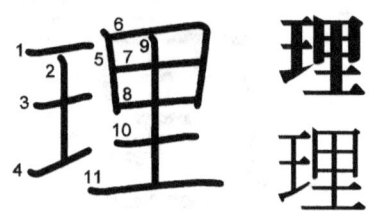

Meaning(s): **arrangement/reason**

理	ことわり reason, logic, sense
理	リ reason, principle
理科	リカ science (medicine, etc.)
経理	ケイリ accounting

Meaning(s): **body, substance**

体	からだ build, physique
体	タイ body, physique
体育	タイイク physical education
風体	フウテイ appearance, look

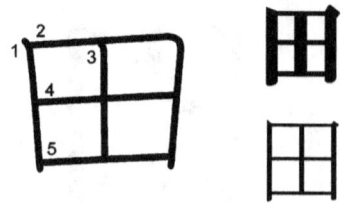

Meaning(s): **rice field, rice paddy**

田	た rice field
田畑	タハタ fields (e.g. rice etc.)
田園	デンエン countryside
田植え	たうえ rice planting

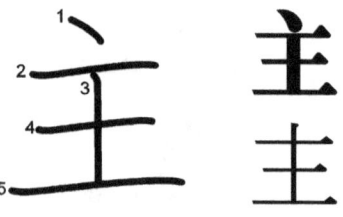

Meaning(s): **lord, chief, master**

主	ぬし head, leader, master
主	おも chief, main, important
主	シュ main thing, majority
主に	おもに mainly, primarily

Meaning(s): **topic, subject**

題	ダイ title, subject, theme
題材	ダイザイ subject, theme
表題	ヒョウダイ title, headline
命題	メイダイ notion, theory

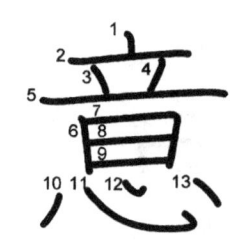

Meaning(s): **idea, mind, heart**

意	イ feelings, thoughts
意外	イガイ unexpected
賛意	サンイ approval, assent
総意	ソウイ consensus

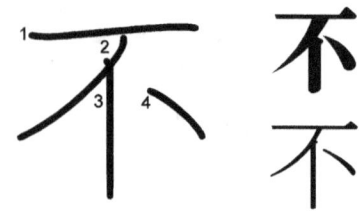

Meaning(s): **negative, non-, bad**

不	フ un-, non-, neg. prefix
不安	フアン anxiety, worry
意味不	イミフ ambiguous
不気味	ブキミ weird, ominous

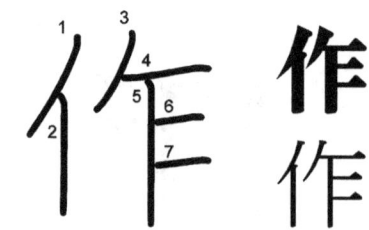

Meaning(s): **make, prepare, build**

作る	つくる to make/produce
作	サク work (e.g. of art)
作業	サギョウ work, task
作る	つくる to raise/grow/train

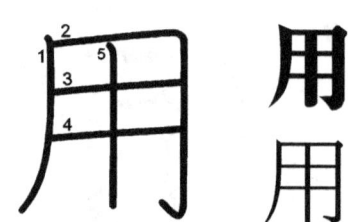

Meaning(s): **business, service**

用いる	もちいる to use/make use of
用	ヨウ task, errand
登用	トウヨウ appointment, promotion
用意	ヨウイ preparation

公

N4 Level Kanji

Radical	八
Strokes	4
Parts	ハ ム
Kun	おおやけ
On	コウ

強

N4 Level Kanji

Radical	弓
Strokes	11
Parts	ム 弓 虫
Kun	つよ(い)
On	キョウ、ゴウ

度

N4 Level Kanji

Radical	广
Strokes	9
Parts	一 又 广 口
Kun	たび、た(い)
On	ド、タク

以

N4 Level Kanji

Radical	人 (亻)
Strokes	5
Parts	｜ 、 人
Kun	もっ(て)
On	イ

野

N4 Level Kanji

Radical	里
Strokes	11
Parts	亅 矛 里
Kun	の
On	ヤ

持

N4 Level Kanji

Radical	手 (扌 )
Strokes	9
Parts	土 寸 扎
Kun	も(つ)
On	ジ

世

N4 Level Kanji

Radical	一
Strokes	5
Parts	一 ｜ 世
Kun	よ
On	セイ、セ

家

N4 Level Kanji

Radical	宀
Strokes	10
Parts	人
Kun	いえ、や、うち
On	カ

思

N4 Level Kanji

Radical	心 (忄, )
Strokes	9
Parts	心 田
Kun	おも(う)
On	シ

度

Meaning(s): **occurrence, time**

度	たび	time (e.g. 3 times)
度	ド	degree, extent
法度	ハット	law, ban
中度	なかたび	mid/halfway (through)

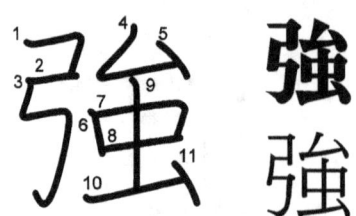

強

Meaning(s): **strong**

強い	つよい	strong, competent, skilled, knowledgeable, being able to handle
強	キョウ	one of the biggest
強盗	ゴウトウ	robber, robbery

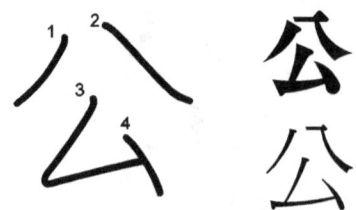

公

Meaning(s): **public, prince, official**

公	おおやけ	official, public (use, etc.)
公	コウ	government matter
公廨	クガイ	government office
王侯	オウコウ	noble rank

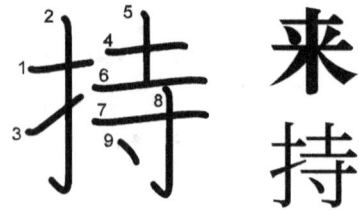

持

Meaning(s): **hold, have**

持つ	もつ	to hold, take or carry
持久	ジキュウ	endurance, persistence
持	ジ	draw/tie (contest)
持てる	もてる	to be popular

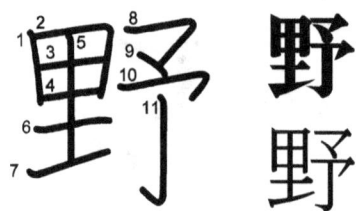

野

Meaning(s): **plains, field, rustic**

野	の	plain, field, wild
野	ノ	plain, field
野外	ヤガイ	outdoors, outside
在野	ザイヤ	out of office

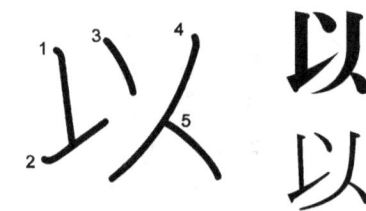

以

Meaning(s): **by means of, because**

以て	もって	with, by, because of
以降	イコウ	from ... onward
以下	イカ	not more than ...

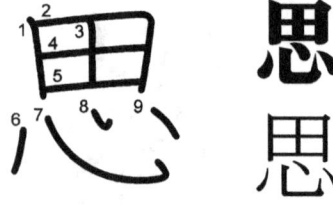

思

Meaning(s): **think**

思う	おもう	to think, to believe
思考	シコウ	thought, thinking
相思	ソウシ	mutual affection
哀思	アイシ	sad feeling

家

Meaning(s): **house, home, family**

家	いえ	house, home, family
家主	やぬし	house owner
家	カ	-ist, -er
家	うち	house, one's home

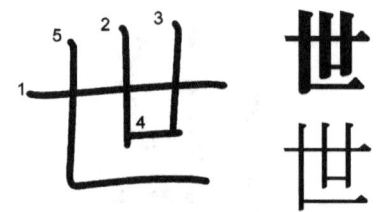

世

Meaning(s): **society, world, public**

世	よ	world, society
世	セイ	counter for generations
世の中	よのなか	society, the world
夜店	ヨミセ	night stall/shop/fair

心

N4 Level Kanji

Radical	心 (忄, 㣺)
Strokes	4
Parts	心
Kun	こころ
On	シン

院

N4 Level Kanji

Radical	阜 (阝)
Strokes	10
Parts	二儿宀阝元
Kun	
On	イン

正

N4 Level Kanji

Radical	止
Strokes	5
Parts	一止
Kun	ただ(しい)、まさ(に)
On	セイ、ショウ

文

N4 Level Kanji

Radical	文
Strokes	4
Parts	文
Kun	ふみ
On	ブン、モン

教

N4 Level Kanji

Radical	攴 (攵)
Strokes	11
Parts	子老乞攵
Kun	おし(える)、おそ(わる)
On	キョウ

界

N4 Level Kanji

Radical	田
Strokes	9
Parts	个儿田
Kun	
On	カイ

近

N4 Level Kanji

Radical	辵 (辶, 辶)
Strokes	7
Parts	込斤
Kun	ちか(い)
On	キン

重

N4 Level Kanji

Radical	里
Strokes	9
Parts	一丨ノ日里
Kun	おも(い)、かさ(ねる)
On	ジュウ、チョウ

元

N4 Level Kanji

Radical	儿
Strokes	4
Parts	二儿元
Kun	もと
On	ゲン、ガン

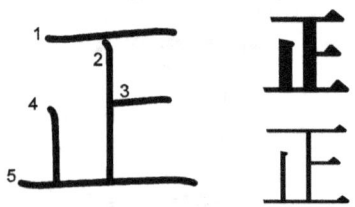

Meaning(s): **correct, justice**

正しい	ただしい right, correct, honest
正	セイ (logical) true, regular
正解	セイカイ correct answer
正(に)	まさ(に) exact(ly), precise(ly)

Meaning(s): **temple, school**

院	イン house of parliament (congress, etc.), graduate school
院長	インチョウ director
棋院	キイン go club, go hall

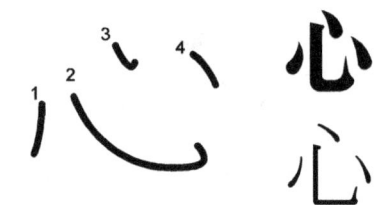

Meaning(s): **heart, mind, spirit**

心	こころ mind, heart, spirit
心	シン heart, mind, spirit
我が心	わがこころ my heart
会心	カイシン satisfaction

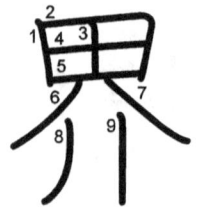

Meaning(s): **world, boundary**

界	カイ community, world
界隈	カイワイ neighborhood
球界	キュウカイ the baseball world
経済界	ケイザイカイ economic world

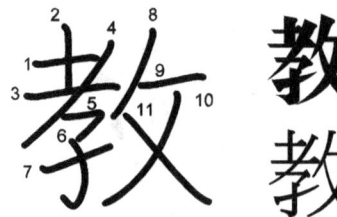

Meaning(s): **teach, faith**

教える	おしえる to teach, to tell
教わる	おそわる to be taught, to learn
教育	キョウイク education, training
政教	セイキョウ religion & politics

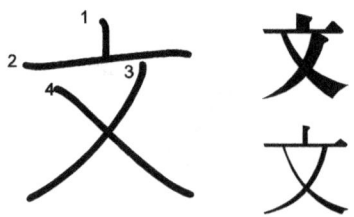

Meaning(s): **sentence, literature**

文	ふみ letter, writings
文	ブン sentence, text
文化	ブンカ culture, civilization
文	モン letter, character

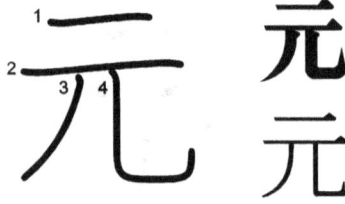

Meaning(s): **beginning, origin**

元	もと origin, source, basis
元	ゲン unknown (in equation)
元日	ガンジツ New Year's Day
元祖	ガンソ originator, inventor

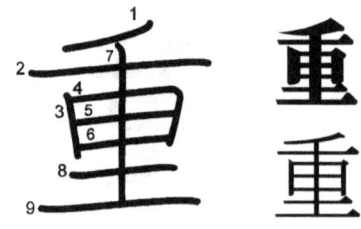

Meaning(s): **important, respect**

重複	チョウフク repetition
重い	おもい heavy, uneasy, slow
重ねる	かさねる to pile/stack up
重	ジュウ serious, -fold, -ply

Meaning(s): **near, early, akin**

近い	ちかい near, short, soon, friendly, intimate
至近	シキン very near
近海	キンカイ coastal waters

海

N4 Level Kanji

Radical	水 (氵, 氺)
Strokes	9
Parts	汁 母 毋 乞
Kun	うみ
On	カイ

画

N4 Level Kanji

Radical	田
Strokes	8
Parts	一 口 田
Kun	かく(する)
On	ガ、カク

考

N4 Level Kanji

Radical	老 (耂)
Strokes	6
Parts	勹 老
Kun	かんが(える)
On	コウ

集

N4 Level Kanji

Radical	隹
Strokes	12
Parts	木 隹
Kun	あつ(める)
On	シュウ

知

N4 Level Kanji

Radical	矢
Strokes	8
Parts	口 矢 乞
Kun	し(る)
On	チ

売

N4 Level Kanji

Radical	士
Strokes	7
Parts	儿 冖 士
Kun	う(る)
On	バイ

使

N4 Level Kanji

Radical	人 (亻)
Strokes	8
Parts	一 ノ 化 口
Kun	つか(う)
On	シ

物

N4 Level Kanji

Radical	牛 (牜)
Strokes	8
Parts	ノ 勹 牛 勿
Kun	もの
On	ブツ、モツ

別

N4 Level Kanji

Radical	刀 (刂)
Strokes	7
Parts	刈 力 勹 口
Kun	わか(れる)、わ(ける)
On	ベツ

Meaning(s): **consider, think over**

考える	かんがえる to think (about, of), to believe
考え方	かんがえかた way of thinking
備考	ビコウ note/remarks, N.B.

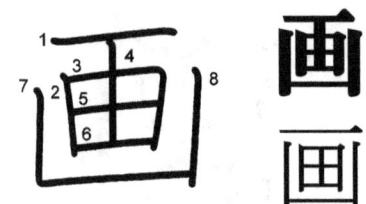

Meaning(s): **brush-stroke, picture**

描く	えがく to draw, to paint
画する	かくする to draw (a line)
画家	ガカ painter, artist
画	カク stroke (of kanji, etc.)

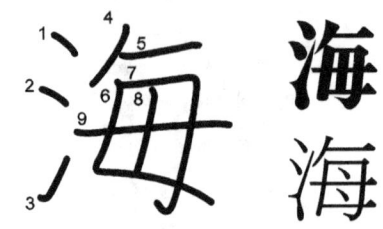

Meaning(s): **sea, ocean**

海	うみ sea, ocean, waters
海辺	うみべ beach, seaside
公海	コウカイ international waters
内海	ないかい inlet, gulf, bay, lake

売

Meaning(s): **sell**

売る	うる to sell
売れる	うれる to be well known
売却	バイキャク selling off
転売	テンバイ resale

知

Meaning(s): **know, wisdom**

知る	しる to know, to learn (of), to find out/discover
知恵	チエ wisdom, wit, sense
認知	ニンチ recognition

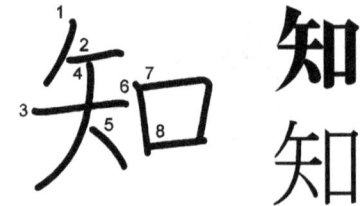

Meaning(s): **gather, meet**

集まる	あつまる to gather/collect
集	シュウ collection, compilation
集める	あつめる to assemble/gather
集う	つどう to meet, to assemble

別

Meaning(s): **separate, branch off**

別れる	わかれる to part from/with
別	ベツ distinction, difference
告別	コクベツ farewell, leave-taking
分ける	わける to divide (into)

物

Meaning(s): **thing, object, matter**

物	もの thing, object, stuff
物	ブツ stock, products
財物	ザイブツ property
幣物	ヘイモツ present to a guest

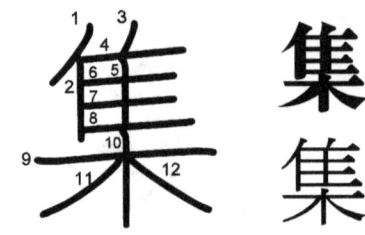

Meaning(s): **use, messenger**

使う	つかう to use (a tool etc.)
使者	シシャ messenger
使い	つかい errand, mission
使い方	つかいかた way of using (a thing)

死

N4 Level Kanji

Radical	歹 (歺)
Strokes	6
Parts	一 ヒ 夕 歹
Kun	し(ぬ)
On	シ

計

N4 Level Kanji

Radical	言 (訁)
Strokes	9
Parts	十 言
Kun	はか(る)
On	ケイ

品

N4 Level Kanji

Radical	口
Strokes	9
Parts	口 品
Kun	しな
On	ヒン

始

N4 Level Kanji

Radical	女
Strokes	8
Parts	ム 口 女
Kun	はじ(める)
On	シ

私

N4 Level Kanji

Radical	禾
Strokes	7
Parts	ム 禾
Kun	わたくし、わたし
On	シ

特

N4 Level Kanji

Radical	牛 (牜)
Strokes	10
Parts	土 寸 牛
Kun	
On	トク

終

N4 Level Kanji

Radical	糸 (糹)
Strokes	11
Parts	夂 小 幺 糸
Kun	お(わる)
On	シュウ

運

N4 Level Kanji

Radical	辵 (辶, 辶)
Strokes	12
Parts	冖 込 車
Kun	はこ(ぶ)
On	ウン

朝

N4 Level Kanji

Radical	月
Strokes	12
Parts	十 日 月
Kun	あさ
On	チョウ

品

Meaning(s): **goods, refinement**

品	しな	item, thing, goods
品	ヒン	elegance, grace
品位	ヒンイ	grade, quality
品目	ひんもく	item, commodity

計

Meaning(s): **plot, plan, scheme**

計る	はかる	to measure, to weigh
計らう	はからう	to manage/arrange
計画	ケイカク	plan, schedule
計	ケイ	measuring device

死

Meaning(s): **death, die**

死ぬ	しぬ	to die, to lose spirit
死	シ	death, decease
死因	シイン	cause of death
死ぬ気で	しぬきで	all out, desperately

特

Meaning(s): **special**

特産	トクサン	local specialty
特異	トクイ	unique, peculiar
快特	カイトク	rapid express (train)
在特	ザイトク	Special Permission to Stay in Japan

私

Meaning(s): **private, I, me**

私	わたくし	I, me, private
私	シ	personal matter
私案	シアン	one's own plan
私	わたし	I, me

始

Meaning(s): **commence, begin**

始める	はじめる	to start, to begin
始発	シハツ	first departure
始業	シギョウ	start of work
創始	ソウシ	creation, founding

朝

Meaning(s): **morning**

朝	あさ	morning, breakfast
朝方	あさがた	early morning/hours
朝刊	チョウカン	morning newspaper
朝	チョウ	dynasty, reign

運

Meaning(s): **carry, luck, fate**

運ぶ	はこぶ	to carry, to move
運	ウン	fortune, luck
運営	ウンエイ	administration
機運	キウン	opportunity, chance

終

Meaning(s): **end, finish**

終わる	終わる	to come to an end
終局	シュウキョク	end, conclusion
終える	おえる	to finish/graduate
終	つい	end, final, never

住

N4 Level Kanji

Radical	人（亻）
Strokes	7
Parts	丶化王
Kun	す(む)
On	ジュウ、チュウ

広

N4 Level Kanji

Radical	广
Strokes	5
Parts	ム广
Kun	ひろ(い)
On	コウ

台

N4 Level Kanji

Radical	口
Strokes	5
Parts	ム口女
Kun	うてな
On	ダイ、タイ

有

N4 Level Kanji

Radical	月
Strokes	6
Parts	一ノ月
Kun	あ(る)
On	ユウ、ウ

真

N4 Level Kanji

Radical	目
Strokes	10
Parts	一八十目
Kun	ま、まこと
On	シン

無

N4 Level Kanji

Radical	火（灬）
Strokes	12
Parts	一｜ノ杰無乞
Kun	な(い)
On	ム、ブ

工

N4 Level Kanji

Radical	工
Strokes	3
Parts	工
Kun	
On	コウ、ク、グ

料

N4 Level Kanji

Radical	斗
Strokes	10
Parts	斗米
Kun	
On	リョウ

町

N4 Level Kanji

Radical	田
Strokes	7
Parts	一丁田
Kun	まち
On	チョウ

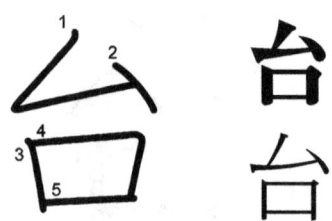

Meaning(s): **pedestal, a stand**

台	ダイ stand, rack, table benchstage, holder
台	うてな stand, pedestal
台	タイ Taiwan

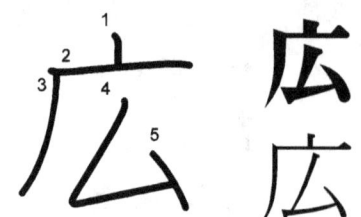

Meaning(s): **wide, broad, spacious**

広い	ひろい spacious, vast, wide
広告	コウコク advertising
広域	コウイキ wide area/view
広がる	ひろがる to spread (out)

Meaning(s): **dwell, reside, live**

住む	すむ to live, to reside
住	ジュウ dwelling, living
住居	ジュウキョ house, address
住まう	すまう to live, to inhabit

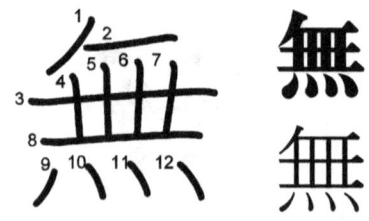

Meaning(s): **nothingness, none**

無い	ない nonexistent
無	ム nil, zero, un-, non-
無	ブ un-, non-, bad ...
皆無	カイム nonexistent, none

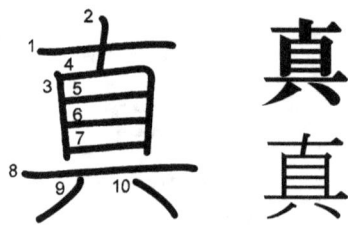

Meaning(s): **true, reality**

真	ま just, right, pure
真	シン truth, reality
迫真	ハクシン realistic, true to life
実しやか	まことしやか credible (lie)

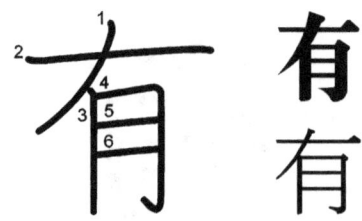

Meaning(s): **possess, have, exist**

有る	ある to be/have, to exist
有	ユウ existence, having
有無	ウム existence or nonexistence
有意義	ユウイギ significant, useful

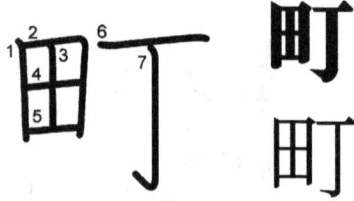

Meaning(s): **town, village, street**

町	まち town, block
町	チョウ town, neighborhood
町議会	チョウギカイ town council
街角	まちかど street corner

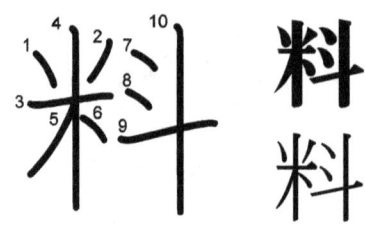

Meaning(s): **fee, materials**

料	リョウ fee, charge, rate
料金	リョウキン fee, charge, fare
史料	シリョウ historical records
使用料	ショウリョウ use fee, rent

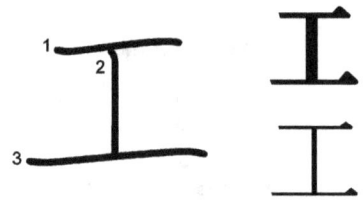

Meaning(s): **craft, construction**

工	コウ (factory) worker
商工	ショウコウ commerce/industry
工夫	クフウ inventing, figuring out
竹細工	タケザイク bamboo work

止

N4 Level Kanji

Radical	止
Strokes	4
Parts	止
Kun	と(まる)、とど(まる)
On	シ

急

N4 Level Kanji

Radical	心 (忄, 小)
Strokes	9
Parts	ク ヨ 心
Kun	いそ(ぐ)
On	キュウ

建

N4 Level Kanji

Radical	廴
Strokes	9
Parts	廴 聿
Kun	た(てる)
On	ケン、コン

研

N4 Level Kanji

Radical	石
Strokes	9
Parts	一 丨 ノ 亅 二 口 开 石
Kun	と(ぐ)
On	ケン

切

N4 Level Kanji

Radical	刀 (刂)
Strokes	4
Parts	刀 匕
Kun	き(る)
On	セツ、サイ

送

N4 Level Kanji

Radical	辵 (辶, 辶)
Strokes	9
Parts	一 二 并 込 大
Kun	おく(る)
On	ソウ

楽

N4 Level Kanji

Radical	木
Strokes	13
Parts	丷 木 白
Kun	たの(しい)
On	ガク、ラク

究

N4 Level Kanji

Radical	穴
Strokes	7
Parts	儿 九 宀 穴
Kun	きわめる
On	キュウ

転

N4 Level Kanji

Radical	車
Strokes	11
Parts	二 ム 車
Kun	ころ(がる)
On	テン

  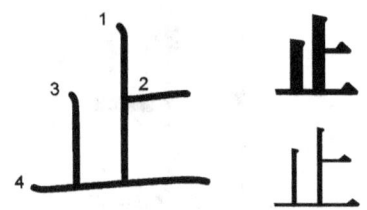

Meaning(s): build

建てる	たてる	to build/construct
建て	たて	contract, commitment
建立	コンリュウ	(act of) building
建議	ケンギ	motion, proposal

Meaning(s): hurry, sudden, steep

急ぐ	いそぐ	to hurry, to rush
急	キュウ	sudden, abrupt
急ぎ	いそぎ	haste, hurry
快急	カイキュウ	rapid express (train)

Meaning(s): stop, halt

止まる	とまる	to stop (moving)
止まる	とどまる	to remain, to abide
止める	とめる	to turn off, to park
解止	カイシ	termination

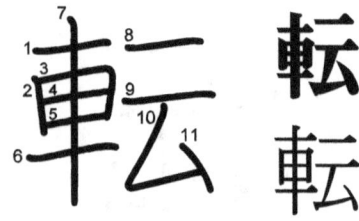

Meaning(s): escort, send

送る	おくる	to send/transmit (a thing), to see off (a person)
送球	ソウキュウ	throwing a ball
移送	イソウ	transportation

Meaning(s): cut, cutoff, be sharp

切る	きる	to cut/open, cut through, disconnect
切	セツ	eager, earnest, kind
家財一切	カザイイッサイ	set of household goods

Meaning(s): polish, sharpen

研ぐ	とぐ	to sharpen, to polish
研究	ケンキュウ	study, research
予研	ヨケン	Nat. Institute of Health
研究員	ケンキュウイン	researcher

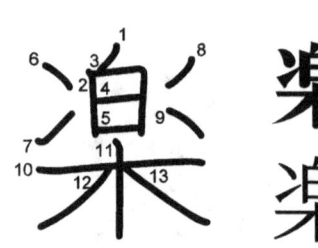

Meaning(s): turn around, change

転	テン	change in pronunciation or meaning of word
転がる	ころがる	to roll, to roll over
転ぶ	ころぶ	to fall down/over

Meaning(s): research, study

極める	きわめる	to master
究明	キュウメイ	investigation
究竟	クキョウ	conclusion
究竟	クッキョウ	finally, ideal

Meaning(s): music, comfort, ease

楽しい	たのしい	enjoyable, fun happy
楽	ガク	music
楽	ラク	comfort, ease, relief
行楽	コウラク	outing, excursion

病

N4 Level Kanji

Radical	疒
Strokes	10
Parts	一人冂疒
Kun	や(む)
On	ビョウ

着

N4 Level Kanji

Radical	目
Strokes	12
Parts	ノ并王目羊
Kun	き(る)、つ(く)
On	チャク

起

N4 Level Kanji

Radical	走(赱)
Strokes	10
Parts	土巳走
Kun	お(きる)、おこ(す)
On	キ

試

N4 Level Kanji

Radical	言(訁)
Strokes	13
Parts	工弋言
Kun	こころ(みる)、ため(す)
On	シ

待

N4 Level Kanji

Radical	彳
Strokes	9
Parts	土寸彳
Kun	ま(つ)
On	タイ

質

N4 Level Kanji

Radical	貝
Strokes	15
Parts	八斤目貝
Kun	たち、ただ(す)
On	シツ、シチ

早

N4 Level Kanji

Radical	日
Strokes	6
Parts	十日
Kun	はや(い)
On	ソウ、サッ

銀

N4 Level Kanji

Radical	金(釒)
Strokes	14
Parts	艮金
Kun	
On	ギン

族

N4 Level Kanji

Radical	方
Strokes	11
Parts	方矢乞
Kun	
On	ゾク

起 / 着 / 病

Meaning(s):	**wake up, get up**
起きる	おきる — to get up, to wake
起源	キゲン — origin, beginning
起こる	おこる — to happen
起こす	おこす — to raise/raise up

Meaning(s):	**arrive, wear**
着る	きる — to wear, to put on
着く	つく — to arrive at, to sit on
着	チャク — arrival, arriving at ...
決着	ケッチャク — conclusion, end

Meaning(s):	**ill, sick**
病む	やむ — to fall ill
病	やまい — illness, weakness
病	ビョウ — disease, -pathy
病院	ビョウイン — hospital, clinic

質 / 待 / 試

Meaning(s):	**substance, quality**
質	たち — nature (person)
質	シツ — quality, value
質	シチ — pawn, pledge
質す	ただす — to ask (about

Meaning(s):	**wait, depend on**
待つ	まつ — to wait, to await
待遇	タイグウ — treatment, service
歓待	カンタイ — warm welcome
待機	タイキ — standing by

Meaning(s):	**test, try, attempt**
試みる	こころみる — to try, to attempt
試	シ — testing, examination
試す	ためす — to try (out)
考試	コウシ — test, exam

族 / 銀 / 早

Meaning(s):	**tribe, family**
族	ゾク — tribe, clan, family
族長	ゾクチョウ — head of a family
皇族	コウゾク — imperial family
王族	オウゾク — royalty

Meaning(s):	**silver**
銀	ぎん / ギン — silver coin/medal, silver color
銀色	ギンイロ — silver (color/colour)
世銀	セギン — World Bank

Meaning(s):	**early, fast**
早い	はやい — fast, quick, prompt
早	はや — already, now
早急	ソウキュウ — immediate, urgent
早速	サッソク — immediately

験

N4 Level Kanji

Radical	馬
Strokes	18
Parts	人亻口杰馬
Kun	
On	ケン

親

N4 Level Kanji

Radical	見
Strokes	16
Parts	亠并木立見辛
Kun	おや、した(しい)
On	シン

映

N4 Level Kanji

Radical	日
Strokes	9
Parts	ノ冖大日
Kun	うつ(る)、は(える)
On	エイ

仕

N4 Level Kanji

Radical	人(亻)
Strokes	5
Parts	化士
Kun	
On	シ

医

N4 Level Kanji

Radical	匸
Strokes	7
Parts	匸矢乞
Kun	
On	イ

英

N4 Level Kanji

Radical	艸(艹)
Strokes	8
Parts	ノ冖大艾
Kun	
On	エイ

写

N4 Level Kanji

Radical	冖
Strokes	5
Parts	一冖勹
Kun	うつ(る)
On	シャ

味

N4 Level Kanji

Radical	口
Strokes	8
Parts	丨二一八口木
Kun	あじ
On	ミ

去

N4 Level Kanji

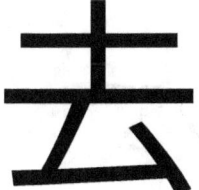

Radical	ム
Strokes	5
Parts	ム土
Kun	さ(る)
On	キョ、コ

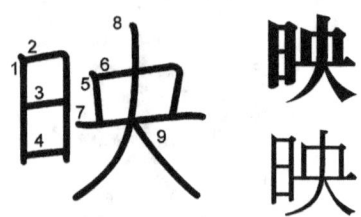

Meaning(s): **reflect, reflection**

映る	うつる	to be reflected
映す	うつす	to cast (shadow)
映える	はえる	to shine, to glow
映画	エイガ	movie, film

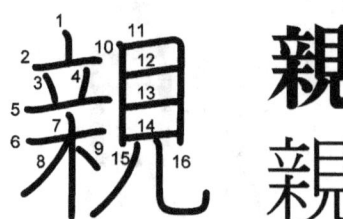

Meaning(s): **relative, familiarity**

親	おや	parent, parents
親しい	したしい	friendly, intimate
親	シン	close relative
親方	おやかた	boss, supervisor

Meaning(s): **effect, verification**

徴	しるし	sign, indication
験	ゲン	effect, omen
霊験	レイゲン	miracle
筆記試験	ヒッキシケン	written examination

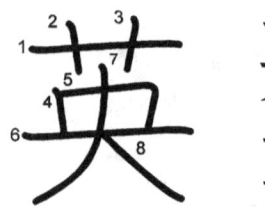

Meaning(s): **England, English**

英	エイ	United Kingdom
英語	エイゴ	English (language)
和英	ワエイ	Japanese-English (dictionary)

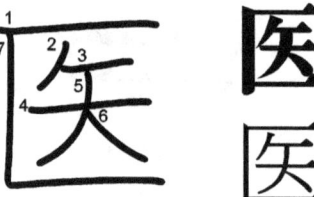

Meaning(s): **doctor, medicine**

医	イ	medicine, healing, doctor
医院	イイン	doctor's office, clinic
軍医	グンイ	military physician
校医	コウイ	school doctor

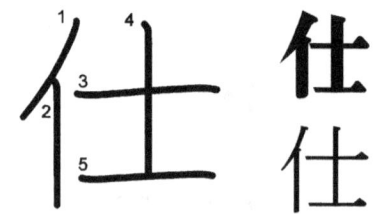

Meaning(s): **attend, doing, official**

仕	シ	official, civil service
社会奉仕	シャカイホウシ	voluntary soc. service
致仕	チシ	resignation, 70 (age)
仕込み	ジコミ	learned at ...

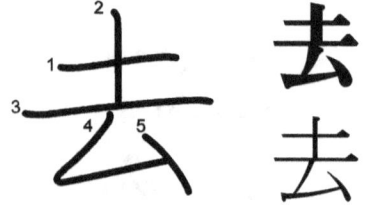

Meaning(s): **gone, past, leave**

去る	ぎんこう	to leave, to go away
去年	キョネン	last year
大過去	ダイカコ	past perfect tense
去就	キョシュウ	leaving or staying

Meaning(s): **flavor, taste**

味	あじ	flavor, taste
味	ミ	counter for food/drink
味覚	ミカク	taste, palate
味付け	あじつけ	seasoning, flavor

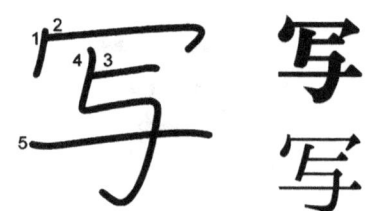

Meaning(s): **copy, describe**

写す	うつす	to duplicate
写る	うつる	to be photographed
写真	シャシン	photo, picture
活写	カッシャ	vivid description

夜

N4 Level Kanji

Radical	夕
Strokes	8
Parts	亠化夕
Kun	よ、よる
On	ヤ

答

N4 Level Kanji

Radical	竹 (⺮)
Strokes	12
Parts	一个口竹乞
Kun	こた(える)
On	トウ

字

N4 Level Kanji

Radical	子
Strokes	6
Parts	子宀
Kun	
On	ジ

帰

N4 Level Kanji

Radical	巾
Strokes	10
Parts	亠刈巾ヨ
Kun	かえ(る)、かえ(す)
On	キ

注

N4 Level Kanji

Radical	水 (氵, 氺)
Strokes	8
Parts	丶汁王
Kun	そそ(ぐ)、さ(す)
On	チュウ

音

N4 Level Kanji

Radical	音
Strokes	9
Parts	日立音
Kun	おと、ね
On	オン

図

N4 Level Kanji

Radical	囗
Strokes	7
Parts	囗斗
Kun	はか(る)
On	ズ、ト

悪

N4 Level Kanji

Radical	心 (忄, 㣺)
Strokes	11
Parts	一丨口心
Kun	わる(い)
On	アク

歌

N4 Level Kanji

Radical	欠
Strokes	14
Parts	一亅口欠
Kun	うた、うた(う)
On	カ

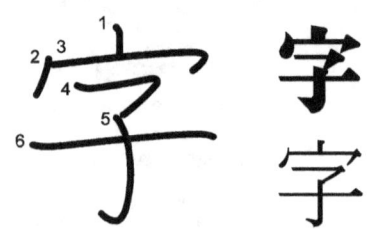

Meaning(s): **character, letter, word**

字	ジ character (esp. kanji) handwriting, penmanship
字形	ジケイ character style
英字	エイジ English letter

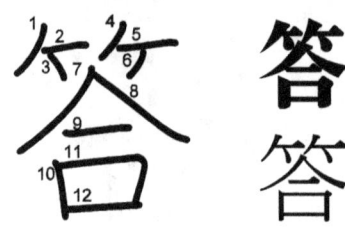

Meaning(s): **solution, answer**

答える	こたえる to answer, to reply
答申	トウシン report, reply, findings
答え	こたえ answer, reply, response
正答	セイトウ correct answer

Meaning(s): **night, evening**

夜	よる evening, night, dinner
夜明け	よあけ dawn, daybreak
夜	ヤ counter for nights
同夜	ドウヤ the same night

Meaning(s): **sound, noise**

音	おと/オト sound, report, fame
弱音	よわね complaint, whine
音楽	オンガク music
音信	オンシン correspondence, news

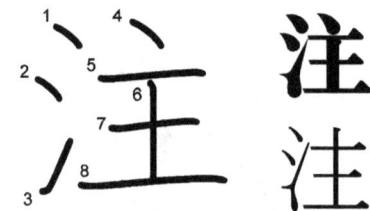

Meaning(s): **pour, irrigate**

注ぐ	そそぐ to pour (into)
注す	さす to pour (e.g. drinks)
注	チュウ annotation, comment
注意	チュウイ notice, caution

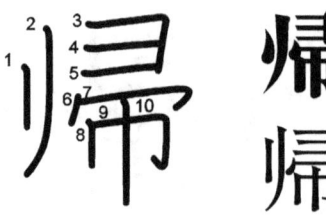

Meaning(s): **lead to, result in**

帰る	かえる to return, to come home
帰還	キカン return (home)
帰す	かえす to send (someone) back
回帰	カイキ return (to), revolution

Meaning(s): **song, sing**

歌	うた song, singing
歌劇	カゲキ opera
歌曲	カキョク melody, tune, song
歌う	うたう to sing (of love)

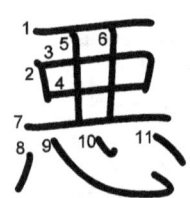

Meaning(s): **bad, evil, wrong**

悪い	わるい poor (quality), inferior
悪	アク evil, wickedness
好悪	コウオ likes and dislikes
悪し	あし bad, evil

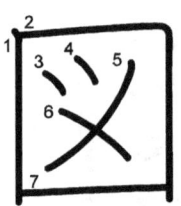

Meaning(s): **map, drawing, plan**

図る	はかる to plan, to attempt to aim/strive for
図	ズ diagram, illustration
図書	トショ books

風

N4 Level Kanji

Radical	風
Strokes	9
Parts	ノ几虫風
Kun	かぜ、かざ-
On	フウ、フ

歩

N4 Level Kanji

Radical	止
Strokes	8
Parts	ノ小止
Kun	ある(く)、あゆ(む)
On	ホ、ブ

室

N4 Level Kanji

Radical	宀
Strokes	9
Parts	ム土宀至
Kun	むろ
On	シツ

春

N4 Level Kanji

Radical	日
Strokes	9
Parts	一二人大日
Kun	はる
On	シュン

黒

N4 Level Kanji

Radical	黑
Strokes	11
Parts	杰里黒
Kun	くろ
On	コク

紙

N4 Level Kanji

Radical	糸 (糸)
Strokes	10
Parts	小幺氏糸
Kun	かみ
On	シ

館

N4 Level Kanji

Radical	食 (飠)
Strokes	16
Parts	｜口宀食
Kun	やかた
On	カン

青

N4 Level Kanji

Radical	青 (靑)
Strokes	8
Parts	二亠土月青
Kun	あお(い)
On	セイ、ショウ

赤

N4 Level Kanji

Radical	赤
Strokes	7
Parts	土赤
Kun	あか(い)
On	セキ、シャク

 室 室

Meaning(s): **room, apartment**

室	むろ	greenhouse, icehouse, cellar
室	シツ	room, wife (of someone of high rank)
同室	ドウシツ	same room, sharing a room

 歩 歩

Meaning(s): **walk**

歩く	あるく	to walk
歩む	あゆむ	to walk, to follow
歩	ホ	step, counter for steps
歩合	ブアイ	rate, ratio, percentage

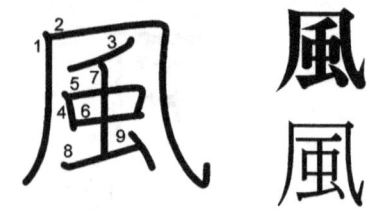 風 風

Meaning(s): **wind, air, style**

風	かぜ	wind, draught, manner
風	フウ	method, manner, way
風格	フウカク	personality, style
涼風	りょうふう	cool breeze

紙 紙 紙

Meaning(s): **paper**

紙	かみ	paper
紙	シ	newspaper
紙上	シジョウ	on paper, in the papers
製紙	セイシ	papermaking

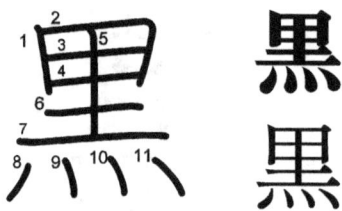 黒 黒

Meaning(s): **black**

黒	くろ	black, guilt
黒煙	コクエン	black smoke
黒衣	コクイ	black clothes
黒い	くろい	dark, sun-tanned

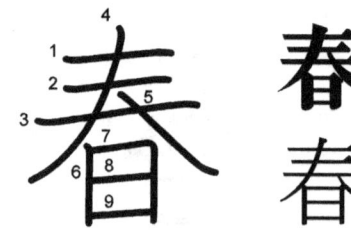 春 春

Meaning(s): **spring**

春	はる	spring, springtime
春秋	シュンジュウ	spring and autumn
春季	シュンキ	spring season
毎春	まいしゅん	every spring

赤 赤 赤

Meaning(s): **red**

赤	あか	red, crimson, scarlet
真赤	まあか	bright red, deep red
赤らむ	あからむ	to redden, to blush
赤銅色	シャクドウイロ	brown, tan

青 青 青

Meaning(s): **blue**

青	あお	blue, green light (traffic)
青い	あおい	blue, azure, green
青果	セイカ	fruit & vegetables
緑青	ロクショウ	verdigris, copper rust

 館 館

Meaning(s): **building, mansion**

館	やかた	mansion, palace
館	カン	(large) building, hall
公館	コウカン	official residence
館長	カンチョウ	director, curator

走

N4 Level Kanji

Radical	走 (赱)
Strokes	7
Parts	土 走
Kun	はし(る)
On	ソウ

色

N4 Level Kanji

Radical	色
Strokes	6
Parts	ク 巴 色
Kun	いろ
On	ショク、シキ

屋

N4 Level Kanji

Radical	尸
Strokes	9
Parts	ム 土 尸 至
Kun	や
On	オク

習

N4 Level Kanji

Radical	羽
Strokes	11
Parts	丶 白 羽
Kun	なら(う)
On	シュウ

夏

N4 Level Kanji

Radical	夂
Strokes	10
Parts	一 夂 目 自
Kun	なつ
On	カ、ゲ

秋

N4 Level Kanji

Radical	禾
Strokes	9
Parts	火 禾
Kun	あき
On	シュウ

服

N4 Level Kanji

Radical	月
Strokes	8
Parts	卩 又 月
Kun	
On	フク

旅

N4 Level Kanji

Radical	方
Strokes	10
Parts	ノ 方 乞
Kun	たび
On	リョ

洋

N4 Level Kanji

Radical	水 (氵, 氺)
Strokes	9
Parts	井 氵 王 羊
Kun	
On	ヨウ

屋

Meaning(s): **roof, house, shop**

屋	や shop, store, restaurant roof, house
屋	オク house, building, roof
屋外	オクガイ outdoors, outside

色

Meaning(s): **color**

色	いろ color, hue, tint, shade
色	ショク counter for colors
色彩	シキサイ color, hue, tints
色合い	いろあい shade (of color), hue

走

Meaning(s): **run**

走	はしる to run, to drive to travel, to move
走	ソウ run, race
快走	カイソウ fast moving / running

秋

Meaning(s): **autumn, fall**

秋	あき autumn, fall
秋季	シュウキ fall / autumn season
秋風	アキカゼ autumn / fall breeze
秋口	あきぐち start of autumn / fall

夏

Meaning(s): **summer**

夏	なつ summer
夏季	カキ summer season
夏至	ゲシ summer solstice
初夏	しょか early summer

習

Meaning(s): **learn**

習う	ならう to be taught, to learn
習性	シュウセイ habit, behavior
演習	エンシュウ practice, exercise, drill
見習い	みならい apprenticeship, trainee

洋

Meaning(s): **ocean, sea, foreign**

洋	ヨウ Orient, foreign, sea, Western, European
洋画	ヨウガ Western film/movie
南氷洋	ナンヒョウヨウ Antarctic Ocean

旅

Meaning(s): **trip, travel**

旅	たび travel, trip, journey
旅客	リョカク passenger, tourist
旅先	たびさき destination (for trip)
修旅	シュウリョ excursion, field trip

服

Meaning(s): **clothing, admit, obey**

服	フク clothes (esp. Western)
服役	フクエキ penal servitude
私服	シフク civilian clothes
呉服	ゴフク cloth, kimono fabrics

曜

N4 Level Kanji

Radical	日
Strokes	18
Parts	ヨ 日 隹
Kun	
On	ヨウ

借

N4 Level Kanji

Radical	人 (イ)
Strokes	10
Parts	二 化 廾 日
Kun	か(りる)
On	シャク

夕

N4 Level Kanji

Radical	夕
Strokes	3
Parts	夕
Kun	ゆう
On	

堂

N4 Level Kanji

Radical	土
Strokes	11
Parts	冖 口 土 尚
Kun	
On	ドウ

貸

N4 Level Kanji

Radical	貝
Strokes	12
Parts	化 ハ 弋 目 貝
Kun	か(す)、かし
On	タイ

肉

N4 Level Kanji

Radical	肉 (月)
Strokes	6
Parts	人 冂 肉
Kun	
On	ニク

勉

N4 Level Kanji

Radical	力
Strokes	10
Parts	ル カ ク 免
Kun	つと(める)
On	ベン

飯

N4 Level Kanji

Radical	食 (飠)
Strokes	12
Parts	厂 又 食
Kun	めし
On	ハン

鳥

N4 Level Kanji

Radical	鳥
Strokes	11
Parts	杰 鳥
Kun	とり
On	チョウ

Meaning(s): **evening**

夕	ゆう	evening
夕刊	ゆうかん	evening paper
昨夕	さくゆう	last night
春の夕	はるのゆう	spring evening

Meaning(s): **borrow, rent**

借りる	かりる	to borrow, to rent/hire
借家	シャクヤ	rented house
賃借	チンシャク	hiring, renting, leasing
借地	シャクチ	leased land

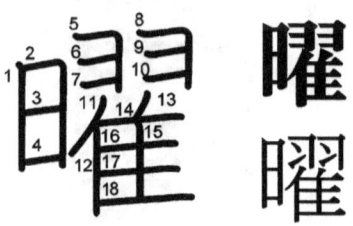

Meaning(s): **weekday**

曜日	ヨウビ	day of the week
曜霊	ヨウレイ	the sun
晃曜	コウヨウ	dazzling brightness

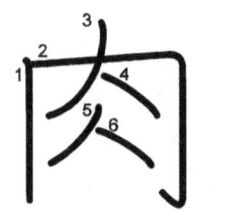

Meaning(s): **meat**

肉	ニク	flesh, meat, pulp / flesh (of a fruit)
食肉	ショクニク	meat (food)
中肉	チュウニク	medium build

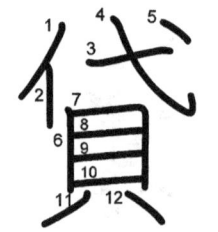

Meaning(s): **lend**

貸す	かす	to loan, to rent out
貸与	タイヨ	loan, lending
貸借	タイシャク	lending & borrowing
転貸	テンタイ	subleasing

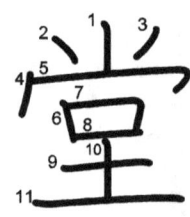

Meaning(s): **public chamber, hall**

堂	ドウ	shrine, chapel, hall
堂々	ドウドウ	magnificent, grand / impressive, dignified
殿堂	デンドウ	hall, shrine, temple

Meaning(s): **bird, chicken**

鳥	とり	bird, bird meat, poultry
鳥居	とりい	torii, Shinto archway
鶏肉	トリニク	chicken meat, poultry
鳥獣	チョウジュウ	wildlife

Meaning(s): **meal, rice**

飯	めし	cooked rice, meal/food
飯店	ハンテン	Chinese restaurant
米飯	ベイハン	cooked rice
握り飯	にぎりめし	rice ball

Meaning(s): **exertion, effort**

勉強	ベンキョウ	study, working hard
勉学	ベンガク	pursuit of knowledge
猛勉	モウベン	studying hard
努める	つとめる	to endeavour/try hard

茶

N4 Level Kanji

Radical	艸 (艹)
Strokes	9
Parts	个 艾 木
Kun	
On	チャ、サ

昼

N4 Level Kanji

Radical	日
Strokes	9
Parts	一 丶 尸 日
Kun	ひる
On	チュウ

冬

N4 Level Kanji

Radical	冫
Strokes	5
Parts	丶 夂 夊
Kun	ふゆ
On	トウ

兄

N4 Level Kanji

Radical	儿
Strokes	5
Parts	儿 口
Kun	あに
On	キョウ、ケイ

牛

N4 Level Kanji

Radical	牛 (牜)
Strokes	4
Parts	牛
Kun	うし
On	ギュウ

弟

N4 Level Kanji

Radical	弓
Strokes	7
Parts	｜ ノ 丷 弓
Kun	おとうと
On	テイ、ダイ、デ

姉

N4 Level Kanji

Radical	女
Strokes	8
Parts	亠 女 巾
Kun	あね
On	シ

妹

N4 Level Kanji

Radical	女
Strokes	8
Parts	｜ 二 丿 八 女 木
Kun	いもうと
On	マイ

犬

N4 Level Kanji

Radical	犬 (犭)
Strokes	4
Parts	丶 大 犬
Kun	いぬ
On	ケン

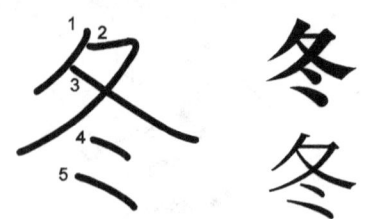
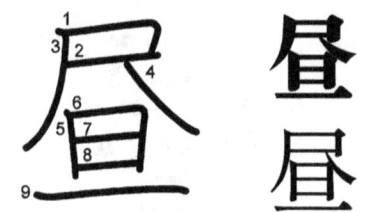

Meaning(s): **winter**	Meaning(s): **daytime, noon**	Meaning(s): **tea**

冬	ふゆ *winter*	昼	ひる *noon, midday, lunch*	茶	チャ *tea, tea making, brown*
冬季	トウキ *(season of) winter*	昼食	チュウショク *lunch, midday meal*	茶色	チャイロ *brown, light brown, tawny*
冬場	ふゆば *wintertime, winter season*	夜昼	よるひる *daytime/during the day*	煎茶	センチャ *green tea, green leaf tea*
毎冬	まいふゆ *every winter*	昼間	ヒルマ *left hand*	喫茶	キッサ *tea drinking, coffee shop*

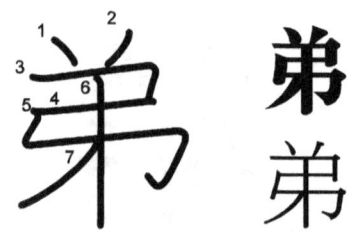
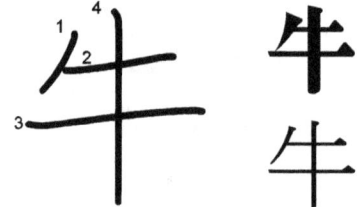

Meaning(s): **younger brother**	Meaning(s): **cow**	Meaning(s): **elder brother**

弟	オトウト *younger brother*	牛	うし *cattle, cow, beef*	兄	あに *older brother*
弟子	デシ *pupil, disciple*	特牛	こというし *strong bull*	兄	ケイ *you, Mr, older brother*
弟	おとうと *younger brother*	肉牛	ニクギュウ *beef cattle*	兄弟	キョウダイ *siblings*
兄弟	キョウダイ *siblings*	去勢牛	きょせいうし *ox, bullock*	父兄	フケイ *guardians, parents*

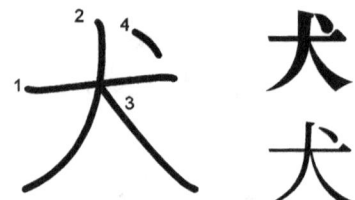
妹
妹

Meaning(s): **dog**	Meaning(s): **younger sister**	Meaning(s): **elder sister**

犬	いぬ *dog, informant, spy*	妹	いもうと *younger sister*	姉	あね *older sister*
野良犬	のらいぬ *stray dog*	妹君	イモウトギミ *(younger) sister*	姉妹	シマイ *sisters*
柴犬	シバイヌ *shiba inu (dog breed)*	弟妹	テイマイ *younger siblings*	大姉	おおあね *eldest sister*
柴犬	しばいぬ *shiba inu (dog breed)*	妹君	いもうとぎみ *(younger) sister*	姉さん	ねえさん *older sister, miss*

漢

JLPT Level	N4 Level Kanji
Radical	水 (氵, 氺)
Strokes	13
Parts	一 二 口 大 汁 艾
Kun	
On	カン

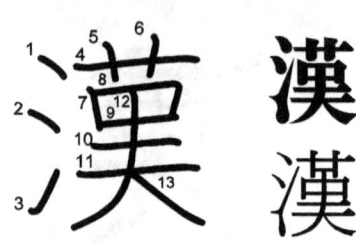

漢

Meaning(s): **China, Sino-**

漢	カン	China, man, Han (Dynastsy)
漢字	カンジ	kanji, Chinese character
門外漢	モンガイカン	amateur, outsider, layman

Meaning(s):

___
___
___

Meaning(s):

___
___
___

Meaning(s):

___
___
___

Meaning(s):

___
___
___

Meaning(s):

___
___
___

Meaning(s):

___
___
___

Meaning(s):

___
___
___

Meaning(s):

___
___
___

spare	spare	spare

JLPT Level	JLPT Level	JLPT Level
Radical	**Radical**	**Radical**
Strokes	**Strokes**	**Strokes**
Parts	**Parts**	**Parts**
Kun	**Kun**	**Kun**
On	**On**	**On**

spare	spare	spare

JLPT Level	JLPT Level	JLPT Level
Radical	**Radical**	**Radical**
Strokes	**Strokes**	**Strokes**
Parts	**Parts**	**Parts**
Kun	**Kun**	**Kun**
On	**On**	**On**

spare	spare	spare

JLPT Level	JLPT Level	JLPT Level
Radical	**Radical**	**Radical**
Strokes	**Strokes**	**Strokes**
Parts	**Parts**	**Parts**
Kun	**Kun**	**Kun**
On	**On**	**On**

Meaning(s):

Meaning(s):

Meaning(s):

Meaning(s):

Meaning(s):

Meaning(s):

Meaning(s):

Meaning(s):

Meaning(s):

Thank you

Congratulations on your progress with the Japanese language! I really appreciate that you chose this book from the selection of other available titles and hope that you found this special *JLPT N4 Kanji* volume of the *Japanese Made Simple* series valuable and enjoyable. I have always aimed to pack my books with lots of practical information that is easy to follow, providing readers with excellent value for money.

This series continues to be a labor of love, but the process of writing and independently publishing books is challenging. While I try to produce accurate language guides, little details are easy to overlook - I would be grateful if you could alert me to any problems or mistakes so that I can promptly fix them for future readers!

Lastly, I need to ask you for a favor.

Nothing would make me happier than for more people to learn Japanese with my books, and it would be really helpful if you could spare a moment to leave your review or feedback on *Amazon*. The hard truth is that we all rely on reviews to guide purchasing decisions, and your positive feedback can make a huge difference to 'the little guys' and writers like me.

Be sure to let me know how I might improve the content or what you would like to see in future follow-up books. *I'll look forward to hearing your thoughts.*

Until next time, *arigatōgozaimasu!*

ありがとうございます!!
Dan.

DanAkiyamaJP@gmail.com

Notes

Kanji for Beginners Vol. 2
Learning Japanese Made Simple

Learn how to read, write and speak
Japanese with the JLPT N4 Level Kanji

A Workbook for Self-Study

Dan Akiyama

www.ingramcontent.com/pod-product-compliance
Lightning Source LLC
Chambersburg PA
CBHW081708100526
44590CB00022B/3698